Radical
Feminist
Therapy

■

Radical Feminist Therapy

■

WORKING IN THE CONTEXT OF VIOLENCE

BONNIE BURSTOW

SAGE Publications
International Educational and Professional Publisher
Newbury Park   London   New Delhi

For information address:

 SAGE Publications, Inc.
2455 Teller Road
Newbury Park, California 91320

SAGE Publications Ltd.
6 Bonhill Street
London EC2A 4PU
United Kingdom

SAGE Publications India Pvt. Ltd.
M-32 Market
Greater Kailash I
New Delhi 110 048 India

Printed in the United States of America

Library of Congress Cataloging-in-Publication Data

Main entry under title:

Burstow, Bonnie, 1945-
    Radical feminist therapy : working in the context of violence / Bonnie Burstow.
        p. cm.
    Includes bibliographical references and index.
    ISBN 0-8039-4787-9 (cloth). — ISBN 0-8039-4788-7 (pbk.)
    1. Abused women—North America. 2. Feminist therapy—North America. 3. Women—North America—Crimes against. I. Title.
HV6250.4.W65B87   1992
155.6'33—dc20   92-30005
                                                                        CIP

93 94 95   10 9 8 7 6 5 4 3 2

Sage Production Editor: Tara S. Mead

Contents

Acknowledgments

As with almost everything that is worthwhile, many wonderful women have helped make this book possible.

The single largest contribution is from Kali Munro. Kali's uncompromising feminism instructs me. Kali is the only other person I know who has clearly integrated feminist therapy and antipsychiatry; it was a relief to have had her to talk with throughout the long two and a half years of writing. Thank you for painstakingly reading each chapter as it was written and for offering sensitive and astute feedback. Most of all, thank you for being there.

Linda Advocaat scrupulously read each section as it was written and provided ongoing, down-to-earth feedback. Margot Smith, as always, encouraged me, was supportive, and cared about what I was doing.

My editor at Sage was a "goddess-sent." She recognized the value of the manuscript, moved with lightning speed, and had the guts to back a book that challenges so much. I am in debt as well to Don Weitz for his uncompromising antipsychiatry understanding and solidarity.

My students and supervisees throughout the years have guided me. The questions and dilemmas of, to name just a few, Kathy Canter, Robin Black, Jan Peltier, and Carol-Anne O'Brien gave me further insight into what needed to be written. The Native and immigrant students at Winnipeg Education Centre and the program itself taught me about work with Natives and immigrants. Special thanks to Kay Johnson and the other women of color at Carleton University who "confronted the hell out of all faculty." It is women of color who have taught me the most about difference.

Finally and most particularly, I would like to acknowledge the contribution of my clients over the years. While I cannot name them for reasons of confidentiality, I know and they know that they have taught me what no one else conceivably could. It is to them—as women who resist, as survivors, as warriors—that I dedicate this book.

Introduction

The context in which this book is written is the fundamental unhappiness and alienation of women. I am referring here not simply to the angst and pain that are inevitable parts of our human condition or primarily to the unhappiness that arises from individual circumstance. It is that *unnecessary yet unavoidable, individual yet common, suffering born of the patriarchy and other systemic oppression.*

Civilization as we know it is based on the violation and domination of subordinates by elites. All women are subordinate. Working-class women, women of color, lesbians, and women with disabilities are doubly or triply oppressed. Civilization is based as well on male hegemony, that is, on viewing, understanding, and naming the world from a rigidly male elite point of view and seeing this view itself as something that is neutral and given in the nature of things.

Violation, domination, and hegemony are common to all oppression. All oppression is heinous, dehumanizing, and confusing. And all has its own special torments and deceptions. What is especially insidious and psychologically destructive about sexism is its closeness. We do not have distance from it. It is in our homes and in our own families from the earliest years, and it comes under such baffling and seductive disguises as nurturance and romantic love. We are so mystified by it and caught up in it right from the start that it takes an incredible struggle for us to win back even the beginnings of our lost humanity. For a long time, individually and collectively, women have been waging this struggle. Feminist therapy or counseling may be seen as one small but very real part of the fight.

Feminist therapy is rooted in women's knowledge, in women's help and ways of help. The word *therapy* comes from the Greek word meaning "to attend" or "to minister" and only derivatively became connected with medicine. Our ancestors or precursors are women who attended to others. We date back to the witches, the midwives, the wise women who defied the patriarchy and brought women's help to those who wanted it. It dates beyond the patriarchy itself to the spiritual women of all classes and colors who were compassionate and gave counsel.

The immediate context for the emergence of feminist therapy was the growth of the women's movement. The larger context is the obscuring of our roots by male and malelike professionals and a growing dissatisfaction with the increasingly patriarchal counseling that resulted. Sadly, for some time now, especially in the Western world, an enormously high percentage of women who "give counsel" have taken training from and identified with the androcentric, racist, and classist "mental health establishment." The woman's movement provided an opportunity to begin reexamining and disidentifying from that establishment. Individual women both inside and outside consciousness-raising groups targeted the "mental health system" as a particularly misogynous and oppressive substructure. Feminist researchers began studying the area. Their findings left us in little doubt. The so-called "mental health system" served the interest of the patriarchy; that is, it pathologized the socially created problems that women face and reinforced the sex roles that the patriarchy prescribes.

A particularly influential study that helped substantiate the claims of those of us who denounced the "help" given by "mental health professionals" is Inge Broverman's now classical research into sex role stereotyping by psychiatrists, psychologists, and social workers (see Broverman, Broverman, & Clarkson, 1970, pp. 1-7). The research was based on a questionnaire that contained listings of bipolar traits associated with sex role stereotypes—such bipolar sets as "very assertive/not at all assertive." The research indicated that both male and female clinicians equate "socially competent adult" with "socially competent man" and see women as socially competent only when not acting like a competent adult. Feminists were quick to point out the implications of Broverman's study. Whether conducted by men or by women, therapy was a patriarchal institution whose vision and goals contributed to the infantilization and disempowering of women.

A second important study is by Phyllis Chesler. In her book *Women and Madness*, Chesler (1972) demonstrated psychiatry's role in the subordination of women. She saw psychiatry as a fundamentally androcentric institution whose purpose is to enforce sex role stereotypes. She argued convincingly that women are in double jeopardy: Women are institutionalized both for veering from their socially proscribed role and for overly conforming to it. Women of color are particularly jeopardized.

These denunciations and this research helped clarify the importance of pioneering a different approach to counseling even though the approach did not highlight the significance of our earlier history. It became abundantly apparent that the "mental health" professionals' claim to neutrality was androcentric myopia. Psychiatry was fundamentally patriarchal. And therapy clearly was not and could not be neutral. A counselor/counseling approach has either establishment beliefs/values and supports systemic oppression or liberatory beliefs/values and struggles against oppression. Feminists saw the humanistic approaches as preferable to everything else but concluded that a strictly humanist orientation was inadequate. No existing approach did not pathologize, did not individualize, and located itself fundamentally on the feminist side.[1] Feminist practitioners and writers responded by attempting to create one.

Within a few decades self-declared feminist therapists and feminist therapy referral centers were in every major city in North America and Europe. Then came the articles and books. Particularly noteworthy in this regard is Greenspan (1983), who spelled out important practice differences among psychoanalysts, humanist therapists, and feminist therapists; and Sturdivant (1980), who articulated differences in underlying beliefs and values. Later Brown and Root (1990) and Fulani (1988) pushed farther, incorporating an understanding of racism and stressing multicultural approaches.

From the outset the new feminist approaches were based on the belief that the relationship between client and counselor must reflect female values and female ways of relating. The role of therapy was to help women understand their oppression and to find new, more empowering ways of dealing with it. The therapist-as-expert stance was defined as a masculine way of being, and ongoing serious attempts were made to overcome it; symptoms were partially redefined as resistance; and a link was established between feminist therapy, consciousness-raising, and political action.[2]

The theory and practice of feminist counseling have continued evolving and redefining themselves over the past few decades. Important theoretic contributions have been made, and many women have been helped. Mothers who might otherwise have ended up with traditional family therapists who would have sacrificed them in the interests of the "family system" instead found allies and advocates. Families led by strong Black women stopped being called "dysfunctional." And many incest survivors who might otherwise have been called "hysterical" and ended up institutionalized and drugged were recognized and helped to remember and reclaim self. We may legitimately be proud both of the individual work that has been done and of the theoretic groundwork that has been laid. At the same time, as in all human movements and activities, serious shortcomings and problems exist. These problems and shortcomings form one of the principal motivations for writing this book.

Despite the many achievements, despite the women who have been well served, a number feel profoundly betrayed and still more feel deeply dissatisfied. I have no doubt that some of the anger and disappointment and certainly some of the intensity with which it is felt stem from misogyny and traditional woman-blaming. Feminist therapists are blamed for charging for their services even though everyone knows that making a living is a necessity and that men charge considerably more without feeling guilty. Feminist therapists are blamed for not being the all-giving, perfect mothers that patriarchy has conditioned everyone to expect of women.[3] This unfairness notwithstanding, some anger is also very legitimate, for some very serious problems exist.

Some women psychiatrists oppose the sexism they see, yet they try to hold onto psychiatry, mistakenly viewing themselves as "feminist therapists." Some feminist therapists use "diagnoses" freely, including the phallocentric diagnoses of the psychiatric profession.[4] A new rapprochement has even arisen between some streams of feminist therapy and psychiatry, with the result being co-optation in such psychiatrically defined and controlled areas as "eating disorders" and "multiple personality disorders." Although a few are deeply sensitive to the damage wreaked by psychiatry and truly extend themselves to keep people out of the system, even some of these feminist have helped commit their clients involuntarily, without the client posing any threat whatever to the therapist or to any third party. Many do not open their doors to ex-psychiatric inmates. In fact I have been told by women working in a feminist therapy referral center that most of their counselors specifically list "psychiatric patients" as a client type that they do not wish to see. Many feminist counselors imitate their male counterparts by overcharging or by consistently charging what most women could not conceivably afford. Some seldom or never recognize when they are dealing with an incest victim or a battered woman, and others recognize but avoid. Many of those who do not avoid them nonetheless approach survivors in a heavy-handed or sensationalistic way and harm them in the process. Many feminist therapists violate their clients' boundaries, sexually or otherwise. Many continue to try to patch together marriages that are profoundly oppressive. Most feminist therapists sometimes, and some feminist therapists often, draw indiscriminately from different counseling modalities without examining their compatibility with feminist principles. Most heterosexual therapists have their own lesbophobia and do not understand lesbian existence. Most of the white therapists do not understand racism, superimpose mainstream norms, and miss the interconnections between racism and sexism. Most counselors use highly direct modes of communication even when working with women from cultures that rely more on context and find such communication intrusive. Many counselors do not understand the special problems faced by poor women. And in North America the vast majority of feminist therapists do not have a clue how to work with women who mutilate themselves, with prostitutes, with women in conflict with the law, and with women with eating and/or drug problems.

These problems exist for a number of reasons. First, as with other professions, women who become feminist therapists are generally white, middle-class, heterosexual women who are not victims of racism, who have never prostituted or harmed themselves in ways that exceed societal norms, and who have never been institutionalized. Most have received no formal training in a feminist therapy orientation. Most have been trained, say, as a gestalt therapist or as a bioenergetics therapist or, more commonly, "eclectically" and have added feminist therapy to their already "busy" repertoire, sometimes actively striving to keep it all together, though often just going on faith that it will all work out. Others are not really feminists but use the label because it gives them access to referral centers and think that this is all right because they are, after all, "against sexism." Many are feministically inclined but do not have a clear position. Others have a position that is clear but still preradical. Many are very good theoretically but are confused about what to do practically and so end up acting like either traditional therapists or no kind of therapist at all. Workers in feminist counseling centers avoid a number of these mistakes because more come from the working class, more are lesbian, and more are of color. Consequently these counselors have a solid, practical bent and are often among the most helpful workers that women in trouble encounter. Nonetheless they frequently lack an overview because of the piecemeal nature of their training (experience while being overworked plus sporadic workshops). And they do not have an understanding of process. Workshops themselves give help while also adding to the problem. With new understanding coming rapidly, we naturally turn to workshops for new information and approaches. The workshops that are attended by therapists and counselors alike leave us with the illusion that we understand more than we do. And they range from excellent information and approaches on one hand to sensationalism, fad, and heavy-handed intrusion on the other. Additionally, despite their backgrounds, most therapists and counselors have received no training in how to depathologize and have been given no information about the nature of psychiatric "treatments." All are in a profession and a society "spooked" by psychiatry. The training received by most is ethnocentric. It promotes directness, explicitness, confrontation, and individualism over the implicit, nonintrusive, and communal. All have the opportunity to violate their clients as professionals. And the legitimate feminist attempt to get away from the rigid boundaries of mainstream counseling can itself result in blurred boundaries and violation.

Therapists with any of these difficulties, and we all have some, can find help in many of the feminist therapy books written to date. Unfortunately, though, valuable and powerful as much of the literature is, it is marred by a number of the same flaws and shortcomings. The literature too has been written primarily by white, middle-class, Anglo-Saxon women who have not prostituted, have not damaged themselves in ways that exceed societal norms, have never been institutionalized, are able-bodied, and have not suffered from racism. Progressively writers are stretching themselves as indeed we all must in the attempt to understand and to articulate, and this is wonderful to see. Much more stretching, understanding, and articulation is needed, though. Until recently lesbian existence was excluded from a great deal of the literature; the implications of lesbian existence for heterosexual women are still never spelled out. Although there is now more inclusion of lesbians and recognition of woman-woman love as "healthy," with only a few exceptions (e.g., Goodrich, Rampage, Ellman et al., 1988) the inclusion and validation of woman-woman love is generally compromised by lesbian-relating being viewed through a psychoanalytic lens that reduces it to the pre-Oedipal.[5] Except in works written by women of color and Jewish women, and I am thankful for these contributions, white, Gentile clients are generally assumed. Sporadic references are now being made to differences, for most feminists are trying to do better. Still a tokenism generally exists about such references. Although we encounter the occasional delimiting statement and some clearly well-meaning apologies, what is true of white Gentile women is generally treated as The Truth about women in this society. Some of the books are not very feminist. None take a radical feminist line, although Greenspan (1983) and Sturdivant (1980) come very close. Prostitutes, ex-inmates, women who are drug dependent, and women who self-mutilate are generally given short shrift, if they are mentioned at all.

The guidance given in regard to psychiatry is more problematic. Rosewater and Walker's (1985) amalgam of psychiatry and feminism is misleading and confusing. Rivera (1988) writes in a psychiatry-identified way about the "mental illness" called "multiple personality disorder," referring in detail to psychiatric "discoveries." Feminist theoreticians like Caplan (1989), whose opposition to mother-blaming and to the notion of female masochism represents an important feminist thrust, nonetheless fail to see the inherent sexism and oppressiveness of psychiatry and treat it simply like any other field that needs to be tidied up. Having identified the diagnosis "masochistic personality disorder" as sexist, and having worked hard to remove it from the *Diagnostic and Statistical Manual of Mental Disorders (DSM)*, Caplan (1987, pp. 241-269) expressed dismay when it reappeared under the new label "self-defeating personality disorder." She continued to write, however, as if this were simply the fault of individuals at the convention and as if reform were possible and sufficient. Neither Rosewater nor Rivera nor Caplan objects to such diagnoses as "borderline personality disorder" and "schizophrenia."[6] Rosewater just asks that we distinguish between "real borderlines" and "schizophrenics" on one hand and battered women who only look as if they are "borderline" or "schizophrenic" on the other. Unlike the "borderlines" and the "schizophrenics," Rosewater tells us, battered women really are the victims of overwhelming violence and should be treated accordingly. Treatment for the "schizophrenic" woman, says Rosewater, should be "based on helping her, at whatever pace is suitable for her, to deal with the discrepancies between her own perceptions and her external realities" (Rosewater & Walker, 1985, p. 224). This is worrisome advice in itself because most so-called "distortions" have at least a kernel of truth and because women's history is already seen as deficient and discounted. It is especially worrisome if we consider the equation that Greenspan and Chesler make between rejecting sex role stereotypes and being diagnosed "borderline" or "schizophrenic." Counselors who give credence to Rosewater's writings would approach only some women with a feminist orientation, while continuing to invalidate and "correct" others. They would be compounding oppression and adding to the disempowerment of those women whom the patriarchy most stigmatize and most fear—all this, confusedly, in the name of feminism.

Theorists like Greenspan and Sturdivant stand in sharp contrast to Rosewater and Rivera. Greenspan (1983) and Sturdivant (1980) offer sharp critiques of psychiatry and are good at cutting through diagnoses to expose the sexist core. Even these theoreticians, however, are limited in their psychiatric critique; they offer few practical suggestions on how to work with women who have already been psychiatrized or who are at strong risk of being so. Feminist therapists looking to them for guidance in the psychiatric area would be benefitted but would still come up short.

Still more significant, feminist counseling literature has not provided the concrete guidance needed. The literature is divided between weak theory with detailed practice suggestions on one hand and powerful theorizing with only general remarks and examples about how to put it into practice on the other. This deficit is a sizable one, for good feminist counseling is itself the concretization of good theory. As counselors we need good theory, and we need to know how to work with it.

Additionally, although specific types of violence against women are the topic of many feminist counseling books, violence against women overall is seldom given centrality in generalist feminist counseling texts. Violence against women is central to our existence as women and as such is an issue that we can no longer afford to marginalize.

THIS BOOK

Radical Feminist Therapy attempts to radicalize feminist therapy further and to offer detailed and grounded guidance. It is written for feminist practitioners both new and experienced who are open to unlearning and relearning. It is written for the feminist counselor, the therapist, the supervisor, the educator, the student, the client, for anyone, in fact, who wishes to make her or our feminist counseling more truly feminist and is reaching out for orientations and understandings that embrace more and more women. A large book that covers many areas in depth, it attempts to address the needs both of students who want a comprehensive introductory text and of practitioners who want something that can be used as an ongoing resource.

The central emphasis of the book is violence against women. The operant premises are:

1. Women are violently reduced to bodies that are for-men, and those bodies are then further violated.
2. Violence is absolutely integral to our experience as women.
3. Extreme violence is the context in which other violence occurs and gives meaning to the other forms, with which it inevitably interacts.
4. All women are subject to extreme violence at some time or live with the threat of extreme violence.

Considerable emphasis is placed on childhood sexual abuse, rape, and battery continuums, as well as on women's responses to this violence (depression, cutting, splitting, troubled eating, and protest). In line with the commitment to inclusion, the book also includes detailed exploration of feminist ways of working with women and issues that are generally either omitted or pathologized in generalist feminist counseling texts. Examples include Native women, Jewish women, women with disabilities, prostitutes who are battered by pimps, women who self-mutilate, psychiatrized women, women with drinking problems, and women who are considering killing themselves.

The second half of the introduction and the first two chapters lay initial foundations. The remaining 12 chapters rigorously integrate theory and practice. Each chapter ends with a list of suggested readings to assist learners who have a special interest in the area.

Each practice chapter is grounded in and includes reference to concrete interactions with clients. Contrary to standard practice, references are kept short and general for purposes of confidentiality. Features from different clients have been combined together, and stories have been purposively altered.

Different Theoretical Perspectives

Radical Feminist Therapy is grounded in a number of related and interconnected perspectives that combine to shape the understanding and guidance offered.

The first and by far the most important perspective is *radical feminism*—the perspective highlighted in the title. Radical feminism sees oppression against women as connecting with but not reducible to all other systemic oppressions and places special emphasis on the physical violation of Woman as Body. With our growing awareness of partner and child abuse and other forms of male violence, the importance of this perspective for feminist therapy is becoming increasingly clear.[7]

A secondary though important perspective also found in the book's title is *radical therapy*. Radical therapy is the counseling and political movement that grew out of transactional analysis. It starts from the premise that problems in living are rooted in systemic oppressions—classism, sexism, and racism in particular. It involves consciousness-raising and leads to action. It is built on two basic equations (Wyckoff, 1980, pp. 15-16):

Oppression + Lies + Isolation = Alienation

Action + Awareness + Contact → Power

The third perspective is *antipsychiatry*, and it is one that is officially endorsed by radical therapists.[8] Antipsychiatry is a combined movement/perspective that views psychiatry as a fundamentally oppressive institution propped up by hegemony and built on mystification, subordination, and violence. It involves analysis, demystification, and liberation.

All three perspectives are grounded theoretically in a more general perspective called *structuralism*. Structuralists see power deferential and "power over" as figuring significantly in the problems that people have in living. All see traditional therapy as oppressive.

The final perspective and one that somewhat qualifies the structuralism is *existentialism*. Existentialism views the human being as freedom that is severely and often brutally conditioned but not totally "determined" by our social and human situation. Such prominent existentialist themes as *otherness, freedom, objectification,* and *alienation* have already entered into feminist thinking via de Beauvoir (1964) and into liberationist thinking generally.

Personal Grounding and Purpose

I am a therapist, consultant, supervisor, and social work professor who has spent many years working with and helping others work with violated women. I am grateful to clients and students, for they have taught me more than books and articles ever could. I continue to develop my understanding out of my ongoing interaction with them.

More personally and just as significantly, I have been subject to hardships and oppression that predispose me toward certain types of understanding and that have made me the kind of feminist therapist, educator, and thinker that I am. I am of lower class origins. My childhood was forever being interrupted by those ongoing desperate financial crises that characterize the welfare class. For long periods the four of us lived in a small one-bedroom flat. I remember having to use windows as exits to avoid the debt collectors who were waiting at the door. We were forever moving, beating hasty retreats because we could not pay the rent.

My father was a "psychiatric patient" who went from hospitalization to hospitalization. My family was thrown into crisis after crisis by the frequent "committals," by his threats and mood swings, and by the important things that he kept forgetting as a result of the memory loss caused by ongoing electroshock.

I am an incest survivor. I am also a survivor of extreme childhood battery more generally, and like many other abused children, I coped for years by withdrawing, by distancing, by self-mutilating. Needless to say, this left me at risk of psychiatrization, and indeed attempts were made to "interfere with" me in my earlier years, but I had seen enough, thankfully, to protect myself.

Except during those vulnerable times that we all have, the worst aspects of my childhood seem very distant to me now. I am glad that they are remote, for I would not wish them on anyone, myself included. At the same time, I am strangely grateful that I can call on them, for they tremendously benefit me as a practitioner. I have seen many incest survivors and have worked well with them at a time when they were still considered a rarity by most feminist therapists and when most of my colleagues were floundering with these women.

Both adult and child experiences that were nowhere near as tortuous have similarly instructed me. I have the knowledge that comes from being a Jew in an anti-Semitic Christiancentric world. I have the knowledge of being disabled and in physical pain in a world built for the able-bodied and the pain-free. And I have the knowledge that is forced on you when you are a woman with a woman partner in this lesbophobic society, in which heterosexuality is compulsory and in which woman-woman love is often punished, is always marginalized, and is at best tolerated.

Like the more formal schools of thought already delineated, this knowing that exists at the core of my being enters into my understanding of patriarchy and of feminist therapy. And it too underlies the redirections and the deepening in this book.

I am also white. I know that having white privilege distorts my vision and detracts from the book. As a counselor, teacher, supervisor, and writer, I have been struggling to access other vision and believe that this book has been greatly enriched through that struggle. At the same time, I am painfully aware that my section on Jewish women is considerably more powerful than my section on African American women despite the extra efforts devoted to the latter.

From the opposite side, I know as well that the very oppressions to which I am subject sometimes blind me to the experiences of women on the opposite side of that oppression. As Audre Lorde (1982, 1984) so astutely points out, although seeing from the outside in allows the oppressed to understand the oppressor better than the oppressor understands the oppressed, it too is a limited vision involving its own bias. From both sides, I regret whatever misrepresentation or insensitivity has resulted. And I look forward to correction from women who are differently situated.

NOTES

1. One possible exception is transactional analysis. See Steiner (1975).

2. Theorists, like practitioners, vary on their degree of political understanding and commitment. For a particularly strong position, see Greenspan (1983).

3. At the Tenth International Conference for Human Rights and Against Psychiatric Oppression, for example, feminist therapists were repeatedly criticized for not giving of their time for free, for pretending that they had any knowledge, and for not making themselves completely and always available.

4. See, for instance, Rosewater and Walker (1985), pp. 215-225.

5. In this regard, see, for example, Burch (1982, 1985) and Chodorow (1978).

6. Caplan's recent antipsychiatry speeches suggest that she is becoming significantly more radical. I applaud the shift and look forward to future books and articles that reflect it.

7. Readers wanting to know more about radical feminism are referred to Daly (1978); Koedt, Levine, and Rapone (1973); and Redstockings Collective (1978).

8. Antipsychiatry's most famous and most articulate spokesperson is Thomas Szasz. See Szasz (1974, 1977, 1987). For radical therapy statements on antipsychiatry, see Agel (1973). For inmate statements, see any copy of the current Canadian magazine *Phoenix Rising* or the now defunct American publication *Madness Network News.*

1

The Radical Feminist Foundations

Radical feminism begins with the existential. It is concerned with the fundamental issues of power, freedom, subjects and objects, and human existence itself.

As existentialists have demonstrated, our human existence is predicated on our ability to project meaning, to embark on projects, to create world.[1] As subjects, we are forever creating and re-creating world by making new choices and by ordering what is around us. This world-creating ability and the transcendence of self and other that is involved distinguishes us from objects and, to a lesser extent, from other species. Objects cannot know but are known, cannot act but are acted on, can never be more than they are but are always exactly and only what they are. Their mode of existence is one of being locked into self and has been called accordingly the *in-itself.* Other species have consciousness and very definitely know. What they know, however, is not fully "world," for their actions are not full-fledged projects. Similarly they do not have the reflective awareness of self that allows them to alter self. For better and, as we are rapidly learning, for worse, human existence transcends situations. In thought and action and in the dialectic between them, we move beyond both self and what is given and change both self and world in the process. Existentialists have called this transcending dimension of our being the *for-itself* and have called this mode of our existence our *being-as-being-free.*[2]

Our being-as-being-free does not mean that anything is possible or that we can have what we want. We exist in concrete situations that are largely not of our own making and that offer resistance to our projects. Every situation in which we find ourselves involves aspects that we could not possibly change. I could not change, for instance, that I have a gender and that I bring the lived experience involved in growing up female into every new situation I face. Other aspects, such as living with misogynous people, I may be able to change. Every such change is a re-creation involving reflection, naming, and acting. Human power is our capacity to do this. *Power* comes from the word *posse,* meaning "to be able." People have power insofar as they are able to realize their projects—insofar, that is, as they are able to define/change the world.

Although this power is uniquely human or allegedly so, we are not fully human if we exercise it primarily in isolation. Insofar as we act as discrete individuals, we are negating the aspect that makes us more than isolated for-itselfs and that confers humanity on us—that is, our being-as-being-with. We are most authentically human when we appreciate our connectedness with everyone else, when we embrace the other as subject, when we engage together in world-creating dialogue. We are most authentic, correspondingly, when we realize our connectedness with all that exists and allow this ecological understanding to help form our dialogue and to guide our projects.

Oppression—the domination of certain "others" by elites—runs counter to dialogue, to being-as-being-with. It is made possible by the human being's dual status. As human beings we not only have a for-itself dimension but, like the rest of existence, we have an in-itself. When another person looks at us or thinks about us in the absence of encounter, our in-itself is seized and we become an object under his or her gaze. The existence of other consciousness means that each of us can at any time become objectified, can at any time be robbed of our freedom. It means that we have an outside that is always in the other's hands and that leaves us forever vulnerable. This "outside" from which we are alienated and that renders us alienated from ourselves allows us to be categorized and used the way objects are, and it extends to both our bodies and our consciousness. We are not fat, greedy, or "a good lay" innately or because we choose this but because others see/use/reduce us this way. Just as each of us can be turned into an object, each correspondingly can be a subject who objectifies. We can forego encounter with any consciousness, seeing "it" as "other" than ourselves. We can turn any being into another object in our means-ends network, reducing that being to something pleasurable or unpleasurable, serviceable or unserviceable.

Everyone is so determined; everyone is periodically robbed of his or her freedom. Not everyone, however, is oppressed. With oppression, we are not simply determined but "overdetermined"; that is, we systematically have qualities imposed on us and/or are defined negatively by virtue of membership in a group that may or may not be of our choosing, and our projects are thwarted with these qualities used as justification. Anyone may be seen as fat or stupid. Jews, however, are thought to be avaricious just because they are Jews, Blacks as simple and needing "hard work" just because they are Blacks, lesbians and gays as child molesters just because they are gay, the elderly as irrelevant and expendable because they are old; they may be denied position and liberties accordingly. The oppression of human groups arises from and mirrors our oppression of other species and involves a similar reduction, domination, and "animalization" of the total being; and both are rooted in our disrespect for and rape of nature. Oppression itself involves the systematic overdetermination of one group by another. It involves spiritual and material domination of one group by another. With oppression, one group—the elite—systematically reduces the "others" to objects to be characterized, used, and in some cases even disposed of. With oppression, one group has the power to realize their choices and to name the world in order to change the world, while the other has these choices, these names, and this world imposed on them.

The oppression of women, like all oppression, begins with this objectification and domination. We are not dealing with anything as simplistic as sex role division but something as complex and fundamental as the dehumanization/animalization/reification of one entire sex.

As de Beauvoir (1964) suggests, this reification characterizes civilization as we know it. I think that she is wrong in dismissing the notion of matriarchies, and certainly it is important to make distinctions and to remember that some groups, such as the Keres and the Hopi, have traditionally valued women.[3] She is right, however, when she maintains that we are living in man's world, in which woman is relegated to the position of absolute Other. Man is seen as transcendence, woman as immanence; man as for-itself, woman as in-itself; man as human, woman as nature; man as positive thrust, woman as lack. Man looks on woman from his vantage point and reduces her to a being that is not for-itself but for-him. He establishes ideologies and hierarchies that reproduce and legitimate his own objectifying stance. In the world that elite males create and that other men and elite women are at once privileged and victimized by, women are less than men; Black and Red men are less than white men; "Black and Red men's women" are less than the "white men's women"; the working class are less than the ruling class; nature is an expendable commodity to be exploited; and the objectifying stance on which all this is based is celebrated as the scientific method and seen as the *sine qua non* of human progress.

WOMAN AS BODY—PHYSICAL VIOLATION

The oppression of women, like all oppression, includes the objectification and exploitation of both mind and body. The oppression of women, however, centers fundamentally on Woman as Body, with the objectification of our consciousness figuring partly as extension of and partly as metaphor for the objectification of our body. As women, we are reduced primarily to Body by men, and that body is fetishized: Woman's body is treated not as for-itself or for-herself but as for-him. We are not seen as a living being with directions and functions of our own but as a collection of parts that exist to please and serve the male. Traditionally women's pleasure is seen as irrelevant, undesirable, uncomely. Insofar as we are seen as having pleasure, correspondingly, we are seen as insatiable and are "bestialized" just as all blacks are by some whites and as other species are by so much of humanity generally. Being woman and Black, Black women are particularly bestialized.

Woman as Body performs many services for men. Unlike with other oppressions, the principal service appears to be sexual and erotic servicing. Women's bodies are arranged, maimed, jeopardized, and tailored for the purposes of men-defined eroticism. In China, for hundreds of years men were turned on by small feet, so upper-class women—women not used in labor—had their feet bound and crippled. In many African countries Black women from all classes are given clitorectomies so that their pleasure will not interfere with men's, and infibulation is forced on them—a practice clearly geared to male pleasure at the expense of female agony.[4] Westerners are often shocked by these activities, ethnocentrically seeing their own culture and themselves as more "enlightened." At the same time, women in Western countries undergo dangerous breast surgery so that their breasts will fit the erotic standard of adult males, shave their legs because men like smooth skin, and have bum tucks, face lifts, nose bobs, and electrolysis. We dye our hair, smear our lips, paint our cheeks, stop our sweat, perfume our genitals, unkink our hair, and pluck our brows. And white women in particular are forever starving themselves because, although we are reduced to body, we are body that is expected to occupy as little space as possible. Women lose in all of this, for our body is being divided, degraded, damaged, and stolen from us. Men benefit overall, although that benefit, paradoxically, is also a loss. The male ruling elite receive extra benefit primarily at the expense of women, although also to a lesser extent at the expense of other men because the women that the elite "own" are the "ideal" and because the elite profit financially from the commodities associated with the eroticization of woman.

Despite the mystification that surrounds it, the eroticization of woman is a form of rape in its own right. It involves the violation of one body for the sexual pleasuring of another. It is a prelude to and reinforces the further violence inherent in patriarchal sex. I am referring here not only to exceptional cases but also to the violence of everyday sexual practices under the patriarchy.

As Women Against Violence Against Women (WAVAW) has clearly demonstrated, despite the mystification in which it is shrouded, the classical heterosexual sex act as practiced in the patriarchy borders on conventional rape.

In the common vernacular man "takes" woman; man "possesses" woman. This domination is graphically realized in the popular missionary position, in which man, who is demonstrably on top, straddles and thrusts himself into woman, who is on the bottom. His virility is measured by his forcefulness, by the decisiveness of his thrusts. Significantly, penetration remains the *sine qua non* of patriarchal heterosexuality regardless of its irrelevance to female orgasm and of the health hazards that it has been shown to pose for women.[5]

The violence that is implicit here is made explicit in pornography, which in turn serves to reinforce and normalize it. Women appear in chains, are shown whipped, mutilated, and tortured. Man emerges as conquering pain-giver and woman as "enthralled" sex slave. Male violence is thereby normalized; it is turned into an ideal toward which men strive and by which women are "taken."

From vision to preparation to act, the story of woman as sex object is the story of violence defined as love. What the traditional male finds erotic, significantly, is what reduces woman to body and weakens, distorts, and otherwise damages all parts of that body. It is ravishing, correspondingly, that defines heterosexual man's sexuality and that is being experienced as sexual pleasure. The violence, it would appear, is not coincidental but essential, not a by-product but part of the goal. Traditional patriarchal heterosexuality emerges as a form of domination, as an act of conquest and humiliation, as the practice of misogyny. If scrutinized closely, it reveals itself as both violence and domination in the service of male-gratifying sex and, even more worrisome, as male-defined sex in the service of violence and domination.

What is thought of as conventional rape serves as a paradigm for this sex. It also provides us with ready-made scapegoats. As long as rapists are around, the dichotomy between "good" and "evil" men is maintained. This dichotomy serves to camouflage everyday male violence and allows most men to continue "sexploiting" women, while being seen and while seeing themselves as good, kind, and caring.

Other services to "mankind" also follow from this more blatant sexual terrorism. As women we are in fear of our lives, knowing that any of us can at any time be attacked. We are not and do not feel safe in the streets or in public generally, especially at night. Some will not go out at night "unescorted." Others, who have no choice, do what they must and then proceed quickly home. Women thereby are "kept in their place."

Even at home many do not feel safe. We worry about someone breaking in, about the man we do not recognize who is peering up at our window. Most women feel safer and either publicly or privately breathe a sigh of relief when there is "a man around the house."

Men respond by providing protection. Some men, that is, protect us from the violence of other men, but the protection is not free. Although the extent varies according to culture and individual circumstance, those protected are at least to some extent humbled and grateful. White women buy protection from male

oppressors at large at the price of submission to our own individualized viola-
tors. In a white-dominated society, a woman of color, by contrast, is often joined
with an individual male with whom she shares an oppression. The home
functions as a refuge in the midst of racism. This difference needs to be
acknowledged. On the gender level, nonetheless, the man with whom she is
joined is her oppressor just as certainly as he is an oppressed ally. Although the
different types of oppression and alliances make the situation highly complex,
on a very important level she too is buying protection from men at large at the
price of submission to an individual violator. Barry (1979) understandably calls
this setup *sexual slavery.*

The privatized woman and the public woman—the wife and the whore—are
the principal forms that sexual slavery takes, and they are mutually reinforcing.
The wife is maimed, violated, beaten, and protected by her man. The prostitute
is beaten, raped, and otherwise violated by a pimp who valiantly protects her
from all other pimps.

Prostitutes exist, correspondingly, partly to guarantee the rights of safe
sexual violence to single men, although more fundamentally to allow "attached" men freer expression of misogynous violence without jeopardizing the
additional servicing provided by partners. Men who practice unbridled sexual
violence on their "women" would clearly jeopardize the relationship, which
after all does include genuine affection and intimacy, and they would also
jeopardize the more delicate emotional servicing that goes with it. With whores,
greater violation is possible, just as it is in conventional rape and without the
inherent danger.

Significantly, sex with whores is exclusively tailored to male desire, with the
pleasuring of the female never entering at all except by way of male-serving
fantasy. Even today, when more and more prostitutes are claiming their power
and are setting clearer limits to what they will and will not do, what is being
bought is nonetheless comparatively less restricted and more condensed sexual
violence. The money exchanged turns the violence into a business and effectively absolves the violator from responsibility and guilt, much as the financial
support given the partner magically transforms domestic violence into wifely
duty. The fantasy often provides an additional, even if contradictory, form of
absolution. And the racism and classism that support prostitution and that help
separate the "good" and "bad" women offer still further absolution. The hierar-
chical division between "good women" and "bad women" in turn legitimates
the conventional raping of prostitutes, "sluts," and women of color; together
they serve to terrorize both the "good woman" and the "bad woman," keeping
both in line.

The overall reduction of women to sexual object as described here underlies
and gives shape to sexism generally. As MacKinnon (1982) has argued, the
female "sex role," together with its limitations, has clear roots in sexual
servicing.

If the literature on sex roles and the investigations of particular issues are read in light of each other, each element of the female *gender* stereotype is revealed as, in fact, *sexual.* Vulnerability means the appearance/reality of easy sexual access; passivity means receptivity and disabled resistance, enforced by trained physical weakness; softness means pregnability by something hard. Incompetence seeks help as vulnerability seeks shelter, inviting the embrace that becomes the invasion. . . . Socially, femaleness means femininity, which means attractiveness, which means sexual availability on male terms. Gender socialization is the process through which women internalized themselves as sexual beings, as beings that exist for men. . . . Women who resist or fail, including those who never did fit—for example, Black and lower-class women who cannot survive if they are soft and weak and incompetent, assertively self-respecting women, women with ambitions of male dimensions—are considered lesser female, lesser women. (MacKinnon, 1982, pp. 16-17)

Whether the role played by sex is as absolute as MacKinnon suggests, woman as sexual object is clearly foundational for the gender role and serves as prototype.

If the sexual domination of women is operant in all forms of sexism, and if all center on woman's body as in-itself, it is clear that all sexism involves mind as well as body and for-itself as well as in-itself. Were "thing" or "dead body" precisely what was being found attractive, necrophilia as traditionally understood would be the preferred practice, as opposed to a mode that is hauntingly familiar.[6] As well, more women would be killed or rendered unconscious during patriarchal sex. For the most part it is a live being that is being sought throughout, albeit one that is alienated, that is no longer totally for-itself. It is for-itself that is en route to but that never reaches in-itself. Sexploitation involves the partial, not the complete, reduction of woman. We must be sufficiently objectified to be a body that is for-men and at the same time sufficiently our-selves to have human grace and movement. Correspondingly we must have certain thoughts and attitudes—the types, of course, that accommodate exploitation but that nonetheless leave us with a quasi-human status.

The territory that is relegated to us is a narrow strip halfway between subject and object, human and nonhuman. It is "no man's land" but somehow is expected to be woman's land. Insofar as we accept it, we remain confused and confusing, always in danger of losing our footing or overstepping our bounds.

WOMAN AS BODY—LABOR EXPLOITATION

Just as we are reduced to a body tailored for the sexual servicing of males, we are reduced or quasi-reduced to a body to bear men's children, a body to nurture and raise men's children, a body fit for "mindless" household drudgery. Few women totally escape this drudgery. Tragically a number of those who escape it partially do so only because they have conditional access to their husbands' money (and those conditions are mammoth) and only at the unacceptable expense of other women's double labor. Although the oppression clearly is not equal and the dominant woman is herself oppressing, the slave who has her own slave is still a slave, despite her illusions to the contrary. The slave of a slave who works in other women's houses, correspondingly, is also a slave in her own. Black and low-income women who do household service for middle- and upper-class whites still drag themselves home to do it in their own.

As Marxists have demonstrated, women are very much slave labor—labor that is neither recompensed nor regulated but is owned. Like the traditional slave, we serve others, are a being-for-others. We are given menial work that requires that we be for-itself but keeps pulling us toward in-itself. Unlike most slaves, though, we are presumed to be doing this freely, out of our own bountiful love. The mode of being allowed us in patriarchal society—being-for-others— is contradictorily envisioned as a destiny given us by nature and as a human project freely chosen. The project of giving, correspondingly, is seen as arising from our own caring and generosity—qualities, curiously, that are viewed as determined and yet that are demanded of us whenever we act differently.

As body, as labor, we are owned ultimately by the patriarchal state, as the state's involvement in abortion makes only too clear. *Fetal rights* means that the state can condemn pregnant women to 9 months of hard labor and to the ongoing life problems and directions that ensue. Our bodies are held captive, and the human right to say no is denied.

It is in the traditional home that Woman as Body and as labor is owned most consistently and most personally. The fruits of our reproductive labor are claimed by the father. In the traditional family, which brings with it not natural motherhood but "the institution of motherhood," moreover, woman as wife and mother becomes personalized slave. She does not have her own world but instead has the world of others thrust on her. She is there to take care of everything and everybody, to accommodate, to straighten everything up.

On the physical side, woman as drudge takes care of others by performing the household routines that are undeniably important and that give her and could give anyone else grounding but that are as deadening as a steady diet. All too often her work is not transcendence but monotonous, repetitive tasks that change nothing and that need to be done again and again. Day after day she sweeps the floor, makes the beds, washes the dishes, dusts the furniture, prepares the food. Although the advent of 20th-century feminism has meant more men "chipping in" and some movement toward equality, and although significant differences certainly exist between households, even among the so-called "progressives," equality is generally more of a pretense than a reality. Man characteristically does not notice certain messes, and woman obligingly picks up after him. Physically, woman remains domestic laborer.

On the emotional side she is the nurturer. She is always there, outside of herself, thinking about what others need. She calms, she reassures, she supports, she makes certain that everyone else is all right. The personal intimacy and the giving are undeniably wonderful. Women are the richer and more fully human for being able to be intimate and to give, and men are the poorer for not developing this side of themselves. Insofar as this intimacy and personal giving are compulsory, one-sided, and all-encompassing, however, they are fundamentally dehumanizing and are a tyranny. They mean having no Self. They mean having all the responsibilities and none of the rights. They mean being taken for granted and being blamed by professionals, family, community, and state alike when anything goes wrong. They mean not mattering, not being important. They mean having the little child that is inside all of us forever sacrificed.

This caretaking and nurturing service is expected not only from mothers and wives but also from almost all women and not only in the home but in society at large. If a lone child somewhere needs nurture, whatever woman is present is almost invariably the one to respond. If a meeting is being held and someone asks whether anyone will take notes, all eyes turn toward the women. Most women spend countless hours listening to the monologues of male friends, hearing their bragging, and empathizing with their tales of woe. It takes active and ongoing refusal to make a dent in the imbalance. Women who refuse to listen or who demand some semblance of equality are dismissed as "cold bitches" by the average man, as well as by male-identified women, and are often seen as problematic even by those who pride themselves on being politically aware. These problems are still very pervasive. Social life has not changed as much as we had hoped.

Despite the changes in the last few decades, many women today are still trapped in the home, are still isolated and submerged. A great many more than was once the case are leaving the home to work in outside jobs, and this is sometimes good. For women even more than men, however, the external labor force is not now and never was the deliverance that educated, white, middle-class feminists supposed, though it is clearly better for those with privilege. For Black women, Natives, immigrants, and for poor women—a category that is rapidly increasing—work outside the home has always existed, and work outside tends to mean assembly lines. Assembly line work, whether in factories or in typing pools, is every bit as monotonous and soul-destroying as household drudgery. Monotonous work in sexist and racist workplaces is piled on top of women's work at home. As Black feminists have pointed out, many indeed would give their eyeteeth for the opportunity to stay at home. Women, especially women of color, remain cheap labor. Despite the liberal talk of equality, the truth is that the majority of women are saddled with work that most men do not want and at salaries that even oppressed men are not forced to accept. Many women find demeaning domestic duties slipped into their jobs even though these are not included in the job descriptions. Almost all women are subject to some form of sexual harassment from bosses or male colleagues. Most remain at the lower end of the hierarchy, while men who know demonstrably less receive greater respect and more authority. Those women who manage to get a bit of authority are generally resented. Most married women, correspondingly, find themselves with two full-time jobs—one at the workplace and one at home.

UPBRINGING

Home and school are the earliest institutions responsible for facilitating that internalization of sexism known as *female upbringing*. Individual parents and teachers vary, of course. Some try hard to combat societal sexism, and some are better at doing so than others. Others clearly exceed the sexist norm. All, however, are affected negatively by the sexist society in which we live, and all correspondingly pass on some type of sexism.

As decades of feminists have demonstrated only too clearly, the paradigmal little girl is treated differently from the paradigmal little boy. While the boy is encouraged to venture out into the world, to explore, and to go about his projects, the girl is encouraged to stay home, in some cases to be absolutely adorable, and in almost all cases to help mother and teacher and to be very, very obedient. She receives less attention than male students. She is taught androcentric history. Generally she receives less nurture than her brother. And she is the one forced into household chores. The result is both deprivation and the clear message that "serious" learning and nurture are not for her. She is being primed to be body that caretakes and body that exists for the pleasuring of others.

If from a dominant, and often even a nondominant, Western culture, very early on, she is initiated into romantic love—an ideology that glorifies men and both glamorizes and enforces heterosexuality—all at the expense of women. If from North America, she is likely read misogynous, racist, and classist stories like *Cinderella* and *Snow White*. Whether she is white or of color, the stories create cognitive dissonance, but far more if she is of color. What she learns is that mother/woman is inherently wicked but that, thankfully, she (the fair blonde-haired daughter) is not really related to mother at all but rather is a princess in disguise who will one day be rescued by a handsome prince. Later, when she is a teenager, societal influences coming from home, school, peer groups, and community groups converge powerfully on the romantic ideal. She is encouraged to date boys and to measure her success in life by her popularity with "guys"—something often achieved at the expense of her female friends with whom she is truly close. Insofar as this encouragement is successful, she periodically competes for boyfriends with her female friends, and she breaks appointments with them when a date pops up. She feels complimented if her boyfriend is jealous, extra attentive, and possessive, because this means that she is "truly loved," in other words, DESIRED BY A MAN, HENCE DESIRABLE, HENCE WORTHWHILE. She is primed to seek out a possessive, domineering male partner and to become significantly isolated from her female friends and from acquaintances generally. Later she may be railed at, constantly accused of infidelity, locked in the house, and battered mercilessly, while continuing to see her man as someone who needs her and deeply loves her. Wife battery, it is important to realize, is only the romantic ideal carried one stage further. Insofar as her childhood includes seeing her father shouting at and beating her mother, she is further primed to accept ongoing abuse.

The power of example and of covert messages that prepare the young woman to accept an abusive partner mitigates what feminist or womanist elements exist in her upbringing. Most girls, as I have observed, do not receive the undiluted sexist upbringing that is paradigmal. The young girl is more likely to be given an impossible array of liberated and oppressive messages that hopelessly contradict one another and confuse. The vast majority of Black women are given the message that they need to work if they are to survive and indeed were given that message long before white women took up feminism. They are taught to be capable, to be survivors. Unlike white women, they are taught to be strong. These days, a Black women may also be told that she can do anything that her brother can. Chances are, however, that if any money can be saved to further any of the children's education, it will go to her brother. The covert message is that while strong, capable, and equally destined to work, she is not as important. Correspondingly a white woman may continually be complimented on how lovely she looks, while her brother is complimented on his mathematical acumen. At the same time, she is told that women are every bit as bright as men and that she can be anything she wants when she grows up. She is getting both a direct and an indirect message. Unfortunately, indirect messages are more influential than direct messages. The indirect message that is given by the mother's and other women's management of their own lives, correspondingly, is very forceful indeed. Despite the overt messages, the examples provided generally tell the girl that mathematics is not for her, that she is to cultivate men sexually, that she is to identify her welfare and indeed her cultural group's welfare with the men's; and she is likely to comply at least to some degree.

DIVIDING WOMAN FROM WOMAN

The division between women on which the patriarchy so fundamentally depends is effected initially in the patriarchal household. Girls are drawn to their mothers in a profound way, this being at once the body out of which they came and the body that reflects back their own image. The identification and attraction generalize into woman-woman attraction and identification generally, and they constitute and have always constituted a profound threat to patriarchal rule. The patriarchy responds by promoting disidentification and separation.

Even in Black families, in which female bonding tends to be so much stronger, the early fairy tales and the early glamorizing of heterosexuality separate most girls from mother/woman, who is her first love and quite likely her sexual preference. Separation from mother (women) and the switching of allegiance and love to father (men) are also furthered by the institution of motherhood. Bearing most of the responsibility for raising and disciplining the children, mother is set up to appear like the domineering shrew. The absent, good-natured father looks very attractive by comparison, unless, of course, he is not good-natured and/or his violence is too obvious. Even the father who lives on his own, whether he has deserted or not, stands a good chance of being preferred, for he is absolved from discipline and can buy children with gifts and good times, although this is somewhat less likely to happen in the poor family, the Black family, and/or the newly formed lesbian family in which positive female co-parenting exists. Anyone can see that identification with mother means drudgery and powerlessness. Collusion with father is an obvious pull, and father generally is only too ready to collude. The daughter's live intelligence after all is attractive, compared to the dullness of his exhausted wife-turned-drudge; and in the early years this intelligence is not sufficiently threatening that it need be snuffed out. Often father and daughter look down on mother (woman) together. They exchange meaningful glances when she misses a point. They agree that she is not bright as they are, cannot reason as they do. This collusion does not save the daughter from the mother's fate. Much to her horror, she finds father progressively acting in accordance with a different set of rules. As she gets older, she is more often lumped with the mother (woman) to whom she feels superior. Intermittently she feels furious with father for going along with the unfair status change and in the process may switch affection to others. More fundamentally, however, she blames mother for passing on the curse of womanhood, often while continuing to see father (man) as a possible ally or savior.

The father's preference for the daughter intellectually is paralleled by a preference sexually and emotionally. Mother as drudge may be performing the labor function expected of Woman as Body, but in the very process of doing so she falls short of being the ideal sex object. The daughter is softer, more malleable, more infantile, by domineering male standards, far more desirable. Mother is set up as rival in a mother-father-daughter triangle, and the daughter is primed for further seduction.

Incest as we know it is the extreme, albeit an extreme that is very common indeed. Despite the romanticization in which fathering is clouded, it is an extreme that is prepared for and that exists latently in the traditional father-daughter relationship. Some individual fathers, of course, are not seductive, do not violate, and offer a vision of a better future, just as some individual male partners are benign, but even the best generally sexualize in some way. If we are to get a handle on what is happening, we must stop looking at incest as a separate deviant category as the patriarchy has taught us to and dare to see its relationship with traditional fathering.

The patriarchal father-daughter relationship exists on what might be described as an *incest continuum*. The entire continuum is intrusive, with the degree of intrusion increasing from left to right. On the left (least intrusive side) is the preferring and the sexual innuendos already described. These compliment daughter and effect a quasi-sexual father-daughter relationship at mother's expense and at the expense of woman-woman relating more generally. Further along the continuum is sexual behavior that is more direct and more problematic. Here we find overt flirtation and physical contact that is clearly sensual and that borders on the sexual. This flirtation and this contact drive a formidable wedge between mother and daughter, often leaving daughter with a combination of titillation, frustration, fear, and confusion.

Incest as characteristically defined is on the more intrusive side of the continuum and is characterized by some form of genital contact. Despite our pretense to the contrary, it is frighteningly common although hidden, and it humiliates and subordinates mother and daughter alike. It gives the wife the message, "You are no longer any good and are lucky I keep you," and the daughter the message, "Ultimately you are good for one thing only." Both are immobilized by it, though the daughter especially is held captive. If it is repeated a number of times, as it is further along the continuum, the daughter becomes horrified and confused; she wants to flee, but being already at home, has no place to go. The paradigmal incest survivor desperately wants to tell an outsider, but she remains silent out of the conviction that she will not be believed and/or out of loyalty to the family. She is tormented by the thought that it is really her fault for being so seductive. She may tell mother, only to hear mother deny it or blame her, for mother too is trapped. She suspects that mother knows. She may believe that sleeping with father is the only way to keep him from deserting the family, and so, curiously, it is her duty. She generally blames mother for not rescuing her, for not being interested in sex, and for not being a proper partner for father and thereby dumping her with the task. Later she may flee sex. Alternatively she may become highly promiscuous because she has been taught that sex equals love. Besides, as father has made only too clear, "this is all that she is good for anyway."

Repeated infant violation and frequent and ongoing brutal violation in childhood are the extreme, and they are absolutely devastating, whether the father figure is actual father, mother's boyfriend, uncle, parenting brother, stepfather, or some combination thereof. They are acts of terrorism that leave the child existentially overwhelmed, petrified, and alone. Inevitably this existential devastation goes with her into adulthood. The paradigmal incest survivor lives in a perpetual state of siege. Nothing is safe. Anything and anybody can hurt her, can rip her open the way father did. Anyone can abandon her as mother did.

The separation between mother and daughter that is implicit here prepares for the larger separation between woman and woman generally, and that larger separation is the cornerstone of male supremacy. Divide and rule, quite literally, is the formula. The mother and daughter, as has already been demonstrated, are separated through paternal acts of preference, seduction, and collusion. Rape is paradigmal of and metaphor for what is happening, as is epitomized in the Greek myth of Persephone.

Persephone, the daughter of Ceres (an earth goddess), is violently abducted by her uncle, who is Ruler of the Underworld. He steals her from her mother and motherland, ravishes her, and forces her to live in the Underworld as his wife, far from the love and company of Ceres. Mother and daughter pine as a result.[7] Although father/husband is disguised as uncle here, it is frighteningly clear what this myth is revealing/concealing. The patriarchal father-daughter relationship is being depicted as an incestuous act of violence that diminishes female power and adds to male dominion. At its center is the brutal separation of mother and daughter. Separation by the excluding "husband"—a violation of the woman-woman bond that continues the violation by the father—is similarly conveyed.

Wherever it may be on the continuum, father-daughter incest works to separate mother and daughter in the patriarchal household. Separation correspondingly is ensured by making mother responsible for both disciplining and for patriarchal policing, whether this policing takes the form of overseeing foot binding and clitorectomies, as in China and Africa, or of pushing crippling shoes or diets, as in America. Daughter/victim is set up to hate mother/tyrant. Envy of the younger woman who is treated so much better in the patriarchy and whom the mother is thereby being set up to resent can enter into and dreadfully complicate what is happening. In most cases, though, mother (woman) is primarily doing what she thinks she must if daughter is to get by. Woman is associated with the injury and blamed, while man appears to have nothing whatever to do with it, benefits, and is absolved.

Women more generally are separated from each other by overresponsibility, co-optation, and the horror of female existence. We are separated from each other by ongoing male violence, male-serving ideologies, patriarchal marriage, and the threat of poverty, which helps keep these marriages intact. From a different vantage point we are also separated from each other by our own and by others' racism, ageism, and ableism.

On the geographic level the overall gender separation translates into the dispersion of women into the various homes of the oppressor. On the sexual/ emotional gender level, where sexism so fundamentally resides, it translates into compulsory heterosexuality and homophobia in the broadest understanding of the terms.

Essentially, as radical feminist Adrienne Rich (1986, pp. 33-75) has helped us all see, the nascent threat that mother poses to the patriarchy in the early years, female lover poses in the later years, for both "realize" and symbolize woman-woman love in its intensity. The patriarchy's response is to separate lesbian existence from the broad continuum of physical and emotional woman-woman intimacy in which it is embedded, for which it serves as paradigm, and to which it lends its power. Lesbian existence is isolated from what Rich meaningfully calls the rest of the lesbian continuum, and then is effectively stigmatized, punished, and pushed underground. In the process, woman-woman relatedness is severely weakened and male domination more securely entrenched.

By striking at the paradigm of woman-woman love, the patriarchy is robbing woman-woman love of fullness, meaning, and continuity. It is thereby weakening the bond between women generally. It is countering a general threat to male domination. It is suppressing a very direct and very specific threat to the heterosexual monopoly on which the patriarchy fundamentally depends. The point is that if women were not compelled to see themselves as primarily loving/needing men, the heterosexual monopoly could not exist. By forcing women to equate heterosexuality with naturalness and lesbian existence with the unnatural, men are effectively keeping women to themselves and away from each other. The concept of *natural* camouflages the violence involved.

The current liberal conceptualization similarly camouflages the compulsion. Calling compulsory heterosexuality "heterosexual choice" or "preference" creates the impression that we are free and open, but it does not change reality. *Heterosexual preference, it is important to realize, is not preference or choice by any ordinary understanding of the terms.* We cannot speak of choice or preference when only one option is allowed. Although in a different society, it could be a real and meaningful choice, heterosexuality as we know it is a form of coercion dictated by male ideology/propaganda, by force, by stigma, by the erasure of lesbian existence, and by the erasure of the coercion itself, so that what is imposed is made to look like the natural unfolding of our inclinations. The truth is that despite our seeming or avowed clarity, most women do not authentically think through their sexuality but accept the heterosexual preference that we have been programmed to assume. The quick questioning that the more progressive allow themselves and the quick reassurances and/or easy compromises that they give themselves do not alter this fact. Women everywhere are railroaded into strict heterosexuality, while thinking that they are making free choices or are acting in accordance with their own personal proclivity. Women thereby are kept from sensing and following their own inclinations. We are being given a "straight-forward" path that is not ours and that blinds us to the complex matrix of affinities that is "woman's".

Compulsory heterosexuality and the larger separation between women that it symbolizes are a female tragedy. They are a tragedy of isolation, of limited alternatives. More personally and more profoundly, however, they are a tragedy of identity and of self. As long as we do not know who we are, as long as we do not know the complexities of our feelings, understandings, and inclinations, we easily become/remain a being with no self—not a for-itself but the for-men into which the patriarchy has fashioned us. By blinding us to the complex matrix of affinities that is woman's and by not letting us see our selves as reflected in our sisters and in our attraction to our sisters, the patriarchy effectively keeps us from knowing who we are. Woman in a profound and meaningful way is being kept from knowing self by being prevented from knowing woman.

LATER YEARS

As women age, the harsh realities of ageism and sexism combine. In some cultures, like the Native, older women are valued and respected. Not so in the dominant and most nondominant North American cultures. Not attractive by male standards, no longer "of service" sexually or domestically, we are not valued. Our wisdom is not recognized. Many an older woman is deserted by a male partner who prefers younger women. Older woman as despised or inconvenient mother or mother-in-law may be barely tolerated in her children's home. Having earned very little money throughout their lives and having very little pension, the majority of older women are poor. Many face the violence and infantilization of the nursing home. Unhappy, alone, and no longer able to put up the pretenses expected, many end up subjected to antidepressants and electroshock.

RESISTANCE

Resistance is rooted in woman's being for-itself. On the visionary side, it begins with women's ability to see through hegemonic pretensions despite the mystification and confusion. All oppressed groups have dual vision because all must keep moving between their own nascent understanding and the oppressors' if they are to survive. Women's dual vision leads to confusion because we keep losing wherever and whoever we are. This notwithstanding, there are times when all women are keenly perceptive. Each one of us has moments when, intuitively at least, we see the ego, the posturing, and the self-deception that underlie male creation. At times every woman, at some level, is painfully and furiously aware of the sexual violence that permeates male-female relations and is disgusted by it. All women—even those who see men as vastly superior—have an essential disrespect that never completely disappears.

This disrespect has enormous existential significance. When we experience disrespect, while we are in no way altering systemic oppression, we are momentarily turning the tables on the "other." We become the subject under whose penetrating gaze the "other" is objectified and found inadequate. The transition involved is much like the transition that occurs when the slave who is being whipped by his master suddenly whirls around and glares at him with contempt. The rape victim who gets in touch with her anger casts a similar glare. It does not in itself change the external situation, but it is the ground on which analysis and action are built.

When "seeing through" is coupled with analysis, our resistance becomes truly powerful and genuinely threatens the patriarchy. Access to empowering analysis, correspondingly, is part of what it means to be women in this society.

Analysis varies from the sporadic, which is an important beginning, to the rigorous and systematic. Early on it may extend only to a few practices. It may amount, say, only to identifying the systematic biases and omissions accompanying chore divisions. Whatever it may be, it is ground on which to build. Toward the middle of what might be called the *awareness continuum,* women progressively and more consistently see through the myths, propaganda, and institutions. Women see and have a meaningful analysis of the subordination and the violence that underlies it. Many have trouble moving on. Some feel that they would lose too much if they sustained their present vision, and they flee from what they know. Others, especially those whose early upbringing involved being treated as honorary males, have difficulty letting go of the male identification. Their new vision still centers on male values, although it "appears" to eliminate sexism by turning all women into men. They are nonetheless decidedly "en route."

Women further along the continuum offer the vision of the visionary. While rooted in the present, they project themselves concurrently into the future and into the past so that their "having-been" helps form their "becoming." Women with such vision value and cherish many of the characteristics associated with women—with working-class women, with women of color, with lesbians— seeing and proclaiming them as the pivotal values on which a better society can be built. They cherish and attempt to promote such values as life-affirmation, nurture, cooperation, adaptation, respect for aging, environmental connectedness, process foci, and power sharing, and many create liberated zones where these values are realized at least for a time. Here we go beyond analysis to imagination, synthesis, renaming, and action.

Women's vision may be seen as an act of resistance in its own right. Seeing out of our own eyes is itself disobeying the patriarchy. Women also resist more concretely. As women we are beings who act and whose actions can be our own. We can and to some extent always do wage a war of active/passive resistance.

The resistance that is action similarly varies in degree, effectiveness, and scope. Some women's acts are limited, individual, and border on resignation, but even here is a core of resistance that is poignant and meaningful. In this category we find the housewife who stops cleaning up and just sits there unhappy and "unable" to do anything. In the past psychiatry would have said that she is having a nervous breakdown. Today it would say that she is "chronically depressed." These "diagnoses" are not so much wrong as horrendously limited. She is clearly "sick to death" of the endless repetitive chores that befall her as woman. She is fundamentally exhausted, worn out, bored; she "cannot take it anymore," and her being is rebelling. Her exhaustion is not phoney but absolutely genuine. At the same time, as the contradiction inherent in linking *cannot* with *rebelling* implies, "cannot take it anymore" to some degree means "*is not* and *will not* take it anymore." Although the refusal may not be happening on a reflective plane and refusal is only one dimension of what is occurring, this woman in her own way is going on strike. The wife who always has a headache similarly is on strike. She may not think, "Sex with my husband is like being invaded and I'm not going to take it anymore," but she is taking action, however, and on some level is aware that she is taking action. Here too are many of the women who are thought of as whiners, criers, manipulators, and underminers. Feeling powerless in a situation in which they clearly do not have equal power and in which power exists over them, they use indirect means. They access underground power. What we have here is nothing less than the strength of the survivor.

Other women more blatantly resist, albeit sporadically and tentatively. This resistance prepares for more decisive stands in the future. Naysaying is essentially a practiced skill that women learn by doing.

Toward the end of the continuum is more consistent, deliberate, and systematic action. On the personal level, every day throughout the world women engage in decisive acts of resistance. We protect our daughters from incestuous fathers. We leave unsatisfactory relationships. We dress and talk in ways that repudiate sexual objectification. We refuse to paint or mutilate our bodies. We force our way into male-dominated professions. We demand nonsexist division of chores. On the political level women throughout the world analyze with other women, speak out, write, act. We enter consciousness-raising groups. We tear up pornography. We push for pay equity. We march with our sisters in take-back-the-night marches. We form women- and age-affirming groups like Crones of Ottawa. Many women are actively engaged on one or both of these levels. On both levels what we are doing is actively refusing to be a body-for-men, whether in the primary sexual way or in the secondary menial way. We are demystifying, renaming, and battling against our oppression and the violence on which it depends. We are daring to reclaim our alienated bodies, our stolen selves. The personal empowers us as women and prepares us for the political. The political itself is empowering as a process and leads to the societal change without which fuller personal liberation is impossible.

More complex vision and action are accessed and taken in addressing dual oppression, triple oppression, and quadruple oppression. Bit by bit, women are teasing out the classism, racism, and ableism in mainstream feminism; the sexism, heterosexism, and ableism in communities of color. As Jewish women, women of color, and women with disabilities, we form our own collectives. We do educationals. We both join with and challenge others with whom we share oppressions. In the process, we are beginning to create/re-create a women's movement that serves all women.

If woman's vision—all women's vision—is the guide to concrete resistance, woman-woman relating is at once an act of resistance and the space in which woman's vision and action flourishes. It is, as it were, the basic building blocks from which liberated zones are created. Despite the terrorism and divisive tactics of the patriarchy, this relating similarly exists and has always existed. Wherever they may exist on the lesbian continuum, women have always been and continue to be profoundly drawn to each other. We turn to one another. We hear each other's secrets. We share our innermost thoughts with each other. Physically and emotionally we comfort one another in times of distress. We explore together. We take joy in each other. We co-mother together. In all of this, whether we are fully aware of it or not, we are engaging in a pivotal act of resistance. We are disobeying the patriarchal "prime directive" to be a body for-man and are ignoring the order to disperse. Toward the farther end of the lesbian continuum are many women who commit the ultimate act of treason— choosing a female partner. Today this choice is being made more openly, more defiantly. The importance of this resistance can be measured by the patriarchal reaction to it. Both actually and symbolically, by loving one another, women are demonstrating their independence of men. We are choosing self and are affirming the full range of affinities and connections inherent in being woman. By relating to each other personally and intimately, no matter what form this relating may take, women are reaffirming the essential bond between women that patriarchy so brutally violates and on whose violation patriarchy so fundamentally depends. By coming together correspondingly we are creating room for women's vision, for feminist analysis, and for action.

SUGGESTED READINGS

Barry, K. (1979). *Female sexual slavery.* New York: Avon.
Daly, M. (1978). *Gyn/ecology: The metaethics of radical feminism.* Boston: Beacon.
Hooks, B. (1984). *Feminist theory: From margin to center.* Boston: South End.
Koedt, A., Levine, E., & Rapone, A. (Eds.). (1973). *Radical feminism.* New York: Quadrangle.
Lorde, A. (1984). *Sister outsider.* Freedom, CA: The Crossing.
MacKinnon, C. (1982). Feminism, Marxism, method, and the state: An agenda for theory. In N. O. Koehane, M. Rosaldo, & B. Gelpi (Eds.), *Feminist theory: A critique of ideology* (pp. 1-30). Chicago: University of Chicago Press.
Rhodes, D., & McNeill, S. (1985). *Women against violence against women.* London: Onlywomen Press.
Rich, A. (1986). *Blood, bread, and poetry: Selected prose 1979-1985.* New York: Norton.

NOTES

1. This existential analysis borrows from Sartrean and Freirian existentialism. Sartrean existentialism is fundamental because it is the grounding out of which de Beauvoir wrote, and through de Beauvoir it underpins much of feminist thought. In my analysis, I make explicit much of what de Beauvoir left implicit. My use of Sartre and Freire in no way implies an acceptance of the sexism of either. For Sartre's and Freire's own articulation, see Sartre (1956) and Freire (1970).

2. For a more detailed discussion of the for-itself, see Sartre (1956), pp. 119-298.

3. For an analysis of the woman-centered nature of Native life and an attempt to recover the gynocentric traditions that have been erased, see Allen (1986).

4. For a more detailed portrait and discussion of these practices, see Daly (1978), pp. 135-177, and Dworkin (1974), pp. 95-117.

5. For a detailed analysis of heterosexuality as violence, as developed by Women Against Violence Against Women (WAVAW), and for commentary on the health hazards posed, see Rhodes and McNeill (1985).

6. Dworkin (1974, pp. 34-36) discusses the necrophilic nature of patriarchal male heterosexuality, using the *Sleeping Beauty* fairy tale as a paradigm.

7. Many feminists have discussed the Persephone story. For a particularly insightful discussion of it, see Chesler (1972), pp. xiv-xix, 17-18, 22, 26, 27-30, 264-266, 267-268, 275, and 281.

2

Psychiatry

Psychiatry is fundamentally problematic. The problem is more basic than the obvious difficulties posed by drugs, electroshock, and incarceration. Psychiatry has no viable scientific or even conceptual foundations. It is based on the concept of *mental illness*. We have talked about mental illness for so long and so many government initiatives are devoted to curing these illnesses that the concept seems natural to us. It is nonetheless illogical, unscientific, and indeed almost unintelligible.

Illness by definition is "of the body," and it is characterized by verifiable lesions or swelling—scientifically observable pathology, in other words. The mind is not the body. The mind is an activity of the body. Activities cannot have diseases. The brain is physical, and so there can be and indeed are brain diseases. Alzheimer's is a case in point. With genuine brain diseases such as Alzheimer's, there are observable lesions or swelling. People with "mental illnesses" such as schizophrenia, however, have no such brain lesions or swelling. Moreover, as psychiatrist and psychiatric researcher Peter Breggin (1983) clearly demonstrated, despite years of attempting to prove chemical imbalance, the only chemical imbalances that people called "schizophrenic" and "manic-depressive" can be shown to have are those that psychiatric drugs themselves produce.

As Szasz (1974) pointed out years ago, what we have here essentially is a metaphor. It is, however, a metaphor that is treated as if it were a literal truth and that is backed up by the power of the state. The state hires doctors called "psychiatrists" and empowers them to decide who has these "diseases." It gives psychiatrists the horrendous power to name and lock up people who may or may not be having emotional difficulties and to treat them for diseases that have no basis in fact.

It is difficult to be clear when thinking about psychiatry. It has so shaped our thinking that the categories betray us. We find ourselves asking what to do with people who are "mentally ill." We ask how to "treat" "life-threatening depression." If we are to cut through the hegemony, we need to step behind these terms and come at psychiatry from perspectives that do not already fall under psychiatric control. A helpful place to start is with psychiatry as it began and as it evolved, for it is out of the past and its transformations that the oppression of the present is born.

THE HISTORY

Psychiatry is a white patriarchal European invention. In early Europe far fewer people were declared mad, and doctors were only one of a number of groups who catered to people seen as mad or people with problems in living. Slowly this elite male medical group sought for and gained control over the madness turf, shaped it to suit their own ends, and successfully expanded the terrain.

The early medical explanation for "madness" stemmed from the theory of humours. The body was seen as containing four very fine substances called *humours.* Mental difficulties were credited to an imbalance in the humours. Doctors attempted to restore the alleged imbalance of the humours, much as psychiatrists attempt to restore alleged chemical imbalances today.[1]

From the Middle Ages onward, a second and very powerful group with jurisdiction in this area was the Church. The Church attributed madness to possession by the Devil and regarded possession by the Devil as punishment for evildoing. Help consisted of casting the Devil out of people and was accomplished by such torturous measures as confinement, beating, reciting chants over people manacled to chairs, and hurling insults at the Devil within.

Businessmen were the third group. Initially it was primarily businessmen who ran asylums. There was no "treatment" in the asylums because there was no "illness."

A fourth significant group and by far the largest and most sought-after was the powerful female healers called *witches, midwives,* and *wise women.* These women ministered to emotional as well as to physical problems, bringing natural herbs and counsel to those in distress. Unlike physicians, who relied on books and authority and who worked abstractly, the wise women operated empirically, using what they discovered and altering their approach to fit individual need. The common folk relied on the wise women extensively because, unlike the doctors, they were affordable, reliable, and actually helpful.

This last group is a remnant—a core—of female power in the midst of patriarchy. The witches and midwives were women-identified women, often lesbian. They were the inheritors of early religions, of earlier ways of being. For century after century they defied the patriarchy, bringing women's knowledge, spirituality, and ways of healing to those in need. They represented a very real threat to the patriarchy generally. They were a special threat to male doctors, whose male ways of curing were not nearly so popular, and to the patriarchal Church. The doctors initially responded by condemning these healers and by arguing successfully that they be outlawed. The Church responded by massacring them.

On December 9, 1484, Pope Innocent VIII issued a Bull, naming Sprenger and Kramer chief inquisitors and giving the Inquisition extensive powers to confine, try, torture, and burn people accused of witchcraft.[2] The Bull ushered in more than a century of torture and killing—all of it in the name of help. Inquisitor after inquisitor brutally extracted confessions from our foremothers. Once the women confessed, the Church consigned them to the flames, allegedly to save their immortal souls.

Without a doubt the Inquisition was a massive gynocidal enterprise based on the hatred and fear of women. The vast majority of people tried were women. The "hideous crimes" attributed to those women are clear reflections of male insecurity. Witches, it was said, made the penis disappear, and they smote men with impotence. Male disgust at Woman as Body correspondingly can be found in the vivid descriptions of the "disgusting" sexual acts committed by witches, together with Sprenger and Kramer's pronouncement: "All witchcraft comes from carnal lust, which in women is insatiable" (Sprenger & Kramer, 1948, p. 123).

Significantly, despite the frequent recitations of the "terrible crimes" committed by the witches, it was the power to do good, not so much the power to do evil, that the clerics and the doctors explicitly objected to. Many argued that the bad witch might be spared because she was so hated that she was of minimal danger but that the good witch or healer was much sought-after and appreciated and therefore should be put to death.

The persecution of the witches left the male-dominated Church and the male-dominated medical profession more securely in charge of the madness turf. The doctors wrested further control by discrediting the Church. They argued that madness was not caused by demons but by somatic imbalances and consequently should be treated by medicine. Correspondingly the doctors maintained that the women accused of witchcraft were deluded, pathetic creatures—not consorts of the demons. They objected to the Church's torturing of these women, saying it was inhumane, and advocated "treatment" instead. The doctors' viewpoint eventually prevailed. The victory was a victory for the doctors, who now had a securer turf; it was not a victory for the healers/women—the supposed recipients of the doctors' generosity. It was massive disempowerment. Although the Church had persecuted these powerful women, it did not deny or trivialize their power. Psychiatry went one stage farther. *It transformed women therapists or healers into mental patients.* As Szasz (1977, p. 92) points out, a role reversal was effected—one with enormous repercussions. Before long the male physician had rewritten history by casting the witch as madwoman and himself as healer. In so doing he created a legend out of his own prehistory and hid the truth: THAT WOMEN ARE THE REAL MOTHERS OF PSYCHOTHERAPY. What is equally significant is that he effectively pathologized the strong woman and placed her under his control.

The doctors eventually triumphed over the businessmen too. The growing medical establishment convinced government that "madness" was a medical problem. Laws were passed, giving supervisory authority to doctors only. Doctors ended up with the singular authority to confine and to intrude.[3]

Who the Mad Were and Where They Went

As the labeling theorists have made only too clear, from the outset madness was a relationship with power at its base.[4] People are mad when others with credibility declare them mad, whether they do or do not have problems in living. Someone is generally declared mad when she deviates from societal norms or from the norms of the person with authority. It is almost invariably in a number of people's interests that a given person be declared mad. It is usually in the interests of the male elite. It is often in the interests of the person seeking to have another so labeled—the discontented husband, for example—and it is always in the interests of the labeling authority—again an elite male establishment. This being the case, not surprisingly the mad came from all segments of society, although increasingly from the poor, from womenfolk, and from people whose way of being posed a problem to "others."

In the Middle Ages and the Renaissance, complete confinement was rare. Come the late 17th century, attitudes and practices changed. Advanced capitalism brought with it the demand for uniformity and intolerance toward the unemployed and toward people who were poor, were different, or broke the law. Its "solution" was massive institutionalization. Progressively these people were locked up. The age of the asylum began.

Rule by Doctor: The Dual Role

Two roles came together to form the modern-day psychiatrist. The first role is doctor as patriarch. From the 17th century onward, madness was associated with irresponsibility or lack of discipline and was seen as contributing to the collapse of family control. The psychiatrist duplicated the patriarchal family, with himself cast as disciplining father and the patients as children requiring socialization. The disciplining father did not primarily nurture, this being a female value, but had the staff observe and control. Inmates were watched scrupulously, with every "deviation" noted, discussed, and acted on. Inmates were taunted brutally for every error. They were threatened and tortured when they did not act in "gender appropriate" ways or when they resisted the hard work that was seen as essential to sanity and was in fact only essential to patriarchal capitalism. This mode of "treatment" was called "moral management." Some of the devices used in moral management were the very devices used to torture the witches.[5] Frequent use was made, for example, of the witch chair—"an iron chair with studs all over it in which the accused was fastened, while a fire was lit below the seat" (Szasz, 1977, p. 149).

The second role is doctor as scientist. The role of a scientist was progressively stressed, for it is by defining madness as a scientific medical problem that doctors were able to secure a monopoly over the asylums.

The distancing and control inherent in moral management were not softened but intensified by the increasing stress on science. The ascendancy of the scientific method meant further eclipse of such female values as care and interconnectedness and further entrenchment of the distancing and the "power over" that characterize patriarchy. Under the objectifying gaze of the doctors, the "mad" ceased being subjects to dialogue with or even to fear and became objects ruled by the laws of cause and effect. Behaviors that were not in the interests of patriarchal capitalism became diseases with antecedent causes. The job of the doctors was to find the causes and to counter them.

Psychiatric Assault on Women
in the 19th and Early 20th Centuries

During the 19th and early 20th centuries, psychiatrists became increasingly complicit with husbands and fathers. Dissatisfied husbands and fathers wishing to discipline or get rid of their troublesome female dependents sought the assistance of psychiatrists. Psychiatrists were more than willing to comply. Women like Mrs. Packard, whose religious beliefs differed from her husband's, and women who generally had been molested by their fathers were routinely invalidated, assigned diseases, and institutionalized.[6] The percentage of women among the psychiatrically institutionalized grew under medical rule. By 1872 in England, there were considerably more "certified female lunatics" than "certified male lunatics" (see Showalter, 1987, p. 52ff).

Physicians made their fame and fortune by specializing in exotic disorders of females. Hysteria is one such "disease." "Hysteria" is a "mental illness" peculiar to women. It was invented by the early Greek physicians. *Hysteria* means "the rising of the womb." The doctors believed that women's uteruses kept rising up and causing problems. If the womb rose sufficiently high, it would press against the stomach, creating swoons, unreason, and the general hysteria that the patriarchy has always associated with women.

Hysteria was all the rage in the 19th century. In France, Charcot filled an entire asylum with "female hysterics." The women walked about half-undressed, periodically swooning and falling into the highly sexual involuntary movements known as "hysterical attacks." Although I have no reason to believe that the women were pretending or feigning distress, they were clearly given covert instructions on how to express that distress. The walls of Charcot's asylums were filled with pictures of women engaged in just such attacks. In his grand rounds, Charcot daily exhibited the women to male interns and other doctors. He installed a photographic department in the asylum so that the women's poses could be easily captured on film, and he disseminated the photographs to his male colleagues. The existence of the sexual symptoms themselves depended on the physicians who specialized in them and disappeared in their absence. The reduction of woman to body for the pleasuring of the male is clearly operant. Sadly it is likely that many if not most of these women were severely injured survivors of childhood sexual abuse.[7]

Another popular malady that pathologized women's distress and resistance was "bad nerves." Women wearied by their terrible lot in life were seen as suffering from bad nerves, which were depicted as an inherent part of the naturally inferior female body. The dissatisfaction of talented women such as Virginia Woolf was attributed to the effect that undue ambition has on the delicate female nerves. Such women, as Showalter (1987) documented, were ordered to cease their activity and to resign themselves to a rest cure that went on and on.

Freud is particularly noteworthy among the pathologizers of women. As Masson (1984) demonstrated, at the threat of ostracism from the medical community, Freud suppressed his discovery that women labeled "hysterics" had been sexually molested in childhood. He declared the complaints of molestation pure fantasy, and he came up with a cause that male scientists eagerly embraced—excess libido. Freud further pathologized women by suggesting biological foundations for "female inferiority" and by his theory of penis envy.[8]

Further Medicalization

Bit by bit, all of the language of madness and of human experience itself was medicalized. Medical terms like *mental illness, symptoms, diagnosis,* and *differential diagnosis* became linguistic coinage; complex psychiatric taxonomies were invented, using the format and thinking found in medical texts; and psychiatric associations were formed around the world that ruled and legitimated incoming mental "diseases."

Curiously, Freud himself both furthered and threatened this medicalization. He furthered it by creating new ailments himself and by essentially pathologizing everyday life. Just as significantly, he threatened it by inventing the "talking cure" and by suggesting that nonmedical people could also do "psychotherapy."

Within a few decades the threat became formidable indeed—so formidable that the future of psychiatry was in jeopardy. Many varieties of psychotherapy were created. They were popular, and most of the practitioners were nonmedical. The success of psychotherapy endangered the credibility of the medical explanations, and the success of the nonmedical therapists posed a special problem. Although psychiatrists also practiced psychotherapy, overall they were simply not as good at it as the psychologists and social workers.

The answer to the doctors' problems was further medicalization. Further medicalization was made possible by an alliance with the drug companies. The initial inroads were made by a French pharmaceutical company named Rhone, Poulenc and its American marketer, Smith, Kline, and French. The company had spent 10 years developing what became known as chlorpromazine. Chlorpromazine was not invented to "cure schizophrenia," as is now generally believed. The documentation by Smith, Kline, and French as quoted by Scull (1977) proves that chlorpromazine was intended as a cure for nausea and itching and as a general anaesthetic. It became clear in 1953 that the company might sustain a great loss because there was no market for chlorpromazine. Smith, Kline, and French responded by hiring 50 salesmen to convince psychiatrists and others with power that chlorpromazine would cure mental illness.

The psychiatrists "bought the line." They bought it, I would suggest, because (a) chlorpromazine sedated "patients" and made them easier to manage, (b) giving drugs made the treatments medical and themselves bona fide doctors, and (c) it secured their turf. The drug companies bombarded state legislatures and hospitals with propaganda, convincing authorities that "mental patients" had medical problems and were in dire need of drugs—something that only doctors could prescribe. En masse, psychiatrists began chemically altering their "patients" despite the lack of identifiable physical illness or chemical imbalance. They touted the highly controlled behavior of their drugged patients, together with their very use of these chemicals, as evidence of the alleged imbalances.[9] The circularity of their logic was ignored, as was the widespread misery that they caused. The drug revolution was under way.[10]

Psychiatry Today

Psychiatry today is the institution that we might expect, given its history. It is framed in the language of medicine; it is justified on the basis of science, societal safety, and such female values as caring and compassion. This notwithstanding, it is fundamentally androcentric and is committed to control. Psychiatrists see themselves as serving their "patients" and society at large. They appear to be decent people, offering medical help to those in need and only forcing it on those who are "dangerous." Take off the psychiatric blinders, however, and a very different picture emerges. Psychiatrists are people authorized to pressure others into taking "medicine" in the absence of a medical problem. They are legally mandated to intrude and imprison "the problemsome" on the grounds of dangerousness, whether "the problemsome" are truly dangerous or not and despite the fact that psychiatry's own research and amicus briefs indicate that psychiatrists have no reliability whatever in predicting dangerousness.[11] Although many of their clientele clearly have problems, psychiatrists as a whole are not serving the "sick," the needy, or even the "general good." They are serving their own vested interests as entrepreneurs in a massive growth industry. They are serving the interests of the multinational pharmaceutical companies, which significantly provide the funding for most psychiatric conferences and journals.[12] More fundamentally, they are serving the interests of patriarchal capitalism, which has little tolerance for differences, believes in quantification and control, and seeks to imprison, infantilize, correct, or incapacitate those who deviate from the assigned roles.

DSM III R, the third and revised edition of the *Diagnostic and Statistical Manual of Mental Disorders* (American Psychiatric Association, 1987), is the official psychiatric diagnostic manual of the American Medical Association and is the manual typically used in North America. With every new edition of this manual, many new disorders are added to the already sizable collection. The *DSM III R* is a virtual cornucopia of "illnesses," containing hundreds of "diseases,"—a number that is not difficult to arrive at because no proof of disease need be given. *I have never met anybody who would not fit at least two or three of the diagnostic categories in the DSM III R.* Such normal behaviors as not speaking in situations that you consider dangerous (official diagnosis: elective mutism) or grieving a dead spouse for a number of years (official diagnosis: adjustment disorder) figure as significant "symptoms."[13] People who are a bit unusual or who belong to a counterculture or who are the wrong gender are likely to find even more pathologies and indeed more *serious* pathologies specially tailored for them. Not surprisingly, people from oppressed groups—the working class and immigrants, for example—are disproportionately represented in psychiatric institutions.

The pathologization of deviance or of different life-styles is blatantly evident in DSM disorders. Under *borderline personality disorder* (*DSM III R*, p. 345ff), for instance, are such identifying "symptoms" as "frequently changing sex partners" and "confusion over sexual identity"—behavior typical of the gay community and obviously a threat to the patriarchy. The very names of many of the disorders—"oppositional defiant disorder" and "conduct disorder," to note just two—connote the correction of deviance that is at their base. Typical gender-prescribed female behavior is pathologized under such disorders as "histrionic personality disorder" (*DSM III R*, p. 349ff) and "dependent personality disorder" (*DSM III R*, p. 353ff). Correspondingly, despite the cultural disclaimers, definitions of *schizophrenia* and *schizoid personality disorder* (pp. 197, 339) fit the traditional Native who hears voices, who receives messages from beyond, who sees himself or herself as having a mission, and who is understandably uncomfortable living in a white racist society.

The *DSM III R* generally reveals/conceals the fetishization and objectification of subjective impressions underlying psychiatric symptoms, diagnoses, and definitions. According to the *DSM*, to qualify as pathological, a syndrome or pattern "must not be merely an expectable response to a particular event" (p. xxii). The phrase suggests that something is inherently "expectable" or "not expectable" regardless of the beliefs and the status of the person doing the "expecting." Psychiatrists expect people to finish their grieving within about a year. Longer grief thereby becomes "unexpectable" and a symptom. Nothing is inherently "unexpectable," however, about longer grief. It is only that psychiatrists do not expect it. IT IS OUT OF THIS DIFFERENCE BETWEEN WHAT THE ELITE GROUP CALLED "PSYCHIATRISTS" EXPECT AND WHAT OTHERS DO THAT PSYCHOPATHOLOGY EMERGES.

Much of modern treatment is the approach of yesteryear dressed up in scientific names. Imprisonment is now called "custodial treatment." Moral management is still rampant, but it is now known as "behavior modification." What are new, although they do have historical predecessors, are drugs and electroshock. With these "treatments" psychiatry moves invisibly beyond simple control and occasional torture into overwhelming and ongoing incapacitation and destruction.

Psychiatric inmates and ex-inmates routinely receive large ongoing dosages and combinations of highly potent and toxic psychotropic drugs. Other psychiatric "patients," if drugged, are more likely to receive the milder drugs known as *minor tranquilizers* (also called *antianxiety medication*). Minor tranquilizers are relative lightweights, but they can be extremely problematic nonetheless.

They are highly and quickly addictive (3 weeks in the case of Valium). They often cause the very addictive symptoms that they are used to alleviate—sleeplessness, anxiety, terror, and rage, to name a few. (For more details see Bargmann et al., 1982.)

For the most part the major drugs prescribed to inmates and ex-inmates fall into two classes—the neuroleptics (also known as *major tranquilizers* and *antipsychotic medication*) and the antidepressants.

Neuroleptics are by far the most commonly prescribed, and the phenothiazines are the neuroleptic family generally used. Neuroleptics block the production of the neurotransmitter called dopamine. DA (dopamine) receptors are found in different areas of the brain, and so different types of functioning are affected. DA blockage in the extrapyramidal system, which governs movement and perception and affects feeling, impedes perception, movement control, and affect. DA blockage in the frontal lobes serves as a chemical lobotomy, as psychiatrist Peter Breggin (1983, p. 110-146) demonstrated. Note also the following admission of traditional psychiatrist Sterling (1979):

> The blunting of conscious motivation and the inability to solve problems under the influence of chlorpromazine resembles nothing so much as the effects of frontal lobotomy. Research has suggested that lobotomies and chemicals like chlorpromazine may cause their effects in the same way, by disrupting the activity of the neurochemical, dopamine. . . . A psychiatrist would be hard-put to distinguish a lobotomized patient from one treated with chlorpromazine. (pp. 14-18)

DA blockage in the higher areas of the brain generally serves to diminish affect and all levels of cognitive functioning.

An early side effect of the DA blockage in the lower regions is Parkinsonism—a condition whose symptoms include the facial rigidity, tremor of extremities, limb spasms, and shuffling gait for which "psychiatric patients" are famous (Breggin, 1983, p. 87). Parkinson's disease, significantly, is caused by insufficient dopamine. Thirty to fifty percent of the people subjected to this blockage for 2 or more years develop tardive dyskinesia (TD). TD is a severely degenerative neurological disease that is irreversible; is characterized by facial and body tics, drooling, and loss of limb control; and often culminates in blindness. TD arises from a rebound hyperactivity that occurs in the system that has been medically impeded. Curiously the standard psychiatric treatment for TD is high dosages of the causative agent itself—the neuroleptic.[14] This treatment serves to mask the symptoms of TD, while furthering the disease. Anyone discontinuing the drugs experiences the rebound activity without the masking. Ironically this is conventionally deemed a "return of the original psychosis" and is treated yet again with high dosages of the causative agent.

DA blockage in the higher areas has even more dismal consequences. In the long run DA blockage in the limbic and frontal lobes can lead to severe neurological disease—organic brain syndrome, general brain syndrome, and irreversible psychosis. The standard psychiatric treatment for these medically created disorders similarly is masking the symptoms through higher dosages of the causative agent.

The long-term results associated with rebound hyperactivity are not being deliberately sought, albeit they are predictable. DA blockage, however, with its retarding effect on motor functions, perception, feeling, and thinking, is the desired goal that psychiatrists actually specify. Their rationale for the treatment is:

1. Neuroleptics render schizophrenics tame and manageable.
2. Neuroleptics block dopamine.
3. Therefore schizophrenics must have a chemical imbalance characterized by excess dopamine, which these drugs correct.

The invalidity of the syllogism is obvious. The truth is:

1. Neuroleptics are used on many people not diagnosed schizophrenic.
2. No evidence suggests that people so diagnosed have more dopamine.
3. Because all "patients" treated with neuroleptics develop conditions associated with insufficient dopamine, there is every reason to believe that these patients' dopamine levels are normal and are being chemically rendered abnormal.

It is tragically clear that lobotomy-like indifference and manageability are what is actually being sought. Impairment of thinking and feeling is the valued "therapeutic effect."[15]

The second major class of psychiatric drugs—antidepressants—primarily affects the higher regions of the brain. Antidepressants block dopamine, although not to the degree that the neuroleptics do. They also block other neurotransmitters, such as norepinephrine. These blockages serve to produce the following:

1. Lobotomy-like effects, although not to the degree of the neuroleptics
2. Severe neurological and movement disorders known as akinesias
3. Generalized brain disorder and acute organic brain syndrome

Psychiatrists use antidepressants when treating people labeled "depressed" or "manic." Their rationale is that mania is caused by excess amine activity, and depression by insufficient amine activity. Antidepressants correct both imbalances, diminishing amine activity in mania and increasing it in depression. The problem with the rationale is that it is illogical to think that the same drug would produce two opposite effects. Evidence exists for neither excess amine activity in "mania" nor insufficient amine activity in "depression"; the drugs only reduce amines.

Antidepressants essentially are amine inhibitors that are given to people who have no chemical imbalance so as to impede thinking and damage the brain. A study by Davies, Tucker, and Harrow (1971) indicated that organic brain syndrome (indicative of severe brain damage) is very common during "routine antidepressant therapy." Psychiatrists Goodwin and Ebert (1977) explicitly advised administering antidepressants in sufficient dosage to produce "confusion" and other signs of toxicity. The intention was clear.

The primary evidence for the antidepressant effect is evaluations by raters who observe the greater "liveliness" of people taking antidepressants. Psychiatrists like Baldessarini (1978) allude to such second- and third-person observations. They suggest that these observations invalidate both "patients'" claims that they do not feel less depressed on the antidepressants and the substantiation of these claims presented by increased suicidal risks. Evidence that antidepressants increase rather than reduce depression is simply being dismissed. Such dismissal amounts to saying, "Everyone else—doctors especially—knows better." Tragically, as Breggin (1979) pointed out, what observers are interpreting as greater liveliness appears to be simply the jitteriness, restlessness, and hence greater movement of people inflicted with akinesias.

Electroshock (ECT) is the most damaging and intrusive of all "conventional" psychiatric treatments. It consists of passing sufficient electricity through the brain to create a grande mal seizure. Both the electricity and the seizure cause general brain damage, often of a very severe nature. Physical indicators and results of brain damage are the presence of ghost cells in CAT scans, EEG abnormalities, capillary hemorrhage, ganglion cell changes, and gliosis; mental indicators and results are both temporary and permanent antegrade and retrograde memory loss, diminished affect, and diminished intellectual capacity. These results in turn are indicative of acute organic brain syndrome.[16] "Modified shock" stops the back from breaking through the use of muscle relaxants and localizes the damage in one hemisphere through the placement of both electrodes on the same hemisphere, but it does not decrease the brain damage.

Psychiatrists are quieter about the brain-damaging capacity now that damaging brains is unrespectable. They know, however, and have always known that ECT works via brain damage. Originally, in fact, ECT proponents used the high capacity to damage as a "selling point." Meyerson (1942), for instance, cited ECT's superiority in this regard, adding:

I believe that there have to be organic changes or organic disturbances in the physiology of the brain for the cure to take place.... I think ... that these people have, for the time being at any rate, more intelligence than they can handle and that the reduction of intelligence is an important factor in the curative process. (p. 39)

We are clearly not talking side effect here; we are talking, strange though it may seem, about "therapeutic effect."

Short-term memory loss invariably accompanies treatment. Although for some the memory loss is temporary, many survivors lose their ability to concentrate and to take in new information. And many survivors forget much of what they experienced and learned before shock. Shirley Johnson (1984, p. 21A) tells of forgetting friends and family. Her son, a musician who was given shock, lost his ability to play and consequently killed himself. I have had clients who permanently lost all awareness of their lives prior to shock. They could not read. They could not talk. Their very identities had been erased.

Research backs up individual claims. By measuring survivors' scores on the Wechsler memory 60 to 90 days after modified ECT, Small, Sharpley, and Small (1968) found that a significant number showed memory defect. Research by Templer, Ruff, and Armstrong (1973) correspondingly indicated that ECT causes permanent memory loss and general intellectual impairment.

As with so many other treatments, insofar as depression is alleviated (and the long-term results here are very dismal indeed), alleviation is extremely temporary and, as Breggin (1979) showed, it stems from brain damage.[17] For a while people whose memory has been impaired simply are not depressed over what they cannot remember.

PSYCHIATRY AND WOMEN TODAY

Psychiatry today is the misogynous institution that it always was. The psychiatric family is the ultimate backup for the patriarchal families of origin and of marriage and the ultimate enforcer of patriarchal norms. Women who are not living up to the expectations of patriarchal capitalism are sent to the psychiatric family where they are infantilized and their behavior corrected. Statistics Canada (1988) reported that 63.7% of Canadian women have "mental disorders," compared with 36.3% of men. In other words, almost twice as many women as men are seen as mentally disordered. And indeed women outnumber men as "patients" by about that number. This difference speaks both to the greater oppression of women and to male hegemony. It speaks as well to the conditioning that prepares women to see their misery as stemming from their own personal deficiencies and to accept "treatment" for it accordingly. Sadly, many women today give their consent; others continue to be treated/institutionalized against their will.

Psychiatrist as father presides over this family just as father/husband presides over the families of origin and of marriage. Significantly, 97% of all psychiatrists are male; those few who are female do not upset the workings of the patriarchal institution, for as Smith (1975) has argued, they maintain their positions by thinking and acting like honorary men.[18] Nurses and social workers, who correspondingly are predominantly women, play the role of mother under the patriarchy. They handle almost all of the emotional and physical caretaking; they mete out the discipline; they preside over bodily injury (toxic drugging, etc.); they force "patients" to comply with the order of the male authority; and they attend to all facets of the "patients'" existence. They are always around, giving orders and pushing "treatment" on the "patients." By contrast the seemingly benign psychiatrist (absentee father) drops by for a few minutes a week, smiles kindly at the "patients," and reassures them. Nurses and social workers receive most of the resentment accordingly, and the psychiatrist is obeyed, while being saved from disapproval, the work, and indeed the very reality of his patients' existence. Put all this together, and a clear picture emerges. Psychiatrist as absent but powerful father resocializes woman as sick infant, with Woman as Laboring Body functioning as servant and scapegoat— all this for the greater good of the patriarchy.

Women from all positions along the lesbian continuum are psychiatrized, although treatment varies, becoming more obviously brutal as we progress along the continuum. The cooperative male-identified woman who readily agrees that her problems stem from within is likely to meet with a "kind" father. The psychiatrist gently explains her problems to her. He perhaps gives her a rest because of her frail nature, while inevitably encouraging her to reassume her full role as mother and wife. He smiles his approval as his "good little patient" takes in and integrates what he tells her about "her problem." He gives her Valium (minor tranquilizer) or, if need be, a major tranquilizer to help her deal with "her stress." He institutionalizes her when and only when she is clearly not performing/coping/acting "appropriately." She looks up to this man, just as she has been taught to look up to men generally and paternal men in particular; she consults him again and again and is likely to regard his treatments as lifesaving.

As we progress along the continuum, as women more deliberately and blatantly resist, the oppressive and brutalizing nature of psychiatry becomes more obvious. Women who characteristically act "inappropriately"—who defy their role as a being-for-man generally and as body-for-man in particular— stand a very strong chance of being labeled "borderline personality disorder" or psychotic and of being institutionalized. Although she did not use radical feminist categories, Chesler's (1972) comparative figures on the length of hospital stays suggest that defiant women get institutionalized longer. My knowledge of my untraditional sisters as clients, friends, and colleagues, and interviews that I have conducted with psychiatrized women, tell me that they are also more likely to be subject to the bullying tactics now known as "behavior modification." Routinely, defiant women are blamed, are punished, and are threatened with perpetual sickness and perpetual "treatment" if they do not dress as they are supposed to dress, if they do not shave their legs, if they do not stop swearing, if they do not become the pleasurable and docile body-for-men that patriarchy requires. Women who publicly display their defiance—our open lesbians and our other rebels—run a special risk of severe physical damage. Paradigmal in this regard is the lobotomization of Frances Farmer in the early part of this century. Of more direct relevance today is the electroshocking of Sheila Gilhooly—a Vancouver woman who was committed for being a lesbian, despite the official removal of homosexuality from the *DSM III R*. Tellingly, after each electroshock, Sheila was asked, "Do you still not want to be cured for being a lesbian?" (Blackbridge & Gilhooly, 1988, p. 44ff). Frances gained her freedom when she was so brain-damaged that even her lobotomization struck her as a good thing. Although the conditions of release are not generally so transparent, for a frightening number of resistant women, seeing/pretending to see the error of their ways or at the very least dressing and acting more like a body-for-men is the surest way and sometimes the only way out. A damaged brain and diminished mental capacity are the penalty for endurance.

What is at issue here is the type of functioning that is sanctioned by patriarchal capitalism. What is at issue just as significantly is the elite male vision that accompanies this sanction and that inherently shapes psychiatric thought and practice.

When psychiatrist as elite male looks on woman, he is looking at someone who "appears" problematic right from the start. The more completely and successfully she functions as a body-for-others, the saner she looks. Correspondingly the less successfully she functions as a body-for-men and/or the more untraditional, resistant, and indeed intelligent she is, the less normal she will seem to him and the more in need of extreme psychiatric intervention. A woman who is very distraught seems very ill, for the male medical eye has no other way of taking her in. The male, generally white psychiatrist does not have that much relevant experience to draw on even if he were attempting to go against his training and his privilege. He has no immediate experiential understanding of what it means to lead a woman's life and generally even less sense of what it means to lead the life of a poor and/or Black woman and/or lesbian. He does not know woman's pain, and he does not understand her confusion, resistance, and suffering except as the "correctable" pathological symptomology that it becomes under his androcentric medical gaze. Individual psychiatrists, of course, may sometimes see more, despite their conditioning as medical males. Psychiatrists as a group, however, see what their lens allows them to see. That lens has been specially fashioned out of their own professionalism—that is, out of their own gender, position, and mandate—to pathologize women's resistance/thought and to filter out women's reality.

Further repercussions follow from this vision/reduction of women. One very important repercussion is that psychiatrists more readily resort to treatments that impede thinking and cause serious brain damage when they are "treating" women. Significantly, in North America two out of every three prescriptions for psychiatric drugs are written for women. Women receive the vast preponderance of the drugs most likely to result in acute organic brain syndrome—the highly neurotoxic antidepressants. And women receive electroshock—the most brain-damaging treatment in the entire repertoire of modern conventional psychiatry—two to three times more often than men. Women who matter least to the elite male—poor women, Black women, and the elderly, for example—receive the highest percentage of the most damaging treatments.[19]

The reduction of woman to body-for-man underlies gender differences and legitimates the injury. Because woman is a body-for-man, because she is not for-herself but for-him, the impeding of her thinking is at worst unfortunate and at best the optimal choice. Her thinking, after all, does not matter much, and diminished thinking capacity could even make her more serviceable. Impeding the thinking of older women, of working-class women, of women of color matters still less.

Covert and Overt Sexual Abuse

Covert and overt sexual abuse is an underlying dimension to the psychiatric violation of women, as well as an additional abuse. Exotic diseases of females have historically served to amuse psychiatrists and to guarantee their fame at the expense of our already most victimized sisters. "Eating disorders" are a modern version. Women diagnosed with such "disorders" are "managed" and "displayed."

Our incested sisters, as before, are the most promising exhibits. In the 19th century, Charcot paraded these women, then called "hysterics," exaggerating and promoting their sexualized movements, while all of psychiatry denied that childhood sexual abuse had occurred. Now that psychiatry can no longer deny the reality of child sexual abuse, it has typically credited itself with a discovery that women made and set up a growth industry on the basis of it, with entrepreneurial psychiatrists in charge. The deeply injured and fragmented women whom psychiatry calls "multiples" have proven particularly serviceable in this regard. The paraded hysterics of Charcot are the paraded multiples of modern psychiatry.

There is absolutely no question that abused women who have undergone very early and repeated sexual assault forget, split, and fragment. The forgetting, splitting, and fragmentation are real—not a pretense. Typically, however, psychiatry absolutizes and reifies the forgetting, treating lack of reflective awareness as no awareness at all. Moreover psychiatry actively promotes splitting, despite talk of "integration." At the behest of the psychiatrists, the individual woman who formerly called herself "I" now habitually says "we." In one "hospital" in Ottawa, individuals diagnosed MPD (multiple personality disorder) are routinely put to bed a number of times each night—a separate time for each "personality." The disintegrating effect is obvious and horrifying. What is equally serious is that psychiatrists throughout North America film their "multiples," looking for, subtly encouraging, and catching personality changes. Then they exhibit the films at special Incest Conferences, to the fascination/education of onlookers. The circus goes on.

The eroticization evident in this abuse has parallels on the one-on-one level. A frightening number of female incest survivors have told me that their original psychiatrist (male) treated them very differently from subsequent feminist therapists. The psychiatrist, they said, dwelt on the sexual abuse graphically, continually pressing them for minute details. The voyeuristic use of women for male sexual excitation is implicit.

Overt sexual abuse also occurs. As Masson (1988) and others have shown, many psychiatrists and indeed many male therapists habitually have sex with their female "patients." By their own reports, 10% to 13% of male therapists repeatedly have sex with their clients.[20] The sex itself is often described as a vital part of the "cure." As Chesler (1972) has demonstrated, women comply for many reasons: out of bewilderment, out of naïveté, out of neediness, out of fear of abandonment, sometimes out of the very realistic conviction that this is the quickest way to gain their freedom. Others are blatantly forced.[21]

However it occurs, what we have here is victimization and a profound betrayal that is akin to incest and that similarly wounds. The psychiatric daughter, like the incest victim, has been violated by the man set up as her nurturer. Like the incest victim, she is left confused, ashamed, not knowing where to turn, afraid to lodge a complaint, and often not believed if she does.

The seduction and sexual violation are significant in themselves. They are also a meaningful metaphor for patriarchal psychiatry overall. It lets psychiatry be seen for what it is—self-serving male violation masquerading as care.

SUGGESTED READINGS

Breggin, P. (1983). *Psychiatric drugs: Hazards to the brain.* New York: Springer.

Chesler, P. (1972). *Women and madness.* New York: Avon.

Conrad, P., & Schneider, J. (1980). *Deviance and medicalization: From badness to sickness.* St. Louis: C. V. Mosby.

Showalter, E. (1987). *The female malady: Women, madness, and English culture, 1830-1980.* New York: Penguin.

Smith, D., & David, S. (1975). *Women look at psychiatry.* Vancouver: Press Gang.

Szasz, T. (1974). *The myth of mental illness: Foundations of a theory of personal conduct.* New York: Harper & Row.

Szasz, T. (1977). *The manufacture of madness: A comparative study of the Inquisition and the mental health movement.* New York: Harper & Row.

NOTES

1. For a thorough discussion of early medical understandings and treatments of madness and the various changes undergone up to the present day, see Foucault (1988).

2. For a translation of this Bull, see Sprenger & Kramer (1948), pp. 29-32.

3. For informative accounts of this rise, see Foucault (1988), pp. 189-299, and Conrad & Schneider (1980), pp. 1-72.

4. For a helpful rendition of the labelist position, see Becker (1973).

5. For a discussion of these, see Szasz (1977), p. 137ff.

6. For an account of the psychiatrization of Mrs. Packard, as well as a number of other female dependents, see Chesler (1972), pp. 5-17. For an account of the pathologization of incest survivors, see Masson (1988).

7. For an informative account of Charcot discussing these and other details, see Showalter (1987), p. 145ff.

8. See Freud (1973a), p. 360ff, and Freud (1973b), pp. 145-169.

9. For further discussion of this point, see Breggin (1983).

10. For further information on what happened, see Scull (1977).

11. Most mental health acts in Canada and the United States list "dangerousness to self or others" as a criterion for involuntary hospitalization. There is no evidence, however, that people so hospitalized are any more dangerous than the average citizen, and there is reason to suspect the opposite. Recent studies moreover indicate that psychiatry has no success in predicting dangerousness; see Hucker (1985) and the 1982 American Psychiatric Association's amicus brief to the Supreme Court, as cited in Savage & McKague (1988), p. 84.

12. For a good book on the relationship between psychiatry and the pharmaceuticals, and the conflicts of interest involved, see Bargmann, Wolfe, Levin, et al. (1982).

13. For the two diagnoses in question, see *DSM III R*, pp. 88 and 329.

14. For further details, see Breggin (1983), p. 99ff.

15. For these and other details on the neuroleptics, see Breggin (1983), pp. 7-184.

16. For these and other details on the effects, see Ontario Coalition to Stop Electroshock (1984), pp. 2-51; Burstow & Weitz (1984), pp. 10A-12A; and Breggin (1979), p. 135ff.

17. For a review of the effectiveness literature, see Ontario Coalition to Stop Electroshock (1984), p. 46ff; Brill, Crumpton, Eiduson, et al. (1959); Lambourne & Gill (1978); and Johnstone, Deakin, Lawler, et al. (1980). For a discussion of the relationship between brain damage and temporary alleviation, see Breggin (1979).

18. For this statistic and the ensuing argument, see Smith (1975), p. 2ff.

19. For statistics on the drug ratios, see Cooperstock (1980). For statistics and breakdowns on the electroshock ratio, including gender, age, and province, see Ontario Coalition to Stop Electroshock (1984), p. 82ff. For other relevant statistics, see Burstow (1982).

20. For further details and incomplete but telling statistics, see Chesler (1972), Appendix; Kardener, Fuller, & Mensh (1973), pp. 1077-1081; Pope, Keith-Spiegel, & Tabachnick (1986), pp. 147-158; and Holyroyd & Brodsky (1977), pp. 843-849.

21. Significantly, women who have sex with their psychiatrists are released quicker than women who do not. For the relevant statistic, see Chesler (1972), Appendix. For personal statements by women who have had sex with their psychiatrists, see Chesler (1972), p. 136ff.

3

Basics and Beginnings

Properly understood, feminist therapy or counseling is a highly personal and fundamentally political encounter or series of encounters between women. It is grounded in woman-woman solidarity and is dedicated to client empowerment. The counselor's job is to help sisters who have become clients with their personal problems in ways that politicize rather than depoliticize. The counselor herself is political both inside and outside of counseling. She has some understanding and is committed to furthering her understanding of how systemic oppressions combine to frame the personal problems that women face. She is aware of the centrality of violence against women, and she integrates this understanding into her practice.

An explicit premise on which feminist counseling is based is that personal problems are both created and exacerbated by societal power imbalances. Correspondingly, helping women make the connections and resist is key to what feminist counseling is about.

A second premise is that people similarly situated are in a better position to understand each other than people differently situated. It follows from this that we are called on both to draw on our common experience in attempting to understand the women whom we see and to stretch to understand difference. It follows as well that it is generally preferable that women clients see women counselors. Men simply cannot draw on the shared experience of being or growing up woman in a man's world. Even those men who are more aware and have good intentions inevitably impose male vantage points on women clients. Moreover, as Chapters 1 and 2 make clear, women need to be talking with other women, not receiving more "male help." A similar principle holds with other oppressions. All else being equal or even close to equal, it is preferable that lesbian counselors work with lesbian clients, that women of color work with women of color, that disabled women work with disabled women, and that working-class counselors work with working-class clients. When making referrals, we need to keep such pairings in mind. I am not suggesting that we totally buy into identity politics or deny the possibility of understanding difference, but I am suggesting that we recognize the value of shared experience.

In light of the empowerment goal, the power dynamic within the counseling relationship itself is of key importance. Traditional counseling duplicates the power imbalances in society as a whole. Therapists who are generally male, white, heterosexual, and middle or upper middle class bestow their expertise on clients who are generally women and often women who are subject to multiple oppressions. Part of the feminist power shift is to alter who is doing the counseling, as already discussed. An equally critical part is to alter the process. It is to reject the "expert" stance and work cooperatively together. This alteration is sometimes referred to as "equalizing the power" between counselor and client. A more accurate description is "reducing the power differential."

Examples of typical therapist power tactics that it is important for us as workers to watch out for and to curb are as follows:

- Forever pushing our own goals, definitions, and solutions
- Confronting in that pointed and heavy-handed way that conveys "Whatever I am seeing is accurate, is critically important, and you had better attend to it."
- Implying or acting as if the client's well-being were utterly dependent on "staying in counseling"

When the client herself relinquishes power that she should properly have (and in light of women's socialization, this often occurs), it is important for us to address what is happening. Examples of such relinquishments include the client acting as follows:

- Making such statements as, "You know so much more than I do; so tell me, what should I do?"
- Complying with everything we suggest—being a "good girl," in other words
- Crediting us with the hard work that she herself has done
- Responding to us as if we were a superior species that did not have dilemmas and limitations that human beings are heir to

In some cases we may use what has happened as an opportunity to highlight power issues and to begin co-investigating messages about power. Whether we do so or not, minimally we need to state that we do not know. We need to point out that solutions reached together are infinitely better than anything we could come up with single-handedly. We need to make it clear that we make all sorts of mistakes ourselves and indeed to give examples. We need to invite women to own and value their own work, their own insight, and the special knowledge that they bring.

Statements that clarify the importance of co-investigation and mutual knowledge should be made from the very beginning because they set the stage for co-responsibility and for dialogue. From day one, the client should be provided with the information she needs if she is to make informed choices and is to play an active role in shaping the therapy. From day one, correspondingly, it is important to truly engage her in dialogue. To be clear, dialogue does not preclude disagreeing or challenging. As feminist workers we must be ready to challenge, especially when faced with statements and positions that suggest internalized oppression. A commitment to dialogue, however, does mean respecting this women, truly listening to and considering her point of view, and being prepared to problematize and question not only her response but also our own.

From the outset, we are called on to demythologize our skills, our presence, our selves and to continue to do so. On the level of observation, this means letting clients know what we base our observations on, thereby cutting through the mystery. More generally it means letting them know how we operate, how our approaches may differ from other people's, what our beliefs are—the feminist perspective in particular—and how these beliefs and approaches are likely to affect them. Toward the end of the first session, if they are interested in continuing, it is helpful as well to provide more detailed written information and to encourage them to come back with whatever questions, concerns, disagreement, or points of negotiation they may have. (See Appendix A for my own information sheet.)

The first few sessions are a critical time for mutual questioning and negotiating. Doing this allows worker and client to make informed choices about whether to work together. It allows the client to make an informed choice about whether to pursue therapy at all. And it helps ensure that the initial contract that is agreed on has genuinely been framed by both and is at least initially satisfactory. The questioning and negotiating set the stage for ongoing client monitoring and client power.

We can open the door to questioning and negotiating by discussing the importance of it. Explaining the importance alone, however, does not suffice. Many women will hear what we are saying, acknowledge the importance, and still not actively participate in the framing. They do not know what to ask. They do not know what to insist on. They may not have a sense of the broad spectrum of arrangements from which to choose or on which to improvise. Insofar as we want more than nominal client empowerment, we must actively facilitate the participation needed.

Examples of comments and questions that I find myself making in the process of facilitating client questioning and negotiating and that I see as helpful are:

- When you first thought of seeing a therapist, what did you hope to get out of it?
- Most people are at least somewhat ambivalent about therapy. And I can sure see why. There's much to be ambivalent about. What specifically worries you about therapy? What would you absolutely never want to see happen?
- As I work with people, we try out different exercises. If people feel good about the exercises, we may do them again. If they are allergic to them, that's okay too; we move on. If we get into something that you really don't want to be doing, please let me know. Don't just go along. Also, if there is anything that you do not want that you could identify now, I'd really appreciate knowing about it.
- You say that you've seen a number of therapists before. What did you like about them? What didn't you like? And what bugged the daylights out of you?
- Pursuing therapy is only one of the choices available to you, and it is not necessarily your best choice. How about our exploring some of the other options and looking at the positives and negatives in each?
- Right now the lowest pay slot I have available is $30.00. Is that a problem for you? What *could* you afford?
- I've been asking all the questions. What would *you* like to ask? What do you need to know about me?
- Many people assume that counseling has to be done weekly. There's nothing sacrosanct about once a week. It's a question of what works for you.

We should not suggest arrangements that primarily protect us while boxing the client in—"no suicide" contracts, for example. Any contract that we arrive at should be flexible. Contracts and decisions should at least be compatible with empowerment.

QUESTIONS TO ASK OURSELVES

What kind of therapy we do is largely but not exclusively a function of the questions we ask. Unfortunately, although it helps, having a sound theory is no guarantee that we will ask sound questions. The questions we ask the women themselves are especially important, and these are discussed in detail in Chapter 4. Underpinning these, and arguably just as important, are the questions we ask in the privacy of our own heads. If we are to be doing empowerment counseling, it is vital that a high percentage of the questions we ask ourselves bring into focus the oppressions the individual woman bears, the ways she internalizes oppression, and her modes of resistance.

One source of information available to us is the physical being in front of us. The ways in which our bodies are formed and are held are at least partially a consequence of our feelings, decisions, and situation. As long as we do not reduce people to their bodies and guard against stereotyping, the body can legitimately be used as a guide.

Although a source of information to all counselors, the body is particularly instructive to us as feminist workers. Our oppression as women is rooted in the body. By attending to and querying the body, we can begin finding out about oppressions that the client may be subject to and how they are responding. The tentative ideas that we thereby form help frame further exploration.

Questions and ideas that I find myself posing and that I see as helpful include the following:

Initial Questions	*Tentative Thoughts/ Further Questions*
Is this woman from a "visible" or "audible" minority?	If yes, which? What are some of the group values, customs, and body language that I need to be aware of? What types of oppression is she likely to be subject to? What types of accommodation might she need or want?
Does this woman look exhausted?	If yes, I may have reason to be concerned about her status as laboring body. Is she being worn out as a mother and wife? Does she do menial work for slave wages?
Does she wear lipstick, mascara, and/or other traditional makeup? Does she wear high heels? Does she wear tight clothing?	If yes, the sexualization of woman is apparent, but the question remains, What does it signify here? Is the woman male-identified? Is she heterosexual or lesbian? Is she in the sex trades? What power is she getting from making use of this resource allowed her by the patriarchy?
Is her clothing loose and comfortable?	If yes, this is likely a very good sign. She seems to care for herself. What else might be going on?

Does she look frightened when I come near her? Does she wince when I raise my hand? Do her arms hug her body in front of her?

If yes, this woman may well be a survivor of extreme childhood sexual assault and/or extreme childhood battery. She might also be a battered spouse. This is something for me to follow up. She is at the very least a vulnerable and violated human being, and I should be as gentle and supportive as possible.

Is she bruised? Has she been bleeding? Is anything broken? Does she have scars?

If yes, in all likelihood this woman either is being battered currently or is a survivor of abuse who is currently hurting herself. If they are razor blade scars, it is most likely self-injury. I need to get in touch with my caring and my compassion, and I need to find out more about the injury.

Is she extremely thin?

If yes, it may be that she is or has been ill. The family may not have enough food to go around, and like most women, she is putting herself last. On the other hand, she might be anorexic. Does she hate her body? Is she repelled by her flesh? Again a strong possibility of childhood sexual assault.

Does she look away from me? Does she avert her eyes whenever I look at her?

If yes, she may simply be scared in this specific situation. Or she may generally be scared. Her fear may be so deep and so early that she is quite unaware of it and defensive stances like looking away have become habitual.

Does she look me straight in the eyes?

If yes and she is not glaring, this woman is likely relatively comfortable with herself-in-the-world and has direct strengths on which she draws. The possibility is also strong that she is highly woman-identified and/or lesbian. If yes and she is glaring angrily, she is strong enough to show her anger, and that is well and good. Whomever else she is angry at, she is probably also angry at me.

Whether in conjunction with the initial body-focused questions or not, there are also some general questions related to oppression, internalization, and resistance that we do well to ask ourselves. Examples of such questions are:

- How is society generally and the people around her in particular specifically blocking the aspirations of this woman?
- What are the different oppression groups to which she belongs? What values do these bring? Which of these values are important to her? What conflicts in identity and loyalty arise for her? How does she deal with these conflicts? What is won and what is sacrificed in the process?
- Does she associate with people with whom she shares a number of oppressions? If so, which oppressions are shared? Which oppressions are given most recognition, and which are kept subordinate?
- What might she do now to increase her power in the various disempowering situations in which she finds herself?
- Is this woman male-identified or woman-identified? Where is she on the lesbian continuum?
- What are her thoughts about sexism? About classism? About racism? About ableism? About ageism? About any other oppression that she is subject to?
- Is she aware of her attractions to other women? How does she feel about these attractions?
- In what ways does she ally herself with other women? In what ways does she distance herself?
- To what degree does she internalize her sexual objectification as woman, and what form does this internalization take?
- Does she do typical women's work? What if any are her options in the short run? What would she like to be doing in the long run? How can she get there?
- What kind of wages does she receive? What actions might help change this situation?
- Is she surrounded by people who expect her to accommodate and nurture them constantly? What does she think of their demands? What price does she pay when she refuses? Should the price be exacted? What could she do in return?
- Is she forever trying to please others and/or take care of them? Is she trying to please me now by being a "good patient"?
- Is she being physically abused currently? How serious is this abuse, and what form does it take? What are her escape routes?
- Where is she on the childhood sexual abuse continuum? Was she battered as a child? What does she think about this abuse?
- What messages did her parents overtly and covertly give her about her role as a woman? As a Black woman? As a Jewish woman? As a "disabled woman"? What messages does her culture or community give her overtly or covertly? What are the positives? The negatives? What are the sanctions for disobeying?

- How does she relate to food? What does she get, and what does she lose in the process?
- Does she see herself as valuable and competent or low in worth and ability?
- Is she ashamed, and if so, to what does this shame relate?
- What is she proud of?
- Can she let herself get angry? Is she stereotyped or otherwise punished for getting angry? What response do her colleagues and her friends have to her anger? What form does her anger take? How does she stop herself from getting angry? Where and in what ways does her anger work for her, and where and in what ways does it work against her?
- Does she ask for what she needs? Does she negotiate? How do the people around her respond to her requests and her negotiations? How does she respond to their responses?
- Does she make her own decisions? If not, to whom does she defer on which issues and why? What is the current price of refusal?
- Does she suffer from any of the physical/psychological conditions that stem from giving oneself away? Headaches? Depression?
- What are her modes of protest and resistance? When does she use them? How successful are they? What does she get from them? What do they cost her?
- What are the other sources of power or control that she draws on? How does she use them? How else might she use them?
- What are the untapped potentials for power in her situation?

Such questions as these begin sensitizing us to difference and to the power dynamics and the possibilities for change that are inherent in the woman's situation. They highlight internalization of oppression and resistance. They help clue us in to the complex combination of strengths and problems that our clients bring.

COUNSELOR ETHICS

Many of the ethical principles held by humanist counselors and traditional social service workers are ones most feminist counselors would totally concur with. At the same time, some of those principles are ones most of us would strongly disagree with. Some we would agree with in principle. Additionally some ethical issues for us would not be issues for counselors who see the world as liberals do. This being the case, it is important for us as feminists to evolve our own codes.

Ethics can never be a closed subject that we make decisions about, codify, and then question no more. We do not and cannot know enough. Codes are imperfect. They overstate. They understate. They distort. They leave out. They address only issues that are already part of our consciousness. They are necessarily limited by the modes of thoughts of the era. They reflect systemic and personal biases. They say nothing about situations that have never arisen.

We can and should learn about counseling ethics from each other—especially from others with less privilege and from clients. At the same time, every feminist counselor is necessarily her own ethicist who must answer to her own conscience.

We begin with our own work. As human beings who work with others at their most vulnerable, it is our responsibility to question continually the ethicality of our approaches and our decisions, despite how many years we have been working this way, how many counselors operate similarly, and how many revered theorists have written that it is right. As we dare to question and to face, we continually broaden our understanding of counseling ethics.

My own positions as I now understand them are evident in the book as a whole and indeed are teased out throughout the book—some of it in this chapter. As a more concise statement, I offer the following:

1. In our dealings with clients, their empowerment and general well-being are our first obligation. Except where a third party is in serious jeopardy, this obligation takes precedence over our obligations to our workplace, to our colleagues, to other parties, and indeed to any cause or special interest that we have.

2. Except where a third party is in serious jeopardy, interference with our client's freedom of being or of choice constitutes unethical behavior. This includes but is not limited to cooperating in any way with psychiatric interference (not warranted under any circumstances) and physically preventing the client from carrying out decisions that we consider harmful—including the decision to kill herself. The bottom line is that as long as they do not do it in front of us, although they have no right to injure another, people have the right to injure themselves.

3. We are acting unethically when we engage in behavior or make or condone remarks that are sexist, racist, classist, lesbophobic or homophobic, ableist, ageist, or religiously oppressive. Correspondingly we are obliged to incorporate an awareness of the different systemic oppressions into our counseling and to work at making our own counseling approaches and style less ethnocentric, androcentric, heterocentric, ablecentric, Christiancentric, middle classcentric, and youthcentric.

4. Society should be ensuring that an ample amount and variety of free quality services are available for people wanting counseling, and we should be working toward that end. Fees in private practice are an ethical issue because

of where the funding comes from. Ethicality here requires (a) basing fees on a sliding scale, (b) if at all possible, accepting at least one client at any given time without charge or for a nominal fee, and (c) agreeing to earn at least somewhat less than our counterparts in the social services. Barter is acceptable when and only when it does not interfere with the counseling and does not subordinate the client.

5. Counselors have a right to the primary counselor benefits (wages or fees, the joy of helping people, increased understanding) that arise from counseling. Any significant secondary benefits (those that do not intrinsically arise from the job we are doing or the financial arrangements we have made) constitute a violation—generally a boundary violation. Examples of such violations include having sex with the client, turning the client into a friend, accepting either expensive or ongoing gifts, having her run errands for us, dumping our problems on her, and having her take care of us in any way.

6. Having a counseling relationship with a person precludes having any other major relationship with her, whether it be as friend, employee, or colleague.

7. Sexual violations are enormously damaging. We are obliged not to engage in them ourselves, to report staff who do, and to help women take action against offending counselors. Although not all of this would be recognized as abuse in a court of law or by the counseling community as a whole, all of the following constitute sexual violation: genital contact of any form, sensual or erotic contact, unwanted physical contact of any sort, sexual invitations, sexual remarks, sexual looks, sexual terms of endearment, nudity in counseling, putting clients "on display" whether directly or through photographs, sexual disclosures on our part that are not relevant or that exceed what is needed for counseling purposes, queries about the client's sex life that are not relevant or that exceed what is needed for counseling purposes, asking for or dwelling on the details of a sexual violation beyond what is needed for counseling purposes, traumatizing clients by dramatic reenactments of former sexual abuse, and use of such heavy-handed approaches as psychodrama when working with survivors of childhood sexual abuse.

8. It is unethical to deliberately frighten or traumatize a client, to willfully or neglectfully push beyond her comfort level, or to work in ways that put her at serious risk of flooding.

9. We have a responsibility to minimize the power differential that exists in therapy and to work cooperatively together.

10. Cooperating with the psychiatrization of our clients or using the medical model ourselves is unacceptable regardless of what shape our client is in.

11. Except when a third party is in serious danger, we owe confidentiality to our clients even if they are suicidal and even if we are extremely worried about them. Breaches of confidentiality include talking about clients beyond what is needed for supervision, consultation, or referral purposes; going outside the circle of confidentiality that we have specified to the client; and giving or getting specific referral information that the client does not wish us to give or get. It is also unethical to ask clients to sign sheets that give us open-ended permission to disclose information on her to funders and referral sources.

12. Dishonesty or misrepresentation constitutes unethical behavior. Examples of counselor dishonesty and misrepresentation, most of which are additionally self-serving, include telling a client that (a) we know that the counseling will help her, (b) we are highly experienced in some area that we are not experienced in, (c) she could afford therapy if she "had her priorities straight," (d) if she is staying with a man who batters her, she must want to be battered, and (e) she can do anything she wants to in this world.

13. We are obliged to seek supervision or consultation or to refer clients when we are aware that we are not serving them well. We are obliged at least to suggest termination when we think that the client is now getting highly diminished returns and that continuing in counseling is no longer her best option.

14. Acting in ways that make the client more dependent on us is unethical. Examples of dependency-making dynamics include marathon sessions, extremely frequent sessions, and counseling that involves only depth work.

15. We are obliged not to encourage a client's idealization of us—referred to by some as *positive transference*—and to counter it insofar as possible.

SUGGESTED READINGS

Browne, L. (1989). From perplexity to complexity: Thinking about ethics in the lesbian therapy community. *Women and Therapy, 8,* 13-26.

Greenspan, M. (1983). *A new approach to women and therapy.* New York: McGraw-Hill.

Hill, M. (1990). On creating a theory of feminist therapy. In L. Brown & M. Root (Eds.), *Diversity and complexity in feminist therapy* (pp. 53-65). New York: Hawthorne.

Rosewater, L., & Walker, L. (Eds.). (1985). *Handbook of feminist therapy: Women's issues in psychotherapy* (pp. xxix-xxxi). New York: Springer.

4

General Empowerment Work

Feminist counseling inevitably involves some type and some degree of political exploration, although what is appropriate varies greatly. Co-investigation and empowerment begin with solidarity in the face of an oppressive world.

Solidarity sometimes demands action from us. Solidarity always demands allegiance and the expression of that allegiance. It can be voiced by expressing honest outrage at what has been done to this person in particular and to her community generally and by joining with her in the face of this injury. Insofar as these statements involve joining on an emotional as well as an intellectual level, they are a form of political empathy (political empathy moves beyond, while including the more individual empathic responses that would be made by a strictly humanist counselor); insofar as they shed light on the world, they are a form of analysis; and insofar as they are a joining at all, they are a way of identifying.

Solidarity can be expressed in especially empowering ways in the cases of oppressions that counselor and client share. We-statements and us-statements are particularly helpful. By way of example, we can respond to a woman who has been saddled with most of the housework by making a statement like, "Yes, men are always using us that way, aren't they?" In one brief remark we have begun to (a) identify our commonality as women, (b) proclaim our bond as women, (c) empathize with our sister client, (d) identify oppressor and oppressed groups, (e) analyze the sexist situation, and (f) invite ongoing solidarity and analysis. A solidarity-based encounter between a disabled counselor and a disabled client, correspondingly, might go:

> **Client**   I'm kind of down today. Miskouri is my favorite singer, and I would have loved to go to that concert, but it's the same old story. It wasn't wheelchair accessible.
>
> **Counselor**   I'm really sorry about the concert. And I can understand your disappointment. What an ableist society we live in! We keep being excluded from event after event. It's frustrating all right. Damned irritating too!

Where the client is subject to an oppression that we as counselors are not, we have to work harder to find/express solidarity, and we must be committed to this work. One way that we can begin is by looking for similarities in our own oppression that can serve as touchstones and by speaking out of what we find. Although such statements cannot have the power of the clearer we-statements, if done authentically and sensitively they do have a power of their own.

By way of example, a client in one of my classes who was counseling an older learner searched inside and came up with, "I've never been your age. So I can't really know what it's like. I'll tell you, though, as a Black, I too have often been excluded from decision making, and I find it fuckin' exasperating!" As she went on to acknowledge the differences, to explore the unique disentitlement that seniors meet in our society, and to brainstorm ways of resisting, a solid connection was forged.

That connection hinged critically on the counselor's honest acknowledgment of the differences. Where we are bridging oppressions, it is important that we acknowledge differences as well as similarities or else the joining itself becomes unauthentic and authentic exploration is sabotaged. It is especially critical when the client's oppression is one to which we will never be subject.

For many clients, making a few statements is as much politicizing as it is helpful. With some, in fact, we will never focus on these statements, and the statements will contain only a bare minimum of analysis. With many others, however, fuller co-investigation is feasible and desirable.

Fuller co-investigation involves unearthing and exploring the oppression themes that make up the client's thematic universe. By *oppression theme* I mean the woman's hopes and aspirations, together with what concretely blocks those hopes and aspirations. A theme is a social contradiction. *Thematic universe* refers to all of the themes as they open up into each other and combine together to form the oppressive situation.[1]

We help clients identify and explore oppression themes through the questions we ask and the statements we make. As a radical feminist therapist, I typically make certain kinds of statements and ask certain kinds of questions. It is not so much that I follow a formula, for dialogue is more spontaneous than that, but an identifiable pattern can be discerned that I tend to keep tucked away at the back of my mind.

Examples of simple questions and question-statement combinations that facilitate this exploration are:

- What do you want? What stops you from getting it?
- This is an interesting setup that you've just described. Let me ask you, Who wins and who loses if things are left this way?
- What contradictions do you see in your life?
- In whose interest is it that things are the way they are?
- Do you think it is harder for you at your ____ (workplace, school, etc.) than it is for ____ (men, non-Natives, straights, etc.)? What makes it harder?

The we-statements discussed earlier similarly help our sisters explore their thematic universe. Examples of other types of statements and statement-question combinations that help, that are more challenging, and that can be used to further and deepen the inquiry are:

- You say you want to be a better wife and mother and that your own inadequacies stop you. I don't know what other people are telling you, but let me assure you that I don't find you the least bit inadequate. Personally I find your resourcefulness amazing, and I know that if I were in your situation, I could not manage anywhere near so well. But let me ask you, What else do you want? Is there anything you want that you think being a better wife and mother will bring you? Are you sacrificing anything that you want, however happily, in the effort to be a perfect wife and mother?
- No, I don't find it surprising that you are depressed, and I don't think it's because there's something wrong with you. As a working-class Jewish woman, you don't have the same options as most of your friends, and that's damn depressing. Here are some advantages that I see them having. . . . What would you add to the list?
- There's a contradiction that I just can't hold together here. On the one hand, you tell me that your father was a caring and good man. And I can understand your being fond of him. On the other hand, you've recounted time after time when he molested you. I think of that adult man who had that little girl in his charge, and I think of that little girl who kept getting hurt, who was terrified, and who even now goes into panic, and I don't see that good and kind man. I see injury, I see violation, I see a violating father backed by a whole society of fathers. And I see a vulnerable little girl who deserved a whole lot better than that.

If done competently and caringly, the question-answer combinations cannot only affirm solidarity and further the analytic inquiry but can also nurture; and it is vital that at least some of them nurture. We nurture whenever we make room for the child, whenever we attend to the child, whenever we express any caring or support for the child.

The incest example is an instance of a challenge that includes and opens the door to nurturing. In the process of clarifying the seriousness of the violation, the therapist is letting the hurt child know that she is being seen and that the therapist feels for and is concerned about the injury, the pain, the terror. In her own quiet way the therapist is promising the hurt child that she will be there for her.

On top of the damage inherent in oppression per se, we are damaged by the cover-ups/lies/myths that we are fed and by our internalization of these. They confuse us, they humiliate us, they undermine us from within. By helping women see the lies for what they are, we are helping them decontaminate and reclaim their selves.

In a number of the previous examples, the issue of internalized oppression was raised somewhat obliquely. At times it is also good to be far more pointed and direct. Examples of more directed or pointed queries into lies/myths and internalized oppression are:

- When fathers violate their daughters, they often present what they are doing in ways that make them look good and us look bad. What did your father tell you about what he was doing? What did he tell you about yourself? How did you feel about him as a result? How did you feel about yourself?

- What are your family myths? What did your parents tell you the family or family members were like? How do you feel about these descriptions? What do you believe?

- You must be believing something about yourself if you are taking these psychiatric drugs. What do you believe? In whose interest is it that you believe that?

Examples of more challenging statements and questions are:

- You say the incest was your fault, that you dressed seductively, that you flirted with him. Four-year-old girls do not flirt in the way that you understand it, and they certainly do not invite their fathers to ram a penis down their throats.

- You don't think that you have internalized any of the lesbophobic garbage thrown your way. On a purely abstract level, I am sure that is true. But as you talk about your relationship, I see something different in your face. Let me tell you what I see.

- I feel sad at what you are saying and angry at what has been done to you. You have told me that you stay away from Natives because Natives are not good and because the Native within makes you bad. You are not bad, and Natives are not bad. Natives have been mistreated and lied to for years. What I see is someone who has been beaten by white stepparents and has been lied to ever since she was a child. And I would really like us to do something for that abused Native child within.

In the process of exploring internalized oppression, we need to focus on the current internalization as it arises out of current oppression and not simply on the past. This notwithstanding, as many of the preceding examples illustrate, at times—indeed at many times—we will want to focus on the client's childhood because so many of the obstacles, the lies, and the scripting begin in childhood.

Identifying childhood oppression means identifying the legitimate wants and needs that women had in childhood and the obstacles that they encountered at the time. Humanist psychotherapists would also explore childhood wants and obstacles. They would not, however, be on the lookout for those wants and needs that are forced to remain invisible in this sexist, lesbophobic, classist, racist, and ageist society. *We* need to be. Correspondingly, although humanistic psychotherapists tend to individualize childhood wrongs as if they stemmed from the isolated foibles and shortcomings of individual parents or caregivers, it is our responsibility to politicize. We know and need to remember that parents are part of a larger system, that parents are also socialized and are also oppressed. To be clear, this does not mean that we dwell on society. Nor does it mean that we either absolve offending parents of all responsibility or ask our client's hurt child to forgive her parents. It means that we have a clear social analysis in our own heads and that we should be prepared to bring in that social analysis when and where it is helpful.

The very process of identifying these early wants/needs and blocks involves us in unearthing and challenging lies. Many clients will see the legitimate needs and wants that they had in childhood as illegitimate because long ago their parents/community/teachers/peers/social service workers in some way invalidated them. We can counter by exposing the invalidation and by validating.

An example of a powerful and empowering counter is:

No, I don't find anything perverse about your attempt to pass as a boy. Passing as a boy opened up all sorts of possibilities that were not available to you before—possibilities that you had every right to want and to go after. Let's be clear here. Your parents told you that you were wrong to want to date girls and pal around with boys. But it is perfectly normal for a woman to be attracted to women or to enjoy any other supposedly "male" activities. It seems to me that even the more aware social workers who were trying to be on your side were also being less than honest with you. They told you that the rest was okay, that it was only wrong to pass or want to pass, and that once you cleared up this pathology, you could have everything you wanted as a liberated out-of-the-closet lesbian. You believed them and started seeing yourself as sick. But where's the sickness and where's the mistake? As a visible 11-year-old lesbian, could you really have dated girls without being sneered at, rejected, or attacked? And would you really have been accepted in the society of boys?

The counselor here is validating invalidated wants or needs. She is untangling the complex of lies and misrepresentations. And she is helping the client both retrieve her own eyes and reach for more information.

SCRIPTS

Scripts are a function of oppression and lies and of our own internalization of these. A *script* is an alienated existential blueprint for the living of our lives. Its origins are an oppressive society that controls us from the outset via parents, schools, social workers, government departments, and other socializing agencies. Generally the blueprints that we are given and internalize are overwhelmingly in the interests of the elite, although they also can bear the individualized marks/needs/fears of the socializing agents, whether those agents are part of the elite or not. The combined influence of both has to be considered. Scripts generally begin in childhood and continue throughout life, although socializing agents continue to script us throughout life. Scripts as well can begin later on and may even run counter to early and/or parental scripts. Ourselves, our kin, or our oppressed community can also impose *counterscripts* on us—that is, scripts intended to counter the scripts given us by society yet that limit us in turn and may still serve the interests of the elite. Generally counterscripts work both for us and against us. They are a form of resistance with a power of their own, yet they also sabotage us. Some are in the interests of the males within our oppressed communities, while running counter to our own interests as women.

Central to the formation of scripts are attributes and injunctions. *Attributes* are qualities that a socializing agent claims that we either individually or as a group have. Attributing young girls with the quality *pretty* is a case in point. It works essentially as an indirect command. As little girls we are instructed to spend inordinate time on our appearance—on our being as it appears to others—and to tailor and warp our bodies in the interests of male gratification.

Injunctions, by contrast, are direct commands—direct instructions on how to live, which once again are in the interests of the elite. By way of example, it is not uncommon for a corrections official to tell a working-class inmate to get her priorities straight, to get a 9-to-5 job when she is released, and to work hard. That inmate is being given a direct "work-to-death injunction" in the interests of the capitalist. When a Native parent tells a Native child not to make a fuss but to accommodate the white man, that parent is also providing the child with an injunction. In this case, ironically, it is an injunction that is congruent with Native culture, that is not inherently internalized oppression, but whose internalization demonstrably serves the interest of the white elite.

Examples of typical scripts for us to watch for and to help our clients at least temper are "The Woman Behind the Man,"[2] "Supermom," "Just a Good Fuck," "The One Good (Lesbian, Woman, Native, Black, etc.)." Examples of counterscripts given us by our oppressed community that may also need to be addressed are "Tough Dyke," and "Prostitute as Feminist Extraordinaire."

Helping the client temper the script means helping her do the following:

- Unearth and analyze the script
- Recognize the lies, the exaggerations, the attributes, the injunctions, and the internalizations
- Progressively become aware of the concrete ways she lives it out
- Access what these responses are costing her
- Make new decisions that in some way alter the script
- Put those decisions into action and monitor those actions

Counterscripts—especially community-based counterscripts—have to be addressed with particular sensitivity and a respectful recognition of their duality and ambiguity.

Just-Like-Us: Special Cases of Scripting and Bonding

A special type of script to be on the alert for is something I call "just-like-us scripts." By way of clarification, the life course of a just-like-us script involves any formidable combination of imitating the oppressor, obeying the injunction to ally with the oppressor, obeying the injunction to accept that everything is equal, and obeying the injunction to cover up differences between oneself and the elite when in the presence of the elite. Just-like-us scripts may be separate scripts in their own right or may be an underside of or an addition to other scripts.

Liberal versions of just-like-us scripts are particularly pervasive. The paradigmal liberal-scripted woman sees all ideology as dangerous and believes that she has no ideology. While acknowledging that injustice exists and occasionally fighting against it, she believes that society is essentially just and that for the most part we need only point out injustices and appeal to people's better nature and everything will be okay. Insofar as she acknowledges and protests against severe injustice, it is generally in some other part of the world and in reference to an oppressed group to which she does not belong. She believes that all positions are equally flawed, that there is equal right and wrong in just about everything anyone says, and that everyone has an equal burden to bear. Her most cherished attributes include being open-minded, being fair, being reasonable, seeing both sides, and being nonjudgmental.

The liberal-scripted woman is paradoxically both very easy and very difficult to work with. Her tendency is to graciously agree with the counselor, while not shifting. She "knows" that there is a great deal in what you say, while "understanding" that you exaggerate. She does not want to offend anyone by pushing anything too far. Even while concurring with you, correspondingly, she is "aware" that "this is just one side of the story" and that the other has equal validity.

Helping the liberal-scripted woman involves finding, addressing, and joining with whoever inside understands the violation and knows that she is being sold out. It means asking questions like, "Who is it that praises you for being so open-minded?" and countering the appearances of fairness with challenges like, "I don't call cheating yourself being fair." It means surfacing both sides of the contradictions that she holds and highlighting the contradiction involved.

A second type of just-like-us script I call "honorary just-like-us scripts." The woman with this script has been assigned and has accepted attributes that are traditionally identified with the oppressor. She has been treated like an "exception" by one or more significant others who belong to the oppressor group. And she has been rewarded for joining with them in belittling the oppressed group to which she actually belongs.

A highly significant subtype is women who go through life like "honorary guys." Honorary guys have male best friends with whom they spend most of their time. They join with the men in laughing at womankind. They both see themselves and appear to be accepted as "the exception." Often, albeit not invariably, the script begins in childhood, with father palling around with daughter and both together quietly snickering at silly, incompetent mother, who is, "God love her, just like a woman." The attributes of the honorary guy include "fantastic for a woman", "tough", "intelligent", "cynical", and "one of the guys". The more obvious injunctions include "imitate me", "pal around with me", and "put down women". Hidden injunctions and other messages include "you are not okay insofar as you are a woman"; "you are not quite a guy and not quite a woman"; "your being okay depends on me, so stick by me"; "adore me"; and "do not cross me".

The honorary guy is in an enormously precarious and frustrating position. Being even more critically divided from women than the traditional woman is, she has no women friends on whom to rely. She keeps finding herself fundamentally betrayed. "Inexplicably" she is periodically robbed of her "male" status and is demoted to "woman" again. It is not only the world at large that robs her. Every now and again her very pals dismiss her. She gets hurt. She is angry. She continually reconnects with her male friends, while blaming the world at large and women in particular for the indignity of being saddled with a woman's fate.

As counselors we need to understand and validate this woman's pain and her anger. She has been harmed dreadfully. Her very ability to question traditional women's roles is being used to deceive her. She is being tied in knots by the one plight that she most hoped to avoid—the plight of women in this society. By empathizing with her both personally and politically, we can help comfort her and begin the political task at hand. By encouraging and validating her fury, even in those instances where it seems misdirected and/or excessive, we can help her to move beyond fury and frustration, to focus her anger where it truly belongs, and to change her situation. Central to our work with our honorary-scripted sister is helping her loosen her male-identification and begin forming solid friendships with women. The process is a slow one, and the client will need ongoing help as she reassesses her relationships and explores new ways of relating.

A third type of just-like-us script I call "keep-it-hidden just-like-us scripts." They are imposed on people by "liberal" members of the dominant group. As with the liberal scripts, the presumption is strong that the dominant group has a modicum of decency, although only the liberal subset of the dominant group is seen as totally decent. As with the honorary scripts, the person so scripted is deemed okay, while some other members of the oppressed group are not. The differences are:

- People so scripted need not criticize their group overtly and indeed might be challenged if they do.
- They can act differently from the liberal mainstream as long as they are discreet about it.
- Rather than being depicted as exceptions, they are given the message that most members of their group are okay. It is the indiscreet members of their oppressed group who are disapproved of and are seen as "exceptions."

The attributes that the "liberal" members of the dominant group impose on people with keep-it-hidden scripts are fairness, discretion, and the attributes of the dominant liberal group. Injunctions and other messages that are given include the following:

- Act like us "in public."
- You are totally okay only as long as you act like us "in public."
- All members of your group are totally okay only as long as they act like us "in public."
- Not acting like us "in public" is unfortunate, indiscreet, and blameworthy.
- We are being nice by accepting you the way we do.
- If we did not accept you or you did not appreciate us for accepting you, you would not be totally okay, so do appreciate us for being nice and compliment us when you can.
- Although you can see or imply that your group is being oppressed by other members of the dominant group, do not see or imply that you are oppressed by us liberals.

Native women and men who are derogatorily known in the Native community as "apples" (red on the outside and white on the inside) are people laboring under this script. So too are lesbians who (a) almost never refer to lesbian encounters in straight company even when that company are friends, (b) never engage in shows of affection around their heterosexual friends, (c) see lesbians who do so as risky and as irresponsibly jeopardizing the responsible lesbian image that the rest of the community is trying so hard to build, and (d) are enormously grateful to their straight friends for their open-mindedness and largesse.

Helping a women loosen the grips of such a script involves the following:

1. Finding, comforting, and inspiriting the child within who got hurt and frightened and decided to accommodate
2. Co-investigating what is being sacrificed and who is gaining in the process
3. Encouraging her to take pride in and affirm her identity as (lesbian, Black, Native, etc.) and celebrating all steps in this direction
4. Supporting her as she begins relating to her liberal friends differently and struggles with the conflict and/or tension involved

STRENGTHENING/REPAIRING THE BOND WITH WOMANKIND

Our part in mending the woman-woman bond begins with relating as one caring woman to another. Analysis, ongoing political empathy, and making connections between this woman's individual situation and the systemic oppression of women are also integral. We further the mending whenever we help our client empathize with or understand other women. We further it by helping her join with her sisters in protesting their situation and/or demanding their rights. We further it more fundamentally by encouraging and supporting female friendships and by helping women explore their multifaceted attractions to women.

One very clear point of entry is our clients' putdowns of themselves and other women. Misogynous descriptors and antiwoman injunctions are often at the base of these criticisms. By surfacing and co-investigating these, we can help our clients amend the descriptors and increasingly free themselves from the injunctions. Such explorations could in turn culminate in a fuller examination of misogyny, a clarification of rights and violations, increased anger, a movement toward women (sometimes also mother), and action.

Our clients' friendships and relationships are also an important point of entry. We can strengthen their bond with women by helping our clients explore the following:

- What their male friendships and/or intimate relationships are like
- What their female friendships and/or intimate relationships are like
- How and why they differ
- How and why their relationships with women are undermined
- The part that everyone plays in the preferring of men and the sacrificing of female-female relationships
- Ways in which they are harder on women friends and why they are harder
- What they now give to and receive from women
- What they would like to give and receive
- Their relationships with their mothers

Helping women explore the fuller range of emotional/physical affinities to women is more sensitive and is frequently not possible. Many women are far too frightened and far too lesbophobic to open up that dimension of themselves. We must respect the enormity of the pressure and the scripting and not push. Many of the women who have pushed down their attractions to other women nonetheless want to explore their attractions despite their fear and do so when we provide an opening. Ways of making it easier for them and of providing that opening include:

- Periodically using phrases like "whether with a woman or with a man" when discussing relationships
- Commenting on the richness of their relationships with women where appropriate
- Gently challenging lesbophobic statements
- Affirming the centrality and richness of the woman-woman bond
- Accepting the sexual diversity that women bring

WORKING WITH THE BODY

We can assist in the physical side of liberation in many different ways. We can encourage women to enjoy their natural bodies. We can point out gently and supportively when they are looking at their bodies through patriarchal eyes or white people's eyes or Anglo-Saxon eyes and help them find/regain their own eyes. By engaging them in breathing and other energizing exercises, we can help women to experience the joy of energy coursing through their bodies and to feel both physically and emotionally.[3] By touching, warming, and caring for what is numb, we can help bring back life. By engaging women in anger exercises, we can help them get in touch with their anger and their strength. By encouraging and nurturing women as they dare to feel sexually and as they explore those sexual feelings and inclinations, we can help them find/build/enjoy a sexuality that is their own.

More specific and more intense body work can be helpful, and the body-related questions that we initially asked ourselves may give us direction in this regard. If a client is emaciated and not eating, for instance, we will want to work harder on body image. Slowly, in the long run, we will also want to help her alter her eating pattern and find other ways of exercising control. (For more details, see Chapter 12.) If the client is holding her body in ways that choke off breath, feeling, memory, and anxiety, one option to consider is applying pressure to those areas and encouraging expression. The aim here is to help her open up the areas that are choked off, get in touch with body memories, and protest.

Intense body work such as this is powerful stuff; it can legitimately be used to help unearth issues and get in touch with feelings. At the same time, if done carelessly, it can harm and even revictimize. This can and does happen even with highly skilled and benign feminist therapists and even with the best of intentions, for what is powerful can powerfully harm as well as powerfully help if we are not careful. Moreover, momentums and biases that work against us occur within therapy itself. Counselors can get caught up in the drama and go farther than they should. Therapists generally have a bias in favor of vulnerability and accordingly can easily intrude and leave the client in a state of terror, while believing that truly excellent work has been done.

Insofar as we do intense body work, we have a profound obligation to be aware of this problem and to monitor our work accordingly. Some cautionary pointers in this regard are:

1. Get trained in body work before doing it. Also modify what you learn to fit what you know about women.
2. Check in every case and at every turn to see whether the client wants to do the work that you are suggesting.
3. Do not push. We need to accept even a quiet or hesitant no and to assure the client that a refusal does not make her "bad," "resistant," or "doomed."
4. Make sure that the client understands the importance of letting you know whether she is becoming overstressed.
5. If the client is becoming really scared or overwhelmed, or if she begins blurring, confusing who you are, spacing out, or splitting, *discontinue physical work immediately, comfort her, and help her reorient herself.*
6. It is a mistake to combine intense body work with psychodrama. We risk traumatizing the client.
7. The more violated the client has been and the earlier the violation, the more vulnerable she is and the more important it is that we proceed slowly and carefully.
8. Generally go slowly and pace your session. Do not overload the client. Do not go deeper while the client is still struggling with the current depth.

9. Discontinue and process body work well before the session finishes. The client needs time to process, reorient, and ground herself before leaving.

10. A session of intense body work should generally be followed by lighter sessions. When intense body work occurs session after session, clients usually end up becoming far too vulnerable; their overall well-being is threatened.

DEPRESSION

Working with women in a patriarchal, racist, and classist society inevitably means dealing with depression much of time. It is not surprising that women are depressed. Oppression is depressing, and depression paradoxically is often the strongest protest that people can muster in a dehumanizing situation.

When depression is extremely severe, when the woman, say, hardly speaks, is always sleeping, or barely moves, the physical reality of depression itself demands our attention. Who we have here is not only a "dis-couraged" but also a "de-energized" human being. On a purely physical level we can help her energize herself by helping her to get moving, to take in more food, and to breathe more deeply. These are things to be encouraged, of course, not demanded or pushed.

Whether the depression is obviously severe or not, it is absolutely essential to nurture depressed women. We need to care for and validate them. In many cases it is also important to provide practical assistance so that what is clearly an overwhelming load is lightened. Good work generally involves a number of the following:

- Directly advocating for more money for day care or other services
- Helping women access what resources are available
- Creating a space in which women can rest
- Helping them become more entitled—that is, become clearer about their rights, learn how to assert what they want, learn to say no, and put this into practice in situations where it is physically safe for them to do so
- Helping them get in touch with and express anger
- Helping them extricate themselves from brutal and demoralizing life situations
- Countering false attributes
- Helping them reconceptualize so-called "personal failures"
- Helping them become aware of and truly appreciate their strengths
- Helping them get a critical handle on their situation
- Helping them forge links with members of the different oppressed communities to which they belong—to other women in particular

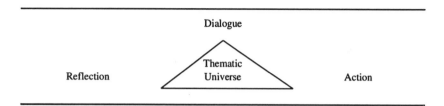

Figure 4.1. Empowerment Model
SOURCE: Burstow, 1991

IDENTITY AND ACTION

Oppression, lies, and isolation serve to alienate, confuse, and disempower. Awareness/emotional work helps women cut through the lies, become less confused, and rid themselves of internalized oppression. It is equally important to help women forge links with other members of their oppressed communities (women, Black women, women with disabilities, etc.) and take action, whether individually or collectively. Joining with and dialoguing with multiple others who are similarly situated, on equal footing, and intent on empowerment help forge a positive identity and cut through the alienation in ways that dialogue with a single counselor cannot. It also facilitates common analysis and common action.

Action itself is as vital to empowerment as the reflection and dialogue that go into analysis. Empowerment in its fullness looks about as depicted in Figure 4.1. Some action is inherent in the work already discussed. The stage for additional action is also set by the co-investigation, the exercises, and both the individual and the multiple joining.

Questions that help identify the oppressive situation and eliminate internalized oppression have already been discussed. Examples of questions that help identify and facilitate action include the following:

- You describe yourself (or your community) as the loser in this situation. What would a *good* situation look like?
- What needs to be changed here? What would you like to see changed?
- What concrete tasks would have to be done for this change to occur?
- What if any small steps can you see taking that would begin moving things in that direction?
- What help would you need if you were to try this?
- Whom or what might you turn to or ally with?

Although some of the answers given will inevitably have to be problematized, such questions as these help overcome surplus powerlessness and lead to action and sometimes also to joining. The action and the joining in turn are the ground from which new and meaningful reflection and dialogue emerge.

SUGGESTED READINGS

Burstow, B. (1991). Toward a Freirian approach to counselling. *The Canadian Journal for the Study of Adult Education, 5,* 55-69.

Freire, P. (1970). *Pedagogy of the oppressed.* New York: Seabury.

Wyckoff, H. (1975). Banal scripts of women. In C. Steiner (Ed.), *Scripts people live: Transactional analysis of life scripts* (pp. 210-234). New York: Bantam.

NOTES

1. These are Freirian terms. For further elucidation, refer back to Chapter 1. See also Freire (1970).

2. This particular script has been identified by and discussed in transactional analysis. As the reader familiar with T.A. will recognize, I am using some of the T.A. concepts, while pushing them farther and radicalizing them further. For a discussion of women's scripts from T.A.'s viewpoint, see Wyckoff (1975). Other scripts listed here, like most of the scripts referred to in this book, are my own conceptualizations and bear my own names.

3. For valuable energizing exercises that can be drawn on, see Lowen (1976).

5

Difference: Working With . . .

LESBIANS

Lesbians place special faith in feminist therapists, and they disproportionately use our services. This is understandable, for feminist therapists have been better than their nonfeminist counterparts. This notwithstanding, for the most part heterosexual feminist therapists are light years away from understanding the special issues and dilemmas that lesbians face and so do not provide what is needed. Although lesbian feminist therapists tend to do better work with lesbian clients and are the preferred matching, lesbian therapists too are often amiss.

Indeed, in its own quiet way, feminist therapy has tended to duplicate many of the heterosexist assumptions of society and of traditional therapy. It has depoliticized lesbian existence, often reducing it to a life-style. In the literature lesbian relationships are frequently described as immature and the counselor's job depicted as redressing that immaturity. Everyone is careful to point out that lesbianism is normal. Tellingly, though, the very word sounds like a disease. Feminist therapy theoreticians correspondingly are forever portraying lesbians as pre-Oedipal, enmeshed, and maladapted.[1] More politically aware counselors in turn often automatically assume that "internalized lesbophobia" is the central and overriding issue to address with any lesbian who comes to see them, regardless of presenting issue and regardless of "where the client is at." Internalized lesbophobia is indeed a critical issue in our work. Nonetheless, when such an assumption becomes automatic, it is another way of pathologizing lesbians or of finding lesbians inadequate. In the process the power and complexity of lesbian lives are overlooked, as are the differences.

By contrast, good work with lesbian clients involves the following:

- Recognizing and rejecting pathologizing and infantilizing theories and approaches, however covert or subtle the pathologizing and infantilizing may be
- Accepting and respecting lesbians as courageous, mature adult women who are affirming and defying
- Talking out of an awareness of the centrality of the woman-woman bond
- Understanding and talking out of an understanding of the daily dehumanization and violence that lesbians face
- Acknowledging heterosexual privilege
- Recognizing the diversity of lesbians and, when appropriate, co-exploring the special problems faced by Black, Jewish, Native, disabled, and other lesbians who are members of two or more oppressed communities (increased tension, extra invisibility, not knowing where to belong, and not belonging anywhere)
- Advocating wherever helpful
- Privately and publicly protesting lesbian oppression
- Challenging and inviting clients to challenge the current minimization of lesbian issues in the women's movement

It is critical that counselors be able to co-investigate compulsory heterosexuality and its impact on their lesbian clients' lives. It is important to empathize with them and to explore together the impact and possible ways of dealing with (a) invisibility and erasure, (b) the lack of role models in the schools or the media, (c) the experience of being rejected, ridiculed, assaulted, or terrorized because of sexual preference, (d) the lack of social and legal recognition of relationships, (e) the perception by others of being sick or perverse, (f) the inability to publicly enjoy or "flaunt" relationships as heterosexuals typically do, and (g) the comparative economic liability of two female salaries.

Examples of stereotypes and images that lesbians face and that it is important to be able to co-address are:

- Lesbian as sick
- Lesbian as man-hater
- Lesbian as undesirable woman who is unable to land a man
- "Lesbianism" as a "phase"

- Lesbians as evil plotters who will take over and ruin any good organization, given half a chance
- The image of the aging, lonely, despairing "dyke," often depicted as the inevitable fate of lesbians

Coming Out to Self

Coming out to self is a particularly important area for counselors working with lesbians to be knowledgeable about. Women in the early stages of a lesbian identity are often terrified at the prospect of being lesbian. Women who have been neither feminist nor lesbian-positive and women who have had a narrow religious upbringing may be utterly scandalized by what they are feeling. Even if they did not have a narrow upbringing and even when they are feminist and avowedly lesbian-positive, they may harbor the secret suspicion that they are not quite "all right." They may suspect that "lesbianism" is not normal. They may wonder whether their early molestation by their father might have "caused" them to be lesbian.

Many lesbians who escape the very early self-doubt while caught up in the original "high" of new life and new possibilities doubt later. As the enormity of the lesbophobia around them begins to sink in, many become frightened; they become self-conscious, and they begin to question themselves. Surrounded by a society that cruelly marginalizes, pathologizes, indeed even vilifies lesbian existence, they do not quite know what to think. The fact that these self-doubts themselves may seem politically incorrect can add to their isolation, for they may not be able to share it with their lesbian friends.

At the outset many of the women exploring a new identity have trouble even broaching the issue with their counselors, especially counselors who are straight or whom they believe to be straight. They may drop only the occasional clue and go no farther unless we pick up on that clue. They might, for example, scrupulously avoid using any words that clarify gender when referring to an attraction or relationship.

We can help by picking up gender-neutral terms and other clues and then asking her directly and openly whether she is referring to a woman or a man. Our openness and directness convey the message, "*I* am okay with what is being discussed here, and *you* are perfectly normal." Therapists who are lesbian can also make a painful issue much easier by coming out and by being willing to share.

When clients are unsure of their identity, as very often they are, it is important to validate the uncertainty itself. We can assure them that confusion is commonplace in a society that lies about sexual attraction. Of course they are confused. How could they be otherwise? We can assure them that all women are attracted to other women, albeit to varying degrees, and that all choices remain open. They need to give themselves the time and permission to explore.

Whether clients are unsure about their identity as lesbians or not, clients in the early stages of lesbian identity generally need clear assurances from us that they are "all right." Examples of helpful and empowering responses are as follows:

- I keep getting the feeling that you think something is wrong with you and this is why you are lesbian. Women often have those fears at first. Do you think you could share just a few of those fears with me? If we started talking about them, I might be able to be of help. I can promise you at the very least that I am not going to think badly of you for having these worries and that I'm not going to belittle you in any way.

- You say that you feel like a freak. I can sure understand feeling that way. It's awful. Your parents, your school, your friends, the movies you watch all tell you that what you want isn't normal. The truth is, though, that *all* women are attracted to other women—some more, some less. Most, though, don't let themselves become too aware of that love because it's so threatening; it's so different from what we've been led to believe.

- I hear your worry, but no, I sure don't believe that the early sexual abuse that you underwent "caused" you to be lesbian. You're a complex human being with her own network of meaning—not some cause-and-effect mechanism. Besides, most incest survivors are heterosexual. And no one asks whether their early sexual abuse caused them to be straight.

- You are reluctant to act on your attraction to Helen because you suspect that it is abnormal. Looking at where our suspicions come from can sometimes help us. Where do you think the idea comes from? And whose interest do you think this suspicion and this reluctance serve?

Sometimes early lesbian liaisons and/or thoughts about liaisons are "one step forward followed by a hasty retreat." The client tells herself and she tells us: She really is heterosexual after all. When this happens, it is important not to push. This woman is scared and needs our reassurance and our patience.

Another way we can help women who are exploring their sexuality and/or are in the early stages of lesbian identity is by providing much-needed information. They need to be aware of the lesbian resources around them. Books can be a great resource—especially books about lesbian sex. Not surprisingly, given how heterocentric and sexist this culture is, many do not have a clue how to make love to another woman even though it is a body just like their own, and they are both nervous and embarrassed by the ignorance. They will feel better and will be more likely to act on their attractions if they read something first. Explaining the relationship between self-pleasuring and giving pleasure to another woman also helps. They can benefit as well from knowing about the coming-out groups and the women's bars and clubs in their community. So do familiarize them with lesbian resources in the area.

Coming Out to Others

Decisions around coming out to others are major issues for lesbians, and it is critical that you be able to help them with it. Women in this position unfortunately have less than ideal options because society is less than ideal. Invisibility is disempowering and sickening. It means always having to be quiet about what is central in our lives. It means having to dissemble. It means living with the constant risk of unexpected exposure. Coming out, correspondingly, can mean loss of jobs, loss of friends, ridicule, violence, and being subject to that nauseating "liberal" tolerance that always misses the point. Coming out nonetheless is an important and vital assertion of self. It is the beginning of lesbian pride.

It is our responsibility to help our clients understand the profound disentitlement involved in being "in the closet" and the entitlement and pride that become possible when out. It is critical in this regard that we not fall into liberal thinking. Although it is important that our clients make their own decisions, this does not mean that all decisions are equally valid or equally freeing. We know that hiding disempowers and that coming out empowers. It is up to us to share that knowledge and to do whatever we can to nurture lesbian pride.

At the same time, we need to be up-front about the difficulties involved in being out—especially of being out before one is ready. We need to assure the client that it is not only all right but preferable for her to take her time. Taking time is a way of caring for self. She may need our assurance that absolutely nothing is wrong with coming out selectively and that in some situations selectivity is wise.

Many clients in this situation also need help determining whom to come out to and when. Questions that we can ask in this regard include the following:

- How do you think ____ will react if you come out to her or him?
- Are you comfortable with that reaction?
- What is the best that you are hoping for?
- What is the worst case scenario?
- How likely is it?
- Do you feel up to dealing with the worst case scenario at this time?
- If you do come out to ____ now, what extra help do you want from me?

When a client is nervous about coming out to someone else, I generally get a lot of mileage out of role plays and can recommend them. It takes what is abstract and makes it concrete, and it lets women experiment in safety. Frequent role switching further helps in surfacing the different problems that might arise and in exploring different ways of dealing with them.

Couples Work

Some feminist therapists see lesbian relationships as similar to heterosexual relationships and treat them accordingly. And some theoreticians concur. This is a false egalitarianism and indeed a good example of just-like-us scripting.

Our lesbian relationships are not "just-like-the-hets." The reality is that, unlike heterosexual relationships, lesbian relationships are characteristically very intimate because women value intimacy more than men; they are a "naysaying" to the patriarchy; and they are an expression of our fundamental bond as women.

They are also stigmatized relationships that are severely punished, marginalized, and pathologized by the patriarchy in which we all live. Even the women's community and the lesbian community encroach on lesbian couples. Lesbian couples are often treated as if the relationship were casual and short term, when indeed it is serious and long term. Lesbian couples are frequently criticized for being monogamous or for doing *n* number of things that are deemed "politically incorrect."

Insofar as society abuses and marginalizes lesbian couples, it is our responsibility as counselors to befriend them, to safeguard them, and to support them. Insofar as the relationships are uniquely female, it is vital that we not judge them by heterosexual/male standards. Common mistakes in this regard are (a) treating their greater intimacy as if it were infantile "fusion" or applying concepts like *codependency* to it and (b) treating their close relationships with former lovers as inherently problematic and an example of weak boundaries.

These much-maligned tendencies are part of the beauty of lesbian existence. They stem from women's strength—from women's caring and inclusiveness—and they should be celebrated and emulated, not corrected.

Inherently valuable though they are, greater intimacy and closeness can, of course, bring special problems of their own. They can trigger issues from earlier times when we experienced greater intimacy and were more vulnerable. When this happens, it is up to us to address those problems squarely and honestly. It is critical, however, that we do so while remembering what we know as women and not devaluing, pathologizing, or in any way infantilizing the intimacy and closeness themselves.

Ways of safeguarding, supporting, and befriending lesbian relationships include (a) demonstrably valuing the strength and caring in the relationship, (b) not putting as much pressure on lesbian relationships as we would on heterosexual relationships, (c) empathizing with the special pains and difficulties they face, (d) dealing gently with internalized lesbophobia and its impact on the relationship, and (e) actively allying with them against an oppressive and heterocentric society.

Lesbians With Children

Lesbians with children sometimes need help dealing with their children's lesbophobia. Where children are involved, an advocacy role may be called for. Social service agencies are notorious for taking children away from thoroughly competent and loving lesbian mothers. Where co-mothering is occurring, help may be needed in sorting out respective roles and rights.

NATIVE WOMEN

(This section is written for non-Natives who may find themselves counseling Natives. I write it with the awareness that I know little and that we must turn to our Native sisters for guidance.)

It is generally preferable for Native clients to work with Native counselors. Referrals should be made with this in mind. When those of us who are non-Native work with Native clients, it is our responsibility to ensure that the relationship is not oppressive and that we conduct ourselves as knowledgeably and skillfully as possible. Becoming aware of differences is a good place to begin.

Knowing about the specific First Nation that the woman comes from and its history can be important, for there are considerable differences between Nations. Knowing about some of the general differences between Native and white European cultures is critical.

A fundamental truth about traditional dominant white North American (TDWNA) counseling that it is important for non-Natives to know is that it clashes seriously and in many ways with cherished Native values and ways of being. TDWNA counseling, on the one hand, places an emphasis on changing the world to realize our choices. Natives, on the other hand, traditionally emphasize accommodation. TDWNA counseling is predicated on the importance of individuality. For the traditional Native, it is the community, not the individual, that is central. TDWNA counseling operates in terms of "progress toward." For traditional Natives, well-being is a "return to." TDWNA counseling embraces the secular. Traditional Native life is rooted in connectedness and spirituality. TDWNA counseling can ignore elders. Traditional Natives look to the elders for guidance. TDWNA counselors markedly confront. Marked confrontation, for traditional Natives, violates the fundamental rule of noninterference. TDWNA counselors follow the lines of linear logic. Natives think more circularly and allegorically. TDWNA counseling works via clarification, directness, and making explicit. Traditionally much of Native communication is implicit. It is in the silence between the words, the suggestive image, the story that gives itself to us, while never directly addressing our situation.

Some of these differences are not as marked where the non-Native counselor is political. We are learning from our Native sisters and brothers and are attempting to discard, for instance, the cult of individualism. We are coming face to face with the connectedness of all beings and with the havoc wreaked by our power over and by instrumentality. As non-Native women, moreover, many of our preferred ways of being and our values are closer to the Native's than to the white male oppressor's. By acting out of our deeper knowledge as women, we begin to bridge.

The problem and the solutions nonetheless are not simple. White male processes help form much of our thinking and our communication as counselors. Moreover, what we ourselves are bringing as feminists—our emphasis, for example, on analyzing the concrete social situation—is rooted in the verbal, the direct, and the explicit. As such, unless tempered, it can be off-putting, bewildering, and downright intrusive. And we need to grapple with Native women's critique of white feminism and preference for terms like *womanist*.

Ongoing domination, Christianization, and subjugation to whites has led to disentitlement, humiliation, and severe problems in living. These problems are a current reality for Native clients and need to be addressed. Insofar as we pretend they do not, we are being no kind of counselor. Insofar as we address them while ignoring the political roots, we are pathologizing, oppressing, and contributing to disentitlement. Insofar as we address them in white European ways generally, even where we do not pathologize, we can injure deeply.

What makes a complex issue still more complicated is that centuries of white domination and disentitlement and centuries of sexual and other violence against Natives have led to increased misogynous violence within the Native communities themselves—incest in particular. Violence against women is now a colossal reality of Native life and of Native culture as lived, however different the reality was before the advent of white oppression and however much this conflicts with traditional Native values. Not to honor Native ways is to oppress fundamentally. To ignore the violation against Natives is to fail fundamentally as counselors. At the same time, we owe it to our Native sisters not to forget that we are dealing with suboppression, as well as oppression, and not to ignore or minimize the reality of suboppression.

A further complication arises from what white oppression has made of a Native value that whites would do well to emulate—accommodation and adjustment. Like traditional women, traditional Natives accommodate. Accommodation was not dictated by the oppressor. It comes from a deep respect for all beings and from a fundamental sense of connectedness. Accommodation is wonderful, and it is unproblematic in a cooperative world. Whites, however, have used it to further oppression. Native accommodation has often meant accommodating the whites as they plunder, steal, and rape what is Native. It has meant accommodating one's own subjugation. While valuing traditional Native culture, radical Native youth are seeing the importance of nonaccommodation within the context of oppression; and this shift is one that we need to recognize and affirm.

Nonpolitical counselors make such blatantly horrendous and racist errors when working with Native clients that most political counselors know enough not to imitate them. Nonetheless, politically aware counselors tend to make two fundamental types of errors in the face of this complex reality. The first is making a few well-intended gestures by way of accommodation and then going about business as usual. Although aware that something is wrong with how we are proceeding, we plow on, hoping that the tried and true will work. Sometimes indeed it does. At other times, however, it does not. Although nothing is wrong with entering tentatively with what we are used to, a great deal is wrong with having this as our only possibility. Insofar as we simply impose our values and our ways of being on our Native sisters, we are oppressors, not helpers, despite our good intentions.

The second error is the flip side of the first. It is either imitating the Native elder or limiting ourselves to what a Native would do or say. As Wolfgang (1984) and others point out when discussing intercultural counseling generally, insofar as we imitate, we are an absurd parody. We insult more than we please.[2] We are not Natives and should not presume to be what we are not, although certainly we need to learn from Natives and adapt. Additionally some of the ways in question are misogynous, and some are self-defeating.

Awareness of these differences and complexities is a good place to begin. From there we need to get to know the individual client herself. Some important questions for us to ask ourselves are:

- Which of my different ways of being and responding is this particular woman most comfortable with? Which is she least comfortable with?
- What are her Nation's traditions and history?
- In what ways is she like a traditional Native? How does she differ?
- How is she oppressed as a Native? How is she oppressed as a woman? How do these oppressions combine? Does she keep sight of both oppressions or reduce one to the other?
- What resources exist for her within the Native community? The women's community? Other communities?
- Which of these does she currently use, and why? Which does she not use, and why?
- What is she proud of as a Native? What is she ashamed of? What is she proud of as a Native woman? What is she ashamed of?
- How has she internalized her oppression as a Native, and how has she resisted?
- How has she internalized her oppression as a woman, and how has she resisted?
- How is she understanding and responding to conflicting loyalties?

Answering these questions gives us some sense of how and when to accommodate, how and when to challenge, and generally how to proceed. As we tentatively accommodate, support, and confront, we find new answers, new questions, and more appropriate ways of responding.

Accommodations that I have found helpful more often than not when working with Native clients and can recommend include the following:

- More carefully observing rituals that connote respect
- Challenging somewhat less
- Challenging either more tentatively or more supportively
- Being more sensitive to conflicting loyalties and helping the client sort through what can be given to each, without simply sacrificing one to the other
- Going with the ambiguity and richness of the image, story, dream, or metaphor
- Taking extra care not to insult, not to intrude
- Checking often to ensure that the client is not simply accommodating me when I am doing or encouraging something that does not fit
- Doing more advocacy
- Respecting the centrality of the community
- Adapting to Native time

Adapting to Native time involves going with more pauses—more breathing time—without hovering over and expecting aha's to result. We adapt to Native time when we let go and allow processes to occupy whatever time they will, when we think more in terms of the long run rather than tomorrow, the next day, or before next session. Setting our sessions so that punctuality is not so very important can also be helpful.

Addressing Colonization

All Natives have been dreadfully oppressed by whites in childhood and continue to be oppressed throughout adulthood. All see dominant white men's ways treated as if these were normal and universal truths. All are invited to be ashamed of the color of their skin. All live in fear of white violence—both by civilians and by police. All encounter racist obstacles in their pursuit of jobs, positions, and residences. Many are gobbled up by the criminal "just-us" system for something as innocuous as shoplifting and come out only to be humiliated again.[3] Many are painfully poor. All have been robbed of land, language, religion, and self-governance.

On top of all this, many were systematically brutalized in childhood. An alarming number of Native children were stolen from their families and communities by white social workers and other agents of racist patriarchal capitalism; and many continue to be stolen. Many Native children found themselves in white boarding schools where whites attempted to preach, teach, humiliate, and beat the Indian out of them. Many were raised by a series of white foster parents who beat them, used them as household drudges, and sexually molested them. Many were and still are molested by the Church. Abuse was presented as a benefit. Christianization itself was presented as something that saved their souls. Many were told that the discipline and beatings were "for their own good." And oh so many were told over and over again that all Natives are savages, that Natives are worthless drunks who exist only by the kindness of whites, that their own parents were totally incompetent, and that the best thing that they can do is imitate the wonderful whites and turn their backs on Nativekind.

Given this reality, not surprisingly, many Natives grow up profoundly injured and alienated from themselves and from their people. Many internalize the oppression greatly and are ashamed. Many feel worthless, many drink, and many inflict ongoing physical abuse on themselves. Some become confused as they go between "Mother Mary" and Native spiritual figures. A number are subjected to psychiatric drugs to help them deal with "their problems."

As counselors it is important that we take in this horror in its totality. We need to listen to, appreciate, comfort, and support the abused and terrified child within. We need to help clients who have internalized much to unlearn gradually the stereotypes and other racist attitudes or beliefs that they have taken in. We need to help clients who are confused to separate the Native from the European, to identify the source of the confusion, and to identify and reject false help and false befrienders. And we must support Natives as they find their power and their way back. It is critical, correspondingly, to affirm Native indignation, Native pride, Native identity, Native resistance, and indeed Native sovereignty and to help Natives link up with Native communities.

Resources to be aware of and to help clients access include local elders; political action groups; spiritual groups and teachings; healing groups, ceremonies, and teachings; and friendship centers.

In cases in which both the hurt and the internalization are particularly severe, clients are reluctant to hear anything good about Natives or anything bad about whites. One of my clients—Emma—is a case in point. She was raised by white foster parents who beat her, molested her, and used her as a household drudge. She was psychiatrized most of her adult life. She cut herself frequently. Her presenting problem was drinking. She told me that all Natives are worthless drunks; that she did not wish to associate with them; that it was good that she was on psychiatric drugs because a Native was still inside and that Native was sick; and that she wanted to get better, not to associate with "a bunch of savages" and get worse.

Moving ahead with a political agenda—even political empathy—in such instances is counterproductive. What I find helpful and can recommend for cases in which both abuse and internalization are this strong is concentrating exclusively on nurture, support, and personal empathy at first. From personal empathy, we can gradually move into looking at the wrongs that this woman underwent at the hands of whites.

Violence Against Women Within the Community

Ideally, Native women who have been violated by Native men and who identify as part of the Native community can find solutions and resources within the community itself. Unfortunately the ideal is not always possible. We sometimes become the primary resource. This is acceptable as long as we do not give up trying to help women link up with or create Native women resources and as long as we guard ourselves against falling into racist beliefs in the process. It is all too easy for white counselors working with obviously abused Native women to make insidious comparisons and to forget about the more hidden violence against women in the white community. It is easy correspondingly to lay all blame on the Native male and to forget about the central role of racism generally and of physical abuse by whites in particular.

Insofar as we are a resource, we need to modify our approach. The rage work that helps white women clashes with traditional Native ways and sensibility. If the particular Native woman with whom we are working can go in that direction and it fits for her, that is well and good. She has been violated, and she has reason to be angry. Many, however, are more comfortable with approaches that are more spiritual or communal. It is up to us to adapt.

A Native resource available on many reserves is communitywide healing groups. Men apologize for the incest and speak about their own sexual victimization. Native women and men cry and talk together. Some Native women find this helpful; as a white woman I would not presume to question its legitimacy for them. For many, though, including those who go along with it as if it were okay, it is very oppressive. It can mean subordinating themselves once again to the needs of the perpetrator, this time with full community support and with the whole community looking on. I recommend caution accordingly. A resource that I feel better about suggesting and that has helped a number of Native incest survivors is the sweat lodges and the "doctoring" that occurs in them.

A wonderful resource for incest survivors in some communities and that I can wholeheartedly recommend is Native women's sweet grass ceremonies. The ground on which these ceremonies occur is, for the moment, a liberated zone—a Native women zone. Here Native women cry and are held by their sisters hour after hour while sweet grass burns and sisters chant. Here they can receive women's spiritual healing without sacrificing any aspect of their identity.

Women who are being or have been badly and repeatedly violated by their partners and have become alienated from the community may need special help.

An example of this occurred in Winnipeg a few years ago. A Native woman was repeatedly beaten by her male partner. One day he started to beat her elderly mother. She called the police. The Native community responded by ostracizing her. This particular community was largely composed of Native males and Native-male-identified women. From the vantage point of both, the woman was guilty of turning in one of her own kind to the white oppressor, and what she had done was unforgivable. Similarly, many Native women have been beaten on the reserves by their male partners and have complained to the chief and other Native authorities, received no help, and found themselves double-bound by the demands of loyalty.

Such instances as these are complicated and require extreme sensitivity. Women are being caught in no-woman's land between two very real oppressions. They are asked to be totally loyal to one oppression, while being hammered by the other. As counselors we need to understand the dilemma, to empathize with the agony, to help women do what they must to protect themselves, and to support them. By helping them unearth the very formidable contradictions and the double binds in which they are placed and by affirming their rights, we can help them get rid of guilt, see farther, and act. It is also important to do what we can to help them link up with other Native women who are similarly discontent. For ultimately it is from Native women thinking and acting together that more empowering and enduring solutions will emerge.

AFRICAN AMERICAN WOMEN

(This section is written with the awareness that I am necessarily limited in my understanding in this area. Ultimately it is to African American women's articulations that we must turn.)

Many of the issues raised in the section on Native women are relevant to African American women. Black women too are subject to overt and covert violence on the basis of skin color. Black women too are robbed of their choices and are subject to white European hegemony. Black women too have strong family ties. Black women too are oppressed not only by elite whites but also by the Black men with whom they share an oppression. Politically aware work is predicated on some understanding of the history and the specific ways in which the dual or triple oppressions combine.

Optimally the counselor should be African American or at least Black. A Black counselor has inside knowledge and is generally more easily trusted. Such counseling relationships moreover benefit from the rich tradition of Black woman bonding.

A problem that Black counselors working with Black clients sometimes face is hyper-criticalness. Black feminist Audre Lorde (1984, p. 158ff) has drawn attention to the phenomenon of Black women being more critical of each other than of anyone else. Where this occurs, internalized racism and sexism are clearly operant. If Black is bad and woman is bad, then Black woman is doubly unacceptable. Conversely, if all women are expected to be all-giving mothers and Black woman is supposed to be "mammy par excellence," then the individual Black woman with her own needs is necessarily an enormous disappointment. Criticalness of other Black women tends to be some combination of deprivation: anger at mother; internalized stereotypes; the worry that whenever another Black woman is less than perfect, it reflects negatively on all Black women; the ever-disappointed expectation that other Black women will be perfect and will fill the unmet needs; and repeatedly encountering supercriticalness from other Black women.

When such criticalness is directed at the counselor, a co-exploration of what it is about is in order. Additionally, extra gentleness and nurturing are called for. This woman may have missed out on childhood because of time and circumstance. She may have watched on as her exhausted mother did double labor, caring for the white folk and the men and having little time for her. She may have received a tough/toughening education from a parent who was painfully aware of the importance of imparting survival skills and who viewed compassion over racist affronts as a softening that could be ill-afforded. This is an opportunity for her to get some of what she could not get in childhood and can never totally get from her peers. By being gentle and nurturing themselves, moreover, Black counselors are able to model a different response to other Black women and to self.

Counselors who are of color but not Black are generally a better fit than counselors who are white. White counselors who are subject to racism correspondingly are preferable over white counselors who are not.

Those of us who are not Black can enhance our counseling by reading works by such Black feminists as Audre Lorde (1982, 1984) and Bell Hooks (1984) and by going to educationals run by Black women. General guidelines that I try to follow and can recommend are:

- Draw on oppressions to which you are subject, and make connections.
- Do not assume that sexism is necessarily the worst oppression.
- Keep in mind the roles of family and church in the Black community.
- Remember that this woman's male kin are oppressed, as well as oppressors.
- Do not overgeneralize from the situation of one group of women—especially middle-class, white women.
- Take in the pain, the cognitive dissonance, and the frustration that inevitably result from having your experiences continually erased or marginalized.

- If you do not like something about the client, inquire into your own racism. Are you being ethnocentric? Are you judging according to standards that do not fit? Are you falling into stereotypes? If so, which?
- Be aware of differences in spatial orientation. What an Anglo-Saxon experiences as a comfortable distance between two people may seem standoffish to a Black woman. What a Southeast Asian woman finds comfortable is likely to feel miles apart.
- If a Black woman's expressions of anger are bothering you, begin by questioning yourself. Are you uncomfortable with direct expressions of anger? Are you expecting the client to adhere to white, middle-class standards when expressing anger? To some other standards? Does a Black woman's anger scare you? If so, what beliefs and images underlie that fear? Have you said or done anything that is racially insensitive? Are you avoiding challenges that you think are important in order to avoid the anger? (I am not excluding the possibility that no may sometimes be the honest answer to these questions, but we should not jump quickly to no.)
- Women from less demonstrative cultures often mistake Black women's assertiveness and banter for anger. If you think the woman is angry, check it out.
- Do not equate with paranoia a Black woman's persistent worry about being attacked. Such concerns are reality based.
- If white, understand that as white women we are privileged, that we are racist, and that suspicion of us is not only okay but also is an invaluable survival skill.

General Counseling Issues

Black women are disproportionately raped and otherwise brutalized by white men, who have always "bestialized" Black women. Again and again, white police shoot or beat up on Black women, calling them "Black bitches" to boot. This is a tragic, racist, and sexist reality. Suboppression is also a huge and tragic reality. As Lorde (1984) has pointed out, despite the silence in which it is enshrouded in the Black community, the tragic truth is that Black men—not just white men—are raping, bestializing, and beating Black women. Helping our violated Black clients mourn the injury, nurture the hurt child within, gain clarity, and resist is critical.

It is important to be aware that poverty and classism also disproportionately oppress Black women. Middle-class assumptions about upbringing and about the liberating nature of work outside of the home are oppressive and should be guarded against. Extra help accessing resources and dealing with bigoted bureaucrats may be necessary. Help may also be needed in dealing with and problematizing the racist, classist, sexist stigmas attached to being a Black welfare mother, to having a Black working-class style, to cleaning other women's (white women's) houses, to doing whatever needs to be done to make ends meet. Correspondingly encourage, join in, and affirm Black woman's protest against being the "slave of a slave"—"the mule of the world."

The Stereotypes

Critical stereotypes to be aware of include Black women as (a) smiling, all-giving mammy, (b) Superwoman, (c) Shrew or Sapphire, and (d) lascivious beast. The bare minimum that our clients have the right to expect is that we not fall into such stereotypes ourselves. Beyond this we need to be able to recognize these stereotypes and to help clients co-explore ways in which they are internalized.

Black woman as smiling, all-giving mammy and Black woman as Superwoman are selfless ideals imposed on Black women. Black women who veer from the role of mammy are often seen as shrews. Black women who veer from the roles of mammy and Superwoman are seen as selfish and irresponsible. While validating their connectedness and their strength, it is important to demystify the ideal of selflessness and to help women co-explore the injury it does to self. It is important, correspondingly, to invite our Black sisters to be vulnerable sometimes, to allow themselves to be needy, to find out what they themselves want. The client may need special help dealing with the pressure to have children, to support THE MEN, to sacrifice themselves in the interests of the Black community generally and Black males in particular.

Black woman as Sapphire or shrew is the other side of Black woman as Superwoman, and it is the product of sexism and racism. Sapphire was a Black character on radio and TV in the 1950s who was always yelling at and dominating her Black husband. Black men conspired with whites in the perpetuation of this image and the value judgments attached to it. What it does is vilify the strong Black woman. It vilifies the woman who does what she must for herself and her family to survive, who sees through the mystification in which sexism and racism are shrouded, and who will not "take crap" from anyone. She is blamed because the Black man has trouble getting work in this racist society and because she is the one supporting the family. She is blamed because she assumes responsibility. She is blamed because she does not smile and "keep her place." The Black man accuses her of being a "castrating bitch," of demoralizing him, of forcing him to desert the family. White professionals lament the "role confusion" and accuse her of creating a dysfunctional family.

As counselors we need to affirm the strength and to co-explore the racism and sexism involved in these images and these rebukes. Where our Black sisters are stomping down their anger, emulating white women, or attempting to live up to the selfless ideal, more detailed co-exploration and reframing are in order. Where they feel that they must follow one of the stereotypical ways of being to escape another stereotype, we need to empathize with the difficulty of the situation and to help them both redefine and defy.

Black woman as lascivious beast is the stereotype used to justify sexual violence. It too contrasts with the mammy image, which is asexual. Most counselors recognize this stereotype in its extreme. We recognize it, that is, when it takes such horrific forms as rape or demeaning comparisons between Blacks and apes. It is important to recognize the stereotype as well when it is subtler and to help women co-explore the double binds in which it places them. Examples of subtler forms are descriptors such as wild and exciting, natural rhythm, untamed, exotic, and sleek as a cobra.

Additional oppressive descriptors and judgments originating from whites that we may need to recognize and co-address are stupid or subintelligent, ugly, lazy, dirty, evil, and in league with Satan.

The White Beauty Ideal

The beauty ideal that presents a problem to all women presents a special problem for the African American woman, for she cannot even vaguely approximate it. All African American little girls grow up bombarded by images of women with blue eyes, lily white skin, and flowing blonde hair. They know that whatever else this adored image is, it is decidedly not them. They conversely are not it. They contrast starkly with it. Therefore they are "not okay." While seeing these images, they hear people tell them that they are "Black and ugly." Some who are darker than other family members are given the message that the difference is a shame and are encouraged by parents to stay out of the sun to avoid getting any "blacker."[4] Many begin to hate the color of their own skin. Many African American women bleach and straighten their hair. Some gouge their cheeks and alter the contours of their faces.

Here is a lifetime of pain. We need to reach for and listen to that pain. We need to help these women tease out their experiences. Nurture of the hurt and hurting child within is critical. So is co-exploration of the oppression and the ways in which it is internalized. It is important at the same time to help our clients take in and affirm the beauty of their own bodies.

Black Lesbians

As noted in the section on lesbians, Black lesbians are marginalized in society as a whole, in the Black community, in the women's community, and in the lesbian community. One or more aspects vital to their identity are forever being criticized, not seen, or trivialized. As counselors it is important that we empathize with these multiple marginalizations and rejections and affirm the enormous importance of being seen and accepted for all of who they are.

Clients in this triple and quadruple jeopardy may need extra help with coming out, with challenging racism, with challenging sexism. They may need help challenging people who minimize the oppression not shared, treating the one shared as the only important one. White lesbians have been known to tell Black lesbians that lesbian separatism is "the only way to go" and that their

Black brothers and fathers are The Oppressors. Black lesbians are forever hearing other Blacks either denying that lesbians exist in the Black community or referring to it as an ailment arising from racism. They need to be able to respond both inside themselves and in the world at large. Two-chair work and role plays can be very useful. Women unfamiliar with the literature may also benefit from reading works by Black lesbians who explore the interconnections of racism, sexism, and heterosexism. So it is important to have such literature on hand.

Resources

Important resources to be aware of and to be prepared to help the women access include racially and culturally sensitive social services; Black women's groups; antiracist films, books, and educationals; antiracist political action groups; and antiracist lawyers.

JEWISH WOMEN

In the Jewish culture, family is stressed, strong women are a norm, and great emphasis is placed on learning. Arguments, as long as pursued logically, are not something avoided but enjoyed. Traditional religious practices are highly patriarchal. Many Jewish feminists nonetheless actively alter the services. Key religious holidays such as Pesach (Passover) are generally observed by atheists and religious Jews alike, for they carry the culture, are part of family tradition, and celebrate our victories over oppression. Commitment, fighting for justice, and taking a stand are seen as an integral part of the Jewish way.

Jewish women of color face the oppression faced by all women of color and indeed are oppressed both by white Jews and non-Jews. The experience of Sephardic Jews is often erased, as if Ashkenazi constituted all of Jewry. Additionally, whatever our color or ethnicity, we face a unique multidimensional oppression simply by virtue of being Jewish women.

The oppression of Jews is rooted in both racial and religious domination. The violence varies from the colossal and dramatic to the subtle.

Obviously violent forms of religious domination include wholesale conversions at threat of death, the pogroms, and other massive slaughters of Jews for the crime of "deicide." Religious prohibitions and expulsions from countries throughout the centuries are another level. Christiancentrism is a subtler form of everyday religious domination that all Jews face in Western society. Christianity is treated as the universal religion. Christian holidays are recognized by law; Jewish holidays are not. At Christmas we are all wished a Merry Christmas, even by people who are aware that we are Jewish. The inevitable result is a sense of invisibility, of cognitive dissonance.

Although a phenomenon that spans millennia, racism involving "Jewishness" was given fullest articulation in late 19th-century Germany. German theorists held that Jews were a single race and that this race had pernicious, inborn characteristics. Included in the characteristics specified were such biological traits as large hook noses and apelike bodies. Included as well were such psychological and behavioral "tendencies" and "proclivities" as shrewdness, miserliness, money grubbing, and plotting to take over the world. As these characteristics were inborn, it made every Jew the enemy. In Nazi Germany these theories, together with the characteristics, served as a warrant for genocide.

The traits and theories are propounded in North America today. Again and again teachers are found instructing students about the Protocols of Zion—the hypothetical Jewish plot to take over the world. And growth continues in such Aryan and white supremacist groups as the Ku Klux Klan (KKK).[5]

The modern stereotypes that afflict Jews owe much to history. We are seen as dirty, money grubbing, cheap, cunning, conniving, dangerous, pushy, boorish, lacking class, too loud, too intellectual, and too emotional.

The negatives are intensified when applied to Jewish women generally and to working-class Jewish women in particular. If Jews are too loud, Jewish women are seen as shrieking and bellowing. If Jews are somewhat pushy and low class, Jewish women—especially working-class Jewish women—are obscenely pushy and utterly devoid of class. What we have here is anti-Jewishness, sexism, and classism combined.

The two most prominent stereotypes of Jewish women are the Jewish mother and the Jewish American princess (JAP). The Jewish mother has its origins in the shtetls of Europe and in early 20th-century North American Jewish communities. In the working-class Jewish community the Jewish woman was a formidable power and was valued as such. She worked in the outside world, as well as in the home. She, not the male, dealt with the outside world. This female strength and authority clashed with the dominant patriarchal values and norms of North America. Jewish women were gradually pushed into the house and into the limiting role of mother. We did not go easily; and we never fit. The loud, complaining, passive-aggressive, double-binding Jewish mother of the stereotype is part exaggeration by a sexist, anti-Semitic society, part Jewish woman's ambivalent response to the sexist strictures that closed in on her. The son as comic, as novelist, as psychologist invited the world to join him in laughing at her; and the world joined in.

The Jewish American princess is the descendant of Jews who were a bit more affluent, who had a foot and a half out of the ghetto. She had better clothes and took on the mainstream female obsession with appearance. She strove to look like the acceptable Anglo-Saxons (often mutilating her nose and becoming bulimic to accomplish this, for Jews are a far cry from the Anglo-Saxon stereotypes).

Tragically it has become socially acceptable to mock the Jewish American princess. The suggestions are that the Jewish woman is rich, self-indulgent, pampered, dreadfully concerned with appearances, and that all of this adds up to something utterly disgusting. Underneath the overt objections are covert anti-Semitism, sexism, and classism.

The Jewish American princess is galling to mainstream society partly because she is trying to fit and does not. Her airs are objectionable because they are the airs of her Anglo-Saxon "betters." She is dressed too prettily, and yet her "coarse" Jewish manners continually betray her. The closeness to the money, the fact that it is not quite at arm's length, correspondingly taints her and makes a mockery of her finery. It is the ape again, affecting manners and dressed in finery.

She is also an irritant for more blatantly misogynous reasons. Remember the joke:

> **Question** What does a Jewish American princess make for dinner?
> **Answer** Reservations.

She is being put down because women are supposed to cook for their husbands and this "uppity Jewish woman" does not. A collusion between mainstream society and the Jewish husband is evident.

Her typically Jewish pursuit of learning is also an irritant, for it flies in the face of sexist society. Note in this regard the Jewish American princess joke:

> **Question** How do you know when a Jewish American princess has an orgasm?
> **Answer** She loses her place in her book.

The young Jewish woman is being mocked because she is not the sex slave that women are trained to be, because she loves books. This translates into "no feeling, no flesh" by non-Jews who laugh at her. Paradoxically she is also depicted as a lustful, insatiable creature, as indeed women from despised cultures typically are.

Violence threatens behind the laughter. As many Jews are painfully aware, slogans like "JAP free zones" and "Slap a JAP," which are currently popular on American campuses, point to danger.[6] Jewish women become the paradigm of Jewishness, and violence against Jews is the threat.

Historically and currently, Jews respond to danger in many ways. On some level, even if we tell ourselves that we are perfectly safe, most of us are aware of not being safe. The Holocaust happened in our lifetime or our parents' lifetime. Throughout the centuries, everywhere, Jews have been persecuted. We live with the terrible awareness that a major outbreak of anti-Semitism can always occur. Although many Jews take great pride in their heritage, terrorization and hegemony take their toll. At some time or other most Jews have attempted to hide their Jewishness, whether from individuals whom they suspect of acute anti-Jewishness or from most other people. Few would actually deny being Jewish if asked, but they would greatly prefer that the subject never arise. The attempts to pass are not always successful. The truth is that although we are generally not a visible minority, we tend to be an audible one. We open our mouths. The words come out in singsong or too loud. And there we are again—Jew, outsider. Many Jews, without exactly hiding, are ashamed of their Jewish traits, having seen them mocked and criticized. Many make a deliberate effort to tone down or eradicate these traits. Some distinguish between the bad or embarrassing Jews and Jews like themselves who are "just like the Gentiles." Most North American Jews are uneasy about making a fuss over anti-Semitism— especially when it is covert. We seldom talk about it. We suspect that we are being a bit too sensitive. Many listen on with surprise but say nothing as the question of anti-Semitism is omitted in conversations about racism or is referred to as a problem of the past. Some listen to and even participate in disparaging JAP comments.

The Counseling

Whether the counselor is Jewish or not, in this age of Jewish invisibility most counselors greatly underestimate the significance of being Jewish when attempting to understand their Jewish clients. Frequently, as a result of internalized oppression, clients similarly underestimate. The client is thereby shortchanged. We need at least to begin by assuming the opposite. Assume that being Jewish in a Christian, anti-Semitic world is a critical lens through which the client's perceptions are filtered even if the client is unaware of it and is ostensibly "mainstream." Then proceed to find out what this means concretely.

Questions to keep in mind that you will eventually want answers to include the following:

- Does this person see being Jewish as part of her identity? If not, what is the disidentification about?
- To what extent did her family of origin identify as Jewish and celebrate Jewishness? Did anyone try to pass or assimilate? Does she try to pass or assimilate?
- How does she feel about being Jewish? How does her family feel?
- What types of anti-Semitism did she experience when growing up? What did other members of her family experience?
- What advice did her parents give her?

* Which stereotypes bother her the most? What do they mean to her?
* How did she respond to the anti-Semitism in her childhood? How did these responses serve her then? How did they impede her? How does she respond now? How do these responses serve her? How do they impede her?
* In what ways has she internalized anti-Jewishness?
* In what ways does she resist and affirm?
* Does she observe Jewish holidays? Which? What do they mean to her?
* Which Jewish values are important to her? Which is she proud of as a Jew? What if anything is she ashamed of?
* How does she feel about her mother as a Jewish woman? What does being a woman and a Jewish woman mean to her?
* Does she take anti-Semitism as seriously as other oppressions? If not, what is the minimizing about? What forms does her terror of anti-Semitism assume? How does she deal with it?
* How does she feel about her body?

The object is to challenge internalizations, to process and express what has been hidden or avoided, and to affirm as fully as possible the totality of who she is.

It is important that the counselor herself not be overtly Christiancentric and that she at least be open to learning and working on her own anti-Semitism. Automatically wishing a Jew a Merry Christmas is a way of discounting. Inquiring into her experiences of Christmas is a better idea. Extend good wishes on significant Jewish holidays. Whether the woman observes them or not, it feels good to be seen. If she is uneasy with your good wishes, this reaction itself gives you important information.

If you find yourself strangely irritated by a Jewish client, you may be reacting negatively to valued Jewish or working-class Jewish characteristics. If you find her too loud, too pushy, or overentitled, chances are that you are perceiving and judging according to dominant norms. Take in the difference, and let yourself enjoy the loudness and the entitlement. If you are doing couples work and you find yourself feeling sorry for the husband, check whether you have fallen into any Jewish woman stereotypes. At least part of your response may stem from reading the situation according to dominant gender norms. Do not assume that she is avoiding feeling if she intellectualizes. As Jews we typically both intellectualize and feel. Correspondingly do not automatically back off and assume that she is closed if she vehemently opposes something that you say. She may simply be enjoying stating her point or trying to engage you.

When one or more of the following occur, there is reason to suspect that Jewish oppression has been significantly internalized:

* The woman makes a point of letting you know that she is not "very Jewish" even though the subject of her being Jewish has barely been raised.

- She states that she is "not like other Jews."
- She is quiet, does not interrupt, does not talk with her hands, is low in affect, is reserved.
- When she refers to things she dislikes about her parents, Jewish traits and stereotypes keep popping up.
- She discusses other oppressions at length, while saying nothing about anti-Semitism.
- She refers to anti-Semitism as a lesser oppression.
- She makes anti-Jewish statements herself.

With the exception of the mannerisms, which simply give information, each of these is a possible opportunity for co-investigation. If a Jewish woman says that she herself is not "very Jewish," I might make a comment like: "I understand what you are saying. At the same time, it worries me that it is so important for you to let me know this. As if you were embarrassed or ashamed." When a Jewish client discourses at length on different oppressions while leaving out anti-Semitism, we might point out and problematize that omission. From here, more detailed co-exploration and affirmation can ensue.

A client who resembles the Jewish mother stereotype is likely to be a woman who needs help breaking loose and recovering space for herself. It is important to access and affirm the strong, capable woman within. Correspondingly, when a woman is criticized for being either a Jewish mother or a Jewish American princess, co-exploration of the anti-Semitism, sexism, and classism is in order.

Jewish survivors of childhood sexual abuse or partner abuse are likely to need extra help affirming what has happened. The myth is that all Jewish men are "absolute dolls" and "nothing like this ever happens in Jewish families." While respecting what is special about Jewish families and Jewish men, counter that myth. Correspondingly help her deal with the obligation that she may feel to protect the Jewish man or the Jewish community by being silent.

With women who go along with highly sexist services and with women who totally avoid the holidays because of the sexism, I sometimes mention more feminist practices such as women's seders. This of course is not something to push.

If the woman who comes to see you is a Holocaust survivor and you are not Jewish, it is generally advisable to refer her to a Jewish counselor who works in this area or to a Holocaust survivor program. At the very least, do not work with her yourself without consultation.

Many Holocaust survivors experience frequent bouts of abject terror. They have flashbacks. They keep finding themselves back in the camp again or in hiding. They may go to bed with all of their clothes on—even their shoes—so that they can beat a hasty retreat. They have nightmares. They split and have trouble "coming back." It is critical to affirm the enormity of what happened and really to be there for them. Their needs greatly resemble those of incest survivors, who have also had their world overturned, and similar approaches may be used. Bit by bit, help them learn how to ground themselves, to deal with triggers, to create what safety they can, to distinguish present from past, and to mourn. Many survivors additionally feel enormously guilty about being alive when most of their family and friends have died. Our role is to take in the agony, while helping them redirect the blame and move from guilt to mourning to anger.

Sometimes children of Holocaust survivors also experience extreme bouts of terror and flash back to the camps. Similar help is needed. Children of Holocaust survivors generally need help as well separating themselves from their parents and their parents' experiences. Be aware too that the problems may have more than one source. The client may additionally have been abused.

Often children of Holocaust survivors take on their parents' guilt, grief, and sense of doom. Besides the parents functioning as role models, this is a way of being close to the parents. Initially the child was separated from the parents by the parents' grief and doom. By taking on the grief and doom, the child overcomes the separation. The price is overidentification with the parents and an ongoing tragic existence. Taking on the grief, guilt, and doom may additionally be a way of avoiding frustration with parents whom the child has been trying in vain to comfort. Again our job is to help her loosen some of the overidentification and both identify and feel those feelings that the overidentification has masked. And again we need to proceed slowly and gently. Movement is inevitably frightening and inevitably experienced as betrayal.

IMMIGRANT WOMEN

When working with immigrant women, we are generally in a difficult and sensitive cross-cultural situation. Cross-cultural situations of this kind demand greater learning, care, and adjustment from us.

On the basic level of communication itself, it is important to be aware of differences—especially in body language—and to both match the client's style and reinterpret her messages accordingly. Unfortunate consequences can arise if we do not. By way of example, if we did not know that looking away is a sign of respect in some Asian cultures as with Natives and so interpreted our client's looking away as a sign of disinterest, we might begin to resent her and project wildly. Different cultural groups use space differently. We need to ask ourselves and be able to answer: Is this a culture that would interpret my sitting 2 feet away as welcoming or as invasive? Is this a high- or a low-contact culture? If it is an extremely low-contact culture, we would want to reconsider doing the direct body work discussed in this chapter. Similarly we need to know how to interpret facial expressions. And we need to know some of the key words that are charged with meaning in the culture and the network of words with which they are connected. We can get this information by reading about cross-cultural counseling generally and about the specific client's culture in particular. And we can get it by talking to different people from the culture and by creating our own communications map. Not to do this learning and not to adapt is to be ethnocentric and ineffective.

It is important as well to have some knowledge of what helpers within the client's community do or are expected to do. In many cultures help is more directive, and our clients correspondingly may flounder if we are nondirective. High-context cultures require more attention to context. *High-context cultures* are cultures in which the client has strong community ties and in which there are overriding community expectations—both ceremonial and otherwise. With the high-context culture, besides being obliged to consider the whole community, words are generally less important, and helpers are expected to honor customs and ceremony.

Japan is an example of a high-context culture. A traditional Japanese woman might find it difficult if we did not offer her tea and chat with her over tea. The tea ceremony serves to establish rapport and to create the needed level of comfort. Respect for family ways, nonintrusion, and periods of silence would also be expected.[7]

Dealing with differences in values and ways of being is anything but straightforward, for clients vary in their allegiance and are currently in the process of transition. Immigrant women often need help sorting out what to adopt of the new country and what to keep of the old. At times they may discard too much or too quickly and set themselves off balance. We need to be alert to this problem and help them readjust when appropriate. At other times they may be trying to hold on to something that simply will no longer work. Here again input is needed, but it must be given with clear empathy for the enormity of the difficulty and the awareness that solutions and timing vary from person to person.

For the most part, such extensive uprooting and transition are very traumatic. Initially many are elated with the new country; after a few months, however, the terror, the loneliness, and the loss set in. Eventually so too does the awareness of limits. Some take many years before letting in this larger awareness, for it is far too threatening. Others, however, see quite early on that this is not the great open country they had believed it to be. This is not the country of equality where everyone can make a million dollars and lead the "good life." It is a country where oppression exists and where they themselves are a target. It is important to validate the obstacles they see and their anger at being misled and to help them co-investigate. More fundamentally it is important to invite mourning. A way of life, friends, family, and rooting itself have been lost; the women need to mourn.

Newly arrived immigrants invariably need help learning the language, getting work, learning the customs, making friends, and accessing community, legal, and other resources. As counselors it is our responsibility to be aware of the needs, to be aware of the resources, and to provide information and direct networking as needed.

Wives and mothers are generally in a worse situation than their husbands and children and need considerably more help. The men are off at work and the children are off at school, both learning the language and customs, socializing, and making friends. Stuck in the woman's role, the woman meanwhile is often left in the house, lonely and depressed. The husband and the children gain proficiency in North American life. She never quite learns to speak English, needs them to translate, and progressively finds herself desolate as husband and children spend more and more time away. Not surprisingly, many immigrant women become increasingly alienated and depressed. We can help by caring about her and by taking her learning and her social needs seriously. Practical ways in which we can assist include (a) arranging for language instruction or other skills instruction, (b) helping her link up with community groups—social groups in particular, and (c) lending extra support when needed by going with her the first few times.

Insofar as an immigrant woman is "depressed" and does not behave in ways that are typical of dominant North American males, she is in special danger of psychiatric interference. To our disgrace, psychiatric institutions are full of immigrant women who are having a hard time, despite the warning in the *DSM III R* not to pathologize either community differences or "expectable" depression.[8] Protective measures that we can take include:

- Advising her against using services that have psychiatric backup
- Helping her alter some overt behaviors that are likely to be interpreted as "symptoms"
- Intervening on her behalf should psychiatric intervention occur

The Tortured Refugee:
An Immigrant With Special Needs

People who have been tortured may frequently have night terrors. They have body memories. They flash back to the scenes of torture. We need to be extremely gentle and extremely supportive. A woman in this situation needs help talking about what has happened to her. She needs to express the terror and the rage. She needs our reassurance that it is perfectly normal for her to experience flashbacks and terror in her situation and that she is not losing her mind. She needs both to be safe and to know that she is safe. Many of the approaches suggested in the chapters on childhood sexual abuse are applicable.

With the aid of "professionals," some communities have been developing services for tortured refugees, and some of these may be useful for referrals. I would advise extreme caution, however. Women and immigrants are always at risk of psychiatrization, and when we add *tortured* to the list of descriptors, the risk becomes astronomical. Community services for tortured refugees generally have psychiatric backup and tend to pathologize experiences that are perfectly normal in the situation, some now using the incoming diagnosis "post exile syndrome."

WOMEN WITH DISABILITIES

Empowerment counseling with disabled women begins with an understanding of the situation of disabled women in our society. Such an understanding in turn brings us back to the body, its function, and the social constructs and meanings in which bodies exist.

First and foremost, our bodies are our mode of being and the precondition of our being. It is by virtue of being embodied that we exist, and it is in and through our bodies that we orient ourselves and interact with the world. Our five senses bring in information. Our feet and legs move us from one place to another. Our arms and hands let us reach out and grasp. Our lungs take in air. Our stomach digests organic matter that sustains our life.

In a patriarchal capitalist society a certain level of proficiency in each of these parts and functions or a certain way of using them is considered "normal" or "able-bodied." Communities are basically organized around these levels and these ways. Transportation exists for those who can walk to it. Books exist for people who see well enough to read. Jobs are designed for those who can speak, and hear, and see, and walk, and reach.

Disabled is the name given to people who do not have the so-called "normal" level of functioning in one or more central areas or who operate differently. Women with disabilities find themselves in a world that blocks their attempts to get about and do things. Although some of this blocking is inherent in the disability, most is socially created or is exacerbated by an elite ordering of the world. By way of example, a carpet is comfortable to walk on, but not when you are blind and trip on the edges. Theaters are fine, but not if you have no way of getting there. The disabled are not accommodated systemically but are given handouts for which we are supposed to be grateful. We are ignored in the designing of facilities and machines, even though the purpose of facilities and machines is precisely to enhance and extend the work of the body. Many highly capable disabled people can find no jobs at all or are saddled with boring, low-paying jobs.

Underlying these systemic issues is capitalist/patriarchal psychology. Through capitalist/patriarchal eyes, people with disabilities are not quite people. They are in-valids. In a world built on certain kinds of appearance, the visibly disabled are branded as freaks. They are blemished merchandise. People avoid them or stare at them. Some actively insult.

Sexism combines with ableism to compound the problem. Under the patriarchy, women's value is nullified when disabled. The fundamental reduction that all women suffer is the reduction to bodies tailored for and relegated to the sexual and domestic servicing of males. We are the helpless bodies who are forever helping. The cruel paradox that women with disabilities face is that they are penalized dramatically both for falling dramatically short of this male-serving ideal and for realizing it far too closely.

The first part of the paradox is the most obvious. Insofar as women's value depends on the sexual servicing of the male, and insofar as most disabled women do not fit with patriarchal fantasy, they are fundamentally de-sexed and de-valued. As women's other value is domestic services, and as the disabled are not tailored for domestic servicing, all value disappears.

Under patriarchal capitalism, women with disabilities are the ultimate rejects. Men do not seek them out, and so they do not enjoy even the limited power that women traditionally wield. Ninety-nine percent of men whose female partners become disabled leave their partners. (By contrast only 50% of women whose male partners become disabled leave them.[9]) Disabled women who have female partners are held up to incredible scorn. Institutions not only do not facilitate disabled woman as sexual beings but also tend to regard any sexual activity on their part as disgusting. Because women with disabilities receive neither a male partner's money nor even women's wages, they are devastatingly poor. The unemployment rate for disabled women is 74%. Those who do work earn only 64% of the wages of TAB (temporarily able-bodied) women. And TAB women already earn only 60% of men's wages.

The other side of the paradox cuts just as deeply. To the patriarchal eye, visibly disabled women more closely approximate the helpless child, which is the female stereotype. This "helpless plus" appearance meets with a "stereotypical plus" male response. If all women are infantilized by men, visibly disabled women are severely infantilized. They are treated as if they cannot think. They are kept dependent. They are soundly discouraged from doing anything on their own. By the same token, if women's "helplessness" and vulnerability generally are seen as an opportunity as well as an excuse for male violence, disabled women's vulnerability is seen as a blanket invitation. Disabled women are attacked again and again by partners, caretakers, and strangers. And alarmingly, according to Disabled Women's Network in Toronto, disabled women are sexually assaulted three times as often as their able-bodied sisters.

The Counseling Itself

Our first responsibility to our disabled clients is to recognize and honor their fundamental rights of access and of comfort. If counselors who are working in agencies get together with their colleagues and raise Cain over wheelchair accessibility, ramps will be built.[10] If we object vehemently and repeatedly over the absence of counselors who know sign language, sign language will become an integral part of staff development. It is important that we do this. If we simply raise the issue and leave it at that, management will generally agree that wheelchair accessibility or sign language is important but will not make it a priority. Pushing for rights is one way of honoring rights. Other ways of honoring them include having comfortable chairs, making the written information that we distribute available in tapes or braille, and keeping the pathways clear.

In these days of constitutional challenges, more and more women with disabilities are seeing this ableist and sexist society for what it is, are valuing themselves, and are demanding justice. This notwithstanding, as we might expect with this degree of oppression, most disabled women have internalized a horrendously disempowering view of themselves and are neither demanding nor getting very much. Sadly many see themselves as ugly, as deformed, as incapable; and they act accordingly. They see themselves as a tremendous burden. They are thankful for what little they get. They are forever saying "I'm sorry," as if they owed the world an apology. As counselors it is vital that we assist them in freeing themselves of this burdensome image and becoming entitled. The message that we need to give loud and clear is: You are a capable, intelligent, desirable, sexual human being who is fundamentally oppressed, and you have the right to a better life. It is correspondingly vital to comfort the wounded child within and to co-explore the insults, the humiliation, the objectification, the stereotypes.

Because the body is the basic site of the oppression, the body once again is an important focus. Energizing exercises can help disabled women become less alienated from their bodies and experience the vitality of their bodies. By inviting them to notice the sensuosity of their bodies—the curves, the lines, the special features—we help them see themselves through loving women's eyes. By talking about and taking seriously their sexual desires, we can help them affirm themselves as sexual beings.

Disabled women who have been smothered and are dependent need extra help establishing boundaries and acting independently. Help here includes boundary clarification, ongoing encouragement, and assistance in connecting with other disabled women.

In light of the depth of the disentitlement, some type of assertiveness work is important, although it need not take the form of traditional assertiveness training. A good place to begin is eliminating the apologies. To ask for what she needs or wants without apologizing can be an enormously empowering act for a woman who is forever apologizing. Once the level of apologies is lowered, a client might be asked to choose one or two situations in which she would like to assert herself further. She may need/want to say "I love you, but back off" to a smothering parent. She may want to protest the uncomfortable chairs in her doctor's waiting room. Critical analysis here can be vital. People who are disentitled need to be clear about the grounds of their entitlement if they are to act effectively. Once again, role plays can be of tremendous help. Again it is good to help them connect with other disabled women. It is, after all, easier for any of us to become more entitled when we are part of a group that is affirming our rights and dealing with our grievances.

Because of the increased sexism, disabled women frequently need more help than TAB women in their relationships with men. Sadly, getting and keeping an able-bodied male partner is often considered the pinnacle of success in apolitical disabled women circles.[11] On an individual level, this translates into a disempowering focus on getting an able-bodied man and often means putting up with considerable abuse to keep him. We need to give the disabled client the clear message that she does not need a man—able-bodied or otherwise—and that her worth in no way depends on having one.

Whether they are in relationships or not, because of the alarming prevalence of violence against disabled women, it is important for us to be extra vigilant in noticing violence and in offering assistance. In light of the paucity of women's shelters for disabled woman, advocacy is clearly called for.

General information that is important for you to know and share includes the following:

1. Names, information on, and phone numbers of relevant groups in the area—community action groups included
2. Names and numbers of specialized legal services
3. Names and numbers of accessible women's shelters
4. Types of community programs that exist for disabled women and where to find them
5. What their definite and their possible legal rights are
6. Information on financial subsidies
7. Information about special needs housing
8. Location of wheelchair-accessible buildings in the city and the relative safety of access
9. What self-defense courses are offered for disabled women in the area
10. Books, articles, and magazines on disability issues

SUGGESTED READINGS

Boston Lesbian Psychologies Collective (Ed.). (1987). *Lesbian psychologies: Explorations and challenges.* Chicago: University of Illinois Press.

Brown, L., & Root, M. (Eds.). (1990). *Diversity and complexity in feminist therapy.* New York: Hawthorne.

Doucette, J. (1990). Redefining difference: Disabled lesbians resist. In S. Stone (Ed.), *Lesbians in Canada* (pp. 61-72). Toronto: Between the Lines.

Goodrich, T., Rampage, C., Ellman, B., et al. (1988). The lesbian couple. In *Feminist family therapy: A casebook* (pp. 134-159). New York: Norton.

Green, J. (1982). *Cultural awareness in the human services.* Englewood Cliffs, NJ: Prentice-Hall.

Lorde, A. (1982). *Zami: A new spelling of my name.* Freedom, CA: Crossing.

Lorde, A. (1984). *Sister outsider.* Freedom, CA: Crossing.

McKenzie, B. (1985). Social work practice with Native people. In S. Yelaja (Ed.), *An introduction to social work in Canada* (pp. 272-288). Scarborough: Prentice-Hall.

Moraga, C., & Analdua, G. (1983). *This bridge called my back: Writings by radical women of color.* New York: Women of Color.

Rich, A. (1986). Compulsory heterosexuality and lesbian existence. In *Blood, bread, and poetry: Selected prose 1979-1985* (pp. 23-75). New York: Norton.

Samunda, R., & Wolfgang, A. (Eds.). (1985). *Intercultural counselling and assessment: Global perspectives.* New York: C. J. Hogrefe.

Siegel, R., & Cole, E. (Eds.). (1991). *Jewish women in therapy: Seen but not heard.* New York: Harrington Park.

Wolfgang, A. (Ed.). (1984). *Nonverbal behavior: Perspectives, applications, intercultural insights.* New York: C. J. Hogrefe.

NOTES

1. This is even a problem in lesbian-positive lesbian books written by lesbians. See, for example, Boston Lesbian Psychologies Collective (1987).

2. For a discussion of this and related issues concerning cross-cultural counseling, see Wolfgang (1984) and Samunda & Wolfgang (1985).

3. The discriminatory policies of the criminal justice system and the ongoing criminalization of Natives are important realities for counselors to be aware of. To quote just one figure, although Native women make up only a small fraction of the women in Manitoba, they represent 88% of the jailed women. An Elizabeth Frye worker in Manitoba whom I spoke with had this to say about women who shoplift: "If a woman is white, she is usually not incarcerated for shoplifting until the 10th or 11th time. The Native woman, by contrast, is generally jailed after the 1st or 2nd attempt." The atrocity evident here is compounded if we look at why Natives shoplift. Most are poor and need what they take. Talking with women in the Native sisterhood at P4W (Prison for Women in Kingston Ontario), I discovered that the most common crime was stealing money to buy food for their children. These children, significantly, were placed in foster care after their mothers were incarcerated, and thereafter their mothers were pronounced "unfit."

4. For one example of this, see Lorde (1982).

5. For a more detailed discussion of these theories and their influence in modern-day North America, see Bercuson (1985).

6. For more details on this, see Beck (1991).

7. *High-context* and *low-context* cultures are helpful concepts for counselors doing cross-cultural counseling to organize some of their thoughts around. For more information on these concepts and their application to different cultural groups, see Green (1982). For more details on counseling Japanese, see Ramsey (1984), p. 139ff.

8. For these warnings, see the introduction to the *DSM*.

9. For these and other statistics provided concerning disabled women, see Disabled Women's Network (1990).

10. Ramps should be located at the front doors, not the back doors. Rear door access conveys the message "You are a second-class citizen," and it is dangerous, especially at night. Disabled women are often attacked coming through the parking lot at the rear of buildings at night.

11. For more information on this problem, see Doucette (1990).

6

Problematic Territory

HETEROSEXUAL COUPLES

After years of exasperation and serious qualms, many feminist therapists have chosen not to work with heterosexual couples. This decision stems from honest doubt about whether we were helping in the long run. Again and again, we found ourselves wrestling with relationships that were just plain bad for the woman. We started seeing what we were doing as patchwork only. By giving false hope and by effecting just enough changes to make unbearable relationships seem bearable, we were perpetuating the oppressive situations in which our female clients found themselves. Deciding not to do heterosexual couples work is a totally acceptable position. Given the sexist context in which heterosexual relationships exist, counselors who do work with heterosexual couples have a profound obligation to monitor what is happening and make a concerted effort to combat sexism. This is not easy, for dynamics pull us in the opposite direction from the beginning.

Most feminist counselors have no trouble keeping hold of and proceeding from a feminist understanding when the man comes in angry and intimidating his partner and the woman enters cowering and crying. This indeed occurs. Often, however, the dynamic is dramatically different. In many cases the man is much more pleasant and much easier to get along with. Not being oppressed or not as oppressed, he may be quite easygoing. He smiles. He puts everything so reasonably. In some cases he may even have been cleaning up the house for the last few months. The overburdened and invalidated wife, meanwhile, who may additionally have been leaving the house a mess for months now, seems irrational, screams, accuses, nags. We may find her hard to be with and can easily understand why he would. In situations such as this, many feminist counselors forget everything they know about sexism and begin colluding with the man and pathologizing the woman. It is important to contextualize both the good nature and the screaming/nagging, both the cooperation and the strike. It is important to keep sight of and operate out of a concrete understanding of the situation from which these spring. Being prepared for this dynamic and period-ically reminding ourselves what we know can help us avoid the trap.

Another formidable pull comes from the unequal commitment to counseling. As counselors know only too well, generally it is the woman who wants couples or family counseling. The man often sees nothing dreadfully wrong with the relationship, and this is not surprising because the arrangements favor him. Whether he is happy with the relationship or not, he does not like the idea of talking to strangers or indeed talking personally at all. He certainly does not like the idea of bringing the problems to a woman and is worried that the two females are going to gang up on him. He may come, accordingly, very reluc-tantly, and only after months of refusing. The counselor knows, just as the clients know, that she has the woman on her side and that the man is in danger of bolting. The man in turn knows that he has this "out," and whether overtly or covertly, he makes sure that everyone else is aware of it. This threat gives the man incredible power. To make sure he does not bolt, counselors generally give more attention and empathy to the man, counting on the fact that the woman is going to "hang in." The counselor therefore addresses the man's concerns first and treats the couple's respective grievances as if they were equally valid. She sacrifices the woman because she can count on the woman to be an ally, while telling herself that by doing this, she is serving the woman's interest "in the long run." Generally the pull lessens over time and counseling becomes less oppres-sive, but "the long run" never fully arrives. Session after session, the pull is to temporarily sacrifice the woman for strategic reasons.

Even if we were not dealing with a highly oppressive relationship, simply going in the direction of the pull is tantamount to betraying the woman. Women are "paying through the teeth" for being cooperative and dependable. What makes matters worse, at least as often as not we are dealing with a highly oppressive relationship. In such instances it is not only wrong but ludicrous to favor the man and add to his power to ensure that he will not bolt.

This notwithstanding, we can and should be gentle with the man when we can do so without reneging on our feminist commitment. We can and should empathize with the man's difficulty in the situation. We cannot ignore men's grievances. We need to be open to the possibility that the man could be the more victimized party in the relationship even though this is rare. We need to take such injury seriously whether it is systemic or not.

Many therapists who conduct themselves like feminists in their individual therapy with female clients believe that sexism should not be dealt with in couples work because it is too explosive. Except where marked violence is occurring, it is far better, they suggest, to work on communication skills and to do general problem solving. I agree that couples work is very sensitive stuff and that it is often advisable to avoid words like *sexist* because such language can arouse defenses unnecessarily. There is no way to avoid sexist issues, however, if we want to do more than patchwork, for sexism underlies other issues. Of course we can help each partner gain skills in articulation and in active listening, and I would agree that it is a good idea to do so. I particularly recommend helping them learn each other's representational system.[1] Sooner or later, however, we need to confront the fact that men tend to avoid personal communication as much as possible. Correspondingly, although we can and should problem-solve around individual problems, eventually we find ourselves face to face with sexist attitudes and power differences. There is no point trying to avoid what we see and what we know. We need to ask, How do we incorporate feminism effectively when it is only in one of the partners' obvious interests? We need to ask, What does feminist service mean in the context of a patriarchal relationship?

With some men, we can rely on the fact that they do not want to lose this relationship or to have it turn sour on them. Here, affirming the valuing and gently clarifying the risks if they do not change constitute feminist services. So does helping them get a sense of the meaningfulness inherent in a truly equal and intimate relationship.

A more pragmatic feminist service that we can sometimes render is relieving the woman of the burden of explanation by assuming it ourselves. Many women have told their male partners clearly and repeatedly what they want. Again and again, they have tried to help the man understand their concerns. Although some men do not listen at all, often the man listens. He seems to be catching on. Then, presto! The understanding vanishes without a trace. He makes almost the identical mistake again and is as bewildered as he was a thousand explanations ago. That is why she is sniping, being sarcastic, and interrupting. In such instances there is no point repeating the spousal ritual or even changing it by adding new words like *feedback*. The woman needs a rest, and the man needs someone who is not frustrated with him. By taking on the mentor role ourselves, we give her that rest and we give him an opportunity to learn from someone who is not his partner and is not "at her wit's end." Where we find progress marred by "I-can't-help-it" games such as Stupid, Schlemiel, or Wooden Leg, we can point these out to him.[2] Initially it may be preferable to introduce him to such concepts in private one-on-one sessions.

Challenges that are primarily argumentative, even if totally logical, are likely to be ineffectual in changing oppressive attitudes and beliefs. We are more likely to be effective if we help the man identify with the woman's position, and vice versa.

When the woman is disturbed by her partner's sexualizing of women and the man does not think that he is doing anything wrong, for example, we can help him understand by making a connection. We can surface and co-investigate some situation in which he has been objectified and then begin making comparisons. Although I have seen counselors fall flat on their faces trying this and know that it is not foolproof, I have also seen men have "aha experiences."

Similarly an aha experience can happen with men who intimidate their wives if we relate it to situations in which they are the ones bullied. A man who yells at his female partner has probably had at least a few experiences of being on the other end of intimidation. However different the dynamics are, generally some similarities can be drawn on. Find out what those situations are, and empathize with him. Does his boss yell and blame him for everything that goes wrong? What enables his boss to abuse him this way? How does he feel when this happens? Yes, of course he is afraid. And it is a terrible experience. Does his wife perhaps have similar feelings when he comes home and starts yelling about the dirty house? Would he like to check this out with her? By pursuing this line of inquiry, we can sometimes facilitate real awareness and the type of communication in which the man genuinely hears and the woman is heard.

When the man is subject to one or more systemic oppressions, it is easier to make the comparisons. The Black man, for example, is sexualized, and we can use this sexualization to help him understand the sexualization of his partner. Everyone nonetheless is objectified, is subject to power over, and accordingly has some experiences to draw on.

Among the supposedly "minor problems" that heterosexual couples bring to counseling, chore divisions is one of the most frequent. Some women raise these issues apologetically, as if they were petty, and except when the man feels cheated, he generally encourages her to regard them as petty. These are not minor issues, however, but ones that relate fundamentally to woman's position as domestic slave. It is good to affirm their importance, even the importance of the seemingly minor details.

Where the couple is open to it, we can do them a service by facilitating a less gendered chore division. Even if it remains gendered, it is important to aim for some type of equality.

A paradigmal situation that we are faced with is this: The man is unhappy about how messy the house is, and he insists that he is doing his share. The truth is that he seldom completes the chores he starts, even though he *thinks* he has completed them; and he conceptualizes housework in terms of a few discrete chores without having an overview of what needs to be done. The woman meanwhile keeps finishing what he starts and is stuck with the responsibility for the house as a whole.

Rather than argue in the abstract, I find it most effective here to help them articulate and write down a clear and reasonably comprehensive list of chores, together with who is to do what. Accompanying each general chore should be a list of the subsidiary tasks involved. We can help in the creation of the list by commenting on deletions and overgeneralizations. We can help the partners monitor the work and improve on the list by checking in on what is happening and by asking such questions as:

- Is anything not getting done? How would you like to solve this problem?
- Did you find yourself having to do something that was not on the list? Would you like to add it? Who is to be responsible for it?

A common pattern to be on the lookout for and to be ready to call is this: The man does his share for a while, is praised for doing so, and then begins to rest on his laurels. Within a month he is "back to normal."

Often the chore problem centers around the man's belief that it is unfair to expect him to do half the household work. When he is the only one who does work external to the house, he has a point. "Less of the household work," however, does not equal by definition "almost no work at all." I know of no hard and fast rule about what exactly is fair in this situation. But when the woman is being burdened by repetitive tasks all day long and the man does comparatively interesting work, comes homes, puts up his feet, and relaxes most every evening, there can no doubt that the situation is oppressive and that we need to challenge what is going on. This man has a female slave; and female slavery, like any other kind of slavery, is unacceptable. Less demonstrable inequality should also be accessed, and when appropriate, challenged.

Another rationale that men frequently give for doing less than half the work is differences in cleanliness standards. "I am content with much lower standards," he reasons. "She's the one who wants the place super tidy. So it's only fair that she be putting in the extra work needed to keep it that way." What is happening is gamey. The man is having his cake and eating it too. Covertly he enjoys this higher standard even though it is less important to him. And he does not have to do anything to achieve it, because (a) he knows that the mess will bother her more and so she can be counted on to keep the place tidy, and (b) his overt position is, "It's got nothing to do with me anyway."

He is missing the point. He would hardly think it fair if anyone suggested that he do twice the work because he devours twice the food. It is opportunistic for a partner to be individualistic whenever it serves his or her interest and to count on the benefits of mutuality at other times. As counselors it is our job to help men become aware of these games and these inequalities at whatever pace feasible and to clarify the power issues involved.

General power issues of relevance in couples counseling and questions that we might ask ourselves regarding them are:

Issues	*Questions to Ask Ourselves*
defining power	Who defines the terms of the relationship? How might this power be equalized?
decision-making power	Who is empowered to make which decisions? Who determined this division? Where is the inequality here? What might be done about that inequality?
violence	Is violence occurring? How safe is the woman? (If you suspect that the woman is being violated by her partner, arrange to see or talk with her alone. For details on working with women violated by male partners, see Chapter 9.)
sexual gratification/injury	In what ways is this woman warping her body in the interest of male gratification? In what ways does her partner encourage this? Does the couple "make love," or do they "fuck"? Is mutual pleasuring happening? Which of these issues should I broach, and how can I best broach them?
financial domination	In what ways if any is the woman currently controlled by the man's earning power? What is a good first step toward equalizing the situation? Are finances trapping her in the relationship? How might this change?

Counselors have to use their own judgment in deciding which issues to push and when to back off.

As with all counseling, it is important to share information. It is a mistake, however, to share information that is likely to be used to oppress. Goldner's (1985) recommendation regarding possible separation is an example of unwise sharing, as well as a position that needs to be problematized.

Women's usable income goes down dramatically after marriage breakup, and men's goes dramatically up. One study conducted in the 1980s indicated that within a year of divorce, women's economic well-being drops 73%, whereas men's goes up 42%.[3] Where a strong possibility of breakup exists, feminist family therapist Virginia Goldner (1985) recommends that we share this economic information with both partners. I see no problem sharing it with the woman. Automatically sharing it with the man is another issue. What Goldner is counting on is that the man will feel for the difficult position that his partner is in and so will make greater efforts to save the relationship. She assumes, that is, that men will use the information benignly. Although I think this may sometimes happen, I find the assumption naive. If men were generally fair and benign in their relations with women, the problem would not exist in the first place. People moreover are generally less benign than usual when they are having severe difficulties with each other. A man who was not so benign could use this information to strengthen his bargaining position in the relationship and thereby increase his power over. It would also make it easy for him to exit from the relationship without making adequate provision. He has just heard that his income will dramatically increase. And he has just learned that in failing to provide decently, he would be acting no differently from most other red-blooded American males. This is information that I would accordingly only selectively share.

Whatever the presenting problem and whatever work we do, we fail if we absolutize the relationship. Heterosexual couples and heterosexually based families are, among other things, products of sexism and heterosexism. Systemically and individually they may also be a refuge against other systemic oppressions. And individually they can be very positive despite their inevitable connection with the patriarchy; and we need to recognize this. But they are not absolutes; they are not human beings; and human beings should not be sacrificed to them. Therefore, although the preservation of the relationship may be an important goal, it can never be accepted as "the prime directive." Sometimes the best thing we can do for our clients is to help them say good-bye.

THE FAMILY

The pull to sacrifice the woman in heterosexual couples work is translated into an incredible drive to sacrifice the mother in family work. This is not surprising. If we have unresolved hostilities with our own mothers, as indeed most of us were raised to have, we can easily project these onto the client "mom." Most mothers moreover not only bring the adult male into therapy kicking and screaming but also often have to coax, cajole, and beg each and every other family member to come. Once again the therapist knows this. Once again the temptation is to join with whoever is reluctant and to abandon her. And once again this solution is oppressive and unacceptable.

Rule number one of traditional family therapy is to help "distant dad" become more central in the family. Rule number two is to strengthen his power as "head of the family" or to return that power to him when he has lost it. Rule number two is clearly patriarchal garbage and should not be followed. Rule number one is itself dicey, to say the least. Despite our myth of the happy heterosexual family, the fact is that an alarming number of men regularly beat their wives and molest their children; and most men are at an unacceptable place on the violence continuum. In the cases of severe sexual and other violence, the last thing we want to do is consolidate father's position in the family. A wiser course of action is to remove him from the family at least temporarily and so protect the woman and the children. Even in the absence of marked violence, moreover, greater centrality is often not desired or desirable. Many families in fact are de facto a single-parent family and are functioning fairly well this way despite the obstacles they are up against. The last thing other family members may need or want is father reasserting his role.

Mother-Children Families

Whether covertly or overtly of the "single-parent" variety, single-parent families need help being affirmed as a family. Despite their viability and their prevalence, they are continually treated as if they are deprived, dysfunctional, and marginal. As counselors it is up to us to counter that message and to validate that family. We can also serve them by helping them explore/enjoy the more flexible female structures that are now possible. Help may be needed, as well, dealing with interference from social service agencies and accessing much-needed resources.

Often families that appear to be single-parented or families with an involved mother and uninvolved father are in reality families with two or more mothers. This womanly arrangement is generally very nurturing. It has worked well in many communities—the West Indian community, for example. It is important that we recognize what exists here and respect it. Good counseling in these cases rarely means involving or further involving the man. It means validating the family that has been created and helping them protect themselves and access resources.

Mother and Father-Led Families

Family counselors often find themselves working with families in which both a mother and a father actively albeit unequally parent, in which it is possible and desirable for father to become more central, and in which family members want this. In such instances it is important to facilitate this greater centrality. At the same time, as feminists we need to make sure that we do not add to misogyny in the process. In many such cases the woman has been saddled with almost all of the family and domestic work, including the policing. She is tired and irritable. She is blamed for everything that goes wrong. What tradi-tional family therapists do in this situation is collude with the family in its conviction that mother has botched everything, and they bring father to the rescue to the general applause of all. Again this is antiwoman, and reframing is vital. When fathers are made more central, it should be with less fanfare and with as little mother-blaming as possible. By overtly empathizing with the mother's situation ourselves and noting how well she has managed in almost impossible circumstances, we can counter the belief in "mother's incompe-tence" and begin some of the necessary reframing.

Helping repair the bond between mother and children generally is integral to feminist family work. It is particularly important that we attend to the violated bond between mother and daughter. Relieving mother of the extra work—espe-cially the policing—is a good first step. At times it may also be beneficial to arrange for special mother-daughter sessions and to help mother and daughter open up to each other again.

Where children are being hurt, are hurting, or are "misbehaving," keeping sight of larger dynamics is particularly important. Children's problems seldom originate with themselves.

The systems approach represents one attempt to work with larger dynamics. Family therapists of a systems orientation see the problems that children have as an expression of problems in the spousal subsystem. They work on the problems in that subsystem. They try to realign boundaries between subsys-tems. And they generally treat all problems as family problems pure and simple.[4] This approach has some merit in some situations. Spousal problems do impact on children, and an emphasis on the family can counter the tendency to pathologize and scapegoat individual members. One way we can help the children is by drawing selectively on the approach. Do be careful, though. The approach is severely limited. It is utterly apolitical and tends to reinforce sexism, as well as many of the other "isms." It assumes the importance of strong boundaries and of a clear "executive" subsystem. It makes female-male rela-tions look way more reciprocal than they are. It is based, in other words, on an unexamined androcentric understanding of the world. And it obviates individ-ual responsibility almost entirely, as well as the individual her- or himself. Unthinking use of it, accordingly, can easily result in deep injury.

By way of example, we would further sexism and injure people badly if we treated incest as if it were a family problem for which everyone must assume responsibility. Systems therapists approach it this way, blame the wife for not satisfying her husband sexually, and sometimes even ask the children what changes they might make. Workers who do this are adding substantially to the abuse and are covering up the reality of oppression. Families do not perpetrate incest. Abusers, who are generally male, do. As counselors we need to ask the man to take responsibility for the violation and to change. By the same token, wife battery is not something mutually created by man and woman. It is not a "subsystem problem." It is violation by the male, and it must be treated as such.

More generally, contrary to the beliefs and preferences of systems theory, it is important to remember that the family is not an isolated unit but an integral part of an oppressive society. That society oppresses certain types of families just as it oppresses certain types of individuals, and that oppression plays a central role in creating and exacerbating many of the problems that we call "family problems." It excludes some families from decision-making power. It denies resources to some. It calls some "dysfunctional," and it uses that label as a further excuse to intervene.

If we are working with a Black family, we keep on track by remembering that all members of that family are affected by racism and may need help dealing with it. Poor families have troubles because they do not have enough resources to get by and they are stigmatized to boot. Black families, poor families, single-parent families, co-mothered families, and lesbian families correspondingly often need help dealing with oppression, dealing with internalized hatred, dealing with interference, and accessing resources.

We keep on track by remembering that families, moreover, are a microcosm of the oppressive patriarchal society in which they are located. Families are the training ground for patriarchal capitalism, and many of the larger inequalities and contradictions are found therein.

It is our responsibility to look for these inequalities and to temper them insofar as possible. Are rigid boundaries around this family? Are roles distributed by gender? Do males have more power than females? Are rigid hierarchies within the family? Do the young have less decision-making power than they are capable of handling? Is heterosexuality compulsory? Do only some define the rules and choose the names, while others have these rules and these names imposed on them? Whenever we answer yes to one of these questions, we have hit on something fundamental—something that is at the roots. Good feminist family work begins and ends at the roots.

SUGGESTED READINGS

Goldner, V. (1985). Feminism and family therapy. *Family Process, 24,* 31-47.
Goodrich, T., Rampage, C., Ellman, B., et al. (1988). *Feminist family therapy: A casebook.* New York: Norton.
Hare-Mustin, R. (1978). A feminist approach to family therapy. *Family Process, 17,* 181-194.
Hare-Mustin, R. (1980). Family therapy may be dangerous for your health. *Professional Psychologist, 11,* 935-938.

NOTES

1. For information on representational systems and ways of working with them, see Bandler & Grinder (1976).

2. These games may be found in Berne (1973). They involve avoiding responsibility by pleading special ignorance or incompetence.

3. For details on this study, see Dollars and Sense Editorial Board (1983).

4. Systems theorists see the family as a relatively isolated system in the way that a feminist or structuralist could not, and they see the family system as the client. For an example of typical systems theory thinking and work, see Minuchin (1974).

7

Working With Adult Survivors
of Childhood Sexual Abuse

TERMINOLOGY

Word	*Definition*
childhood sexual abuse	This term refers to any sexual activity between an adult and a child, whether that activity involves actual sexual contact or not. Implicit in the term is the contention that sex between an adult and a child is always abusive because it is necessarily nonconsensual. Even where the child appears to be a willing or even eager participant, sex is nonconsensual and therefore abusive because children have neither the knowledge nor power necessary to give true consent.
incest	Technically speaking, *incest* refers to any sexual activity between relatives, whether abusive or nonabusive. In this book, as is the case

with much of the therapy literature, *incest* refers exclusively to sex between adult and child and is always deemed abuse. Sex between relatives is the paradigm, although any sex between a child and an adult who acts like a family member is considered a type of incest because the dynamics are similar.

ritual abuse

Ritual abuse is a combination of sexual and other abuse perpetrated by groups of adults against children for the purposes of power over. It assumes symbolic, religious, and ritualistic forms. Overt torture is involved. A child may be forced to kill or eat other children, may have animals parts inserted into her, and/or may be sprinkled with blood.

overt incest/overt childhood sexual abuse

These terms refer to adult-child acts that involve actual sexual touching. This covers, among other things, sexual caresses; deep or held kisses; fondling of sexual parts; forcing the child to touch either her own sexual parts or some else's; and oral, vaginal, or anal penetration.

covert incest/covert childhood sexual abuse

These terms apply to adult-child acts that imply or connote something sexual, while not themselves involving actual sexual contact. Examples are the adult hovering outside the washroom when the child is within, using sexual terms of endearment when referring to the child, and staring at the child's sexual parts.

emotional incest

Emotional incest is deemed to have occurred when a relative or parentlike figure responds emotionally to the child in a manner that is either (a) more befitting a partner or (b) befitting neither a partner nor a child but that would be seen as befitting a partner in this sexist society.

flashback

A *flashback* is any sudden remembering or reexperiencing. In the literature dealing with violence, the word is used in a restricted fashion to refer to any sudden remembering or reexperiencing of a traumatic event.

spacing out

Spacing out is a mode of coping in the presence of danger. A person who spaces out essentially annihilates the threat to self by annihilating self. She takes off, blanks out, is no longer present in the situation, is no longer reflectively aware of what is going on around her. Spacing out is a common coping device for incest survivors and other survivors of assault. Many space out at the time of the original abuse. Many space out in the presence of situations that in some way remind them of the abuse.

trigger

The memory of abuse is said to be "triggered" when a survivor of abuse experiences flashbacks, whether those flashbacks involve concrete details, the reexperiencing of the original panic, or both. For some women, the presence of identifiable and specific situations or aspects of situations is likely to result in flashbacks. These situations or aspects are known as *triggers*. Triggers generally resemble something in the original abusive situation. By way of example, for someone who was originally overwhelmed by the scent of the person raping her, a certain type of sexual smell may serve as a trigger.

flooding

Flooding is said to occur when memories of abuse come one after another in such rapid succession that the person is overwhelmed and cannot adequately deal with them. As memories of the abuse themselves act as triggers for other memories, the very enterprise of remembering can result in flooding.

splitting

In abuse literature, *splitting* refers to a means of coping used in the face of danger; most commonly, it is a flight into a disembodied state. At the time of abuse, children often "split" from their bodies. They project themselves out of their bodies, sometimes into the wall. They "detach" themselves from their bodies and look back (usually down) at their bodies almost as if what was occurring were happening to someone else. Splitting also refers to a general fragmentation of self. Splitting is a normal coping device that all people employ to some degree. Speaking figuratively, and this language *is figurative,* to some extent we all split from our core and develop personas or what psychosynthesis calls "subpersonalities" to attend to particular problems or life situations. A part of us, as it were, "comes out" whenever we have to deal with business matters. It is quite a different part that emerges when we come face to face with a vulnerable child. To the extent that we keep ourselves reflectively unaware not simply of the existence of these different personas or parts but of the very activities we engage in when acting out of certain parts, these parts and these activities may be thought of as "split off" from us.

dissociation/disintegration/ *Dissociation* is the act of splitting. Splitting
fragmentation leads to a disintegration, fragmentation, or loss of integration.

integration *Integration* is the process of reducing splits and coming together.

multiple personality disorder; These are psychiatric labels and concepts.
dissociative disorders; The women so labeled are survivors with
depersonalization disorder splits that are quite expectable and indeed whose splitting constitutes reasonable responses in the face of violence, however strange they may seem. Psychiatry treats the splits as unexpectable. The concepts are context-strippers that pathologize the coping. They also treat figurative truths as if they were literal truths. It is as if consciousness had literal "splits." It is as if the women in question had no awareness of any kind of certain activities—not even vague, innocuous, prereflective awareness. Because of the pathologizing and the misunderstandings involved, these are terms that feminist counselors do best to avoid.

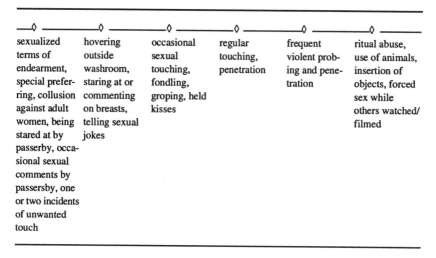

| sexualized terms of endearment, special preferring, collusion against adult women, being stared at by passerby, occasional sexual comments by passersby, one or two incidents of unwanted touch | hovering outside washroom, staring at or commenting on breasts, telling sexual jokes | occasional sexual touching, fondling, groping, held kisses | regular touching, penetration | frequent violent probing and penetration | ritual abuse, use of animals, insertion of objects, forced sex while others watched/ filmed |

Figure 7.1. Childhood Sexual Abuse Continuum

THE WORK

The foundation for work with adult survivors of childhood sexual assault is an understanding of the childhood sexual abuse that is our common plight as women. All women—ourselves included—grew up in a patriarchal world. All women—ourselves included—had some type of sexual awareness forced on them at an age when they had no way to understand it, although the nature and the degree vary. All had their childhood and innocence at least partially interfered with. All correspondingly are survivors of childhood sexual abuse. Understanding this commonality and taking in our own personal violation are what allow us to understand our clients.

Childhood sexual abuse might be thought of as existing on a continuum. One way of conceptualizing the continuum is shown in Figure 7.1.

Continuum differentiations are rough guides only. Indeed the extent and the nature of injury depend at least as much on subjective response as on objective happenings. Continuum differentiations are nonetheless helpful in making rough, tentative assessments and in giving us some preliminary ideas of what to expect.

Generally and very roughly speaking, the farther to the right in the continuum, the greater the emotional injury sustained. Covert sexual abuse (first two points on the continuum) generally results in less fragmentation than overt abuse (the remaining points on the continuum). Covert sexual abuse—which is the norm in patriarchal households—violates the bond between women and systematically and individually nurtures misogyny in our early years. Overt abuse is always beyond the norm, and overt abuse—especially toward the right in the continuum—fundamentally confuses, overwhelms, and terrorizes. It creates a world in which nothing is safe, nothing can be trusted.

Generally speaking, abuse by family or near-family members is more confusing than abuse by nonmembers, for at least initially we expect family members to act caringly. Such abuse moreover shatters our ontological security. Family members are trusted figures. If trusted family members can abuse us, it occurs to us that anyone else can. The location of abusers similarly impacts greatly on us. Insofar as family members or near-family members live in the same house with us, we have no escape. The danger is ever present.

Abuse that occurs or begins in infancy tends to be more damaging than abuse that occurs or begins later on. The infant is more vulnerable, can be more easily and more profoundly hurt. The baby who is molested is overwhelmed by larger-than-life feelings and perceptions that she cannot conceivably understand and that are experienced as life-threatening.

Good work with adult survivors of childhood sexual abuse begins with our own identification of who it is and what it is that we are encountering. Faced with any female client, we can assume some degree of childhood abuse. Proceeding from there, we need to ask ourselves questions like: Did the childhood abuse that this woman underwent exceed the norm? Has this survivor sustained harm beyond the harm that all women experience? "No" answers to these questions, it is significant, do not end our inquiry or render the issue unimportant, but they do make it less pressing.

Sometimes we are quickly provided with answers to these initial questions. Right in the first session some clients introduce childhood sexual assault as the reason or one of the reasons for seeking therapy. Still others wait a session or two but nonetheless tell us early on. More often than not, however, abuse clients say nothing about childhood sexual abuse for many months; and when they do finally get something out, they are confused, speak tentatively, and/or greatly understate.

A major reason for this phenomenon is that women have repressed the abuse so successfully that they have no or almost no reflective awareness of it. In many cases successful repressing means repressing all incidents that might trigger memory of the abuse. Such survivors have large blocks of time absent from their memory. For some women individual stretches of unawareness or what is perceived as individual memory lapses can be as long as a few months, 1 year, or even 10 years. Whenever we encounter a woman who has such large gaps in her memory of childhood, we can usually conclude that she experienced ongoing and severe trauma as a child. The trauma in question might well be the trauma of childhood sexual abuse.

By the same token, women who are terrified, who keep finding themselves in a panic, have clearly been traumatized. If additionally they appear to be covering themselves up, if they always wear layers of clothes, say, or fold their arms over their breasts or cross their legs, we have reason to believe that their terror is connected with their bodies. Overt childhood sexual abuse is one highly plausible explanation.

A number of typical and recognizable ways of coping are associated with childhood sexual abuse. These ways of coping are among the principal indicators of childhood abuse. It is important to be on the watch for them, to understand their significance or possible significance, and to accept them as grounds for further inquiry. Following are a list of some of the ways of coping, together with ways we might recognize them.

Coping Activities	*Indicators/Possible Indicators of Such Coping*
simple repression	The client has periods of her childhood that she cannot remember.
blanking out; spacing out; splitting	The client cannot account for stretches of time. She keeps finding herself in places, not knowing how she got there or what she has been doing. Alternatively, in session she periodically gets a faraway look on her face and does not respond.
disintegration	All of the above. The client additionally may not remember previous sessions. She may seem remarkably different at different times, even having different voices and mannerisms.
eating problems: anorexia, bulimia, compulsive eating	The client tells us that she now has or used to have these problems. In the case of anorexia, the client is extremely thin and has haunting, piercing eyes. In the case of bulimia and compulsive eating, she may express disgust over the amount she eats. With anorexia and bulimia, she may complain of frequent gastrointestinal problems; she vomits involuntarily; she is likely to express revulsion for food and clearly value eating sparingly. In all cases she is unhappy about her weight, and her body image is distorted.

physical mutilation: self-cutting, burning, etc.	The client keeps turning up with cuts, bruises, burns, and other injuries. Alternatively, even in sweltering weather she wears long sleeves.
"slutting" and prostitution (I am using the term "slutting" because women in this situation experience sleeping with different partners this way. Insofar as we ourselves believe in the term or are critical of women for "sleeping around," we are being sexist.)	The client lets us know that she currently sleeps or used to sleep with many strangers a week without pay. The client tells us about continually waking up and finding herself with men that she has no reflective awareness of having seen before. The client tells us that she is/was a prostitute. (A cautionary note: Do not assume that all prostitutes have suffered child sexual abuse beyond the norm or that all prostitution is itself self-abusive.) Alternatively, she frequently contracts such infections as pelvic inflammatory disease.
alcoholism and drug abuse	The client informs us of drug or alcohol intake that we recognize as high. (Again it is important for us to be sensible about this. Grass and hash are not heavy drugs, and a nightly toke in no way constitutes high intake.) The client turns up at one or more sessions drunk or stoned. Alternatively, on a few occasions a friend calls in the day of her session to cancel it.

Other possible indicators of extreme childhood sexual abuse are:

• Discomfort with being touched
• Distress when having sex
• Preference for having chairs far apart
• Seeing sperm or penises everywhere (Again, do not pathologize.)
• The seemingly unrealistic belief that a number of people in her life are out to rape or murder her (Not all seemingly unrealistic beliefs are unrealistic; at any rate, take care here not to pathologize. The belief is minimally a figurative truth or a reexperiencing.)

We can conclude nothing from the presence or absence of any of these responses. Where the client combines a number of these responses, we have a very strong reason to suspect pronounced childhood sexual abuse. If the client comes to think it occurred, her own growing conviction that such abuse happened, whether accompanied by distinct memories or not, serves as confirmation. Her new-found ability to make sense of her life through this conviction constitutes further confirmation.

Once we suspect severe injury from childhood sexual abuse, it is important to take extra care with safety issues and to continue taking extra care, for survivors need safety accommodation. Although important with all clients, it is especially important with abuse survivors that (a) we truly care about the client and are prepared to extend ourselves, (b) we are gentle, (c) we proceed gently, (d) we teach the client how to nurture herself, how to care for herself, (e) sessions not be interrupted, and (f) our office be located in a safe, well-lit part of the city and the client not have to walk through groups of men to reach it.

Our relationship to space and to touch is key. Most women who have been traumatized by childhood sexual abuse are threatened by the same touching that most other clients find reassuring. The pat on the shoulder that less-violated clients generally experience as reassuring can trigger memories of abuse. What is intended as nurturing may be experienced as suffocating, threatening, intrusive. As someone who is used to submitting and hanging on, the client may submit to pats or embraces and even smile faintly, saying that everything is okay, while feeling overwhelmed or invaded. Avoiding this means taking extra care not to touch without clear unambiguous consent and, in some cases, unless the client has explicitly requested us to. And it means continually checking in. When in doubt, we are better to err on the side of distance and to express our caring and our nurture in some other way.

The distance between the counselor and client chair that most other clients experience as either comfortable or too distant is likely to be too close for the average survivor. With the same survivor, what is comfortable or a little too close on some occasions may be dreadfully threatening on others.

The volume and tone of our voice and the actual words that we use may also need adjusting. A loud voice easily threatens. A soft voice may remind the client of the perpetrator's whispers. Often certain tones and certain words are highly associated with the perpetrator.

It is best to keep our approach as gentle and simple as possible. Vivid psychodramas or reenactments of the original abuse unduly risk retraumatizing the client. Probing sessions week after week are unduly intrusive and raise the risk of flooding.

Given the likelihood of splitting and confusion and the possibility of flooding, it is critical that we ourselves be able to deal with and help the client deal with these responses. Grounding work is arguably the most important work that we do with survivors.

If the survivor is spacing out, we can generally help her get back by calling out her name loudly. If she is turning the present into the past, we can help her ground herself in the present by making statements like, "It's okay, Edna. You are safe. ____ is not here. You are 37 years old. You are with me, ____. We are here in the therapy office together. And nobody can get at you."

We can strengthen any toehold on the present and further cool out a frightening situation by engaging the survivor in a conversation about the present or the future. We can make orienting statements ourselves. And we can ask present- or future-orienting questions that require more than yes and no answers—questions such as:

- Where are you going next?
- What is your son Johnathon up to these days?
- You were mentioning that a new house was being built across the street from you. How far has it gotten?

Physically grounding exercises can be helpful in difficult sessions and are an important resource for the client to be able to draw on. Examples of such exercises are (a) the client lying on the floor with legs bent and a foot pressing against the wall and (b) the bioenergetics bow.[1]

When clients remain fragmented or confused and I have reason to believe that this will not add to the confusion, I sometimes draw on psychosynthesis. I suggest, for example, that someone might be inside who can be of help here and ask to talk to her or him.

If the survivor thinks that she is going crazy and/or begins hallucinating, she needs a way of understanding her experiences. Optimally it is good to warn clients in advance that they may reexperience, that they may have flashbacks, that they may flood. Where clients become triggered, are flooding, or are worried about "losing their minds," reassure them that they are reexperiencing and that this is normal. Where they are confused or despairing, let them know that this might be a prelude to remembering.

Direct work with childhood sexual abuse itself begins when one member of the counselor-client team broaches the issue. As often as not, this task falls to us. When we think that the client has experienced childhood sexual abuse that exceeds the norm and/or has been especially harmed by such abuse and the woman herself does not explicitly raise the issue, it is important for us to ask the question directly. The question, asked simply, opens up the area and begins to soften the prohibition against "telling." It suggests that we know something about childhood sexual abuse. It lets her know that we are comfortable with the topic and are prepared to deal with it. And it sends the violated child within the message that we can see her and intend to make space for her. Even if the woman is still repressing or is into denial, and even though our message may also terrify her, on some level this message is comforting and reassuring. It can even be reassuring if her abuse is of a different nature, for it suggests that we are ready to deal with deep vulnerability and injury.

Sometimes we receive quick affirmative answers to this question; when we do, we have obvious material to co-investigate. Unless the client has done extensive work on herself before, however, we are more likely to receive other answers. At least for the time being, it is important that we accept the "absolutely not" answer as a signal to back off, for we are either wrong, too threatening, or both. Answers that express uncertainty also allow us to co-investigate. Uncertainty does not invariably mean that severe childhood sexual abuse occurred or that it took the precise form that the client suspects. Suspicion nonetheless does not come from nowhere. If the client suspects something dreadful, we can almost be certain that something bad occurred. By co-investigating the uncertainty and the unease, we begin to find our bearings.

Remembering is central to work with survivors, for all survivors repress to varying degrees, and it is hard for them to work with what they do not "know." This repression was initially life-saving. As children, they blanked out whatever they had to in order to survive. As adults who are no longer in a powerless position, the vast majority no longer have to repress so rigorously. By helping women uncover what they reasonably can of what has been hidden or put aside, we help them achieve continuity, make sense of their lives, and reclaim power.

Even with the best of intentions, enormous openness, and much hard work, many survivors do not end up remembering very much. Whereas some come close to total recall, others end up remembering only part of one incident. Still others unearth only vague impressions and feelings. The reasons for this limited retrieval include:

- They were abused in infancy and so cannot put together clear memories.
- They were severely ill at the time, and so events were and remain "dreamlike."
- An adult carefully kept them "in the dark."
- Strong repressing continues to be needed.

This is okay, and it is critical that we let the client know that it is okay. We misconstrue/misrepresent reality when we assume that survivors can always remember more and/or that a good life is contingent on remembering all of the abuse or most of the abuse or anything beyond what they are able to remember. This misconstruction/misrepresentation creates pressure that may block what might otherwise come and that sets clients up for trauma, disappointment, and guilt. We need to accept the client's dynamic, invite memory, and then value and work with what is uncovered.

The invitation to remember begins with our initial question(s) about childhood sexual abuse. When we ask a woman whether she has experienced childhood sexual abuse, we are announcing a possibility and are inviting her to co-investigate that possibility with us. By siding with the client, validating her, and caring, we make that invitation less threatening.

More concrete help with remembering and discovering involves asking questions about the past; noting incongruities, puzzles, and worrisome dynamics; and using these as opportunities for further co-investigation. Counselor and client together query, tease out, follow. A client remembers being terrified whenever her mother went out for the day and left her with her father. We ask: Do you have any idea what that fear was about? Can you remember anything that happened when your mother was out? Another's parents told her that an uncle whom she finds frightening was in a different country when she was growing up and that she never met him until she was a teenager. Yet she remembers playing with him when she was 4 years old. The question arises: What is the meaning of this incongruity? Were the parents telling the truth? Does anyone else in the family or the neighborhood look like the uncle? If this is not the truth, why was she lied to? Where was her uncle when she was a child? What is her current fear of her uncle about? And what light can her siblings shed on these questions? This is material for investigation.

Dreams as well open up possibilities and offer clues, for dreams focus in on what we actively forget. For many, the first allusions to childhood sexual assault occur in a dream. Some actually see themselves being abused. One client of mine dreamed that her father gave her a familiar look that had always upset her and then slipped his hand under her skirt. As she related the dream, a tear rolled down her face and she whispered, "Oh, no! Oh, God! That's why that look always haunted me so!" In the process of attending to dreams and of going between dream and memory, clients make discoveries. And both the dreams and the intentional work can lead to further recall.

Our biggest informational resource is the client's current ways of coping. Just as these ways of coping help us co-identify abuse, certain ways of coping provide clues about the nature of the abuse, for they are themselves responses to abuse.

The following interchange is an example of how the client's coping might be used to further co-investigation and discovery.

Client	I'm really scared I don't have any control over the bulimia. You know, I throw up food without even wanting to.
Counselor	I know. And it must be really upsetting. Let me ask you something, though. Does this happen more often with any particular type of food?
Client	It could happen with anything. Well, actually, it's more with things that are runny—you know, like drippy egg whites.
Counselor	The texture bothers you.
Client	It's so messy. Disgusting, really.
Counselor	That's an interesting word that you've used there. You often describe things as "disgusting," and when you do, your mouth wrinkles up.

	Like you really can't stand the taste. When you used that word in our session last week, you were talking about the taste of semen.
Client	Yeah....
Counselor	You are looking disgusted now. Are you okay?
Client	You know, there's something I had forgotten all about. When I first had oral sex, I was like totally grossed out and I started retching.... There's something else, too.... The taste was familiar! I knew that taste from childhood!

As this interchange shows as well, sensory perceptions themselves serve as clues. When working with survivors, it is important to take seriously and co-investigate sensations that are dramatic, whether those occur at a sensual or a metaphoric level. Although we all have likes and dislikes, when an edible that is fairly neutral is experienced as enormously "distasteful" and results in vomiting, there is a reasonable chance that it is associated with oral rape. We can be sure moreover that a client who persistently uses terms like *disgusting* hates the taste of *something*. *Something* has happened that she cannot stomach. Correspondingly, when certain types of body odors figure in seemingly nonsexual memory, it is likely that sex is involved. By drawing attention to sensation, we help clients make connections and flesh out memories. Use of the present tense can be especially effective in helping clients flesh out memories. The past tense distances. When clients describe abuse in the present tense, the distance is bridged. Again routine or extended use of the present is bound to traumatize.

Although this is not invariable, childhood sexual abuse tends to be recalled in layers. A woman remembers one incident or parts of an incident. This opens the door to other incidents. Periodically she thinks that she has come to the end of her memories. Later, confusion and despair set in. The confusion and the despair are followed by a different type of memory. We can help women deal with their feelings and the turmoil by clarifying the process.

Most clients who have been subject to extreme childhood sexual abuse have a hard time acknowledging even to themselves that abuse actually occurred. Incest survivors find it particularly difficult. It is a dangerous truth. Fully taking in what happened can mean losing one's father, losing one's myths, losing one's family, losing one's very foundations. It is, moreover, an utterly outlandish truth. How could adults conceivably do such things to children? And if other adults could, surely not their own fathers! It seems impossible that such things could happen. They tell themselves it did not happen. They begin to entertain the possibility that it did. They have some memories. They flee and/or are confused by what they are uncovering. They decide again that nothing happened. They go back to thinking that it did and try to remember more but cannot. And they continue to go back and forth.

Our training to doubt our own perceptions further exacerbates the problem. Women are taught to be uncertain. The positive we get from this teaching is that we weigh matters more carefully. The negative is that conclusions can be very difficult for us, especially when those conclusions indict men.

The seemingly flimsy and often contradictory evidence before us further aggravates the problem. Survivors feel as if they were indicting an innocent human being on the basis of a few vague childhood memories.

Vacillation, confusion, and flight are a normal part of the process. We help by accepting them as legitimate, by giving the process its due, and by being honest. It is important to let the client know that she is not "being difficult." She is proceeding the only way that she can proceed. Although trying to talk clients into concluding abuse never makes sense, because we can err in judgment and women need to come to their own truth anyway, we can help by responding honestly to her doubts and questions and by giving what information we can. General consciousness-raising about women's situations can also figure in here. Examples of typical doubts that are expressed, questions that are asked, and possible rejoinders are:

Client A   I feel like I'm making everything impossible. I had memories months ago. I should have been able to accept them by now.

Counselor   It's okay, Freida. A few months is not long, and there are no "shoulds." You are trying to feel your way through a horrendously difficult situation. What you are entertaining is very threatening. Whatever did or did not happen, a frightened and confused child is inside you. Let's not pressure that child.

Client A   But don't you think I'm resisting a bit much?

Counselor   I think that you are doing the very best that you can.

Client B   How do I know these are real memories? For years now I've had these episodes in my head. But how do I know that I didn't just make it all up?

Counselor   It's not impossible, but it is highly unlikely. Children don't just invent stories of abuse. I've found that when children remember abuse, even if they have some stuff wrong, I can be sure that something traumatic happened.

Client B   I remember my father molesting me. But my father is a good man. It makes no sense. It just couldn't have happened.

Counselor   No, it sure doesn't make sense. So often, men who "love" us and who seem truly decent abuse us. It's almost impossible to wrap our minds around that. This is one of the awful dilemmas that we face as women.

Client C   Maybe nothing really happened. With people talking about incest so much, maybe the idea simply got planted in my head and it took root.

Counselor	It's awful for you, I know. You want a different explanation, and why wouldn't you? I would too.
Client C	But what do you think? Could I have picked this up by power of suggestion? I want to know what you really think.
Counselor	Maybe, but you don't strike me as that impressionable. I think that it's a whole lot easier to doubt yourself than to doubt your uncle. As women we are trained to doubt ourselves.
Client D	I have all these memories of events that were supposed to have happened this one afternoon. But it's impossible. Just not enough time; and too many contradictions. I couldn't have been attacked first in Flin Flon, then in Winnipeg. And I couldn't both have had the measles and not had them. With all these incongruities, how do I know if any of it is real?
Counselor	I understand the doubt, and it's okay to be in doubt. Let me tell you something, though. We do funny things when we remember—especially when we remember traumatic events. We collapse four events into one. We get the order wrong. We erase some details and highlight others. Almost all survivors remember in this way.
Client E	After all this time, I have nothing but a vague memory of a penis pressed against my lips. What do I do if nothing more comes? How do I know what to believe?
Counselor	It's a very difficult situation you're in, for this may be all you get to work with. Some people end up with only vague perceptions from infancy that have no actual people in them, for this is all the baby saw and all the baby knows. Myself, I can't imagine you having the memory of a penis in your face if nothing happened. You're going to have to see how it sits with you, though. If you assume that someone stuck a penis in your face when you were a baby, do things start falling into place? Does your life end up making more sense? Or are you left with the same muddle? Does it feel right? Or does it feel off?

Some survivors acknowledge the abuse to themselves but have trouble acknowledging it to us. Survivors who share an oppression with the perpetrator are particularly likely to find acknowledgment difficult, especially where the counselor does not share that oppression. This is a racist and classist society, and "telling" in a racist and classist society is a loaded issue.

Many survivors both from dominant and nondominant groups grew up with the onus on holding their family together. They could not tell or father would take off; the family would be in shambles; and it would be their fault. They are still protecting the family.

Others have trouble acknowledging because they have been terrorized into silence. They were threatened with dire consequences if they told anybody, and they are still "spooked."

Still others have trouble acknowledging because they are afraid of being doubted. Originally the abuser may have effectively silenced them by assuring them that no one would believe them anyway. They may have told their mother or someone else in the past, only to be punished for making up such a dreadful lie. They may find what happened so incredible themselves that they are sure no one else will believe them.

Women may additionally have trouble because they do not trust us, they are afraid of a lesbophobic response, or they are afraid of being pathologized.

We help here by doing the following:

- Believing the survivor and making it abundantly clear that we believe her
- Clarifying just how prevalent child sexual abuse is
- Not responding in a racist, classist, or lesbophobic way
- Not pathologizing her
- Understanding the complexities and the agony and fully empathizing with the dilemma
- Assuring the child within that she can relax her vigil with us, that there is no one whom she needs to safeguard, that she will not be punished, that no one can find out that she has "told"
- Offering and/or arranging for protection, as appropriate
- Encouraging loyalty to the hurt child within

Trivialization and self-blame are among the largest obstacles to "working through" and to empowerment. Some degree of each is almost inevitable.

Trivialization takes many forms. Some women trivialize the abuse by defining it out of existence. They may be quite clear, for example, that their father touched their breasts, but they contend that it was not really "abuse" because it only happened a few times and he "never once" touched their genitals. Others define what happened as abuse, while suggesting that they are not "quite" victims because they were never subjected to that heavy-duty abuse that befalls other women. In both cases the woman is telling herself:

1. Men as a whole are respectable.
2. Most of the abuse done to women is either not abuse at all or is not very bad.
3. What was done to me is negligible and unimportant.
4. Women do not matter very much.
5. I do not matter in the least.

Even where they were clearly traumatized by what happened, women toward the beginning and the center of the sexual assault continuum are particularly likely to trivialize the abuse. Where the perpetrator is a male, women tend to transfer blame from the perpetrator to themselves. I have heard clients say, "It wasn't all his fault. I seduced him." Some blame themselves for accepting the money that their father gave them for "favors." Some see the abuse as justifiable punishment for being bad.

Where minimization is occurring, it is important to point that out and to clarify. We can tell the client who is defining the abuse out of existence that we regard such acts as abusive. If she is a mother, we can make use of this relationship by asking her whether she would consider these acts abusive if someone did them to her child. Questions like this often result in "aha" experiences. We can remind the client who sees herself as "not quite" a victim that it does not matter that thousands of women were subjected to "worse" abuse. Her trust was still betrayed. She was still hurt. And that betrayal and that hurt are significant.

The same solidarity, caring, and clarity are needed in dealing with the transfer of blame. It is up to us to assure the guilt-ridden child within that it does not matter whether she flirted or not. She is not to blame. Little girls do not understand sex and cannot consent to it. They do not intend sex when they flirt. The full-grown man who betrayed her innocence is responsible. Along the same line, the woman who feels guilty because she had pleasurable sensations during the abuse needs to hear that she did nothing wrong. Her body sensations are natural and in no way constitute a betrayal of self. The woman who blames herself for accepting money similarly needs reassurance. Although she may feel as if she sold herself, we might point out that she did not sell. HE TOOK. She simply got something for herself in the midst of this nightmare. By the same token, the woman who sees the abuse as justifiable punishment needs to know that there is nothing she could conceivably have done to deserve such abuse. Although she may have been told again and again that she was bad, dirty, or at fault, the reality is that she was an innocent child. Although she may have felt dirty as she lay there with the man's "come" all over her body, there is no contamination and no fault.

The challenging of these beliefs must be accompanied by an appreciation of the child's wisdom and strength for having the very beliefs that we are challenging. The point is that the misogynous and self-depreciating beliefs not only put down self. Initially at least they also served to protect self.

By way of example, when the child tells herself that her flirting caused her to be molested, she is not only protecting the man at her own expense and is not only internalizing oppression, although without a doubt this is involved. She is also giving herself safety in an enormously unsafe world. A world in which fathers molest daughters for no reason is far too threatening. A world in which her own father acts this way is devastating. The child cannot live with a reality this awful and this dangerous. So she does the only thing that she can do to make the world safer. She magically transforms the world by providing a reason.

"Flirtation" is that reason. She tells herself that her father is still a caring father. He only hurt her because she flirted. Now, her father is not a monster. An essentially unsafe world becomes just a tiny bit safer. By the same token, by construing the molestation as just punishment, the child puts a wall between herself and a reality that she cannot conceivably bear.

Specific Survivor Coping and the Work of Therapy

Much of our work with survivors involves addressing the very coping that initially helps us identify them as survivors. It involves addressing the cutting, the burning, the starving, the drinking, the blanking out, the fragmentation, the "slutting," the prostituting.

What holds true of the transfer of blame from perpetrator to self holds true of this coping as well. These ways of being are responses to danger. They provide safety even while encroaching on self. They have positive, not just negative, meaning and purpose. Most if not all initially served the woman well. Of these, many are no longer as necessary, and optimally some shifting could occur over the course of therapy. This notwithstanding, all need to be understood and appreciated. And to the extent that they are modified, it must be only gradually, at the client's instigation and with the client calling the shots.

Chapters 10, 11, and 12 provide detailed analyses of self-mutilation, eating problems, and drinking problems and suggest ways of working with these issues. "Slutting," prostituting, splitting, and fragmenting are discussed here.

"Slutting"

Coping by "slutting" bears some similarity to coping by self-mutilating. When a client responds to childhood sexual abuse by "slutting," she is at once coping with that early oppression and is internalizing the oppression.

The oppressive message that she is internalizing is, "This is all I am good for anyway" or, "This is all women are good for." The original perpetrator has demonstrated what he thinks of her. In some cases he reinforced the behavioral message with verbal messages. Projecting his own guilt onto her, he called her names like "slut," "whore," "puta." For all intents and purposes, he has given her a "slut" or "bad-girl" script. She responds by taking on the script with a vengeance. Correspondingly she sees herself as "bad" and uses the "slutting" as proof of her own "badness."

Not all women who engage in casual sex have a script of this nature. Many women enjoy casual sex, and many of those who do are freer than those who do not. Some survivors indeed are among these. By contrast, survivors with bad-girl scripts do not exactly enjoy what is going on; they feel impelled to have sex. They say yes to every man who asks. They routinely walk into dangerous situations in which they are beaten or gang-raped. They submit to sexual practices that they find repulsive. And they often wake up from a drunk to find themselves in bed in an unfamiliar room with an unfamiliar man who is sneering at them.

Making the connection with the original childhood abuse is central to empowering work with "slut-scripted" survivors. This may require a great deal of effort, for many have blotted out the original memory. The connection helps them make sense of a life that is baffling to them, and it opens the possibility of different choices.

Proceeding from here, it is important to explore more thoroughly what is happening. Issues requiring clarification and exploration include "slutting" as (a) revictimization, (b) obeying the patriarchal edict to be a sex object, (c) a way of shifting blame to self and so protecting her world, (d) resistance and revenge, (e) a way of remembering, (f) a way of tricking the mind and forgetting, and (g) a way of diverting herself from the original feelings surrounding the childhood abuse and/or of giving these feelings partial expression and/or of rising above them.

A shift in coping is contingent on the woman deciding that she is losing more than she is gaining. She is not likely to make this shift unless we accept her precisely as she is and do not push. A "one-small-step-at-a-time" approach is advisable or else the client may fail and use that failure as proof of her own "badness." Small steps that serve to protect her and to undercut the script include:

- Insisting that the men she has sex with use condoms (Do draw attention to the HIV risk.)
- Refusing to perform any sexual act that she finds distasteful
- Not drinking with people whom she does not know
- Declining sexual invitations from groups of men

Prostituting

Many of the dynamics operant in coping by "slutting" are also operant in coping by prostituting, and similar help is required of us. Many prostitutes, of course, are not survivors. And some survivors prostitute without the prostitution figuring as a key way of coping with childhood sexual abuse. For these women prostitution may be a very viable choice. As prostitutes have long argued, it is at least as viable as marriage.[2] Many survivors nonetheless use prostitution as a way of dealing/not dealing with the abuse. Like the women who "slut," they are living out the bad-girl script. They are obeying the perpetrator's edict to be a sex object or are deciding to be what they think the violation has made them.

And like the "slut," they are going one stage further, thereby avenging themselves on the oppressor.

These similarities notwithstanding, the differences, depending on the situation of the prostitutes, can be very formidable. Some prostitute survivors, on the one hand, lead enormously disempowered lives—more disempowered than the average survivor who "sluts." Pimps regulate their movements and their actions and take almost all of their money. If they are street youths, they generally have no home and no money, and they are always vulnerable to attack.

Prostitute survivors who are more affluent and independent, on the other hand, have more control over their lives than either the street prostitute or the survivor who "sluts." They live comfortably. They generally do not submit to acts that they find distasteful. They make it abundantly clear what they will and will not do. They usually take measures to protect themselves. And they do not give themselves away to customer or pimp. Prostitutes charge for their services; these prostitutes keep the money they earn.

These strengths, along with others, make prostituting a far more empowering choice for certain survivors. They also make it more difficult for these same survivors to see the sexual objectification and alienation involved, as well as the connection with childhood abuse. With street youths and with prostitutes who are controlled by pimps and whose money all goes to pimps, the injury and the connections are more obvious. The confusion can be substantial, nonetheless, due to ongoing manipulation by the male controller and the misguided loyalty that it fosters.[3]

Once again we help by co-investigating the connections. More than ever, concern for safety is critical, and in many cases also concern for health. Once again an injured yet resourceful person needs our warmth and our respect.

Splitting

Besides the short-run help discussed earlier, the survivor who copes by splitting needs greater safety overall, further control, and heightened awareness. By working on safety issues, we can help her create a world that she does not need to flee. Our ongoing work searching through the past, putting together memories, and expanding memory is especially apropos; it helps transform an unknown horror that cannot be dealt with into a known violation that can be faced. By supporting the client as she stays with uncomfortable feelings and thoughts longer and longer, we can help her get power over the splitting.

Empowerment is also served by querying the splitting itself. The client's inner experience of the splitting and our own observations of what happens when she splits serve as data. Where the client wishes, she can also draw on other people's observations. Examples of questions that counselor and client might attempt to address together in this regard are:

1. What sorts of events generally precede the splitting?
2. What does the client look like when she is splitting?
3. What does the client look like a split second before she splits?
4. Where does she go?
5. What enables her to return?

The more the client learns about the types of events, tones, or nuances that precede splitting, the more information she has about the original abuse. Such knowledge furthers the principal inquiry. It also gives her power over the splitting. The point is that the greater her knowledge about the splitting, the greater her ability to catch herself before she splits and to respond differently.

Fragmenting

Survivors who cope by fragmenting are likely to need much more concerted help from us. These women protected themselves by fragmenting off parts of their experience and of themselves. In the long run, greater integration is desirable. We can assist initially by helping them gain awareness of the different parts or subpersonalities, by befriending each, and by getting a sense of the relationship between them. What is involved here are:

- Spending time talking to each of them
- Finding out what the part needs and what function she or he performs
- Finding out what knowledge she holds—especially knowledge of the abuse—and what other subpersonalities she is aware of
- Finding out whom she likes, whom she dislikes, and why
- Co-investigating the changeovers from one subpersonality to another
- Accepting, respecting, and caring about each subpersonality

More advanced work involves helping the different subpersonalities communicate and negotiate with each other. The gestalt two-chair exercises that most counselors are familiar with will serve here, although they probably will have to be expanded to five- or six-chair work. Calling up what psychosynthesis calls *the fair witness* and asking this witness to guide the subpersonalities through their negotiations can be particularly effective. The fair witness is nothing but the self who knows. According to psychosynthesis theory, no matter how fragmented we may be, on some level each of us knows and is aware. Psychosynthesis personifies this aspect or level, calling it "the fair witness." Use of the fair witness (a) gives the client a reliable guide and arbitrator, (b) helps her think of herself as a unified human being, (c) helps her trust in her own awareness and skill, and (d) helps her get in touch with and take in her own knowledge of the abuse.

Numbing

To varying degrees, survivors deal with the initial emotional and physical pain of childhood sexual abuse by numbing themselves to it. The child who does not fragment and does not split needs some other way of dealing with a pain that is too great to bear. In many cases, as well, the child who splits and the child who fragments need additional or accompanying distancing strategies. They cope by cutting off or greatly reducing their feeling. They freeze. They go numb. They make the unbearable more bearable by not quite bearing it. This original numbing continues on in adulthood. Although for some the numbing is minimal, many have numbed themselves so effectively that they can recount intricate details of their abuse without registering any feeling at all.

For many this response to the specific trauma becomes a response to everything unpleasant. When the survivor encounters something unpleasant, she goes numb. For others it generalizes into an overall response to the world. Many survivors go for long stretches of time not feeling anything at all. By not feeling anything, they are certain not to feel anything awful.

The coping was essential initially, and it continues to work—but at a price. Survivors are generally out of touch with their feelings. They are out of touch with their bodies in particular. Because the body is the original source of the pain, bodily feeling is perceived as dangerous and so is cut off. Sex and sexual feeling are especially dangerous because they are associated with the original abuse. Most survivors of overt abuse, accordingly, totally or partially shut down sexually. Most avoid sexual intimacy.

We help, as always, by drawing attention to and honoring the coping, while working toward gradual change. By periodically focusing on the client's feelings/sensations in the here and now, we can help survivors become more aware of their feelings and their sensations. By empathizing with the buried suffering that they are just beginning to discern and by encouraging them to stay with it longer and longer, we help them face and work through the agony of the abuse and access their feelings and their bodies in the process. And by providing safety while inviting them to explore their sexual feelings, we help them find their sexual selves.

Enduring

Many of the survivors toward the right on the continuum—especially survivors who were abused on an ongoing basis—developed an attitude of endurance that helped them cope with the abuse. Like splitting and fragmenting, enduring is a combination of compliance and resistance that enabled the child to survive. The violated child told herself that she has no choice but to go along with what is happening (rational cooperation). At the same time, she told herself that it is okay, that if she just holds on, she can make it through (cooperation and passive resistance). Her decision and her belief in her ability to endure served her well in a situation in which she had almost no power. She applied it to other situations. She learned to view most situations as endurance tests, including situations that she might be able to change, and she responded accordingly. This response at once victimizes her and leaves her vulnerable to further victimization.

In light of the nature of the original abuse, survivors who cope in this way are particularly prone to abuse by men—sexual abuse in particular. They are forever submitting to sexual advances that they do not want. Most see sexual submission as woman's lot in life, and many see sexual invasion as man's right. They assume that no woman really enjoys sex. They tell themselves, "Just grit your teeth and grin and bear it; it will be over in no time." And indeed they get through it all just as they tell themselves they will but at the price of their own enjoyment and their own choice. Many submit to sexual acts that they find utterly distasteful. Many submit to more overt sexual violence and battery. Most have trouble saying no to anything: "If I say no," they tell themselves, "I'll just make the situation worse. And there's no telling what might happen then."

Awareness of the pattern and its origin is key to change. Most survivors who cope by enduring do not see the connection between their current coping and childhood experiences. For most, enduring has become so automatic that they are seldom aware that any choice or any possibility of choice is involved. At any given time, they are as likely as not unaware that they are "enduring."

By drawing attention to endurance as it occurs and by co-investigating their endurance with them, we can help survivors become aware of their style of coping and the degree to which this coping pervades their lives. By co-investigating its connection with the early abuse and their responses to that abuse, we can shed light on both their earlier and their current experiences. By problematizing their automatic equation between "enduring" and "preventing worse abuse," we can help survivors use this clearly valuable coping strategy more judiciously. And by helping them "catch" the decision to endure early on and begin making different decisions where appropriate, we can help them retrieve the ability to choose reflectively and broaden their range of response.

Concrete changes, once again, are best approached on a "one-small-step-at-a-time" basis. Examples of viable small steps are:

- Twice weekly saying no to some request that they do not want to grant or even for no reason at all
- Occasionally asking themselves, while in the midst of doing something that they have agreed to do, how they feel about it. If they find that they are just enduring, stopping.

Generally survivors who endure need particular help reframing and gaining entitlement where sex is concerned. The survivor needs to know the following:

1. That sex is not an ordeal to be borne
2. That sex is for mutual enjoyment
3. That it is perfectly okay to either like or not like sex in general, sex with men, sex with women, sex with specific women or men, and specific sexual acts
4. That she has the right, and indeed to the extent that she can do so safely, she has an obligation to herself to decline sex that she does not want or does not enjoy
5. That declining sex is not invariably dangerous and that when it is, that danger can at least sometimes be dealt with in other ways

She also needs to know that survivors are often triggered during sex and that when she is triggered, stopping—not enduring—and getting help from her partner are generally the best thing that she can do for herself. Indeed all survivors who continue sex while being triggered need to know this whether they split, numb, or endure.

Fury

Some survivors use rage as a source of energy, as an avenue to entitlement, as a mode of self-protection. The fury that served them well during the initial abuse also serves them now. It gives them life and is a way of fighting back. Insofar as it is generalized to the whole world, it can prevent victimization. The down side is that it can also close down other feelings—especially sadness. Generalized fury can be a way of avoiding anger at the perpetrator. It can alienate her from others. It can get her into trouble. And it leaves her vulnerable to being judged "dangerous to self or others."

Like all furious women, the furious survivor needs our validation. She needs to express her anger in a safe place. And she needs help channeling the anger and opening other feelings. If she is someone who frequently lands in trouble, more practical assistance may also be called for. Particularly important are direct advocacy and co-exploring other ways of responding to infuriating situations.

Beyond Coping

Whether the abuse was overt or covert, whether the client splits, endures, or self-mutilates, anger at the perpetrator is empowering. We can facilitate the client's anger by inviting it and by problematizing the transfer of blame. We can also facilitate it by expressing our own anger. It is important to tread carefully, of course, especially if the client shares an oppression with the perpetrator.

Misogyny often figures heavily in survivors' readiness for anger and the respective degrees of anger that they feel toward the different people involved in the abuse. Survivors tend to "understand" male perpetrators and to loathe female perpetrators. What is more significant, many survivors are positively livid at the women who indirectly facilitated the injury by doing nothing and are much less angry at the men who actually abused them.

As feminist counselors we are faced with a dilemma. On the one hand, we do not want to collude with misogyny. We know that lateral oppression and internalized oppression are at the core of the special fury felt toward women. On the other hand, we also know that survivors have a right to be angry and indeed need to be angry at everyone both directly and indirectly involved.

This problem has no easy answer, but there are ways of handling it. By giving the psychological its due and by phasing in the political, we can usually make our way through the dilemma.

To varying degrees, I always begin by inviting anger at the perpetrator and continue to invite anger at him or her. Where the perpetrator is male and where the survivor is much angrier at the woman who did not stop the abuse, I accept this anger as an initial focus; that is, I encourage the survivor to express her anger at the woman, and I validate that anger. The message that I give is: As a little girl, she deserved protection; of course she is angry at not getting it. With those few who experience almost no anger at the "uninvolved" woman, I correspondingly encourage anger although not at this point. As time goes on, a more general shift is usually possible. We move to anger at the abuser. The bulk of the anger work concentrates on the abuser.

Our challenging of internalized oppression, our work on anger, and our validating should be part of a larger attempt to help the survivor gain a critical understanding of the oppression. The survivor needs to know what she was and is up against. Integral to that greater understanding is the awareness that the terrible sexualization and invasion that she was submitted to in childhood were not exceptional. They were unique, of course, just as all experiences are unique, and they were horrendous and totally unacceptable. But they were not out of the ordinary. And they do not set her apart from other women. They are something shared with other women. Even the feminist survivor who has a detailed analysis of sexual abuse is in need of assistance here, for there is a level on which she does not know. We need to help her, we need to help all survivors fully take in a terrible truth: That all little girls are violated in some way and to some degree. That her father, uncle, or whoever else molested her is not critically different from other men. That although he may have carried violation considerably farther than others, men generally sexualize and invade little girls. Although differences must be acknowledged, ultimately the woman violated by a woman also needs to understand the profound similarity between her experience and the experience of other survivors. And she needs to understand the

	Private	Public
Few	1 confiding in one's best friend and/or partner and/or children	2 telling known survivors only, or women at a conference
Many	3 telling most/all friends	4 telling the women's community; telling the general public

Figure 7.2. "Telling" Quadrants

larger patriarchal context in which both her own abuse and the overall abuse of little girls occurs.

Telling

Survivors were condemned to silence by the perpetrator and by everyone who turned a blind eye or actively denied. This silence further disempowered them. Taking back power involves breaking that silence. Acknowledgment in therapy can be a critical step in breaking the silence. But it cannot be the only step. The survivor needs to proclaim her truth in the actual world. That proclaiming may be as limited or as extensive as is helpful to her.

Proclaiming may be thought of in terms of four different quadrants and may be diagrammed as shown in Figure 7.2.

All quadrants can be very empowering, and all allow for movement. More empowerment generally comes as women move from top to bottom and from left to right. This is far from invariable, however, so we need to pay close attention to what is happening for the individual client. By way of example, we have all come across clients who are forever speaking out publicly about their abuse and can do so easily precisely because they are cut off from their feelings. Far from empowering them, public telling in this instance is a way of avoiding their feeling and of avoiding the empowering work that they need to do. Good counseling in such instances means helping them move away from the public and into themselves.

We can help survivors develop further within a quadrant and/or move into new quadrants by introducing possibilities and by supporting them as they make tentative shifts. As always, it is important to proceed slowly. It is also important to reassure the client that there is no competition here, that there is nothing that she has to do, and that she should not do anything that does not feel right to her.

Telling People in the Original Family

A Quadrant 1 activity that all overt and many covert incest survivors consider at some time or other is broaching the issue with members of the original family. Except where everyone concerned is dead, survivors are faced with questions such as:

- Should I tell my siblings? Should I find out whether it happened to them too? Should I ask whether they have any memory of something happening to me?
- Should I confront my father? Should I tell him that I remember him molesting me? Should I tell him that his jokes about "the little bumps on my chest" were not innocent? Should I let him know that he has done me immeasurable harm?
- Should I tell my mother what my father did? Should I insist even if she denies? Should I ask her whether she knew about it, and if so, why she did not put a stop to it?
- Should I tell my brother why I have always hated him so?

Some survivors authentically answer no to all such questions. It is critical for us to support that answer, not to pressure them ourselves, and to problematize any pressuring that occurs.

Where siblings were not themselves perpetrators and where there is no enormous conflict between siblings, siblings are usually the easiest to share with. Most incest survivors who choose to share with anyone else in the family begin here. Some begin with a more distant but benign relative whom they see as uninvolved in both the abuse and the "cover-up." This person may be a favorite aunt or a cousin. Such a person is generally a good choice, and it is important to let the survivor know this and know why.

Discussing the abuse with siblings and/or other benign relatives can greatly enhance the work of therapy. The survivor is standing up for herself in the face of possible rejection, thereby announcing to self and relative that she and her truth are vitally important. It is also significant that relatives can provide important validation and confirmation. Simply by believing the survivor, they offer a special type of validation that we as therapists could not conceivably offer. It is one thing to be believed by a therapist who does not know the perpetrator, who has no attachment to this family whatever, and who is committed to believing her. It is quite another to be believed by a relative who has no such commitment, who is intrinsically attached, and who knows intimately everyone involved. Further validation and actual confirmation occur when relatives say that:

- They sort of suspected something because . . .
- They actually witnessed something, namely . . .
- They heard about something.
- The same family member or some other family member did something similar to them or to some other child.

Such confirmation helps the client feel more secure in her knowledge and helps dispel feelings of "craziness." The relatives' sharing in turn furthers the work of retrieval and co-investigation. It can fill in gaps that the survivor is unable to fill in. It can provide substance where there is no substance—just hazy impressions. It can provide significant amendments, such as unfusing two fused memories, thereby making coherent wholes out of incoherent memories. Where relatives respond well, moreover, whether they provide information or not, they can become a significant and ongoing source of support for the client. And they may become allies in the event of confrontation.

Many relatives do respond well, and so this support is a real possibility. Many, however, seem ambivalent or dubious. Some initially entertain the idea and even offer confirmation, only to deny later. Some respond negatively from the beginning. They accuse the woman of making up lies. They may patronize/pathologize her, giving her some version of, "I have always liked you, my dear Emily, and I know that you think that these dreadful things happened, but that is only because you are sick." They may acknowledge that something happened, while maintaining that she was responsible and calling her a "slut." Especially with covert incest or overt incest toward the beginning of the continuum, they may confirm the memory, while totally trivializing what happened. Even those who eventually do respond positively, moreover, are often dubious, dismissive, or reluctant at the beginning.

Where the survivor is considering telling a relative, it is important to familiarize her with these different possibilities and to help her assess the likelihood of different types of responses. Help her explore as well how she feels about certain negative responses, whether she can live with them. Where she decides tentatively or firmly to go ahead, role plays can be invaluable. They make different responses real for her and get her used to dealing with them. Be prepared to support her and indeed to reassure her in the event of a negative response.

Confronting

Confronting is harder than simply telling. Of the confrontations that survivors are most likely to consider, the diciest, as well as the most potentially rewarding, are the two following paradigmal confrontations:

1. Confronting father with what he has done
2. Confronting mother with what father has done and what mother failed to do

Such confrontations are an enormous act of courage. The survivor is breaking the silence injunction right at its source. As an adult whose child is easily triggered by the presence of parents and by what parents say, she is raising issues that trigger her and is saying the very things that are most likely to result in responses that could further trigger her. She is facing the possibility—in fact, the likelihood—of denial. She is risking rejection by both parents and indeed by the entire family.

Where the survivor knows what she is about and has truly chosen this, these paradigmal confrontations can also be tremendously liberating, even where parents respond poorly. The survivor is showing herself and her family just how courageous she is. She is facing someone who abused her and someone who may have spent years protecting that abuser. She is freeing herself from an injunction. She is absolving herself of any wrongdoing and is saying, "You/Dad did wrong." She is saying to father and/or mother, "I and my truth are more important than the family myths." She is saying, "What happened to me is not trivial. It is significant—so significant, in fact, that it is worth upsetting everyone and potentially disrupting the entire family." On a personal level, although she may well not take this in, she is making the most profound feminist statement in the world. She is saying to father, "You—THE MALE CARE-GIVER—are the violator of me—THE FEMALE CHILD. And that violation is one of the most important truths in the universe." She is saying to mother, "I am the credible one and the one to join with. Believe *me* over *father*." She is saying, "Whatever you and I may have done in the past, and however we may have been divided from one another, let's stick together now." She is saying, "Side with *me*. Side with your *daughter*. Side with your FEMALE OFFSPRING over your MALE PARTNER."

Much of the assistance that is needed from us is similar to the assistance needed with telling relatives. With confronting, though—especially paradigmal confronting—our efforts need to be doubled and tripled. More support, more preparation, more clarification, and more role play are needed. It is important that the client be on her own turf or at the very least has support nearby if she is going to confront. Encourage her to give herself this extra support, to set things up in a way that maximizes her control. Her own home is an optimal place for the interchange. If her parents live in a different city, her own city is almost a necessity. If she broaches the issue in a different city and she receives a bad reception, she can easily end up alone with her pain once again; and that is the last thing that any survivor needs. If she is thinking of confronting both parents together, let her know that seeing one at a time gives her more power.

Make sure she is aware that the most likely responses are far from positive, that she can almost anticipate one of the following: (a) denial or disbelief, (b) trivialization, (c) belief or acknowledgment followed by denial, and (d) belief or acknowledgment followed by oblivion of the original conversation.

She is setting herself up for disappointment if she is confronting in the expectation of having the abuse finally acknowledged. Although of course she wants the acknowledgment and will be disappointed if she does not get it, there is an enormous difference between confronting for the sole purpose of acknowledgment and confronting at least partially for the sake of confronting with the added hope of receiving acknowledgment. Confrontation makes sense only if valued in and of itself. It is our job to be clear about this and to help her sort through "where she is really at."

Where the client decides to confront either mother or father, she is likely to need help standing her ground and not rescuing. Where confronting a remorseful perpetrator, especially where the perpetrator has been abused or oppressed, she may need special help dealing with attempts to solicit her empathy and compassion. The perpetrator may plead with her to keep in touch when she does not wish to. The perpetrator may ask her for help dealing with his or her own remorse. The perpetrator may beg for forgiveness, saying that unless she forgives him or her, self-forgiveness is impossible.

Again, although this is certainly not all that is going on, what we are seeing are the dynamics of covert incest. The daughter is being portrayed as special, as a savior, and the pull in this is difficult for her to resist. It is nice to feel special. Our socialization teaches us to care and to want to help. Again our own caring and decency put us in jeopardy.

The remorseful perpetrator, no doubt, is in a painful position and needs help, but the victim-daughter is not the proper source of help. She does not owe this help. She cannot now and she cannot ever afford to accept the special position that the perpetrator puts her in. And initially at the very least, she cannot give help without jeopardizing her own healing. The pressure to give at her own expense reflects and, especially where father is the perpetrator, extends the original childhood injury and is part and parcel of the domination of woman. Woman the victim is being asked to accept victimization and to continue on as the caretaker of man the violator. It is important that we help the survivor understand what is involved here. It is important that she not give herself away.

The daughter may need extra help as well setting the conditions and making the requests/demands that she needs to. Examples of conditions that she might pose are:

- The perpetrator pays the therapy costs.
- The perpetrator provides other financial aid if she is having trouble keeping a full-time job or is/was not able to concentrate sufficiently to do the type of work that would remunerate her well.

- No one in the family is to pressure her.
- All decisions over contact are left to her alone.

Bringing the Family to a Session

As noted in Chapter 6, *families* do not commit incest. *Perpetrators* do. Incest, accordingly, should NEVER be seen as a "family problem." Similarly, although there are some exceptions, and we need to be sensitive to these, generally speaking it is not a good idea to do family therapy with incest survivors and their families, for survivors can be profoundly injured in the process. Meeting a few times with the family in a context in which the survivor alone is our client is a different matter. Sometimes a survivor wants our help broaching the issue with the family and getting her needs met. It is appropriate to accede to this request and see the family a few times so long as we are clear about our role and keep our allegiance firmly intact. We may find ourselves helping other family members in the process, of course, and that is fine. It is not and cannot be our guiding objective, however, and it must never be done at the expense of the client.

Possible ways that we can help the survivor in such sessions include the following:

- Stopping others from interrupting the client when she is saying what she needs to say and helping them take it in
- Stopping anyone else from yelling at her or in any way trying to intimidate her
- Explaining the importance of believing the daughter
- Making it clear that *we* believe her
- Making it clear that we do not see their daughter as crazy, as exaggerating, or as "making a mountain out of a mole hill"
- Explaining how common and yet how much of a betrayal incest is
- Stating unambivalently that terrible harm has been done and that it can never be undone
- In the case of families that share an oppression and/or of perpetrators who are themselves survivors, acknowledging the horror of their oppression, empathizing with what has happened to them or is happening to them, while being clear that this did not cause the abuse in question and does not justify it
- Countering any attempts to blame the daughter and/or helping the daughter counter these attempts
- Noting that the daughter cannot be asked to help the perpetrator with his or her grief
- Suggesting sources of help for the perpetrator
- Suggesting resources/sources of help for a nonperpetrating parent
- Addressing any attempts to transfer to the wife the blame that belongs with the husband

- Unearthing other woman-dividing and woman-harming dynamics in the family
- Explaining/helping the client explain the different ways in which she has been harmed and the type of help she needs
- Advocating for financial assistance and any other kind of assistance that the client needs/wants
- Making it clear that however difficult it may be for everyone, no pressure should be put on the daughter. They need to let her decide what if any contact she is going to have with the family as a whole and with the perpetrator in particular.

The Issue of Forgiveness

Many survivors think that they ought to forgive the perpetrator—that they are somehow not okay if they do not forgive—and some therapists think similarly and present forgiveness as a therapeutic goal. Forgiveness, however, is not the only viable response to injury. It is injurious early on because it curtails working through. And it is not a necessary response at any time. By treating forgiveness as necessary, we effectively pathologize anger, close down the survivor's own process, and reinforce societal messages. We also reinforce the patriarchal pattern of ongoing female forgiveness and ongoing male transgression.

If we are to empower, the message that we need to give instead is that anger must come first. Although the survivor may come to forgive after going through extensive anger work, and this is just fine, it is also perfectly okay if she never forgives the perpetrator. We need to be clear here and to repeat the message or else it will get lost amid the more restrictive messages that the survivor is likely to receive. If in the process we can also shed light on the oppressive nature of the demand to forgive, all the better.

The following is an excerpt from one of my sessions. It illustrates the type of message that I am talking about and the sort of work that may be involved:

Client	Bonnie, I really hate his guts. Like I mean, REALLY HATE. I don't know how I'm ever going to be able to forgive him. . . . Do you think I *have* to?
Bonnie	I want to be clear about this. No, Doris, you *don't* have to. As far as I am concerned, you don't have to forgive him *now*. You don't have to forgive him *ever*. Hating him doesn't make you any less valuable a human being, and it is perfectly natural. Of course you hate him! Why wouldn't you hate someone who crept up on you and molested you night after night!
Client	I feel like spitting every time I think of him.
Bonnie	Feel like spitting now?
Client	You mean right this minute? Right here?
Bonnie	Yeah.

Client	I feel like it. It doesn't quite seem right though. I'm a bit embarrassed.
Bonnie	Of course. It's a difficult thing to do, especially when someone else is present. I'd be self-conscious too.
Client	I don't mind trying it, though.
Bonnie	Go ahead. Place your lips like you're about to spit. And spit.

(A spitting exercise ensues.)

Bonnie	How do you feel now?
Client	*Funny. Good* funny. Like I really did something, though it's a bit weird. . . .
Bonnie	How do you feel when you think of your father?
Client	Let me see. I am more aware of hating his guts. And I feel a wee bit stronger. I also feel somewhat better about hating his guts. Like it's giving me something. It feels nice to hate.
Bonnie	Of course it does. So, it's okay to hate his guts?
Client	Well, it's okay for *now*. But what if I continue to hate his guts 20 years from now?
Bonnie	Then you continue to hate his guts.
Client	Oh, I know. But aren't we *supposed* to forgive?
Bonnie	Sure. We're also supposed to darn men's socks, cook their meals, and accept being sexualized.
Client	You mean it's not okay to forgive?
Bonnie	No. I mean it's not mandatory.
Client	I see what you mean. I'm glad you said that. Cause you know, it *is* more a matter of "should" than "want." I don't actually *want* to forgive him. I want to . . .
Bonnie	Yeah?
Client	. . . I want to . . . SPIT ON HIM. *(laughter)*

Community Incest Work

When working with Natives and others for whom community is central, we need to consider approaches that are more community focused, more sensitive to cultural values and customs, and gentler. Two Native examples of such approaches are:

- The reservewide work with perpetrators and survivors
- The women's use of sweet grass ceremonies

(For more details on these specific approaches, see Chapter 5.)

More generally, as feminists we need to understand and respect the special affinities of women who come from nondominant races or cultural groups. Helpful modifications range from including the spiritual more often, making room for ritual, including family or community members more often, and maintaining a dual focus on the sexual abuse committed against this nondominant group on the one hand and the abuse in question on the other. As always, wherever we include others, it is critical to take extra care that the survivor's needs not be sacrificed.

Legal and Quasi-Legal Routes

For survivors toward the right on the childhood sexual abuse continuum, charging the perpetrator is a significant option. The women most likely to find this option meaningful include survivors who have broken with their families or key members of their families, survivors who are still being bothered by the perpetrators, women whose children are being abused, and women whose abusers are outside the families.

To varying degrees, charging perpetrators is both empowering and disempowering. The empowerment aspect is the most obvious. Charging is a dramatic way of standing up for self. Although more certainly is involved, on an existential level the client is proclaiming/deciding: "I was wronged. You, the rapist, are responsible. I am announcing your wrongdoing to the world at large. And I am holding you accountable." Saying/doing this can help women move from victim to survivor. Accompanying bonuses may be that their safety is enhanced, that others who are at risk stop being at risk, and that the survivor receives remuneration. The down side is that none of these bonuses may materialize. And the existential meaning itself may be undermined by the inimical workings of the justice system. The point is that the justice system is a mechanism of the patriarchal, racist, and capitalistic state, and it serves the interests of the state. The victim may be ignored, humiliated, pathologized, or even vilified in the short run and her interests sacrificed in the long run. The trial itself may be a revictimization in which the offender triumphs. Alternatively it may give the victim nothing, while soundly oppressing the perpetrator and setting the victim up for revenge. Where victim and/or perpetrator come from nondominant groups, the possibility of gross insensitivity and oppression increases.

In light of this combination of possible advantages and problems, it is critical that any survivor considering this route look at the situation realistically and weigh the pros and cons. It is also vital that she construct a strong support group should she decide to proceed.

Although such programs are few, victim-offender reconciliation programs ("vorps") are a possible alternative to the courts. Vorps are legally mandated grass roots community programs that allow the victims to confront the perpetrators and to come to agreements without either side being dragged through the justice system. Examples of the types of conditions that victims and perpetrators might agree on are:

- The perpetrator must never again see the victim.
- The perpetrator must tell his friends and neighbors what happened.
- The perpetrator must never again work with children.
- The perpetrator must provide the following financial assistance. . . .

The advantages of victim-offender reconciliation programs are:

1. The survivor is central to and has far more control over the process.
2. She is not as likely to be revictimized or "avenged."
3. Neither she nor her family is as likely to be subject to gross racism or other forms of discrimination.
4. Because she is actively involved in negotiating the conditions and the conditions have to be acceptable to her, the outcome is at least somewhat more likely to be in her interests.

The major disadvantages are:

1. The process may drag out and may increase the survivor's work in the long run. If the offender does not keep his or her side of the agreement, the survivor is exactly where she was before. And she may no longer feel up to going through the justice system.
2. Victims have sometimes been threatened with impunity right within the negotiations.
3. The very term *reconciliation* assumes a cohesion and a relationship that may never have existed and hints at an ongoing relationship that may not be wanted or desirable.
4. A liberal ideology tends to underpin the conceptualization, and the mediators are usually liberals who are naive about male perpetrators and who do not understand violence against women and the needs of survivors.

We can help the individual survivor with the legal or quasi-legal routes by (a) providing her with relevant information on the different approaches, (b) helping her clarify the pros and cons of each, (c) co-exploring possible questions and responses, (d) providing names of lawyers and mediators who are knowledgeable on the topic and more likely to be sensitive to the issues involved, and (e) facilitating the creation of a viable support network.

Where the client goes to court, we can also give testimony and/or submit affidavits. The attitude required of us as a witness, it should be remembered, differs from the attitude required of us as a therapist. As a witness our job is to be rigorously accurate and as clear as possible about our degree of certitude about anything that we state. The more specific we can be and the more objective we seem, the better. We are most effective when we have been documenting all along. Because of the real possibility of court action where overt abuse has occurred, it is a good idea to start documenting indicators of abuse, including the client's statements about abuse and what we consider the "effects" just as soon as we suspect overt childhood sexual abuse.

A strong case for damages exists where the client has sustained bodily harm. Compensation for psychological damages is possible but is harder to win and requires significant documentation. A somewhat better case for financial compensation exists where the survivor has a history of working part-time at poorly paid jobs, has not been able to complete post-secondary school, and where this can reasonably be interpreted as a "consequence" of the abuse. Helpful points for us to enlarge on in such instances are:

1. The flooding/triggering interfered with the client's ability to work full-time and/or to hold down a demanding and well-paid job.
2. The trauma and flooding made focused, ongoing concentration difficult and consequently interfered with her ability to pursue the post-secondary education necessary for her to get a well-paid job.

The cost of therapy that would otherwise have been unnecessary is also pertinent.

OTHER RESOURCES

Additional resources to be aware of and to provide information on as appropriate include the following:

- Readable literature on incest and other childhood sexual abuse (First-person accounts are particularly affirming.)
- Contacts for survivor self-help groups in the area
- Information on facilitated groups for survivors currently being run in the vicinity— preferably free groups
- Information on relevant consciousness-raising groups—especially groups that focus on violence against women
- Ongoing updates on events of relevance—special workshops, take-back-the-night marches, and so on
- Phone numbers for women's shelters and women's phone lines that are knowledgeable in the area

THE SPECIAL SITUATION OF RITUAL ABUSE

Ritual abuse is at the extreme right on the childhood sexual abuse continuum. Because of the enormity of the terrorizing and terror involved, where ritual abuse has occurred, it is usually the last layer uncovered. Memories of ritual abuse sometimes emerge years after other memories have subsided.

Indicators of ritual abuse include terror at the sight of religious or symbolic pictures; enormous unease with common, everyday routines; enormous difficulty trusting; and such childhood memories as the following:

- Satanic or other demonic images
- Being taken to groups where "dreadful things" occurred
- Sexual and other torture, especially overt torture followed by sex, and especially torture involving mutilation and blood
- Sex in the presence of a group of adults
- Being forced to kill or eat a child or animal
- Observing children or animals killed
- Having animal parts inserted into one's body
- Being smeared with blood

Work with ritual abuse is similar to work with other types of childhood sexual abuse. Extra efforts at creating safety, however, are critical. Some survivors are at risk from cult members who are tracking them, attempting to draw them back in, or otherwise interfering with them. Where this is happening, protective measures should be planned. Generally, though not invariably, the risk is more perceived than real, and the perception comes from programming. Ritual abuse survivors invariably have been threatened with dire consequences if they told. They have been taught that cult members have special powers, will automatically know, and can magically kill or otherwise harm the survivor or the person that the survivor turns to. Greater and ongoing reassurance is needed here. It is particularly important that we demythologize what is happening. We need to help the client see through the bogus power claims and recognize the lies and programming for what they are. Insofar as the child within still believes in the magical power, even while the adult sees beyond it, it is sometimes helpful to engage the client in magical protection exercises. Where this is done, of course, it is important to be absolutely clear that what we are doing is make-believe only, just as the magical power of the cult members is imaginary.

It is also critical to become aware of and to help the client both become aware of and counter hidden programming. A sign of possible hidden programming is the client repeatedly finding herself doing a specific thing that she was unaware of wanting to do and that in some critical way interferes with her. An example of a program: If you start to divulge the cult's secrets, immediately take yourself to a psychiatric institution. The survivor with such a program may frequently find herself entering the doors of a psychiatric institution with no idea why. Uncovering what habitually precedes this surprising event helps uncover the programming. By mutually uncovering programming and constructing other responses to program triggers, client and therapist recover ground and safety.

Ritual abuse survivors tend to have particular difficulty getting from one day to the next. We can help by being more available and by overtly caring. Greater sensitivity to what may "spook the client" and greater accommodation are also in order.

The woman may be terrified by the color black because everyone involved in the abuse wore black. If so, it is important that we not wear black. Unusual requests like removing pictures from the wall and unlocking locked doors tend to have meaning in terms of the abuse. Casual, everyday routines that involve momentary power differentials that we all partake in without thinking about can be threatening to a ritual abuse survivor, for she was subjected to ongoing actions specifically calculated to gain power over her. Except where we sense that something different is called for, it is best to accommodate the special needs and requests insofar as possible and without making an issue of them. As the client feels safer to discuss them, these discomforts and requests can be used as an aid to memory and co-investigation.

Generally more work around guilt is needed as well. Children who were forced to torture, kill, and/or eat other children or animals and then were given the clear message that they were responsible cannot help but feel enormously guilty at some level. It is our job to reassure, to problematize the guilt, and to redirect the blame.

SUGGESTED READINGS

Adams, C., & Fay, J. (1981). *No more secrets.* London: Impact.
Allen, V. (1982). *Daddy's girl.* New York: Berkeley Books.
Bass, E., & Davis, L. (1988). *The courage to heal: A guide for women survivors of childhood sexual abuse.* New York: Harper & Row.
Butler, S. (1978). *Conspiracy of silence: The trauma of incest.* New York: Bantam.
Davis, L. (1990). *The courage to heal workbook.* New York: Harper & Row.
El Saadawi, N. (1980). *The hidden face of Eve: Women in the Arab world.* London: Zed.
Smith, M., & Pazder, L. (1980). *Michelle remembers.* New York: Pocket.
Walker, A. (1983). *The colour purple.* London: Women's Press.

NOTES

1. For a description of the bow and other exercises, see Lowen (1977).
2. For a discussion of the empowering aspects of prostitution, see Bell (1987).
3. For discussions of this confusion and loyalty, see the section on abuse by pimps in Chapter 10.

8

Extreme Abuse by Male Partner

Most of our clients who have ever had male partners are currently being abused by their male partners and/or were once abused by male partners. Currently 25% are being subjected to and/or were once subjected to such extremes as ongoing battery, ongoing humiliation, being forced to perform sexual acts that they find repulsive, and threats to kill.[1]

Possible indicators of extreme partner abuse are as follows:

- The client has a hard time looking at us.
- She seems frightened, confused, or disoriented.
- She winces at every unexpected sound or movement.
- She is bruised or cut, has a broken limb or jaw.
- Her body is extremely covered up.
- She frequently sees doctors or ends up in a hospital.
- In the case of shelters and emergency lines, the very fact that she has called the shelter or emergency line.

Where we suspect such abuse, it is important to ask the woman whether she is being or has been abused and to listen, believe, and take seriously. If her partner is present, arranging to speak with her alone first is the safest course of action.

Where we have reason to suspect extreme partner abuse, our first concern must be immediate safety. The pressing question facing us is: Is this woman currently in a life-threatening situation? Because women typically minimize danger to themselves, if she thinks she is in great danger, we can generally assume she is.[2] Where she is unsure or suspects that things are not quite so extreme, the situation may be just as dangerous. Safety requires that we ask for more information, assess what we hear, and share our assessment.

Walker's (1979) depiction of the cycle of violence is useful for conceptualizing the violence and women's response to it, and it can provide some help in evaluating concrete situations. It is critical to realize, though, that contrary to Walker's somewhat deprecating assumption, denial is not always what is going on for the woman. In the cycle, as Walker describes it, "tension building" leads to violence; the "violence phase" is followed by a "honeymoon period," in which the man is mortified, apologizes, promises to do better, and ostensibly is believed and forgiven. The honeymoon period is followed by a further tension-building phase, and that phase by further violence. And so the cycle continues, with the honeymoon periods characteristically becoming progressively shorter and the violence and the tension-building phases becoming progressively larger. Generally, the farther the violence has escalated and the shorter the honeymoon periods, the greater the danger. We have enormous cause for alarm when the violence and the tension-building phases have greatly expanded at the expense of the honeymoon periods.

Browne's (1987) research into battered women who kill suggests other indicators that might be used. This research is relevant because the killing in question correlates strongly with life-threatening danger to the woman. The research suggests that despite the size of any period in the cycle, the woman is in an imminently life-threatening situation and immediate action is called for where the violence has escalated and any of the following pertain:

- The partner has begun threatening her life.
- Having threatened her life in the past, the partner has just brought a knife or gun into the house.
- The partner has locked her in the house.
- She sustains multiple injuries with each episode.
- The partner has killed her pet.[3]

Where the situation is urgent, it is our responsibility to talk out of that urgency. If she is unclear, as women in situations of battery often are, it is up to us to provide clarity. We need to review the situation with her and make statements like:

> While it is *your* decision, *no, waiting for a week does not sound safe to me.* I know it is hard, but I want you to look at what has happened. He has already broken your jaw. He has threatened to kill you. He has just brought a gun into the house and could use it at any time. Emma, I really wish things were different, but you can't afford to wait around. The time to act is now.

It is critical as well to help her form a concrete and realistic plan of escape and access such necessary resources as (a) a shelter or some other "safe place" to go, (b) people to take her there, and minimally, (c) enough money to get through the next few days. Additionally ask her to repeat any information provided and the steps that she has determined. In the midst of a nightmare like this, it is difficult for anyone to remain focused and clear.

Where children are involved, the exit plan must include them. If children are being brutalized and she is not acting, we may be forced to report the abuse. As feminists, of course, we should not automatically call in the patriarchal state.

Most of the women whom we encounter that are subject to extreme partner abuse are not or not yet in a life-threatening situation. They are nonetheless in an enormously disempowering and indeed brutalizing situation.

The popular image of "the battered wife" is of someone subject to physical abuse that is not overtly sexual. This abuse ranges from slaps, to kicks, to being thrown against walls, to being burned with cigarettes or subjected to other obvious acts of torture. The assumption is that the greater the physical damage, the worse the abuse. This popular image leaves out as much as it shows, and the assumption itself is naive. On the purely physical side, some subtler acts deeply harm because of their psychological impact. These include:

- Subtle disfigurement of any part of the body that the woman takes special pride in or identifies with
- Subtle disfigurement to any part of the body that the woman is already ashamed of
- Being held firmly by some part of the body

Other devastating forms of abuse also occur. Overt sexual abuse and what is called "emotional" or "overt psychological" abuse are particularly noteworthy. These may accompany battery or occur alone. We forget, to women's detriment, that women who are never punched, slapped, or kicked can still be survivors of extreme partner abuse. As abused women have told counselors again and again, it is not the slaps and the kicks that hurt most, it is the ongoing humiliation, the name calling, the isolation, the general degradation.

Sexual abuses that commonly figure in extreme partner abuse are:

- Pressure to have sex
- Pressure to perform sexual acts that she finds degrading or disgusting
- Being photographed in sexual positions against her wishes
- Being forced to have sex with others, with or without the partner watching
- Being called sexual names for purposes of degradation
- Being forced to have sex while hurting from the battery
- Genital/breast mutilation

Common types of psychological abuse are:

- Constantly being told that she is stupid, ugly, or incompetent
- Being compared with women who are depicted as infinitely brighter, prettier, or more competent
- Being told the details of affairs with other women
- Being "punished" for "transgressions" committed by these other women
- Being called degrading names, such as stupid, bitch, witch, whore
- Continually being accused of infidelity
- Being told again and again that *she* provoked the battery and that what is happening is *her* fault
- Being deprived of money
- Being denied the opportunities to take courses or to go places
- Being forbidden to see friends and relatives
- Being locked in the house
- Threats to leave, accompanied by assurances like, "You're so fuckin' ugly now that you'll never be able to get another man."
- Destruction of favored objects
- Violence against loved others, including children and pets
- Continual threats of violence
- The cycle itself

Where the woman comes from a nondominant group, especially where the man is from the dominant culture, racist, ableist, and classist slurs may add to and intensify this abuse.

Like anyone who is systematically tortured, isolated, humiliated, and given highly contradictory messages to boot, the average woman who is subjected to extreme partner abuse has little sense of her own worth and is enormously confused and terrified. She is not sure who the real partner is or whom to believe—the man who woos her or the man who abuses her. She does not know what to expect next and shakes at every sound. She is not even sure where blame lies. She locates faults in herself and keeps trying to "do better." By finding things to alter in herself, she at once undermines herself, protects herself, and keeps herself hopeful. She gets hopeful too whenever he is remorseful—whenever he begs for forgiveness, says her loves her, and promises not to hurt her again. Time goes on. She gradually discovers just how little she can influence the abuse. The honeymoon periods get progressively shorter, and the violence dramatically accelerates. Her hope dwindles, and she becomes increasingly disheartened. She remains, however, and although psychologists keep asking why she remains and pathologizing her, it is hardly surprising that she does.

She remains because she still harbors some hope and/or because she does not know what else to do. She remains because she has bought the line that children need their father and because she cannot imagine raising them alone. She remains because family is central to her. She remains because she "loves" this man and because he "loves" her. She remains not simply despite the jealousy, rage, scrutiny, and violence, but also because of it. (Part of what she fell in love with may have been superpossessiveness, attentiveness to a fault, and the hint of violence. It is these qualities that underpin romantic love, and in Western society the romantic love tradition underpins extreme battery.) She stays because he hurts and says he is lost without her. (Women are supposed to take care of and stand behind their men.) She stays because her culture and community dictate wifely obedience and would blame her if she left. She stays because she has no money, no one to help her, no way to earn a living, and no place to go. She stays because he has threatened to kill her if she leaves, and she has every reason to believe that this is *one* promise he will keep. She stays because he always found her, dragged her back, and beat her whenever she escaped in the past. She stays because the alternative is loneliness and abject poverty. Whether she has an analysis of the larger situation or not, and whether she has many illusions or no illusions at all, she stays because she is stuck in a patriarchal society that creates and mystifies the problem of wife abuse and gives only token help to battered women.

The temptation to rescue, the frustration, and the disrespect are the principal internal problems that counselors encounter when working with this client group. Although other dynamics are involved, the desire to rescue comes at least partially from caring, and it is perfectly understandable. No caring human being wants to sit by while another is being brutalized. No woman-identified woman wants to bide her time while yet another woman is being pulverized. Whatever may be needed in the short run, however, in the long run rescuing simply does not work. Not having gone through their own process, rescued women end up right back where they began. And the counselor ends up exhausted, disempowered, and frustrated.

Frustration comes from caring, overinvolvement, and oversimplification. And it easily turns into disrespect and gets leveled at the client. I have known workers on phone hot lines to exclaim, "But how can you stay with a man who treats you like that! Don't you have *any* self-respect?" I have known workers to berate clients for returning to their abusive partners. Most, of course, are careful not to say anything so overtly oppressive. Even when counselors say all the right things, however, all too often their tones and looks convey the message, "This is not good enough. You have let us down again."

The underlying expectations here are unrealistic and, even when subtle, impede therapy. If we are to work really well with abused partners, we need to appreciate what these women are up against and how very difficult leaving is. And—what is absolutely bottom line—we need to respect battered women more.

We can make progress here if we take in the truly formidable strengths that these women have. Despite the learned helplessness that can occur, "battered wives" are not simply the passive victims that writers like Walker (1979) speak of. As Kelly (1988) points out, they are also women who are surviving daily surveillance and torture. They are not simply submitting, even where submission is key and even though submission is expectable and blameless. They are also making active and critical decisions about how to cope and survive on a moment-to-moment basis. They are deciding to hide certain things. They are deciding to duck. They are deciding not to duck. They are each in her own way also resisting. They are actively and passively resisting violation, whether that resistance takes the form of numbing themselves so that they will not feel the pain, finding ways of avoiding the abuser's ire, or saying no.

The long-range objective with this client group is to help our brutalized sisters become more empowered and better able to prevent and counter brutalization. Short-run goals vary in accordance with the situation. Common short-run goals include helping the client (a) alter a brutalizing situation that she desires to alter, (b) exit from a brutalizing situation, (c) protect herself from the abuser, and (d) start a new and independent life. Subsidiary goals and means that typically figure in empowerment include (a) nurturing and validating, (b) addressing internalized oppression and myths, and (c) co-addressing the very real obstacles in the way. Although some women are fairly clear about the abuse and primarily need empathy, validation, and practical help, for most, work on internalized oppression is critical.

Like incest survivors, women who are subjected to extreme partner abuse often deny the abuse or understate it when describing it to us. Reasons for doing this include but are not limited to the following:

- Self-protection/terror (The partner has threatened to beat her senseless or to kill her if she tells.)

- Loyalty to the abusive partner
- Safeguarding one's situation (If she acknowledges to us the full extent of what is happening, she fears that she may have to act and sacrifice what she now has.)
- Concern that we will not understand what her partner or family means to her and will push her to leave
- Concern that we will not take in cultural differences and will push her to leave

We help by stating gently but clearly what we see, by clarifying, and by offering protection. And often we can make a threatening situation somewhat less threatening by assuring her that we are not going to tell anybody if she does not want us to and that we are not going to pressure her to leave.

Many of the women who do not understate nonetheless trivialize. Women trivialize for much the same reasons that they understate. They may be protecting their men. They may not want to take in the horror of what is happening. They may not want or be ready to act. Additionally, like all women, severely abused women trivialize because of their socialization as women. As women we have been taught to see men as more important. We have been taught that what we do and what happens to us is not all that significant and that it is up to us to bear up and make do. The demeaning and subordinating societal messages are intensified in the abusive relationship. The partner's words and actions daily beat insignificance into the abused woman. Although he may glorify her, he invariably impresses on her that she is nothing, that what is happening to her is nothing, and that she had better learn her place.

We counter by affirming her importance ourselves and by taking the abuse seriously. The message that we need to give and to keep giving is that the abuse is not trivial, that *it* matters a great deal, that *she* matters a great deal. If she is telling herself that her abuse is nothing, compared with what happens to other women, to other women of color, to other disabled women, point out that the abuse is significant and that the abuse hurts. More generally validate the enormous effect of psychological abuse. And spend time co-investigating not only the obvious abuse but also the seemingly less dramatic abuse that may be easy for her to dismiss. Where co-investigation goes well, her very conviction that she and the mistreatment are unimportant may be identified as an indicator and consequence of enormously disempowering abuse. Where abused women minimize the significance of partner abuse generally, as many survivors do, this minimization may itself be problematized. Such problematizing sheds light on and helps counter internalized misogyny. Where racism figures in the abuse and/or the trivialization, co-investigation of that racism is likewise in order.

Self-blame similarly impedes abused women. Women are told that men beat women because women provoke men. Abusive partners are correspondingly victim-blamers par excellence. She deserves what she gets, he tells her, because she is bad, because she is inadequate, because she acts "just like a woman." His continued reference to her so-called transgressions, to real and imagined actions, and to real and imagined characteristics magically absolves him of responsibility and shifts the blame onto her.

Again it is necessary to counter. We need to state clearly and unambiguously that we see her as neither bad nor inadequate. We need to assure her that nothing she has done could conceivably cause him to abuse her or could justify the abuse. She is likely to need this assurance repeatedly if she has been told the opposite repeatedly. If she cannot even entertain the idea that she is not blameworthy, exercises aimed at shifting perspective might be considered. A guided fantasy that I find helpful with some is this: Ask the client to imagine her best friend or her daughter being brutalized for doing something similar. Ask her what she thinks and how she feels. Then invite her to show the same understanding toward herself and to feel the same anger toward her abuser.

Co-investigation of the different purposes served by blaming self is also in order. And the victim-blaming should be revealed as the disempowering ploy that it is. In most cases it is a good idea to spend considerable time clarifying rights and practicing standing up for self.

Second order self-blame may also be a problem. *Second order self-blame* consists of blaming oneself precisely for blaming oneself and/or failing to act. We know that a client is caught up in second order self-blame when absolutely everything redounds to her discredit. A client in this situation sees herself as at fault or as inadequate because she has not left the abusive partner or because she has returned. She may think that she is wasting our time and may guilt herself over this. She may conclude that even if she did not deserve the abuse initially, she deserves it now for ignoring our suggestions. "It would be one thing if I never had any help," she might say, "but I have help and I still fuck up. I'm as stupid as he says, and I deserve what I'm getting." Here again we are called on to counter and to reassure. She needs to hear repeatedly that she is doing the very best that she can in an extremely difficult situation.

In some situations, intermittently putting all the blame on a third party or "the system" is an additional problem, as well as a meaningful coping strategy. The abusive partner may say and the woman agree that the battery is not his fault because he was a battered child himself. Alternatively or additionally, where the abusive partner comes from a disadvantaged group, the battery may be attributed solely to the oppressive system. The advantages of this construction are that it detracts from self-blame and that it targets external forces that are real and formidable. The disadvantage is that it absolves the abuser of all personal responsibility for his action and it further entraps the woman.

Sadly, woman's compassion, her political awareness, and her willingness to accept responsibility work against her here. She excuses her partner because he is in pain and because he was given a "bum deal." She deplores the injustice of what has happened to him. And she sees it as her responsibility to help, nurture, and stand by this highly distressed and oppressed human being. The caring and the understanding are just fine, but she pays through the nose for the exoneration and the overresponsibility. This dynamic can prevail whether the woman shares the oppression in question or not. If she herself shares the oppression, moreover, the bond that comes from shared oppression can further trap her, as can the reactions of the community. And if she does not share the oppression, immobilizing guilt may compound the problem.

If we are to help here, it is critical that we not be classist or racist ourselves. It is also critical that we not minimize the injury of her partner or the culpability of either society as a whole or of a third party. Our client needs to know that we appreciate the dreadful abuse that her partner once endured or now endures. At the same time, she needs to hear :

- His injury does not cause him to abuse her and does not justify the abuse.
- His injury is not her fault, and scapegoating her is not acceptable.
- She is hurt, and he is not helped by her sacrifice of self.
- Neither political awareness nor sensitivity means enduring abuse.
- Being understanding over abuse from male partners who are hurting is part of our oppression as women.

Our clarity over the injuries that her partner once sustained or currently sustains helps her take in these other truths.

DEEPER WORK

Where we suspect that a battered woman witnessed or was subjected to extreme abuse during childhood, deeper work should at least be considered. Deeper work involves a comprehensive co-investigation of childhood messages and models. It takes a lot of time and is not always possible—especially for counselors doing agency or crisis work. Even where time constraints are severe, however, it is good to include this dimension to some degree, for it gives the clients the handle they need to understand themselves and to make substantial, long-lasting changes.

Questions to keep in mind when doing work like this are:

- Did her father beat her mother? Did she see or hear this? If so, what did she see and hear? If not, how did she come to know?
- How did her father justify the abuse? How did her mother respond?
- What reasons did her mother give for staying?

- How did she respond to her father's actions and her mother's response?
- What type of abuse was she herself subjected to as a child? Severe sexual abuse? Battery? Anything else? To what degree and in what combinations? How did the perpetrator "explain" what was happening? How did she respond? Did anyone else know? If so, how did they respond?
- Did she witness anyone else being abused? If so, how did the abuser and the abused respond? How did she respond?
- What similarity and differences are there between her current abuse and her mother's abuse? Her current response and her mother's? Her partner's current response and her father's? Her current abuse and the past abuse? Her current responses and her childhood responses? The responses of anyone connected with the abuse that she witnessed and her current response?
- What light does this early history shed on her current world view and current dilemma?

Some rough guidelines to keep in mind here are:

1. Women whose mothers were abused are more likely to see partner abuse as normal.
2. Women whose mothers were abused tend to act like their mothers (the role model), while assessing their own abuse according to the guidelines (messages) about women provided by their fathers primarily and their mothers secondarily.
3. Women who witnessed any adult male figure abusing any adult female in childhood are more likely to accept abuse by a male as normal.
4. Women who have been abused as children more easily accept abuse from partners, especially abuse that is similar to the childhood abuse, for the abuse seems normal.
5. Women's reactions to their current abuse often mirror their reactions to abuse in childhood.

Abuse in adolescence and throughout childhood might similarly be explored and the connections made.

THE POLITICAL OVERVIEW

Without an overview of partner abuse and violence against women generally, an abused woman can easily be fooled by honeymoon periods. She may keep equating jealous rage with love. Thinking everything is now perfect, she can easily stay or return to an abusive partner. And she can continue pathologizing or blaming herself and making excuses for the man. Alternatively she may see through this particular man and free herself of him permanently, while seeing him as "an exception." This sets her up for bad relationships in the future and for ongoing abuse. She also needs to be able to connect the overview with her own personal experiences or else she will either not take it in or see her own experience as an exception.

Ways in which we can be of help here include the following:

- Familiarizing her with the different stages of the battery cycle and helping her identify the pattern in her own life
- Problematizing the notion of romantic love and gradually uncovering/helping her uncover its relationship to partner abuse generally and to her own battery specifically
- Problematizing beliefs around wifely obedience and duty
- Problematizing notions like "needing a man" and "children need their father" and looking at the impact of such beliefs
- Providing her with relevant literature that addresses these issues—personal accounts in particular
- Encouraging her to talk to other women who have been subjected to extreme partner abuse, especially women who are similarly situated culturally and otherwise
- Familiarizing her with and encouraging her to attend support groups for battered women or consciousness-raising groups
- Encouraging her to go to take-back-the-night marches or other relevant events

TELLING AND CREATING A SUPPORT NETWORK

Like the incest survivor, the battered woman has been ordered not to tell anyone about the abuse and has been threatened with dire consequences if she tells. Like the incest survivor, she is terrified to tell. Unlike most incest survivors, however, who are responding to the past, she has very pressing and current reasons to be terrified, for the batterer may be only too ready to punish her for this transgression. At the same time, she too needs to tell, however slowly and cautiously "telling" may have to be approached. Telling is breaking the silence injunction, joining with others, and standing up for self. Moreover, despite the immediate danger that attends any given act of telling, telling and joining-with are generally the direction in which greatest safety lies.

We help by encouraging her to talk with others without pushing, by taking seriously her perception of danger, and by helping her assess and address the risks involved. Practice sessions telling others, responding to their disbelief, and asking for what she needs are all in order. The latter is particularly important because women subjected to extreme partner abuse need a network of people who understand what is going on and who are prepared to give ongoing, as well as emergency, help. Developing detailed plans on how to handle the situation should the partner discover and begin to retaliate are also critical.

SUBSTANTIALLY CHANGING OR GETTING OUT
OF THE ABUSIVE SITUATION

It would be foolish to pretend that women subjected to severe partner abuse have either free or ideal options. At the same time, it is our responsibility to help women assess their situation and, where appropriate, reassess and rechoose.

Roughly speaking, seven broad options face abused women. (I am simplifying, of course.) And all of these may be formidably and disastrously eroded by poverty and/or the man's ability to "hunt her down" with impunity in patriarchal society. These "options," insofar as they are applicable, are:

1. Staying and hoping for the best
2. Staying but only if some change, however minor, occurs in the abusive behavior
3. Staying but only if substantial changes occur in the abusive behavior; that is, all overt abuse stops
4. Leaving and not coming back under any circumstances
5. Coming back even if no changes have occurred
6. Coming back if some slight changes can be detected
7. Coming back only if the abuser has made specific and very significant changes in his life

Stages that women who seek therapy commonly go through are shown in Figure 8.1.

We come across women at all stages. Generally, though, when we first start seeing abused partners, they are (a) staying and hoping for the best, (b) settling for minor changes, or (c) leaving/left but likely to return with either little or no changes. The choices in question are often made reflectively. At least as often, they are made somewhat prereflectively, with the woman not exactly choosing, not fully clear that she has choices, and not totally seeing or letting herself see precisely what she is "falling" into.

Our conscientization work helps the women see/choose more clearly and make better choices, as do the networking and the general support. Ongoing help with getting in touch with their own strengths is equally important, for women are unlikely to face what they do not believe they can face or to make choices that they see themselves as too weak to carry through. Clarifying and affirming the strengths that they daily exercise can be particularly helpful here, as can assertiveness work—something that battered women tend to need regardless

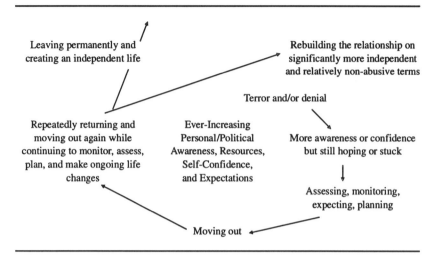

Figure 8.1. Common Stages in Exiting From or Altering an Abusive Partnership

of stage. None of this obviates the need to actually focus in on and flesh out choices and to problematize unsatisfactory and/or "unclear" choices.

Whatever changes they may make in the long run, for some time after seeking help, most women continue trying to improve the situation and to make the relationship work. Our job at this stage is to support the decision, while supplying honest feedback, continuing to nurture and consciousness-raise, and assuring that our client has viable escape plans. At this stage as well, many therapists ask clients to generate two lists: one entitled something like, "My Partner's Behaviors That I Like/Love," the other, "My Partner's Behaviors That I Dislike/Hate." The client is invited to focus on the different items in each list and to figure out how much she gets of each of the behaviors listed. By monitoring the items and noting the relationship between them, women can get a much stronger handle on what is happening.

Change lists can also be helpful at this stage, as well as at other stages. The most effective change lists include (a) specific behaviors that she wants her abusive partner to change, and (b) at least some means that she sees as necessary, *and* (c) time frames for each. We can err badly, of course, by pushing for concreteness and decisions that the woman does not want or is not ready to make.

At the time that she makes a list, the woman may or may not begin to raise some of the issues on her list with her partner and to negotiate, depending on safety, self-confidence, feasibility, and other issues. Whether she raises them or not, she is empowered by the very acts of formulating and monitoring and by the knowledge so generated.[4]

In some cases the monitoring stage is a good time as well to help women begin imagining and thinking through a life without their partners. The types of questions that we might encourage women to consider here are:

- Where would she live?
- What kind of job does she want in the long run? What are her current skills? What new skills does she need? How could she acquire these new skills? What kind of job might she get in the short run?
- Which relatives or friends might be relied on for what kind of help?
- What financial and other help does she need? What specific financial and other resources can she access and how?

Again we need to go slowly, for it can be frightening for a woman to imagine a life without her partner. It becomes less frightening, of course, the more she imagines and plans. And again cultural differences may make it important for us to back off or to modify.

Colleagues working with Southeast Asian and South Asian women report a different dynamic that often transpires at this stage and different help that is needed. Often women continue working on the relationship and staying not because they believe that there is much chance of improvement but because of community pressure. The abuse or the extent of the abuse may be denied by others, and the woman knows that she will "lose face" if she leaves. In such a situation, helping the woman accumulate evidence of the abuse and its extent can facilitate her being able to leave without losing face.

The next stage for some women is moving out permanently. The decision to move out is more readily made by women whose children are clearly being traumatized, and indeed the effect on the children is a motivation that we as counselors can use. For those who do end up moving out either permanently or on a long-term basis, ongoing support, reassurance, and practical help are generally needed.

Few women actually leave permanently the first time they exit. Any given exit is correspondingly unlikely to be permanent.

A woman who leaves tentatively and/or is thinking of returning is likely to need extra help clarifying the changes needed and assessing whatever changes her partner has made. If she appears to be exaggerating these changes or minimizing the problems again, it makes sense to raise our concerns and to attempt to co-explore what is happening. We might also point out that it is easy not to abuse someone who is not around and invite her to compare what is happening now to past honeymoon periods.

Where loneliness is a major problem, the client may need extra help connecting with others, as well as our assurance that the loneliness will lift over time. If she thinks that it would be unwise for her to return but is worried that she may do so out of loneliness or nostalgia, we might suggest reading over her "My Partner's Behaviors That I Hate" list whenever she feels tempted to go back.

Option Seven: Coming Back Only If the Abuser Has Made Specific and Very Significant Changes in His Life

Women who are demonstrably pursuing Option 7 also need help specifying the changes that must be made, assessing the progress, and remaining firm. Where it appears safe, a precondition that we might encourage the women to stipulate is that the abuser—not themselves—be the one deprived of the family home during the separation. Women and children who have done absolutely nothing wrong and are the victims of abuse are forever finding themselves bundling off, relatively homeless, and forced to make do. It is far preferable that the person who actually caused this problem be the one who leaves and "does without." Accepting this consequence can be the beginning of the abuser's accepting responsibility for his actions. Even where it seems safe, he may, of course, "blow" the arrangement by blaming the woman for the loss of his abode, by attempting to get back at her, and/or by turning up when he is not supposed to. Precautionary arrangements need to be made to protect the woman against such responses. Such actions generally mark the end of the arrangement and make it necessary for the woman to leave. Additionally they serve as feedback and may themselves be taken as a significant negative indicator of progress and reliability.

Sometimes women stipulate the partner's seeking help as a condition of getting back together. Although nothing about "help" is magical and a great many women are better off not getting back together under any circumstances, this is a condition that we can reasonably encourage.

Such help is sometimes provided by the woman's own counselor, for many counselors feel okay about seeing both partners as long as they are not living together. Seeing them in joint sessions is nonetheless unwise. It puts the woman in jeopardy and can silence her. In situations like this, moreover, abusers can readily make a mockery out of therapy. Men whose partners have left them often use joint sessions as a way of gaining access to their partners. Even seeing them separately is problematic. Besides the man's motivation being perhaps simply to get his woman back, we are so blatantly a route to the woman that the situation encourages dishonesty. Additionally we have special knowledge about the woman that her partner may want. And seeing us can be a vicarious way of seeing the partner. Sadly, moreover, as women, what we say to a male abuser about battery and misogyny holds far less weight than what a man says.

Referral to male counselors or to male-led groups is generally the best course of action. Again these individuals and groups should not be ones involving joint work.

Points to keep in mind when making such referrals, working with male abusers, or advising women in relation to them are:

- Individuals or groups whose approach includes antisexist education and ongoing confrontation are preferable. In the absence of antisexist education and strong ongoing confrontation, abusers almost invariably lapse back into excuses and justifications.
- The work is insufficient if it does not include helping the abuser become aware of and handle his anger differently.
- The work needs to involve helping him make the connection between his other feelings of helplessness in situations in which he is "one down" and how his partner feels when he comes in shouting and threatening.
- Although it is not generally possible to go as far as we might like here, wherever applicable it is important that some attempt be made to help the abuser begin problematizing romantic love and recognizing its relationship to violence against women—his own in particular.
- An exploration of role models is in order. Any attempt to use these to trivialize or excuse self correspondingly should be confronted.
- Although we need to accept this if it occurs, it is premature for a woman to move back in with her partner or to accept him back into the home a few sessions into therapy.
- Groups co-run by ex-abusers can be extremely effective.
- It is important that the program include consultation with the woman and feedback on how the partner appears to be doing. Where this is not a fundamental feature, the worker may be operating with inaccurate information, and the woman herself has little to go on and comparatively little reason to trust.
- Although a good counselor who is satisfied with the abusive partner's work is promising, it is no guarantee that extreme partner abuse will not resume.
- Where cohabitation resumes, work with the abuser should continue; periodic check-ins with the abused partner become correspondingly far more critical.
- Ideally the program or person chosen should be one that does rigorous follow-up.
- Twelve-week programs for batterers are grossly inadequate.

THE LEGAL ROUTE

Again, as the law is essentially patriarchal, going the legal route can be dicey. Although the law does not officially condone beating, misogynous attitudes, sloppy practices, and lack of enforcement continue to make this route precarious. Police who are called in at the time of or just after a beating often laugh off or otherwise trivialize what is happening. Some improvement has occurred of late, but police historically have been reluctant to lay charges. Their very use of the term *domestic violence* suggests that this is tame violence—violence that is not to be taken very seriously. Even when the police officers perceive danger and remove the abusive partner for the night, they tend to do no immediate follow-up. Many a man returns the next day to thrash his partner for the night of incarceration. Judges pose a still greater problem, for they wield incredible power and it is far harder to hold them to account. Judges commonly display rank sexism. They may find with the man, with little reason to do so. They often dole out token reprimands, accompanying these with such misogynous statements as, "Women! You can't live with them, and you can't live without them!" Where officers charge an abusive partner at the woman's behest and the woman changes her mind, her refusal to testify against her partner is itself sometimes treated as an offense. Although restraining orders are often granted, the order itself is seldom enforced with any rigor.[5]

These problems notwithstanding, going the legal route is a way of publicly standing up for self. Pressure from the feminist community moreover has led to somewhat better education of police officers on the issue of partner abuse. Where appropriate, we can legitimately encourage women to consider the legal route as long as we are clear about the very real limitations.

Points to keep in mind when trying to help women who are considering or actually pursuing a legal route include the following:

- Women need to be aware of their rights, of legal process, and of other official procedures. Battered and traumatized women in particular need readable copies of rights and process literature that they can consult as needed.
- Role plays involving standing up for these rights can be helpful.
- Women need to be aware of the common shortcomings of the legal system. They may need help making decisions in light of these shortcomings and figuring out how to handle different unfavorable responses or outcomes.
- In the long run, spending months or years in jail may make an abuser angrier, vengeful, and more abusive. Where reasonably safe and feasible, accordingly, other routes should be considered.
- Police may offer to do mediation work themselves, but it is usually unwise for women to accept this as a solution. Police receive insufficient education in mediation generally and partner mediation in particular. They do not understand the deep psychological or interactive dynamics involved and come to premature resolution. They do not understand misogyny or the nature of romantic love. And they mediate in the precarious situation of cohabitation. An agreement today is, tragically, easily followed by a broken limb tomorrow.
- Where women are considering going to court, an important resource for us to supply is a list of lawyers who are feminist, sensitive, knowledgeable in the area, and who accept legal aid.

- Women need a friendly face in the courtroom, support before going, and support after returning.
- Prior to any court case, it is helpful if the woman is shown the actual courtroom and is given a run-down of what is going to happen.

POLITICAL WORK

Clearly, major social, educational, and legal changes have to occur if we are to decrease the amount and degree of partner abuse and truly serve the women who are abused. Changes that all of us as women might lobby for, demonstrate for, do deputations on, and otherwise work toward include the following:

- The standard inclusion of violence against women and partner abuse in school curricula
- Adequate public funding for grass roots organizing and support groups in the area
- Sufficient shelters so that any woman and her children needing refuge can gain immediate access
- Far more second-stage housing, with such housing accommodating the needs of children
- Sufficient funding to allow battered women and their children to live comfortably while the women pursue the education that they need to get meaningful and reasonably paid work
- Sufficient funding for individual counseling and for battered women groups
- All current and future shelters and housing being accessible to and catering to women with various disabilities
- The creation and funding of feminist mediation services mandated to address partner abuse
- Enforcement of restraining orders
- A mandate that police remove abusers for an extended period where there is evidence of extreme "wife abuse" and do rigorous follow-up
- Mandatory feminist education on partner abuse for all legal officials—from police to supreme court judges

SUGGESTED READINGS

Browne, A. (1987). *When battered women kill.* New York: Free Press.
Del, M. (1981). *Battered wives.* San Francisco: Volcano.
Kelly, L. (1988). *Surviving sexual violence.* Minneapolis: University of Minnesota Press.

Nicarthy, G., Merriam, K., & Coffman, S. (1984). *Talking it out: A guide to groups for abused women.* Seattle: Seal Press.

Rafiz, F. (Ed.). (1991). *Wife assault: South Asian perspectives.* Toronto: Diva.

Sinclair, D. (1985). *Understanding wife assault: A training manual for counsellors and advocates.* Toronto: Publications Ontario.

Walker, L. (1979). *The battered woman.* New York: Harper & Row.

White, E. (1985). *Chain chain change: For Black women dealing with physical and emotional abuse.* Seattle: Seal Press.

Zambrano, M. (1985). *For the Latina in an abusive relationship.* Seattle: Seal Press.

NOTES

1. For this and other relevant figures, see Sinclair (1985).

2. For research that indicates that women typically understate, not overstate, battery that they have undergone even where overstatement is clearly in their interests, see Browne (1987), p. 15ff.

3. Browne's (1987) research also identifies the man's "beginning to hurt the children" as an indicator. I have left this indicator out because it is not a sign of life-threatening danger to the woman, albeit it does increase the possibility of her killing him.

4. Nicarthy and Davidson (1989) is a particularly good resource for the types of lists that might be generated.

5. For more detailed discussions of these and other problems, see Browne (1987).

9

Working With Women Subjected To . . .

EXTREME ABUSE BY FEMALE PARTNER

For years lesbian battery was seen as nonexistent or necessarily tame by the women's community—feminist counselors included. The rationale was that women are loving beings who could not conceivably violate or at least not badly. This idealization/trivialization limited the help available to battered lesbians and resulted in misguided work. Change has begun as a result of considerable consciousness-raising by survivors.[1] Misconceptions, however, have not disappeared. What further complicates the problem is that some workers are responding to the new information with a "just-like-them" analysis. The assumption is that the lesbian context is irrelevant and that we need simply apply the principles used with heterosexual survivors. This assumption is misguided. Good work with battered lesbians is predicated on an understanding of both the similarities and the differences.

Like their heterosexual counterparts, lesbians who are subjected to extreme partner abuse experience a combination of clear sexual abuse, physical abuse that is not overtly sexual, and severe emotional or psychological abuse. Like their heterosexual counterparts, they are generally hurt more by the psychological abuse. Lesbian survivors similarly are kicked, burned, punched, and may be severely injured physically. Lesbian survivors are humiliated; are told they are ugly, incompetent, and undesirable; and may even be subjected to misogynous tirades. Lesbian survivors too may be accused of infidelity at every turn. They may be picked on, ordered about, and blamed for every little thing. Like their heterosexual counterparts, many lesbian survivors deeply love their abusers and so desperately want to believe that things will work out that they keep staying and hoping, despite ever-increasing violence. The violence cycle itself is similar to the one examined in the last chapter. Lesbian survivors similarly understate, deny, trivialize, blame themselves, and blame the system. Lesbian survivors similarly become traumatized, get confused, and find themselves isolated and trapped. And lesbian survivors too both submit and resist on a minute-by-minute basis.

Lesbophobia generally figures in the extra difficulties that the lesbian couple faces and is a contributing factor. Often the battering partner is profoundly uneasy with lesbian relating. She copes with the self-blame by blaming the partner. Additionally/alternatively she may be having an enormously difficult time with societal pressure and condemnation and may be blaming her partner for furthering an existence that makes her a despised outsider.

Lesbian battery may also bring out and accentuate the battered woman's internalized lesbophobia. The likelihood of such a response occurring increases if the woman is new to lesbian relationships and the batterer is her first lesbian partner. This abused woman may be terrified that she is involved in something unnatural. She sees the battery as implicit and is horrified at the thought that such abuse will now be her lot in life. She is poised between fleeing her lesbian identity and resigning herself to inevitable partner abuse.

Although abuse can be every bit as relentless as abuse by a male partner, commonly it is not. The special affinity that women feel toward women and the love and compassion that is a part of women's culture can restrain and temper abuse.

Although again this is far from invariable, lesbians generally are more assertive, less bound by women's roles, and less affected by the romantic love tradition than heterosexual women. Consequently they are likely to extricate themselves more quickly from a highly abusive partnership.

Additionally, for the most part, lesbian partners are closer in size, weight, and strength than heterosexual partners. Partly because of the physical similarity, partly because of greater equality as women, and partly because of greater assertiveness, lesbian partners who are subjected to extreme partner abuse are more likely to defend themselves actively and physically. This is a real asset, for they are clearly standing up for themselves. The down side is that the self-defense itself is often misinterpreted and leads to an overall misconstruction of the abusive situation. The abused survivor looks at her abusive partner and sees bruises on her. She thinks: "When Mary hit me the third time, I pushed her away; and now she is bruised. I used more force than I had to. How can I call her THE ABUSER! I'm an abuser too."

Abusive partners often define the situation similarly, and many go farther, seeing themselves as the victim and the woman who is defending herself as the abuser. Social service workers similarly frequently misunderstand such situations and define them as co-battery. The local women's community and lesbian community may define it as co-battery likewise or even accept the abuser's assessment that she is the "real victim."[2]

Whether the survivor physically defends herself or not, she may find that it is her partner—not she—who is supported by the community. The community may disbelieve her and/or turn its back on her. Where the abuser has an oppression that the abused does not, the community may oversimplify and see unrecognized privilege as the crux of the matter. If an abused lesbian has left her abusive partner or has sought legal or other protection, the community may construe this as betrayal or a lack of caring.

Where the women's and lesbian communities support the battered lesbian, she is still likely to find the communities less accessible to her. She has almost no place where she can go and feel "okay." Going to events in the women's and lesbian communities means risking bumping into her abusive partner or ex-partner. Not going means confinement to mainstream lesbophobic society.

Societal lesbophobia and heterosexism further deter abused lesbians from telling and from seeking protection. The knowledge of the lesbophobia is a weapon in the hands of an abusive partner. Often, where the abused partner is either fully or partly in the closet, the abuser has kept her "under thumb" with the threat: "You say anything about my hitting you to anyone, and I'll tell your family and your boss that you are a lesbian."

Lesbophobia additionally makes legal routes far more precarious. Police and court may find the whole matter laughable, may even be delighted that a "pervert" is getting what she deserves.

Understandably few lesbians welcome the publicity that a court battle over lesbian battery would bring.

Implications for Counseling

As when counseling heterosexuals, work with lesbians subjected to extreme partner abuse involves:

- Understanding and patience
- Believing and validating
- Taking the abuse and the danger enormously seriously
- Challenging understatement, trivialization, denial, self-blame, and the transfer of all blame onto a third party or to "society"

- Challenging romanticism and rescuing
- Co-investigating the role of oppression and internalized oppression
- Clarifying the cycle of violence
- Helping the client recognize seeming improvement as the return of the honeymoon period
- Helping the client imagine a life without her partner
- Helping the client make emergency and long-term exit plans
- Helping with negotiating and holding firm
- Helping with telling, reaching out, and creating a support network
- Helping to access resources
- Not counseling the battered and batterer together

Both our romanticization and our trivialization of lesbian relationships can easily lead us to ignore the last requirement. Doing so profoundly jeopardizes the well-being of battered clients. What makes the issue more complicated is that it is easy for us to err by accident if running groups for lesbian survivors of partner abuse. According to self-report, many battered lesbians have come to such groups only to find the women who have abused them also attending. No one else knows that anything is wrong, and the group continues, with the battered woman frightened, poorly served, and in jeopardy. More care in screening is clearly necessary. If a potential participant mentions a word like *co-battery,* it is important to find out more, while proceeding as sensitively as possible. She may be either batterer or victim in the relationship in question. She may correspondingly have been in other relationships where her role differed. Having a general rule that no women who are or have been partners can be in the same group is a good idea, for the presence of partners and ex-partners can interfere with the process at the best of times. I advise clarifying this rule at the original interview. Once a list of tentative participants has been created, some kind of check for current and past partners is also in order.

Although differences are relative and may not always apply, generally speaking we can proceed somewhat more quickly with lesbians subjected to extreme partner abuse than with their heterosexual counterparts. Issues like women's roles are seldom as critical. Despite the fact that they are frequently in comparatively less danger, extra attention to safety issues may be appropriate simply because society attends less to the safety of lesbians.

The battered lesbian who is now questioning the validity of lesbian relationships needs our empathy, our gentleness, and our reassurance. She needs to hear that lesbian relating is perfectly natural and that partner abuse is not her lot as a lesbian.

Examples of questions that can be of help with women who see themselves as "co-batterers" are:

- What exactly does *co-battery* mean?
- How does it differ from *blaming the victim?*
- When other people defend themselves, is that co-battery too?
- Who told her this is co-battery?
- Whose interest does it serve if she defines the situation this way?

The message we want to impart is that self-protection is not co-battery, whether she strikes back at the time of the battery or at some other time. And although occasionally using more force than is necessary to defend herself may be something she wishes to avoid, it hardly qualifies as abuse.

Battered lesbians often need considerable help locating and accessing lesbian-positive services and resources. In light of the oppressive attitudes that they may end up encountering, more direct advocacy may also be necessary.

Lesbians who are guilted by members of their own community may also profit from role plays. Survivors who have left their abusive partners are correspondingly likely to need extra help figuring out what to do when they encounter those ex-partners and/or their friends at women's and other events.

Lesbian S/M

As lesbians tend to be more open about their s/m practices than heterosexual women, sooner or later counselors who work with lesbians are bound to encounter a self-identified s/m participant. *Where the s/m is consensual, as lesbian s/m generally is, it is not partner abuse.* S/M constitutes partner abuse where and only where it is not consensual or not fully consensual.

Some typical abuse scenarios are:

- One woman is "into" s/m, the other is not. The latter is coaxed into participating. She may be accused of being a wimp for preferring "vanilla sex" and may be told that she has to stick with the s/m because s/m is "where it's at."
- A partner may have wanted to try s/m initially, found she disliked it, but stuck with it because of pressure.
- One of the partners may like only light s/m but may accept more and more painful s/m at the other's behest.

What is tricky about such situations is that they often look consensual to everyone, while being only quasi-consensual or not consensual at all. Some women who thought that they were consenting at the time realized later that their objections were systematically ignored or ridiculed and that they were abused.

What is happening here is decidedly not the same as the overt and all-encompassing battery discussed earlier. Some of what is occurring in fact may be attributed to error on both people's parts and to ambivalence, as well as to the slippery slope phenomenon. This notwithstanding, some degree of partner abuse is clearly involved, and in some cases that abuse is severe.

Where we suspect that what is happening is not consensual or not fully consensual, it is important to raise our concerns, to co-explore, and as appropriate, to help our client take action. Sensitivity to the complexities of s/m is critical or else we are likely to misstep and alienate our client in the process.

ABUSE BY PIMPS

In this book the term *pimp* is being used in the classical, not the legal, sense to refer to a person who professionally "turns girls out" and whose income is derived from a number of prostitutes. Severe abuse is intrinsic to the prostitute-pimp relationship as defined. Abuse by pimps has much in common with wife abuse. The prostitute is "owned" by the pimp, and the pimp in turn is her protector. As long as he is around, no other pimp interferes with her. Many a prostitute has a deep romantic attachment to her pimp. As far as she is concerned, this is her man—her partner. A pimp may so "work" the prostitute that she deeply loves him and believes that he loves her.

Like the battering husband, this man goes between romance and brutality. At one moment he is romancing her. At another he is either ignoring her, flaunting his relationships with his other "girls," beating her up, raping her, humiliating her, or threatening her.

The pimp-controlled prostitute, like the battered wife, is subjected to enormous control. She is forever being watched. The pimp must know where she is at all times. She is allowed only the friends that he chooses. Just as the housewife must do her housework immaculately and remember every little thing that her partner wants, the prostitute must do what she is told, make her quota, and perform impeccably, or else she is punished. Like the battered wife, she has almost no money. And she is far more dependent on her "man" than she appears.

Like the battered wife, as well, the prostitute who comes to realize that there is no hope has no easy way out. She has no funds and no place to go. If she leaves, she is likely to be found, dragged back, raped, and beaten mercilessly.

For our purposes the critical differences are although the prostitute may think of this man as her partner, he has no such illusions. She is up against a master con pure and simple. He picked her up and dazzled her for the purposes of his trade. Unlike the partner, he does not even think that he loves her. His game is illusion, control, and profit. He is as unpredictable as possible because he knows that unpredictability will keep his "girls" off-balance—more controllable. By way of example, he may show up dressed shabbily and complaining of how little money he has. The next time she sees him, he is in expensive attire, is in a Rolls Royce, and is flashing hundred dollar bills wherever he goes. He works hard at loosening her sense of reality. In the word of illusion that he creates, everything becomes what it is not. He may even turn up poorly dressed and drop the hint that only someone remarkably rich and powerful can afford to look this way. After he beats her, he generally makes love to her. The message sinks in: Violence means love.

Escape can be harder for the prostitute than for the battered wife. The pimp has a vast network of brother pimps and "helpers" who will be on the lookout for her if she disappears and who will beat her and drag her back. She cannot work the street without them finding her, and she probably has no other means of support. Shelters for battered women are correspondingly only temporary refuges and are not ones where she is all that likely to be understood. Besides, pimps tend to know all the shelters in the city.

Implications for Counseling

Much of the work described in Chapter 8 applies to women subjected to pimp abuse. Patience and understanding are of the essence. Here too we need to challenge trivialization, understatement, self-blame, and the allocation of all blame to the system. Here too we need to problematize the "love," highlight external and internalized misogyny, and help the women plan escape routes and access resources.

Many counselors who work in this area not only pressure prostitutes to leave the pimps but pressure them to leave prostitution itself. Applying such pressure is insensitive and indeed counterproductive. It is important to remember that these women too are attached and have less than ideal options. Many prostitutes, moreover, have no desire to leave prostitution and/or are not ready or able to leave. Additionally our knowledge that prostitution can be more empowering than traditional heterosexual relationships should give us pause.

In light of the confusion that the pimp's unpredictably fosters, we need to work harder to establish focus. We need to help create reliable reference points.

To some extent the cycle of violence can be used as a focus and as a point of reference; we can and should use it this way. It is, however, nowhere near as helpful here as it is when we are working with battered wives, for the pimp himself is deliberately unpredictable and deliberately breaks patterns.

Highlighting the sexism, while equally important, is more problematic. If we are not careful, our reference to sexism may simply reinforce the client's identification with the pimp—especially where the pimp is highly skilled. While being frighteningly misogynous and treating/referring to their "girls" like pieces of meat, some highly skilled pimps actually address sexism. They co-opt feminist analysis, using it as a means to further subordinate. As a man of color or as a man from the working class, a pimp may occasionally assure his "girl" that he is oppressed in similar ways. He "understands" what she goes through as a female. They are bonded by oppression, and he is "committed to their joint liberation."

Progress ultimately depends on exposing the pimp game itself. We cannot do so quickly, of course, for we are dealing with attachment, confusion, and extreme danger. By proceeding slowly, by caring, and by being constant, we can ourselves become a reliable point of reference. We can become a touchstone—a locus of clarity. The pimp's effectiveness thereby is weakened. Further exposure and weakening involves uncovering and co-investigating the illusion, the unpredictability, and the reality reversals themselves.

No matter how clear the woman may be, actual escape from the pimp presents many problems. This is another situation where the law can be of service. Removing their pimps from circulation by "signing on the pimp" and then getting out of the city and out of prostitution is one of these clients' most viable options and certainly one that it is important for us to explore with them. Prostitutes who sign on their pimp are in imminent danger, and so immediate and thorough escape plans are vital.

Prostitutes leaving their pimps more generally are in enormous danger. If they decide to stay in prostitution, prostituting in the same downtown core is unwise, and they are best advised to shift their locus of operations. A change in place of residence is absolutely necessary. Equally vital is cautioning them to let as few people as possible know where they now are. The pimp brotherhood is only too willing to beat up sister prostitutes and friends to get the information needed.

During escape, a shelter can be of help as a short-term solution, albeit it is far from ideal. As noted earlier, prostitutes are often not understood in shelters. Shelter staff who are radical and aware can help here by raising awareness among their less radical colleagues and by pushing for staff development in this area.

A longer term and safer answer is the safe houses for battered women. Openness, however, is an issue. Besides there being too few such houses in the first place, staff at most safe houses do not recognize prostitutes as "battered women." Correspondingly they either do not accept prostitutes at all or take in only prostitutes committed to leaving prostitution. When dealing with a specific client in crisis, we have to go for what we can, approach those who are most open, and where feasible, try to talk people into making an exception. In the long run it is our responsibility to educate colleagues and policymakers so that the definitions of *battered women* and *violence against women* are extended and prostitutes start gaining equal access to these badly needed resources.

We might also lobby/work for the creation of safe houses specifically serving prostitutes and run by ex-prostitutes. The homes could help those who want to leave prostitution find jobs and make the transition, while giving safe haven to both those who want to leave and those who want to stay. They might additionally post "bad trick" lists and descriptions of police to be wary of, thereby better enabling the women to protect themselves against some of the other systemic male violence that comes their way.

STRANGER RAPE AND DATE RAPE

As with survivors of childhood sexual assault, when working with women recently subjected to extreme sexual abuse or women who have not yet dealt with adult sexual abuse, we need to proceed slowly and gently. If the woman is in a panic and is worried that she is losing her mind—an extremely common situation—it is important to let her know that she is in shock and that shock is normal and temporary. By explaining what is happening when she has flashbacks, correspondingly, we can help her recover some sense of self and weather the craziness of her inner life.

If she begins having flashbacks of childhood and the flashbacks connote sex or violence, a strong possibility exists that she was abused as a child and that traumatic childhood memories are being triggered by the adult abuse. Checks and tentative suggestions about what may be happening are in order here. Tread carefully, though; the client is already overwhelmed and at risk of severe flooding.

The survivor who went through childhood and adulthood relatively unscathed may be particularly vulnerable. Her self-image precluded violation. Rape, battery, and humiliation are what happen to "other women." Suddenly she is violated. In one evening, one hour, a few minutes, her world disappeared. A similar if less threatening disparity exists with women who had difficult lives but knew that they were strong and figured that they could always protect themselves. In each case the woman's sense of herself as somehow different and/or as inviolable has been abruptly torn asunder. She may have put off dealing with the abuse for years because she does not want the terrible knowledge or the new identity. She may keep trying to piece her old image back together. She can never totally do so, however, because she knows she is not the same. Moreover, she has found out that the world really can "womanize" her, really can intrude on her. *To varying degrees, this in fact is the plight of almost all women who are subjected to extreme sexual abuse for the first time.* Women who were previously raped, correspondingly, tend to reexperience the original shock and loss on top of the current shock and loss and so are dealing with trauma on trauma. We need to empathize with the horror of the invasion, the injustice, the shock. And we need to help our sisters build on firm feminist foundations.

Abused women who do not register terror and who appear to be going about "life as usual" may be seen as in denial. They are denying the enormous impact that this experience has had on them. They are fleeing the terror and the humiliation. Our role here is:

- Reach in, affirm, and empathize with the terror and humiliation that the woman may not be in touch with and is not expressing.
- Define what is happening as flight.
- Empathize with and validate the desire to flee.
- Gently let her know that, as much as we might wish things were different, these feelings are not going to disappear and have to be faced.
- Invite her to get back in touch with self.
- Invite her to feel and to express.

The movement that we want to facilitate is into fear, through the fear, and into anger, analysis, connection, and action. We help with the feelings initially by inviting feelings, by making space for them, and by empathizing personally and politically. Use of the present tense when describing trauma can be very effective.

If the client appears to be stuck in terror, it is usually a sign that deeper trauma is involved. More support and more co-investigation are called for, as well as greater help nurturing self. Prohibitions against anger might correspondingly be co-explored and countered. We can also use our own anger to help fuel our client's anger. Where anger appears to be blocking out the terror, as sometimes happens, it is important to realize that this is occurring and to reach for the fear.

Many women who were raped by strangers see themselves as at fault for having been out alone at night or for having dressed in a certain way. We can help by pointing out the following:

1. We have a right to be out alone at night and to dress as we please without being raped.
2. Women who do not go out alone at night and who dress conservatively also get raped.

Women subjected to date rape—especially women who invited the man back to their place—frequently make statements like: "I should never have invited him back. I was obviously asking for it. It's not like I didn't want anything." Clear distinctions need to be made between wanting company and wanting rape and between interest in romance, in sex, or in adventure and wanting to be raped. And the blame needs to be shifted back to the perpetrator.

Survivors also blame themselves for their inability to protect themselves. Depending on the specifics, we might clarify that (a) not one of us is invincible and (b) it is common to become immobilized during terror and, although this may well be something she wants to work on, it is hardly blameworthy.

At the same time, it is important to help them identify the ways in which they did resist, whether that resistance took the form of counterattack, flight, register of disapproval, submission, or numbing. Appreciating their resistance at once helps survivors feel better about themselves and gets them in touch with their power. It also paves the way for expanding their resistance repertoire.

Where a woman feels bad about not "snapping out of it," we can help by reminding her that it is a slow process and by affirming her right and her need to proceed at her own pace. Affirming her right to abstain from sex is vital and can be the beginning of her reclaiming her body.

Generally women who have been raped need some help phasing in those aspects of their life that they want to retain. Where women appear to be avoiding life, extra encouragement and support are in order. Where women proceed as if they have to be superwoman, co-investigating this demand and helping them slow down are usually wise.

Operating out of and making explicit some version of the violence against woman continuum is a good idea. It is critical that women not view their abuse as exceptional but rather see it as an extension of a misogynous norm. Where the survivors are of color, we might also highlight societal racism and co-investigate the special oppression borne of racism and sexism.

Like survivors of severe childhood sexual abuse, survivors of severe adult sexual abuse need to "tell." Role plays can be very useful, especially where partners, family, friends, or others blame the woman for the abuse.

Linking women up with the types of resources described in Chapter 7 is important. Local rape crisis centers tend to be especially helpful.

SEXUAL VIOLATION BY THERAPISTS

Sexual violation by therapists is a frighteningly common phenomenon that has only begun to be taken seriously over the last two decades and is still minimized. American research by Pope, Keith-Spiegel, and Tabachnick (1986) suggests that 9.7% of male therapists and 2.5% of female therapists (psychologists) have had sexual contact with clients.[3] These findings are similar to findings by two previous American psychologist surveys—Holyroyd and Brodsky (1977), and Pope, Levenson, and Schover (1979). The Holyroyd and

Brodsky research indicated additionally that male therapists who have sexual contact with any client are likely to have contact with *many* clients.[4]

This research at once identifies a large problem and obscures how large that problem is. The figures are based on self-report. People who abuse their power, however, frequently deny or understate the abuse. Our understanding of the problem that we are up against and our estimation of its extent increase dramatically, moreover, if we approach this sexual abuse as we do all other sexual abuse and include covert as well as overt.

Bouhoutsos (1989) suggested that two out of every three therapists will eventually encounter a client who reports "sexual involvement" with a previous therapist. This figure similarly points to a major concern for us, while obscuring the extent. Therapist sexual abuse is broader than "sexual involvement." A therapist may sexually abuse a client without the client being "sexually involved." Additionally, as we know from our work with childhood sexual abuse, often abused clients do not identify what happened as abuse, especially where abuse is covert. And clients are unlikely to raise the issue of abuse with us at all if we are not receptive and aware.

The problem is even greater for us feminist counselors. We exclusively or primarily see women clients. As many more female than male clients are violated by therapists, there is reason to suspect that considerably more of our clients have been so violated.

On the basis of a definition of sexual abuse that includes the entire continuum, my experience suggests that each of us *frequently* encounters clients who have been sexually intruded on by former therapists. If someone has worked for 2 years or more as a counselor and has not met up with such abuse, chances are she has simply failed to recognize it. This is no reason to feel guilty. Indeed it is very understandable, for our education has hardly prepared us to recognize or deal with the problem. It is, however, a reason to increase our awareness and to begin sensitizing ourselves to indicators and possible indicators.

When a client tells us about any sexual involvement with or sexualizing by a former therapist, we can generally conclude that the woman was sexually abused by the therapist in question. In light of the power differential and the dependency involved, significantly, all sexual relating between therapist and client and all "sexualizing" constitute abuse. Correspondingly, just as incest survivors almost never invent abuse where none exits, clients rarely invent tales of therapist abuse.[5] In the absence of such statements, subtler and more allusive indicators can help us.

The same general signs that alert us to the possibility of childhood sexual abuse alert us to the possibility of abuse by a therapist. (See Chapter 7 for details.) The following characteristics of clients are indicators that more specifically raise the question of therapist abuse:

- Has a specific distrust of therapists
- Maintains frequent contact with her ex-therapist
- Appears to be in love with an ex-therapist
- Is enormously ambivalent about an ex-therapist
- Keeps focusing on an ex-therapist
- Refers to letters or gifts received from that therapist
- Is very reluctant or afraid to talk of her ex-therapist
- Alludes to discomfort with the amount of touching involved in previous therapy
- Is enormously confused about the nature of therapy and what is and is not appropriate, even though she has seen therapists before
- Makes reference to an ex-therapist talking a lot about him- or herself
- Repeatedly expresses concern about that therapist's current or past problems
- States that a previous therapist "showed" her how to be a better partner
- Comments about her ex-therapist liking or disliking certain clothes she wears, lipstick she uses, and so forth
- Suggests that a previous therapist strongly encouraged her to be dependent and was angered by her independence
- Makes reference to outings that she and her therapist went on or work that she did for him or her

Caution is needed in interpreting these indicators. A number of them have valid alternative explanations. A conscientious therapist, for example, may well go on an outing with a withdrawn client. Although the nurturing of dependency is inherently abusive, a therapist may nurture dependency without *sexual* abuse being involved. Clients may romanticize and keep focusing on therapists who did not abuse them. Some errors, correspondingly, are comparatively mild and are more likely to be committed by caring therapists who would never deliberately abuse anyone. Being less aloof and more caring than male therapists, a maternal female therapist, for example, may more readily err innocently by hugging a weeping client who is uneasy about touch. Being ultrasuspicious of womanly caring while trusting male aloofness does not make a great deal of sense. Male-like aloofness after all is not itself desirable, and the "aloof" male therapist is far more likely to blatantly molest the client than is the female therapist who is moved to hug her. This need for caution notwithstanding, where the client combines a number of general body trauma indicators with a number of indicators specific to therapy abuse, the probability is that the client was sexually abused in some way by a previous therapist. The likelihood of severe therapy abuse and severe harm correspondingly increases if the client is highly depressed or suicidal. In light of the reality of sexism and the far higher frequency of therapy abuse by male therapists, correspondingly, where a few other indicators of sexual abuse exist, the very fact that the therapist is male is an additional indicator.

Concern over sexual abuse by therapists should be incorporated into our initial interview. In Chapter 3 I suggested that we automatically ask clients what they liked and disliked about past therapists. By attending carefully to the answers, we can get preliminary information about possible therapist abuse, including sexual abuse. Where the answers to these questions and/or other signs suggest therapist abuse, further inquiry is in order.

As with childhood sexual abuse, where the client herself says that a therapist abused her sexually, she needs repeated reassurance that we believe her. She may barely believe it herself and so worry that no one else will. Understandably the very fact that we are therapists exacerbates the worry and raises concerns about our loyalty. Everyone knows that professionals tend to believe colleagues and to stick together regardless. We help by pointedly assuring her that we have no illusions about therapists and that our overriding obligation is to her. By commenting in the initial interview about our own ambiguity about therapy, we can at once invite such sharing and help allay these fears.

As with childhood sexual abuse, direct questions about potential sexual abuse are in order where we have strong suspicions. Where some abuse has occurred, we correspondingly need to inquire into the nature of that abuse.

We can avoid simplistic thinking about therapist sexual abuse by thinking of it in terms of a continuum. One way of conceptualizing such a continuum is shown in Figure 9.1.

Generally the farther to the right on the continuum, the greater the damage. Generally overt abuse (Points 3-6) is considerably more traumatizing than covert abuse (Points 1-3). This notwithstanding, prolonged use of psychodrama with sexual assault victims (Point 2) in which someone role-playing the perpetrator attacks or piles on the client can be every bit as traumatizing as abuse in the 3-5 range.

Point 6 abuse occurs most often in coercive institutions in which the client is under lock and key, and it is more likely to happen to very young adults. It is part and parcel of a general assault on being and is comparable to the worst abuses in childhood.

Some important gender distinctions are:

- Where the therapist is male, covert abuse at Point 3 is particularly likely to reinforce sexual roles and male-identification.
- Where the therapist is female and the client does not identify as lesbian, it can be enormously confusing and result in an identity crisis.
- Where a woman therapist enters into sexual relations with a client, this is generally the only client that she has ever done so with, and love is honestly involved.

1	2	3	4	5	6
Occasional unwanted hugs or pats; use of terms of endearment; occasional comments on sexual attractiveness	Frequent use of terms of endearment; asking for more and more details of sexual abuse where such details are not necessary; use of heavy-handed techniques when working with sexual abuse —prolonged and intense psychodrama, for example	Fascination or enjoyment over hearing details of sexual abuse; probing for details of sex practices; complaining about one's partner; use of sexual terms of endearment; frequent comments on sexual attractiveness and attire; suggesting that a romantic relationship would have been possible if it were not for the present relationship, or might be possible after therapy terminates; commenting on the therapeutic value of sexual relations	Occasional kissing, stroking, fondling; full-fledged sexual relationship immediately or shortly after therapy terminates	Frequent sex, whether presented as romance, as mutual enjoyment, or as a therapeutic technique	Blatantly coercive sex, painful sex, forcing the client to have sex with others, repeating sexual intrusions told to the therapist in confidence; use of photographs, ritual abuse

Figure 9.1. Sexual Abuse by Therapist Continuum

- Female clients who have had sex with female therapists, correspondingly, generally have strong romantic attachments to the therapists and take these therapists as role models. They often become helpers themselves (therapists, social workers, doctors, nurses) and have boundary problems in their professional roles that it is critical for us to be aware of and to help them sort out. (See Wine, 1979.) Women who have had sex with male therapists are more likely to be one of many, to be treated callously, to be enormously ashamed, confused, traumatized, depressed, and suicidal.

Where sexual involvement has occurred, we can generally expect some formidable combination of fear, ambivalence, confusion, shame, distrust, vulnerability, depression, mourning, and suicidal inclinations. We help with the distrust by being trustworthy ourselves (being sensitive, not pathologizing, not sexualizing, maintaining clear boundaries, not betraying confidence, etc.). We help with confusion by being clear and by providing clarity—ongoing clarity about what is and is not appropriate in therapy in particular. The increased vulnerability, the depression, the mourning, the fear, the suicidal thoughts all point to the need for increased support. At the same time, it is critical that we understand the ambivalence around support and attend to it. Often the abusive therapist him- or herself was supersupportive—supportive, in fact, to a fault. The very phenomenon of support has thereby become contaminated and may be experienced as dangerous. We can address this problem by commenting on it, by empathizing with the difficulty, and by helping the client distinguish between clean and unclean support.

The internalized oppression that occurs with overt sexual abuse is very similar to what happens with incest survivors, and similar responses are needed from us. We need to clarify that the professional is the perpetrator, was in a trusted role—indeed, to some degree, a parent role—and is the one responsible. We need to highlight and co-investigate the enormous power imbalance both in this individual relationship and in therapy systemically and the relationship between this imbalance and what occurred. We need to help the client uncover and appreciate the deep similarity between therapist sexual abuse and childhood sexual abuse. It is important correspondingly to familiarize her with how prevalent therapist sexual abuse is and to let her know that victims typically feel ashamed and think that this could have happened to no one else.

Particular sensitivity is called for where the relationship was romantic and where the client still has contact with the offending therapist. I have known workers to err seriously here by referring to the offending therapist as a villain and by pressuring the client to cut off all contact with him or her. Despite our good intentions, when we respond in ways such as this, the client almost invariably is hurt and naturally feels protective, misunderstood, and confused. Correspondingly, one of the following scenarios generally transpires:

1. The client feels pulled in opposite directions and finds a short-term solution to the dilemma, hoping that the situation will somehow resolve itself in the long run. She

tells her current worker that she has cut off relations with "her friend," while continuing to have contact with him or her. One lie leads to another. She feels guilty about lying, guilty about being with her "friend," guilty about not standing up for her "friend." She is not sure what she is doing in therapy.

2. The client leaves the current therapist. It is now harder for her to seek help because she feels more protective of her "friend." She anticipates that future workers will not understand.

3. The client becomes immobilized by the pressure. She is unable to explore what happened and to make any decisions. She becomes increasingly confused and vulnerable.

4. Wanting to please this new parental figure and feeling ashamed, the client succumbs to the pressure and cuts off a relationship that she was in no way prepared to cut off. She becomes progressively depressed, feels guilty, and is plagued by uncertainty. A solution to this crisis is to reactivate the relationship. The solution, if taken, leaves her back with some version of the original dilemma.

We avoid such problems by being clear that we are dealing with a real relationship with all the complications that relationships bring. Without a doubt the "relationship" should never have occurred. It is an enormously serious transgression that has profoundly damaged the client. In most cases the client is much better off without this person in her life. This notwithstanding, what is only abuse to us may be a meaningful relationship to the client, and the reality of that relationship needs to be taken in.

The incest situation can serve as a guide here. Just as we would never pressure an incested client to cut off all relations with an incest-perpetrating father whom she loves, we cannot pressure a client to cut off relations with an offending ex-therapist whom she loves. Our job is to help her co-investigate what occurred, to be clear about the transgression while being sensitive to her feelings, and to help her gradually make her own decisions vis-à-vis her "friend." This notwithstanding, of course, where she is continuing to see the offending therapist professionally, clarification of the contradictions involved and strong encouragement to end the "therapeutic relationship" are in order.

Discussions with other women who have been sexually abused by their therapists have helped many women better understand the transgression, stop blaming themselves, and move toward empowerment. Referral to relevant support groups, grass roots political groups, and therapy groups correspondingly should be considered. Women may particularly benefit from talking with and planning "actions" with other women who were abused by the same "professional." Some become greatly empowered from participating in speak-outs, attending special workshops for survivors, attending public presentations on therapy abuse, and making deputations to professional boards. And we do well to familiarize clients with these options.

Legal and quasi-legal routes that might be considered vary from suing for damages to pressing criminal charges and to laying a complaint and giving testimony to a professional board for purposes of de-licensing or de-certification. A special advantage of the board route is that clients can receive added meaning from denouncing an abuser in front of his or her colleagues and preventing him or her from harming other clients. A disadvantage is that professional boards are often more concerned with protecting the image of the profession and the offending colleague than with protecting clients.

Where the client was referred to the therapist in question by a referral service—especially a feminist referral service—we can also encourage her to lay a complaint with that service. Feminist referral services tend to believe client complaints. They are unlikely to either pathologize the client or put her through a lengthy ordeal. And progressively they have been investigating such complaints and removing offending therapists from their files.

Outside the Therapy Room

As counselors we have a professional responsibility to actively do something about sexual abuse by therapists. Counselors who work in agencies can help within the agency setting itself by doing the following:

* Raising the issue of boundaries more
* Discussing covert, as well as overt, abuse
* Lobbying for improved complaint procedures
* Arguing for stricter guidelines regarding socializing with clients off hours work with clients, discussing one's own problems with clients, touching clients
* Working on subcommittees to address issues of abuse
* Requesting or providing staff development in this area
* Never covering up for an offending colleague, however nice that colleague may be and regardless of whether he or she promises to leave quietly if you say nothing

Meaningful actions that are open to us all include but are not limited to the following:

* Helping women report infractions
* Doing public presentations on overt and covert sexual abuse by therapists
* Doing research into and writing on both overt and covert sexual abuse by therapists
* Educating counselors and lawyers about the effects of therapist abuse
* Running workshops to raise professional awareness of the problem and to help professionals work better with both survivors and perpetrators

- Lobbying the government for increased funding for support groups for therapy abuse survivors, for educational efforts in this area, for advocacy, and for survivor workshops
- Running workshops for survivors
- Presenting deputations to professional boards and government bodies
- Assisting grass roots groups in their political/educational efforts
- Including overt and covert therapist abuse in all of our general discussions about and writing on sexual abuse
- Critiquing those aspects of currently accepted therapies that constitute or border on sexual abuse (aspects of psychodrama, sex therapy, etc.)
- Raising objections at conferences and elsewhere when intrusive approaches such as these are advocated
- Expanding therapist training to include discussions of attractions to clients and how to deal with these attractions
- Conscientiously addressing the sexual abuse committed against trainees and supervisees—abuse, significantly, that at once constitutes profound violation and contributes to boundary blurring overall

SUGGESTED READINGS

Brown, L. (1985). Power, responsibility, boundaries: Ethical concerns for the lesbian feminist therapist. *Lesbian Ethics, 1*(3), 30-40.

Kelly, L. (1988). *Surviving sexual violence.* Minneapolis: University of Minnesota Press.

Lobel, K. (Ed.). (1986). *Naming the violence: Speaking out about lesbian battery.* Seattle: Seal Press.

Pope, K., & Bouhoutsos, J. (1986). *Sexual intimacy between therapists and patients.* New York: Praeger.

Pope, K., Keith-Spiegel, P., & Tabachnick, B. (1986). Sexual attractions to clients. *American Psychologist, 41,* 147-158.

Rhodes, D., & McNeill, S. (1985). *Women against violence against women.* London: Onlywomen Press.

Roberts, C. (1989). *Women and rape.* New York: New York University Press.

NOTES

1. For an informative discussion of the problem and the concomitant consciousness-raising done by lesbian battery survivors, see Lobel (1986).

2. For further information on such responses, see Lobel (1986), p. 183ff.

3. Studies conducted have been on psychologists. Whether the statistics for other practitioners would differ substantially is an open question. My own experience suggests that the more professionalized and hence more powerful and credible the profession, the greater the abuse.

4. Unlike earlier studies that indicated that 75-80% of the therapists who act out sexually do so repeatedly, research by Pope and Bouhoutsos (1986) suggests that 86% of therapists who act out sexually do so only once or twice. Pope, Keith-Spiegel, and Tabachnick (1986) interpreted this new finding as an indication that the problem is lessening. There are, however, other possible explanations. It is men who tend to abuse repeatedly; men typically understate the violations that they commit, and these men may now be more likely to understate in light of the increased seriousness with which sexual contact by therapists is viewed.

5. Admissions by therapists and the existence of similar complaints from other clients almost always validate clients' stories. (See Schoener & Gonsiorek, 1989.) This justifies our believing. A court or employer, of course, would have to use more rigorous criteria to protect those who are falsely accused.

6. Where sex therapy is occurring, of course, asking for such details does not constitute abuse. This notwithstanding, much sex therapy is itself inherently abusive.

10

Self-Mutilation

In patriarchal society all women engage in some type of bodily self-injury, and indeed we are encouraged to do so. *Self-mutilation* is a mode of coping and a specific range of self-injurious acts or series of acts. The term is generally used to refer exclusively to forms or degrees of self-injury that are not condoned, with all other forms or degrees essentially not seen as injurious. The most common forms are scraping, cutting, banging, and burning. Self-mutilation is the paradigm for self-injury over all. Most of what I write about it accordingly applies to the other forms of self-injury.

Some women engage only or almost only in self-mutilation that is encouraged or condoned. Others additionally self-mutilate in ways that are disapproved of. Working with the first is part and parcel of the work we do as feminist counselors generally. Working with the second is the focus of this chapter.

I conceive of the women who self-mutilate in ways not approved of as falling roughly into three groups. The first group is composed of women who self-mutilate lightly. My experience suggests that the vast majority of the women who mutilate in ways disapproved of fall into this category. Many of these women are mistakenly perceived of as engaging in enormously dangerous acts and are treated accordingly. Routine mutilation often translates into deep mutilation in the eyes of uneasy counselors. The frequency of the mode of coping, however, says little about the seriousness of the cut or burn. We can see dangerousness where it does not exist, because the drama of the wound shocks or frightens us. Counselors are particularly likely to become frightened by women who appear at their door dripping with blood and by women who do not wash the wound before seeing them. The drama of the abuse or its presentation, however, is no indicator of dangerousness. We need to see more accurately. Generally what lies beneath the blood are minor scratches and cuts, not wounds that jeopardize life and limb. *Because self-danger is used as an excuse to intrude on women in this intrusive society, it is absolutely critical that we do not invent danger where little or none exists.*

The second group is composed of women who generally self-mutilate lightly and only occasionally hurt themselves badly. The deepness of the injury can be incidental and even unintentional. Often alcohol or drugs play a role here. Having numbed themselves with alcohol or buzzed out on drugs, women feel less pain. They may cut deeper because it is now easier to do so and they want to cut deep. Other common reasons for cutting deeper or burning worse include (a) needing to hurt themselves worse to get the same results, (b) not knowing how badly they are hurting themselves because the pain has diminished as a result of numbing, (c) being less careful, and (d) being atypically furious or frustrated.

The third group is composed of women who frequently injure themselves severely. It is important to take in how small this group is and to stop thinking of these women as paradigmal. My colleagues who have worked extensively with street youths inform me that the group itself includes a disproportionately high number of very young street women, often lesbian prostitutes—women, in other words, who are at the bottom of the hierarchy in street prostitution. Activities commonly engaged in include (a) cutting to the bone, (b) using dirty instruments, and (c) inflicting second degree burns on one or many parts of their bodies. Although women from the other two groups generally restrict their cutting to specific parts of their bodies—often limbs—more women from this group engage in overall body injury, and a higher percentage engage in genital mutilation.

Whatever the group, most of the women self-mutilate alone. They are mortified by their actions. They see the self-injury as separating them from the rest of humankind and let no one or almost no one know about an act that they regard as shameful. Keeping it private additionally protects them against a world that they correctly believe will not understand and may try to stop them. A minority of the women who cut (albeit the majority of those who are street women) do so together with friends. Where cutting is done with others and instruments are shared, the danger of going too far and of HIV infection rises. In this day of AIDS, some of the activities that were once quite safe are no longer as safe.

As noted in Chapter 7, and as many feminist therapists are aware, self-mutilation is a means of coping often employed by women survivors of extreme childhood sexual abuse. Where women self-mutilate, especially where genital and breast mutilation is involved, checking for extreme childhood sexual abuse is important. A far more common background, albeit one that feminist therapists have tended to overlook, is childhood battery. I have found that where a woman copes by self-mutilating, childhood battery is a likelihood. It is critical to check for this and, where battery has occurred, to nurture and reassure the battered child.

Where a client routinely self-mutilates, we know for a certainty that this woman has been badly intruded on in childhood. What we do not know is how.

In the work with this client group, it is critical not to panic, not to intrude, and whatever happens, not to call in the psychiatrists. If you are feeling out of your depths, remember: As a woman you really do have some inside knowledge of these women and their dilemmas. Expertise does not reside in patriarchal psychiatry. No authorities exist—just human beings who are more or less aware and sensitive and who are more or less likely to intrude. *If you are clear about not intruding, you are already a much better person for this woman to be seeing than the majority of "experts" that you might call in.* It is important, correspondingly, that counselors stop scaring themselves. The vast majority of women who self-mutilate have been proceeding this way for years with no dire consequences.

Whether they are in danger or not, and however upsetting the wounds are to us, it is not our place to interfere with their choices. The bottom line is that however much we may want something better for these clients, WOMEN HAVE AN ABSOLUTE RIGHT TO DO WHAT THEY WANT WITH THEIR BODIES. They have a right to nurture or starve that body. They have a right to sell that body, cut that body, even annihilate that body; and although we may and should invite something else, we need to respect that right. The history of sexism is the history of other people—generally males—taking charge of women's bodies. People have already interfered profoundly with these women's bodies. They do not need interference or pressure from us.

Contributing to our misapprehension about self-mutilation and to our abuse of women who self-mutilate is the mistaken belief that self-mutilation is suicidal, quasi-suicidal, or the "royal road to suicide." It is important that we start working in more feminist ways with women considering suicide itself, and I articulate a feminist position on suicide in Chapter 14. Be that as it may, it is critical that we stop confusing self-mutilation with suicide. Although women who self-mutilate may end up killing themselves, just as other women in distress may, SELF-MUTILATION IS NOT A WAY OF DYING or even of edging closer to dying. Though certainly other issues are involved and many of these need to be problematized, SELF-MUTILATION IS FUNDAMENTALLY A WAY OF LIVING. It is a means of getting through the day. In our desire for something better and in our zeal to get women to stop hurting themselves, we forget, to our client's detriment, that this way of proceeding has kept her going for years. For the time being at least, it is likely that we ourselves have nothing better to offer.

A further misapprehension that often results in therapy abuse is the belief that the woman is not really "choosing" or is mutilating herself outside of awareness. Without question, internal and external pullings are operant and the choice is not entirely "free." Neither, for that matter, are the choices to have sex with men or to stay in an abusive relationship—both of which are also risky matters, though I know of no counselor who would forcibly stop women from continuing these courses. The fact that some women numb themselves or split when mutilating does not correspondingly mean that they have no awareness or are not exercising any choice. Of the many self-mutilating clients I have worked with as a therapist specializing in this area, I have never personally come across anyone who could not access some awareness of choosing.

Two instances that I am aware of where the women did not *appear* to be able to and/or to want to access awareness are instructive. In both, the women were seeing a counselor who ordered them to stop hurting themselves. This order placed the clients in an impossible situation. They could not choose to hurt themselves because that choice jeopardized a counseling relationship on which they depended. They could not abstain from hurting themselves, for self-harm was their lifeline. Their solution was to hurt themselves without being reflectively aware that they were either hurting themselves or choosing to hurt themselves. They started "discovering themselves" badly injured. In both cases the injury was significantly more severe than what they had inflicted when operating reflectively. In one case the counselor got the point and rescinded her command to stop cutting. The client returned to normal. She no longer needed to operate out of awareness and now did not need to harm herself as severely. The other counselor took what happened as an indication of "psychosis" and hospitalized "her client." The woman continued to hurt herself "out of awareness."

These examples demonstrate that on some level clients do indeed "choose" to hurt themselves and that they make these choices reflectively as long as others do not interfere. They also suggest how vital the coping is and how damaging interference can be.

Generally, if we are receptive and sensitive, clients who self-mutilate will broach with us the issue of the self-mutilation. They usually do so hesitantly, often initially by way of hints. If we pick up on the hints, are not shocked, and respond sensitively, clients are likely to divulge more. If a client does not raise the issue and we suspect self-mutilation, we do well to raise it ourselves as long as we do so supportively and are prepared to back off.

Although there are exceptions, especially among women who have been talking about their self-mutilation to shelter staff for years, most women who self-mutilate have enormous difficulty discussing it with us. Many have never discussed the mutilation in-depth with anyone. They may have no language to do so. If they have made a point of not thinking about it, as many do, they may have little sense of it and almost no concepts to draw on. We help by offering words and concepts ourselves, while picking up on the words and concepts that our clients "drop."

Two other problems significantly contribute to the difficulties of raising and exploring the issue. The first is the shame that most clients feel about the self-mutilation. Often this shame has multiple levels, each level magnifying the others. The client may be mutilating as punishment for actions or feelings that she is ashamed of. Whether this is the case or not, she is likely ashamed of the mutilation itself even if she also takes pride in it. She suspects that only someone "bad" or "crazy" would do something like this. She may see mutilation as something that no one else or almost no one else does. Even when aware on an intellectual level that they are doing nothing wrong, many who mutilate vilify or pathologize the self-harm. Many feel deeply humiliated and exposed by another knowing of this private act.

A second obstacle is fear of what we are going to do. It is not simply that she is afraid of our humiliating her, though this is a perfectly reasonable fear that clients who self-mutilate often have. She is afraid that we are going to interfere. She does not want to reveal details to someone who is not going to understand and who may decide to stop her. If she has been interfered with by others in the past—especially other "helpers"—this concern is likely be formidable.

These obstacles dwindle if we are patient and continue to respond in ways that normalize and empower. Even passive acceptance helps. Simply by not being shocked, not being alarmist, and not pathologizing, we are sending out the message that we are not going to freak out and that she is okay. Further help comes from making these messages more explicit. It is easier for the client to accept herself and to trust us if we make it clear that we accept and respect her just as she is. Let her know that many women self-mutilate, that she is not doing anything awful. Point out that we all hurt ourselves in some way or other, that as women indeed we are trained to hurt ourselves. Make it clear that you understand that self-mutilation is a way of coping that has served her well and that you have no intention of robbing her of it.

Although certainly not the only way to proceed, contracting in this area can be helpful. It enables women who self-mutilate to see themselves as partners and to establish the boundaries and directions that they need. A stipulation that should be included in any contract is that the counselor not interfere with the client's decisions around self-mutilation. Contracting around co-exploration, as always, is important. Some therapists contract around awareness only, defining "the handling of the self-mutilation" as the client's sole responsibility. A division such as this can be a relief to the client because it seems to safeguard against interference; it is a relief to the counselor because it lightens her load. This notwithstanding, it shortchanges the client who wishes to change her way of coping and wants help with it. Most of our clients who self-mutilate at least partially want a shift, and all are likely to have enormous trouble effecting change. It is our responsibility to offer such help, albeit not necessarily initially, and to be prepared to provide it. Where the client wants it, help of this nature may be stipulated in an initial contract and/or in later contracting. The "provisos" are:

1. The client can change her mind about getting this help, and we have a responsibility to check in with her if we think she might want to.
2. This agreement is not to be used to legitimate pressure.
3. We ourselves will not suggest unrealistic goals, and we will sensitively problematize any unrealistic goals that the client might propose.
4. We will negotiate with the "whole client."

Examples of unrealistic goals are never cutting again, stopping totally by Christmas, and consistently cutting less. Goals such as these set women up for failure and shame. Premature "success" correspondingly leaves the client without a needed way of coping and so often culminates in new or increased use of other types of self-injury.

Negotiating with the "whole client" (Proviso 4) means surfacing the ambivalence that the client is bound to have. Where clients who self-mutilate are very eager to please—and remember, women are socialized to please—they may contract from a place that is tailored to please. They may push down the person inside who does not want to stop self-mutilating, letting the one who does do all the talking and negotiating. It is pointless and indeed damaging to work with half a client. This other half desperately needs to be heard and has to be party to any agreement. We help restore balance by making room for, inviting, and welcoming this the other half.

Not facilitating changes per se but co-exploring what is happening when our client self-mutilates is the center of our work. The co-exploration is furthered by such questions as:

- What does the cutting "mean to you"?
- What do you remember thinking/feeling before you last cut?
- What do you remember thinking/feeling afterward?
- Do you have a sense of what the cutting gave you?

Co-exploration serves many ends. It defines the self-harm as something purposive and meaningful, as opposed to something meaningless or crazy. It helps counselor and client truly appreciate self-mutilation as a valid means of coping. It allows a woman who is not understood and who thinks she is not understandable to receive and take in understanding. Clarity around purposes combined with acceptance additionally gives the client the possibility of exploring alternative avenues for meeting these ends. Invariably as well the co-investigation unearths internalized oppression. It provides material to problematize and opportunities for nurture. It provides access to early injuries and allows us to focus and work on that early abuse.

Keeping in mind the types of meanings and purposes that tend to be served and the possible ways of working with these is helpful. As noted earlier, on some level self-punishment is always involved, and internalized oppression is always operant. The client is telling herself, "I am bad; I am worthless; I deserve to be hurt." It may be that she gets temporary expiation precisely by punishing herself, and this is important to check out. Generally, even where this is the case, the action in the long run adds to her guilt.

My advice is to co-investigate what "makes her bad" or worthless and who early on described her this way. Find out why the body is being targeted for punishment so strongly. In most cases the client is clear that she hates her body and that her body is critically implicated in the "worthlessness." The general disgust over and violation of Woman as Body plays a fundamental role here. Being a devalued color or having a visible disability may contribute to the sense of worthlessness. In the long run, in some way or other, the political issues need to be raised and addressed. In the short run, we need to co-understand this specific choice of punishment and the coping that is involved.

Childhood sexual abuse may figure in the punishment, and this possibility and the specifics should be co-investigated. A survivor of childhood sexual abuse may attack her body or parts of her body because she sees her body generally or these parts specifically as "seductive" and having invited abuse. If she experienced any pleasurable sensations during the abuse, she may be punishing her body for betraying her. A woman who engages in genital mutilation is almost inevitably a childhood sexual abuse survivor who is punishing herself. She is repeating the violation. This is partly self-punishment, partly compliance, partly resistance; it may also be an attempt to remember or to understand.

Whatever the target of the self-violation, over the long run, addressing the internalized oppression and putting blame where it belongs is critical. First and foremost, however, we need to understand and overtly respect the coping. Does punishment provide relief, however evanescent? Does it offer temporary expiation of guilt? There is ample room here for validation.

Checking for possible childhood battery and co-exploring its relationship to the coping are particularly critical, in light of how common childhood battery is to this client group. The woman who has been battered as a child has been provided with a role model. She has been shown how to treat herself and has been told why punishment is necessary. She has been given the messages: You as Body are bad; You as Body ought to be beaten. Because of the difference between male and female socialization, a man who has been battered is somewhat more likely to imitate the batterer by battering others, while a woman imitates/obeys/rebels by battering self. Gently these messages need to be problematized without our saying or implying that she should stop. And together we need to co-explore respectfully the coping that is involved. She may be safeguarding her world by implying that her parents are right. By punishing herself, she additionally is at least to some degree carrying on the work of her abusive parent. Doing daddy's or mommy's work for him or her may be a way of telling herself that she is a help, that she is resourceful, and that therefore she is worth something. It is good that she has found some way of conveying worth to herself, and we need to let her know this.

A second very positive meaning that self-violation often has is proof of humanness. Someone who has been given the message that she is less than human, as all women are to varying degrees, needs her humanness proved. In contrast with Descartes' "I think, therefore I am," she is proclaiming to self and others, "I hurt, therefore I am human." The wound is visible/tangible proof that she feels. Her feeling in turn is proof of her humanity. If she has been accused of being "unfeeling" throughout childhood, her need for such visible and tangible proof may be very pressing indeed.

Whatever else we may think about what is occurring, it is wonderful that this unvalidated woman has found a way of validating her humanity. We need to share our appreciation with her. It is important at the same time to demonstrably respect her humanity and continually invite her to see herself as the full and worthwhile human being she is. If we do so and help her link up with others who treat her similarly, the time may come when she no longer needs this proof.

A third common purpose is bringing back feeling. Women who have numbed themselves in response to abuse have trouble feeling. Inflicting pain on oneself is a way of bringing feeling back—of feeling something, anything! Understanding and validation are called for. As trust builds, other ways of validating feeling may be explored.

A fourth but opposite purpose may also be served. A woman who is extremely anxious—say, a woman who is being triggered and does not want the memories—may cut or burn to put an end to feeling. The pain of the injury puts a cap on or distracts her from feelings that may be hurting her more. The approach used here is similar to the technique that we use when we have a raging toothache and pinch our arm. The slight pain in our arm distracts us from the larger pain of the toothache. As such, it gives relief. Pain may additionally be used to stop flooding or to push down traumatic memories that are beginning to surface. Invariably the woman who copes in this way needs to be reassured that what she is doing is a variation of a common technique, and she needs appreciation of the coping. The reassurance and appreciation must come first. In the long run she needs help exploring what she is afraid to explore. And she needs to learn other ways of deescalating, of dealing with panic, of containing feelings, of stopping flooding. (See Chapter 7.)

A fifth purpose—and one that is almost invariable—is communication. When we are in extreme difficulty and pain, we need to communicate the difficulty, the pain, the neediness to others. To varying degrees self-mutilation is a cry of anguish, an appeal for help. The quandary that these women find themselves in is this: They desperately need to communicate, yet they cannot because they do not feel entitled to speak about the pain or to ask for help. Moreover they are not certain anyone would heed them if they did, and they cannot afford to risk further rejection. Their solution is to communicate indirectly. THEY CREATE WOUNDS THAT SPEAK FOR THEM. In their own way they are reaching out. Sadly this decision seldom results in the type of attention that they want, if it gets them any attention at all. What is equally sad is that their own self-blame frequently interferes with the attempt to communicate. Ashamed both of reaching out generally and of reaching out in this particular way, many women hide the very wounds intended to communicate. They put the wounds in places where they cannot be seen. Often a hint of the wound is nonetheless present, for this conflicted woman still wants to be seen.

We help by recognizing the injury even when it is covered, by taking in the neediness, by affirming. Criticizing the indirectness or calling the cutting "manipulative" is destructive and misses the point. *If their direct communication of neediness had been taken in throughout their lives and had been responded to caringly, they would not now be communicating indirectly.* Respecting and uncovering the personal/political context behind the indirect communication are essential. Beyond this we need to value and respect the communication, whatever form it takes, to help the women communicate more directly and to give the indirect communication of distress the same attention that we would give the direct and vice versa.

A sixth purpose is to get a high—a rush of energy. Women who have been put down and are depressed need energy, a way of feeling strong and good. We can help them acquire this through other means—taking on new challenges, for example, and what is especially critical, making empowering changes in their lives. For the time being, the self-mutilation is giving them a temporary surge and deserves to be affirmed.

Control is a seventh purpose. *Control is a meaning that I have found to be absolutely invariable and the most fundamental.* Women traditionally have been controlled by others. Women who have been violated/controlled in ways that exceed the already devastating norm and/or women who have felt the control acutely desperately need some sense of power. They turn to the one area over which they have control—the area that others paradoxically have both controlled and asked them to control—their own bodies. Self-mutilation is a way of controlling one's body. The woman who burns herself is able to choose how to burn, what to burn, how much to burn, what type of burn. The woman who cuts herself chooses her cutting instrument. She controls when she cuts, how deeply she cuts. Like a sculptor working in stone, she can even determine the exact pattern of cuts that she is going to carve into her limb.

It is precisely the centrality of control that makes our attempt to stop/control her self-mutilation so destructive. The last thing our self-mutilating sister needs is someone to take away her one area of control. We assist rather by respecting this need for control, by not interfering with the expression it takes, and by co-exploring the reality and the difficulty that powerlessness poses. We can assist as well by helping her gain more power in the world and feel entitled to that power. Women who exercise power in the world in which they live and who feel entitled to do so do not need to mutilate/overcontrol their bodies. And we assist by politicizing control itself.

A further meaning for some women—and this relates to control—is strength and success. Many women who have trouble experiencing themselves as strong or successful find strength and success in self-mutilation. As ashamed as they may be by the mutilation, the truth is that many also take pride in it. They tell themselves that most other people do not have the stamina to do what they are doing; and they are right. They know that others do not have the incredible discipline and fortitude to subject themselves to hour after hour of self-torture. By contrast they repeatedly inflict pain on themselves for hours and emerge tangibly and visibly successful. The wound is there—an achievement, a mark of endurance. Endurance has always been encouraged in women, and women have traditionally taken pride in it. Again the folly of interference is clear. We need to recognize the importance of the perseverance and what it gives them. As trust builds, we can invite and help our sisters explore other avenues in which to succeed and to exercise strength.

A final meaning—again one that fundamentally connects with power—is resistance. In a very real way, women who self-mutilate are defying those who attempt to control them, whether that defiance occurs reflectively or pre-reflectively, obviously or unobviously. Even those who were beaten as children and who are taking on the work of the batterers are not simply complying with the wishes of the batterers. They are also taking over control of the battery. It is now in their hands, subject to their choices. Moreover they are demonstrating with their own wounds and their own agony what has been done to them. They are turning themselves into living indictments of the batterers. Also, the women are injuring their bodies in ways that dramatically depart from or exceed what is commanded or even tolerated by the patriarchy. As such what is happening constitutes a defiance of the patriarchy, as well as an indictment of our violation as women. On some level even those who are enormously submissive and who are not reflectively aware of resisting are defying. With others who are angry and know that they are angry, that defiance is enormously blatant.

Sheila Gilhooly's situation again is instructive. Not wearing a dress and not shaving her legs, Sheila was considered unladylike by her psychiatric jailers. Repeatedly they forced her to wear dresses. One day they gave her a razor and commanded her to shave her legs. Sheila took the razor, went to the washroom, and cut herself. She returned, with the same leg hair as before and with visible gashes. The wounds were saying "Fuck you" to her patriarchal tormentors. They were a declaration to self and others that she would not be ladylike, that she would not succumb.

This resistance needs to be recognized and affirmed, however blatant or hidden it may be. Women who are not reflectively aware of the resistance should be given help discovering it and should be encouraged to appreciate its strength and meaningfulness. As trust builds, women are generally able to entertain modes of resistance that do not harm them, that are not "double edged."

Where counselor and client are drawing numerous blanks and/or the explanations arrived at seem incomplete, two-chair gestalt work might be tried. Although gestalt work does not always bear fruit here, I have had self-mutilating clients make remarkable discoveries with it and go on to make dramatic changes in their lives. The metaphor around which I build the work is this: At least two subpersonalities are involved in self-mutilation. One is doing the mutilation, and the other is being mutilated. I set the context and facilitate a dialogue between them. Although situations vary, an important discovery that some women make when doing two-chair work is that it is the person who inflicts the injury who is the underdog. Often the subpersonality who is physically violating the other is retaliating. She feels bullied, pushed into doing things she is not happy about. She is registering what protest she can. She is fighting for dear life. In such instances, if the "top dog" truly listens to the "underdog" and a communication channel is opened, besides self-awareness, all sorts of changes become possible.

Whether women choose to reduce the self-mutilation or not, it makes sense discussing safety issues with them. It is important that they be aware of infection risks—especially HIV—and the risks of combining drugs and cutting. Examples of safeguards that we do well to encourage are:

1. Not sharing cutting instruments
2. Making sure that any cutting instruments they might use are clean

3. Washing, putting antiseptic on, and bandaging wounds

4. Seeking help with the bleeding and bandaging if they have cut to the bone and/or have become too dizzy to take care of the wound themselves

5. Choosing not to drink or use drugs if they feel like self-mutilating and not to self-mutilate if they are drinking or on drugs

The first four are ways of guarding against infection and prolonged bleeding. The fifth is a safeguard against hurting herself more than she wishes. All are modes of self-nurture that could lead to further self-nurture. All are ways of taking care of herself that do not interfere with her choice of how much or how deeply to self-mutilate. All highlight and increase choice.

Where women want to stop hurting themselves, and eventually the majority do, a one-small-step-at-a-time approach is strongly advisable. Examples of small steps that might be considered are:

• Where the client does most of the self-mutilation with friends, *slightly* decreasing the amount or percentage done with friends

• Cutting/burning herself *slightly* less severely

• In individual situations, putting off self-mutilation somewhat longer than she would normally—another half-hour, say, or another hour

• Reclaiming one small part of her body which she currently hurts—declaring one small section that she currently mutilates *a mutilation-free zone*

• Where most of her friends self-mutilate, forming a friendship with one new person who does not appear to self-mutilate

Examples of more advanced steps that might be considered farther down the road are:

• Not mutilating with others

• Restricting the mutilation to a very small section of her body

• Restricting any individual cutting/burning period to 15 minutes

• Cutting less deeply and less often

Progressively, correspondingly, clients may use alternative routes for the purposes currently met by self-harm.

Giving the client positive feedback for every step taken is critical, for psychically each of these seeming small steps is a giant step. Clients moreover are likely to judge themselves critically if we do not. Additionally it is important to let her know that it is perfectly okay and indeed expectable to slip.

Although on some level the women who self-mutilate want to stop, a very high percentage believe that they have little or no power to do so. It is a terrible thing to feel that such torture is going to continue and that you can do absolutely nothing about it. We need to really take in and empathize with this feeling of powerlessness, while gradually and gently encouraging our client to find and exercise some power. Any small step whatever—cleaning the knife before cutting, for example—begins breaking the hold.

The powerlessness in some instances relates to the mutilation seemingly occurring "out of awareness." Women tell us—and they are being honest—that they "find themselves cutting" or alternatively find themselves "already cut." The discoveries naturally terrify them. Our job is to help the women access the awareness that they do indeed have. This means helping them make the prereflective reflective. Repeatedly retracing the steps that lead up to the mutilation and teasing out the awareness of the mutilation itself are a key to reflective awareness. As the stories about the women who mutilated "outside of awareness" make clear, another key is acceptance. If is "okay" for them to mutilate themselves, it is "okay" to be aware of mutilating themselves.

Despite what appears to others as progress, some women continue for a long time to see "real" or "permanent" change as impossible, with their sense of the impossibility increasing with any "slip." They may have trouble regarding slips as anything other than "returning to normal," especially where they have often gone for long periods of "abstinence" before. Women may feel utterly fatalistic about the abuse. They may experience self-mutilation as a curse that is eventually going to strike again no matter what they do.

Gradually co-exploration, problematizing, successes, and heightened awareness serve to increase the sense and reality of choice and to weaken the fatalism. It is important that we ourselves not be spooked by the fatalism, that we be patient, and that we trust in the process. Our own predictable steadiness and support help make hope just a little less scary. Clients indeed are helped by our very belief—by our conviction that they can put an end to the self-mutilation and by our knowledge of others who have successfully stopped. By keeping in touch with our knowledge, sharing what we know, and inviting conviction, we help clients conceive of the "inconceivable" and achieve the "impossible."

Women who self-mutilate dramatically often need help protecting themselves from psychiatric and other interference. And they need advocacy generally. More energy may have to be expended accessing needed resources in light of the bias against the client group.

More global work that we can do includes the following:

- Creating educational events that explore the self-violation continuum and the relationship between women's self-violation and violence against women
- Facilitating the creation of consciousness-raising and self-help groups in this area
- Helping the women organize for purposes of protest and lobbying
- Running workshops ourselves on self-violation and how to work with it
- Including issues of self-mutilation in the groups that we run

SHELTER OR RESIDENCE WORK

Shelter staff are among the workers most likely to be aware of interacting with women who self-mutilate and most likely to be giving help on a daily basis. At any given time a shelter for women generally has at least one woman who self-mutilates in ways that exceed or otherwise differ from the norm. As many shelter staff are painfully aware, where one or more women in the house self-mutilate in this way, and where that mutilation is obvious to others, a number of problems can arise. These problems are largely due to the close proximity of other vulnerable women and staffing and budget limitations. Among the largest of the problems are (a) other residents get triggered or otherwise upset by the abuse, (b) staff have extreme and sharply polarized responses (blaming the woman who self-mutilates, dismissing what is going on as manipulative, and denying help on one hand and "playing rescuer" on the other), (c) attention is insufficient to go around, and other residents do not get what they need, (d) some residents get angry with and blame the woman who self-mutilates, and (e) staff become exhausted and burn out.

These problems have no totally satisfactory solutions in light of the structural limitations. Nonetheless some small structural changes, as well as individual changes, can help.

On the awareness level it is important for all staff to take in that women who self-mutilate really are needy—some of them desperately so—and that woman-blaming concepts like *manipulative* miss the point. Additionally it is important to help fellow staff understand that both rescuing and deserting harm the client. We assure dependence and curtail growth when we always rush in. And we encourage guilt and deny needy women the kindness that they need when we refuse to help them with their wounds or order them to clean up the blood. Workers correspondingly need to be clear about the following:

- All of the women in the shelter have tons of legitimate needs.
- There are *always* more needs that can be addressed.
- Inevitably the needs will sometimes interfere with each other, and it is no one's fault that they do.
- The expectations being placed on them as staff members are impossible, and it is critical that ways be found to lighten their load.
- The residents are not simply a problem. They can also be part of the solution.

Some shelters attempt to minimize upset and triggering by such rules as "No self-mutilating in the presence of others." This is a perfectly reasonable rule and indeed common courtesy. At the same time, it is likely to add to the client's sense of "badness" if she is not reassured that there is nothing wrong with what she is doing and that she does not have to hide the fact that she is self-mutilating. Others make far stricter rules, such as "No mutilating in the shelter." Although the rationale behind rules like these are understandable, they are bound to make the self-mutilating resident feel like a pariah. Beyond this the question arises: Where is she supposed to go? I recommend against such rules.

Treating the self-mutilation as a perfectly "okay" way of coping that "Mary" finds helpful is a good idea. Besides being true and empowering Mary, it reduces the triggering and panic escalation in the house. Insofar as we respond to the coping as normal, other residents generally begin to feel easier and follow suit.

Some systemic/structural changes that might be explored are:

- Assigning more staff to late evening and night hours—the times when women tend to be more vulnerable and are more likely to self-mutilate
- Getting together with staff from other shelters and lobbying for the funding needed to provide the additional staff so clearly needed
- To the degree possible, where difficulties arise, defining them as community problems and helping the residents discuss them and solve them together
- Accessing outside consultation
- Working toward the creation of facilities geared to the needs of this client group

SUGGESTED READINGS

At this point no writings on self-mutilation are available that I feel good about recommending.

11

Troubled Eating

This chapter is titled "Troubled Eating" rather than "Eating Disorders" because there is no disorder here. Trouble with eating can result in medical diseases or "disorders." Trouble over eating nonetheless is not itself a disorder but a psychosocial problem and solution. The word *disorder* moreover connotes the very opposite of what occurs. As anyone who has ever known an anorexic woman is aware, THERE IS NOTHING MORE ORDERLY THAN THE PRECISE REGIMEN THAT WOMEN WHO ARE ANOREXIC FOLLOW.

According to Bemis (1978) and Striegel-Moore, Siberstein, and Rodin (1986), approximately 95% of anorexics and bulimics are women. As the figure suggests, anorexia and bulimia are predominantly, albeit not exclusively, a woman's issue. At one time anorexia and bulimia were relatively minor and almost exclusively limited to the middle and upper classes. In this era of advanced capitalism, the problems are major and transcend class. They are considerably more prevalent among white women than women of color. The gap nonetheless is decreasing. Tragically, in light of the reality of white hegemony, white women are the standard and are progressively emulated. Severe eating problems are correspondingly far more prevalent in highly industrialized societies, like those of the United States and Canada, although the gap is decreasing.[1]

It is common to pathologize a few women, calling them "anorexic" or "bulimic," while seeing most women's eating as more or less unproblematic. This dichotomy belies the reality of our relationship to food. In this society, by age 18, Sternhell (1985) informed us, 80% of women have dieted to lose weight. According to researchers Halmi, Falk, and Schwartz (1981), 79% of female college students have had at least one bulimic episode. As women our relationship to food is clearly a troubled one.

The roots of this troubled relationship can be located in our troubled relationship to our violated, objectified, and driven bodies. It stems from patriarchal capitalism, with racism playing a complementary role. It resides in our reduction to body, our designation as a body-for-others, and our dual function as body for the sexual pleasuring of males and body for domestic services and the nurture of others.

As sex objects we women are expected to violate our bodies in whatever ways are necessary to fit the beauty standards dictated by the white male elite. In North America this means being as pale or light as possible and being considerably thinner than is healthy for any woman to be. As body for the nurture of others and not self, we are correspondingly expected to cater to the physical and psychological needs of others and to have no needs ourselves. Food is a central part of this catering and deprivation, as well as a governing metaphor for what is occurring. On a literal level the traditional woman spends much of her day choosing, preparing, and serving food to others. On a figurative level we are expected to fill others with our love and attention, while we remain needy and starving.

Again our upbringing prepares us for these roles. White little girls are taught to keep themselves trim, to shop carefully, to dress "attractively." Many Black little girls are taught to "look as white as possible." All little girls are taught to see themselves from the outside, to see themselves from elite male eyes, and to alter their bodies accordingly. On some level and to some degree, moreover, we are all taught to cook for others, to fulfil others' needs, and to ignore our own needs.

The fashion industry dramatically exacerbates the problem. We compare ourselves to the slim exotic models and stars and find ourselves distressingly inadequate. What woman has not felt ashamed or at least critical of some part of her body? What woman has not tried to effect some change with at least a bit of desperation? What compounds the problem is that it is in the industry's interest to keep changing fashion. As fashions shift, new paradigms replace old ones, often quite rapidly. The pressure is ongoing to keep making adjustments in our attire and in our flesh.

To understand the dilemma that women called "anorexic" and "bulimic" face, we must proceed from this context. *All women have problems around eating in this society, although these problems vary in significant ways.* Again the metaphor of a continuum is helpful. All women are somewhere on an eating continuum that is itself inherently problematic. On the left are women who only occasionally worry about food intake as it relates to body image. On the extreme right are women who are literally starving to death and/or vomiting up their insides. Both Black and white women are on the continuum; both are plagued by an impossible ideal. Black women are plagued by a beauty ideal that they cannot possibly approximate because it is fundamentally "white." They are less likely to advance toward the right in the continuum and become seriously anorexic and bulimic because the "white" ideal is transparently out of reach. Many nonetheless diet and unkink their hair. And Black women traditionally take on the role of unnurtured nurturer. White women, conversely, are plagued by a combined "deprivation and beauty" ideal that seems almost in reach. They are tantalized by it and pursue it, with it always somehow evading their grasp. The more realistic the goal seems and the higher the woman's sights on one hand, the more desperate she is likely to be around her eating and the farther advanced on the continuum on the other.

As always, power and control are central to our dilemma. The more Woman as Body is infringed on and the more she feels out of control, the more likely she is to treat food and body as areas over which to exercise control. Hence the relationship between childhood sexual abuse and eating problems.[2]

ANOREXIA

Anorexia literally means "loss of appetite." As pioneer Susan Orback (1988) has so astutely pointed out, the name is a misnomer that misses the point of the anorectic struggle. Indeed women who are anorexic fail to eat and as a result become precariously thin. It is not, however, because they lack appetite. *They are purposefully overriding the pangs of hunger and losing weight by an act of will.*

Work with anorexic women has traditionally centered around weight gain. Various types and degrees of force have been exerted toward this end. Many women have been hospitalized and force fed. Hospitalization and forced feeding brutally seize the one area of control that the women have. It is patriarchal victimization/revictimization. It is oral rape! As such it is indefensible, and our cooperating with it in any way constitutes a profound betrayal.

For the most part the intrusion does not even achieve the ends intended. Women are humiliated by the alien weight that has been inflicted on them. Most respond correspondingly either by abruptly losing the weight or by becoming bulimic—that is, binging and vomiting out pounds that they do not want and will not keep. Either way, they feel defeated and lost.

Most feminist therapists who work and write in this area are critical of these practices and argue against them—but only to a point. They point out quite correctly that few women die from anorexia. And they contend that forced hospitalization is seldom necessary and suggest that we hospitalize only if the woman's life is in danger. Feminist therapists disagree about the exact point at which life would be in danger, but most consider anything under 70 pounds as enormously dangerous and warranting intrusion.[3]

My position as always is that as long as a person is choosing, we should not be usurping her authority. This is not to say that we should not strongly warn of dangers and do what we can to influence her. Indeed, where danger exists, we have an obligation to do so. The bottom line is, however painful it may be for everyone, the woman has a right to place her life in jeopardy and even to starve to death; and we counselors do not necessarily know best. Our job is to express our own concern and caring, to encourage and help with better choices as we see them, and to make sure that the client is aware of the danger that she is in.

In light of the anorexic woman's distorted sense of her own body size, this is, of course, not an easy matter. Therapists are frequently concerned that the choice is based on delusion and that concern is legitimate. My experience suggests nonetheless that while we keep hearing from the person inside who is calling all the shots and who thinks that she is too fat, someone is always inside who knows differently. Our job is to contact that person and to help her gain a voice in the decision making.

The traditional emphasis on weight gain generally, as well as on food per se, is also ill-advised.[4] Even where judgment and pressure are not initially involved, the situation all too easily slips into the familiar dynamic of other people attempting to force food on her. What is still more problematic is that such an emphasis reinforces the centrality of food and food intake. Food and food intake are already far too central. They are the metaphor through which anorexic women speak. We need to move behind the metaphor and to co-explore the territory that it at once points to and disguises. We need to deemphasize food and food intake per se.

Deemphasizing food and food intake, it should be pointed out, does not mean not discussing it. Although a balance must be maintained, it is in fact critical to discuss food practices. Anorexic women have made a life out of hiding their food practices. They layer their bodies so that others will not know how little they eat. They take food and dispose of it surreptitiously to give the appearance that they are eating. They spend hours eating the same piece of bread to create the impression that they are eating a lot. They hide both the paucity of their food intake and the rituals used to mask it. And they feel condemned to a life of hiding. They desperately need to be able to come out of hiding, to be seen and

accepted as they are. It is up to us to encourage these conversations, to help the
women come out of hiding, and to accept them as they are. Unless we talk about
the details of food intake, we cannot help them with it.

What deemphasizing food and food intake *does* mean is:

1. Except for brief periods as agreed on, not making food increase a primary goal of
   counseling
2. Accepting women at their current weight insofar as possible
3. Focusing primarily on meaning and purpose
4. No food charts, no weighing in when she comes to session, in fact rejecting
   all paraphernalia and processes designed to make the client "observable and
   controllable"[5]

Ongoing contracting with anorexic women makes sense for the same reasons
that it makes sense with women who self-mutilate. It extends power and control
beyond her body. In this contracting, I always stipulate that I will not hospitalize
the client and that I will not attempt to rob her of her anorectic solution. This
promise and reassurance make it easier for her to come out of hiding and to
share. Contracting around co-exploration is critical, as always.

Not wanting to get into fights over who controls the client's body, and
concerned about dangerously low weight, many feminist therapists stipulate,
and I would suggest mistakenly, some version of the following when contracting:

1. There is a division of labor. The therapist and the client together are responsible
   for exploring meaning. The client alone is responsible for maintaining minimal
   weight.
2. Weight gain will not be discussed in the sessions.
3. Ongoing therapy is contingent on the client not falling below the specified
   minimum—often 70 pounds. (The rationale here is that women cannot think
   clearly when they fall below 70 pounds and so therapy is impractical.)[6]

I disagree with making therapy contingent on the client maintaining a set
weight. Except for safeguarding the therapist against possible legal actions—
something that should not be our primary goal—it serves no positive ends. It
announces loud and clear that when things really get difficult, we are going to
desert her. And it invites hiding and deception, for it is perfectly clear that
openness and sharing are not safe. The rationale moreover is bogus. Emaciation,
without a doubt, interferes with the ability to think clearly. It is not true though
that no woman below 70 pounds can think sufficiently clearly to benefit from
interacting with us. We are merely faced with the onus of working harder.

Defining the handling of weight in such a way that discussions about it are outside the purview of therapy moreover is less than helpful. Although anorexic women understandably fear having control wrested from them, many desperately want help with a pattern that is out of control. It is our responsibility to give such help and to contract for it where the client so desires.

Where the client asks for help in increasing her food intake, once again it is important to surface the ambivalence. Contact both the person who wants to change the eating patterns and the person who does not. And again, a one-small-step-at-a-time approach is highly advisable. An example of an unrealistic step is doubling one's food intake. An example of a feasible step might be drinking half a cup of milk a day. It is important, of course, to find out which foods the woman likes and which she loathes, or else our suggestions may woefully miss the mark.

In all of this it is important that the anorexic woman is making the shifts for herself—not to please us. So determine where her decisions are coming from. Anorexia, it should be remembered, has its origins in the "good little girl" script. It is good little girls who nurture others and try to have no needs themselves who tend to become anorexic. The woman has a long history of pleasing others. She may attempt to please us by eating. Changes that are effected this way, however, will not last. Encouraging her to eat for us moreover reinforces the original script.

With anorexia, it is important to read up on health risks. We want to be aware of what our client is up against and be able to detect health problems. Health risks to be aware of and prepared to discuss with anorexic clients include circulatory disturbances, Raynaud's syndrome, irregular heartbeat, and cardiac arrest. If a client is an advanced anorexic and is also bulimic, recommending a medical checkup for a possible electrolyte imbalance is advisable. Where an electrolyte imbalance is present, addressing it is critical, for the client is at risk of cardiac arrest.

Good work with anorexic clients requires the same steadiness as work with clients who self-mutilate. The client will know whether we are frightened by her gaunt appearance or piercing eyes and will not trust us if we are. An additional attitudinal problem that may interfere with a counselor's ability to work well is admiration. Counselors who have not worked through their own issues around body image may find themselves admiring, even envying, the ultra slim, self-disciplined anorexic client. The admiration interferes with the work.

Like the self-mutilating client, the anorexic client desperately needs our nurture, our understanding, our compassion. She is both figuratively and literally "starving" for it. The dilemma she finds herself in is that she cannot acknowledge the need to herself or to us without admitting that she is needy. And she cannot admit that she is needy without calling into question the entire anorectic enterprise—her deprivational mode of being-in-the-world. The prospect of that is absolutely terrifying! We help by being steady and by knowing when to back off. We help by being compassionate ourselves regardless of how she responds. It is important correspondingly to surface and empathize with the dilemma itself.

Meanings and Purposes

As with any mode of coping, co-exploration of meaning and purpose is central to our work and is likely to unearth a variety of meanings. We need to be on the lookout for common meanings, while taking in the uniqueness.

On one level, as already noted, food refusal is inevitably about denying needs and neediness. While affirming *her right to deny needs,* we help by affirming *her right to have needs.* Some examples of useful questions here are:

- Who told you that you were not supposed to have needs?
- Who benefits/benefitted from your acting as if you have no needs?
- Who benefits from women generally being denied needs?

Uncovering and problematizing the original script is correspondingly critical.

Feeling strong is generally an accompanying meaning. By feeling as if she has no needs or is in some way beyond needs, the anorexic woman is able to feel strong. Being able to override needs is proof of strength. She has the discipline to do what almost no one else can do, and she is proud of that strength. Other women try to diet and fail. She can diet day after day, managing on next to nothing.

We can and should validate the purpose and the strength. At the same time, we should do the following:

- Help her explore other ways of being/feeling strong that do not take away from her
- Problematize the equation: Overriding Needs Equals Strength
- Uncover the tyranny of the superwoman ideal
- Begin co-exploring the sexist messages and conundrums

On some level the denial of needs and the pursuit of strength are inevitably accompanied by a denial of feeling—both physical and emotional—and a denial of the body generally. The anorexic woman is going as far as she humanly can to get rid of her body. She is keeping the body to the bare minimum. The image of woman as spirit and the cult of invalidism are contributing to what is happening here despite the opposing value of being strong. It is important for us to help the client uncover this phenomenon/ideology and begin problematizing it. Whether she is reflectively aware of it or not, on some level the anorexic woman is correspondingly operating out of her own version of the general equation

Body = Feelings = Vulgarity = Needs = Neediness = Unacceptable

Co-investigating and co-problematizing this equation and what underlies it are critical to progress.

The transition to adult womanhood under the patriarchy is generally central to the emergence and meaning of the equation. Many anorexic women grew up taking pride in their intellectual acumen and achievement. As they experienced it—experiences that are not pathological but that point to a very real patriarchal reality—the development of a full woman's body was the beginning of a tragic fall. At one time they were human beings. Then they became "women." Progressively, that is, they were trivialized as thinking human beings. Progressively they were reduced to body. The conclusion that followed is

HAVING AN ADULT WOMAN'S BODY EQUALS BEING A SEX OBJECT; BEING DOOMED TO WOMEN'S WORK (MENIAL, DOMESTIC, CHILD-BEARING); BEING DRAGGED DOWN; NOT BEING ABLE TO SOAR, TO PURSUE DREAMS, TO ASPIRE.[7]

The anorexics' solution was an obvious one. They chose to get rid of the adult woman's body by scrupulously restricting eating. The menses stopped. The breasts began to disappear. The hips lost their unique female curviness. And they began to feel free again.

This is resistance—an insistence on scope and freedom. The sexist plight needs to be acknowledged. And the importance and value of that resistance need to be affirmed. At the same time, it is critical to help our anorexic sister redirect her resistance to the outside world. Help her address communally and politically what she is now addressing individually and internally. Good work in this area correspondingly means helping her take the patriarchy, not her body, as the change target. And it means helping her begin valuing and becoming grounded in her body once again.

In many cases this rejection of sexual feelings, almost all feelings, and the body overall is additionally the legacy of extreme childhood sexual abuse. Many survivors of extreme childhood sexual abuse "forgot" about the abuse until puberty. With puberty comes dramatic female development, sexual feelings, and sexual attention. All of this serves to surface the abuse memories. The woman wishes to get rid of the memories, of the body that is associated with the abuse and is seen as vile, of sexual and other feelings that are likewise associated with the abuse and are seen as vile. At adolescence or at any other time, anorexia presents itself as a solution. Hence the preponderance of anorexia and indeed troubled eating generally among survivors of extreme childhood sexual abuse. In light of this connection, it is enormously important for us to co-explore and co-address childhood sexual abuse when working with anorexic clients.

As already noted, conforming to the attractiveness standards dictated for women additionally is an invariable meaning, and that meaning too needs to be acknowledged. The other side of the conformity once again is resistance. The anorexic woman is far exceeding the mandated thinness and even the thinness that is permitted, and she knows it. She is living up to her own standards in full knowledge that society does not find it attractive and is even appalled by it. On one level she is deeply embarrassed by what she is doing and what she has made of herself, and she attempts to cover it up. We need to empathize with that embarrassment and to reassure her. On another level she feels good, as well she might, about resisting. Part of our job is to validate that resistance. At the same time, we need to help her redirect resistance.

Alongside strength and resistance is, invariably, control. Robbed of control by virtue of being a woman and the particular woman that she is, the anorexic, like the self-mutilating woman, has seized control over the one area that women are encouraged to control, and she is holding on to it desperately. The need for control too needs to be affirmed and avenues for real control explored.

The tragedy of her plight is that the more the anorexic woman controls her eating, the more out of control even her eating practices become. She finds herself progressively unable to choose to eat and/or to put that choice into practice. And she is terrified. Seeking to escape a trap, she has trapped herself. And she sees no way out. Surfacing, empathizing with, and co-exploring the dilemma once again are critical. This is not easy, for it is humiliating for her to acknowledge that she is stuck. Our understanding, respect, and acceptance help. By sharing our own awareness that she can change the patterns, and by helping her change them correspondingly, we help her regain the control that she now vitally needs.

A final purpose is communication. On one level she is communicating that she is strong, that she needs nothing. This communication has already been discussed. On another level she is using her body as an indictment of society. She is saying, "Just look what you have made of me." On still another level she is saying, "I am in trouble. Help."

We need to affirm and co-explore the protest, while helping her protest with her mouth, not her body. And we need to take in and respond to the cry for help, without ignoring the parallel message "I am self-sufficient; back off." By remembering to be both caring and respectful at the same time, we can generally strike the balance needed. When we err, and inevitably we sometimes will, we can recover by taking in the feedback and acknowledging the error.

Resources

Resources that it is important to be aware of and prepared to suggest include the following:

* Books and films on anorexia—first-person accounts in particular
* Names and numbers of any feminist centers that specialize in the area
* Names of doctors who can help with electrolyte imbalances and are unlikely or at least less likely to "take over"
* Names of lawyers who are knowledgeable in the area and are prepared to protect anorexic women from interference by the medical practitioners and others insofar as possible
* Consciousness-raising, support, and therapy groups for women with eating problems
* Feminist educational events related to eating problems
* Feminist protests against the tyranny of thinness, whatever forms these protests may take

BULIMIA

Traditional *bulimia* is characterized by binging followed by purging. Purging is generally accomplished through vomiting or laxative use. Rigorous exercise, however, may play a role, as indeed it may in anorexia.

Where a client does not tell us she is bulimic, we may have a problem identifying the bulimia. Although some bulimics are quite thin, a high percentage maintain the weight seen as average for women in this society. Possible indicators that a client is bulimic include overt preoccupation with food; teeth with the enamel worn off (tooth enamel is worn down by frequent vomiting); the occurrence of or reference to involuntary vomiting; shame; and references to self as greedy or "a fraud."

Bulimia bears a strong relationship to anorexia. Many women who are bulimic are plagued by a thinness ideal. All are at least somewhat preoccupied with weight. Although all are aware of their own neediness, many are enormously ashamed of that neediness and of giving in to it, for they aspire to the same deprivational ideal as the anorexic. Many were once anorexics. In some cases, initially at least, bulimia was a response to interference with their food refusal. Having pounds brutally inflicted on them, they were mortified. And so they purged. Others started increasing their food intake or binging because they were desperately aware of their own hunger—physically and/or psychologically. The conflict between desperately needing to feed or nurture self and extreme discomfort with this nurture or the added weight is expressed in the binge-purge cycle.

In light of the close relationship between anorexia and bulimia, work with bulimics is very similar to work with anorexics, and within reason, counselors may legitimately apply what is learned about one to the other. The similarity notwithstanding, bulimia is its own struggle. Bulimic women are not simply "failed anorexics," although some bulimic women see themselves this way and many counselors follow suit. Good work with bulimic women is predicated on understanding the uniqueness and complexity of the bulimic struggle and integrating that understanding into the work.

This complexity is reflected in the two independent yet interdependent factors that characterize it—binging on the one hand, followed by purging on the other. The binging and the purging need to be co-investigated both individually and as they relate to each other. The bulimic struggle is really a number of struggles, and these struggles are as varied as the different meanings and combinations of meaning.

For purposes of clarification, some counselors distinguish between two types of bulimia—what has come to be called "casual or pragmatic bulimia" on one hand and "compulsive or control-oriented bulimia" on the other.[8] The pragmatic or casual bulimic has no special interest in either binging or purging. *Food intake* primarily means "food intake." It is not laden with emotional and other meanings. She wants to eat amply, while being spared some of the consequences of doing so. Accordingly, she seldom binges. For the most part she merely eats more than what is consonant with her weight ideal. She vomits to get rid of this weight. She likes eating, and her focus is on eating, not on vomiting or binging. The vomiting is pragmatic. She VOMITS IN ORDER TO EAT.

For the control-oriented bulimic by contrast, the cycle is laden with emotional issues, and control is critical. This woman frequently binges, with the binging answering emotional, not simply physical, needs. She almost invariably purges after binging, and the purge is even more emotionally laden. Cooper (1987) and others have identified the purging as a primary value, suggesting that the control-oriented bulimic BINGES IN ORDER TO PURGE. Cooper calls the purging "addictive."

These categories are flawed, but they help us get our bearing as counselors and have some validity. We can legitimately use them as rough guides as long as we are aware of the limitations and distortions involved.

One distortion to be aware of and that we do well to eliminate is the addiction concept. The *addiction model* is based on the premise of a need or activity over which the client has no power once she indulges at all. Hence the A.A. formula, "one drink away from a drunk." The parallel for the control-oriented bulimic would be, "one binge/purge away from hopeless continuous binging and purging." Contrary to this assumption, many clients have gone from what would be seen as severe control-oriented bulimia to occasional bulimia. Cutting back with or without the intention of stopping in fact is the primary route to ending the bulimic cycle. The concept of *addiction,* if taken seriously, would seriously jeopardize the work that needs to be done.

A second problem is the assumption that purging is always the primary goal of the control-oriented bulimic. Although undoubtedly many of these women do "binge in order to purge," for a number of my clients, binging was even more central than purging. It is important to be open here and not to predefine.

The third and most fundamental problem is the dichotomy itself. Although the generalization allows us to see significant differences in emphasis, it makes the differences absolute when they are not. For bulimics whom we would tend to identify as pragmatic, certainly the issues surrounding bulimia tend to be far fewer and less pressing. I know of no bulimic woman, however, for whom "food intake is merely food intake." For all women who are bulimic, in fact for all women period, food intake points to the possibility of becoming a size that is not allowed. For a woman who is bulimic, the bulimic pattern correspondingly means acknowledging while being conflicted over physical need; fulfilling that need despite society's disapproval; generally maintaining an approved weight through disapproved means; and feeling at least somewhat guilty. Additionally, emotional needs are always, to some extent, served.

Rather than dichotomize, it is more helpful to think of bulimia as a continuum. What has been called "casual bulimia" is on the very left, and the advanced "control-oriented bulimia" is on the right. Women may start at different points on the continuum, may stay where they begin, and may move in either direction, although they generally experience a pull to the right. The farther to the right, (a) the more frequent the binging and purging, (b) the more laden with emotional and other meanings, (c) the more critical bulimia as a mode of coping has become, and (d) the greater the physical danger in the long run.

For all women on the continuum, bulimia has a variety of meanings and is a mode of coping.

Good counseling with bulimic women involves assessing where women are on the continuum and what general direction they are headed and adjusting the counseling emphasis accordingly. Good co-exploration, which as always is critical wherever they may be, means investigating the different meanings and purposes. Again it is important to be aware of common meanings and to use them as touchstones, while being open to differences.

The highly pragmatic bulimic has no problem around intake, except her own perception, and for her, purging relates primarily to patriarchal standards. We help by acknowledging her success in both maintaining and sidestepping those standards, while gently problematizing the standards themselves. We need to help her accept that nothing is wrong with her intake and build on her resistance.

Where women frequently binge, controlling or cutting off feeling is frequently a governing motive. Binging or "stuffing down food" is a way of "stuffing down feelings," and it provides relief from those feelings. The feelings being swallowed are generally highly unpleasant feelings, such as terror or heartbreak. Generally the woman is shoving these down because she finds them too awful to bear. Additionally/alternatively she may at some point have been forbidden to feel or express such feelings. The feelings may also be pleasant feelings that are associated with traumatic memories and unpleasant feelings and that act as triggers for these.

Where feelings are being shoved down, childhood sexual abuse is a strong possibility, and it is important to check for it. Whatever the origins of the feelings, we need to do the following:

- Honor the coping that is protecting her from something she could not/cannot bear
- Affirm as often as necessary her right to feel and to express
- Help her begin exploring the feelings that she is now swallowing
- Help her express some of the feelings (Ex-pressing is the opposite of pressing or pushing down. For clients with trouble ex-pressing, expressive bioenergetics exercises involving screaming, hitting, and making noises can be very helpful indeed.)
- Help her find alternative ways of containing feelings (See Chapter 7.)
- Co-investigate the context out of which the feelings arise and to which they are a response

Frequently as well, ongoing binging is a desperate attempt to fill the emptiness. She is attempting to address the felt neediness—the emotional deprivation. The emptiness and the desperation to be filled up needs to be clearly taken in and empathized with on an ongoing basis. We need to care about and nurture the deprived little girl. Affirmation of the coping is also in order. It is critical, correspondingly, to help her find alternative ways of nurturing herself so that eating is not her only way. I like to engage bulimic clients in ongoing exercises that involve giving herself positive strokes, asking for positive strokes from others, and both taking in and holding on to the love given her by self and others.

Women additionally may binge to communicate. They may be communicating distress, protest, the desire for help. Our job here is to take in the communication, help her take it in, affirm and address what is communicated, and help her find other ways of communicating.

Purging, as it functions for the highly pragmatic bulimic, has already been discussed. Purging also serves purposes far beyond allowing women to eat while keeping to the weight prescribed them in this society. Shame expiation is one of these.

After binging, bulimic women often feel profoundly ashamed. They have now done "something utterly disgusting." As they see it, they have lost all control and have indulged themselves "shamelessly." They are greedy. They have been excessive, decadent—exactly the opposite of what is prescribed for women. And they are revolted. Behind the revulsion for indulging this way lies revulsion at having these and other desires and needs at all, revulsion at being human, sometimes the disgust of childhood sexual abuse. Purging reverses what happened by getting rid of the food. More significantly it is a form of expiation, of atonement. By punishing herself the bulimic woman pays for "her sin." She then feels temporary relief. As the name implies, she is now "purged." As words like *sin, purge,* and *indulgence* further suggest, ascetic religious values are clearly operant here even if the woman is not "a believer."

The tragedy of this relief is not simply that the bulimic woman thinks that she has done something dreadful and has to harm herself, though certainly this is tragic. It is also that the relief is temporary and tends to backfire. It is almost invariably followed by greater self-disgust.

The woman looks at the induced shit, at the induced vomit, at the "dreadful mess that she has made," and she is mortified by it. She sees herself AS THE EXCREMENT, AS THE VOMIT, AS SOMETHING PUTRID, MESSY, EXCESSIVE. She knows that society would condemn her, and she condemns herself. Now she has additional feelings that she needs to get rid of. More binging/purging is the obvious solution.

Additionally, if she feels guilty enough, she may seek more overt ways to punish herself and thereby find relief. This can easily lead to a self-aggravating cycle of multiple self-abuse. By ways of example, when they feel especially guilty, some bulimic women self-mutilate after purging. Self-mutilation gives the bulimic woman a renewed sense of strength and self-discipline. It allows her to truly pay for her misdemeanor and feel relief. The kicker is that self-mutilation is also messy, is also disapproved of by society, and is visible proof of her "badness." Once again she has something to hide. Once again she has done something shameful, and she needs to do something about it. And so the cycle of shame and self-abuse escalates.

Significantly, even where shame is not itself a motive for purging, purging frequently results in shame and leads to an escalation of "shameful acts." The messiness is there regardless. Shame arises additionally from the sense of being a sham, from telling herself, "I am maintaining this weight by cheating. And that's exactly what I am—a cheat!" All of this is compounded by demeaning responses from others. Significantly, whereas everyone admires the anorexic, no one exactly "admires" the bulimic. She is more likely to be the object of pity and thinly disguised contempt.

Help is predicated on empathizing with her sense of shame and her overall plight, while being clear with both ourselves and her that she has nothing to be ashamed of. Our bulimic sister needs to know that we appreciate the torturous and self-aggravating cycle that she is in. Just as surely, she needs to know that we do not find her or anything that she is doing repulsive or unacceptable—not her binging, not her purging, not her self-mutilation. She needs to hear that none of her desires or needs are frightening or distasteful. She needs our reassurance that she is being human and that it is perfectly okay for her to be human.

Our ongoing reassurance and acceptance help her accept herself just as she is. Familiarity with others in her plight and being in groups with other bulimic women also help with acceptance, so it is important to let her know that other women struggle with this, to make relevant books or articles available, and to consider group work. Further empowerment comes with co-exploring the roles of society and of concrete others in her life and seeing where real culpability lies. Where religion plays a special role in the shame, co-investigation of the connection and reframing are also called for.

Inevitably, of course, whatever the other meanings, purging is about rejection of something outside of oneself. Like her anorexic sister, the bulimic woman is saying no to food or food intake even though she begins by saying yes. This rejection may primarily be an attempt to retain a set weight or to "atone." Alternatively/additionally, though, she may be revolted by and revolting against something that food or food intake represents. Although she takes the food, she chokes on it; she cannot/will not keep it down.

Where rejection such as this is formidable, food and/or food intake is often associated with abuse, generally early abuse. Although other abuse is usually involved, the abuse that predisposes the woman toward a bulimic solution itself may actually involve food itself and may or may not be something we would normally think of as abusive.

Early feeding habits provide examples of abusive situations involving food which do not necessarily look abusive. Children who were frequently forced to eat food that they did not like or to eat larger quantities or more quickly than they were comfortable with are predisposed toward bulimic solutions. As innocent as the overzealousness may appear to the parent, it is rapish and awful for the little girl who is having food shoved at her, who is being hovered over and ordered to eat it all up "to the last bite." She may begin the vomiting in childhood itself or later. She is not simply getting rid of the food. She is also reacting against the invasion. The anorexic who is force-fed and more blatantly violated similarly may revolt against the invasion that food intake now connotes.

Additionally, even where no abuse exists, where cultures center around food to the degree that the dominant culture does not, the contradictions may pose a problem and may lead to exaggerated feelings of pressure and eventually bulimia. The Jewish experience of bulimia is one example, although there are many others.

As noted earlier, in the Jewish culture the strong mother has progressively lost her role and has found herself confined to the home. The Jewish culture moreover has been traditionally food-centered. The Jewish woman grows up hearing from the larger misogynous world that she has to be thin. At the same time, she hears "eat, eat" from her mother, who is offering her yet another bagel, just a little more cream cheese, a piece of the latest cake that she has baked. On some level she is aware of the double message. And even if she delights in her caring parent, she experiences the ongoing refrain of "eat, eat" as at least somewhat invasive. The more conflicted she is about the double message, and the more invasive she finds what is happening, the more likely she is to seek a bulimic solution.

Abuse that is not overtly connected with food is more typical. As already noted, women who are survivors of childhood sexual abuse are particularly prone to a bulimic solution—especially if oral sex was involved. Foods like egg whites may remind them of the semen. Although they may not be able to put their finger on what is going on, somehow the texture or taste bothers them. They take it in and then reject it. The very act of taking food into the mouth and swallowing may in fact be associated with abuse. The food, like the penis, is taken in. The women feel violated, feel disgusted, choke on it. They want to get rid of the disgusting substance/feel.

Alternatively what is being rejected on a physical level may not have transpired on a physical level either primarily or at all. The bulimic woman may find her overall treatment as a woman utterly "unpalatable." Or she may be reacting to a specific situation.

A case in point is a bulimic immigrant client of mine who worked in a clothing factory. Daily she slaved at boring work for substandard wages, while being ordered about and insulted. She ate during the day and came home and forced herself to vomit at night. She was swallowing more abuse than she could "stomach" and both prereflectively and quietly had found a way of rebelling.

This rejection—this resistance—is meaningful and strong, however unaware the bulimic woman may be of what is going on and however helpless she may feel. Helping our client uncover and affirm that resistance and strength is critical. At the same time, we need to probe the metaphor, to find out what in particular is being protested. Clues may be provided by the following:

- Taste and texture of the food that she vomits, especially where vomiting has become involuntary
- Individual words that she uses to describe her predicament
- Emotionally laden words that she applies both to food and to significant situations

Again, helping her move past the metaphor to the concrete situation is vital, for this situation clearly needs to be focused on and co-investigated. And again it is important to help her explore other modes of protest.

A final meaning complex is strength and control. The woman who purges is also exercising control over her body. She is making it bend to her will. She is forcing it to expel what it would otherwise digest. Insofar as she has little other control in her life, she desperately needs the control that she is now exercising. She is also being strong and, on some level, she values that strength. Even while admiring anorexic women for their strength and feeling pathetically weak herself, the woman who regularly forces herself to vomit knows that she is doing something that few women can do. Other women cannot "work" their bodies this way. They cannot bring themselves to engage in forced vomiting at all. Or they cannot keep it up this long or "work" it this regularly. Despite the overwhelming shame, she takes some pride in this strength—in this achievement.

Again the control and the strength need to be recognized and affirmed. Again the folly of attempting to take over or to rob our sisters of their solution is clear. And again it is important to help our sisters exercise more control in their lives and in the world.

Practical Issues

A one-small-step-at-a-time approach to changing eating patterns is as critical with bulimic as with anorexic clients. Postponing binging or purging by an hour is an example of initial small steps that may be viable.

Women who have arrived at the point of vomiting involuntarily generally need considerable practical assistance. Damage to the esophagus or the stomach lining may be involved, and it is important that such damage be checked for. Whether physical damage has occurred or not, a physical reaction is prohibiting successful food intake. Generally the client is experiencing some type of muscle interference. She may chew the food but gag on it while or almost immediately after she swallows or attempts to swallow. In this instance muscles may be responding involuntarily to block or "choke off" the food route or may be in spasm as a result of prolonged induced vomiting. Alternatively she may swallow the food successfully, only to vomit it up a hour or so later. Again muscle interference is likely. Psychological issues as described earlier are implicated in these problems, and they need to be addressed. The client nonetheless is in dire need of practical physical help.

Where the client is open to it, use of valerian tea or other natural muscle relaxants are a good beginning. She will need to do some experimenting to find out which works best for her. Relaxation exercises and bioenergetics exercises involving ex-pressing might also be considered. With women at an advanced stage of involuntary vomiting, reverting temporarily to a liquid diet is a good idea. The change from liquid to more substantial food should be gradual. Often women who vomit involuntarily are able to digest food that they consider a "real treat," and we can make use of this as well.

Physical damage that may result from bulimia and that we need to be aware of and alert these clients to includes serious electrolyte imbalance, cardiac arrest, damage to the esophagus, rupture of the stomach lining, deterioration of tooth enamel, and rupture in anal membranes. Clients additionally may end up with spastic colon and/or other involuntary spasming.

In light of the seriousness of these problems, we do well to encourage bulimic clients to have electrolyte and other checkups. Again, having a sympathetic and relatively unobtrusive doctor whom we can recommend is a real plus. Help from a naturopath might also be considered.

"OVER"WEIGHT AND "OVER"EATING

The Most Common Problem

Where women see themselves as having a "weight problem," as most women in this society do to varying degrees, there is indeed a problem. In the vast majority of cases, however, neither their weight nor the amount they eat nor what they eat is the problem. *The problem is sexism, capitalism, racism, and indeed ageism.* "Overweight" is artificially created by Anglo-Saxon (and other) sexist standards that infantilize women and deny women space, weight, food, and nurture. What follows from this is that our job as feminist counselors is not to help women lose weight. It is to help them problematize and see through the "weight problem." It is to help women resist. It is to help them cast off the oppressive vision that makes them fat and begin seeing and loving their own unique size, texture, and shape.

Facts critical for us to be aware of and to consciousness-raise in terms of include:

- Women naturally come in all shapes and sizes.
- Women need considerably more fat than men if they are to remain healthy.
- Statistics suggesting that health correlates with thinness are based on research with male subjects, are androcentric, and are irrelevant.
- Doctors who encourage women to lose weight are generally basing their recommendations on such androcentric research.
- The current beauty ideal is not natural or healthy for any woman.
- Although this is not invariable, generally women naturally stop gaining weight when they reach the weight that is right for them.
- Women naturally gain weight as they get older. Fifty-year-old women do not and should not have the weight of an 11-year-old.

- For the most part, people who weigh more do not eat more.
- Size and weight are not ethical issues; only oppression makes them so.[9]

In light of these facts and the impact of the internalized oppression, it is important to encourage our sister clients to eat what and as much as they want with at least some frequency. Like Orback, I encourage clients to experiment with taste, to find out what they really like to eat. My rationale for doing so, mind you, is not Orback's (1979)—that this will help them lose weight, which it might or might not. It is because WE WOMEN NEED AND HAVE A RIGHT TO NURTURE OURSELVES, TO HAVE SUBSTANCE, TO ENJOY.

Exercises in which the client identifies first one then other parts of her body that she likes and what she likes about them are often useful in helping clients progressively appreciate/reclaim their bodies. Where clients have trouble socializing because they "feel fat," you might want to try creative visualization like Orback's (1979), in which women see themselves at their current weight looking attractive, socializing, and appreciated. A word of caution, though. Be careful not to overemphasize exercises like these, for they still involve "being the object of another's gaze." And they can easily foster "magical thinking." Fat oppression plays a major role in social events—especially heterosexual ones. Encouraging magical thinking that denies, minimizes, or "wills away" the reality of fat oppression and its influence on others is not going to help. Fat oppression needs to be honestly acknowledged and combatted.

Other women—their knowledge, their sisterhood, and their resistance—are by far the most important resources that we can draw on when addressing fat oppression and its internalization. Specific woman-woman resources to be aware of and to share with fat-oppressed clients include feminist literature on fat oppression and other forms of "lookism"—first-person accounts in particular; feminist groups like "Hersize," in which women jointly celebrate their bodies and educate themselves and the world about fat oppression; and feminist educationals on shape, size, and eating.

A Less Frequent Problem

Some women who see themselves as overweight actually do overeat and/or are overweight. Where overeating occurs, the sexist deprivational standard already discussed is generally an underlying issue. Compulsory dieting, the tyranny of the thinness ideal, and the emotional and physical deprivation that is woman's lot contribute to making women desperately hungry and needy on all levels. Women frequently address this desperation through desperate eating. They are snatching some comfort for themselves. They are attempting to do something about the tremendous void. The more they diet, the needier they get, and the more desperate their eating becomes. The more desperate their eating becomes, the worse they feel about themselves. The worse they feel about themselves, the needier they get, and the more they want to diet. They are caught in a no-win and self-aggravating situation.

These women need the same type of help that women who only think they are overweight need. They need help seeing through the oppression and the part that it plays in their predicament. They need help loving their bodies, getting rid of "Dieting" with a capital *D,* and finding their own natural eating rhythm. They need our assurance that they are entitled to nurture, that it makes sense that they are needy. And they need help exploring additional ways of nurturing themselves and addressing their needs.

Other emotional and social purposes may also be served by overeating, and it is important to be aware of these and prepared to co-explore them. As with bulimic women, common purposes that the overeating and binging may serve are:

- Shoving down unwanted feelings (These may be feelings associated with childhood abuse, may be feelings that have been "forbidden," and may be feelings of shame and humiliation around being "fat" or having binged.)
- Pushing down frightening memories
- Containing feelings
- Stopping triggering and/or flooding
- Self-punishment

Again it is important to co-explore early and current experiences, to problematize self-blame, and to reassure the client. Again feelings need to be reached for and expressed. And again women need help acquiring other ways of containing feelings and stopping flooding.

Unlike with bulimic women, with nonbulimic bingers, being overweight may be a primary goal of the eating. Where excess weight is a goal, carrying excess weight is itself a mode of coping. This coping in turn can serve a variety of purposes, and those purposes too need to be co-explored and co-addressed. Ways of fleshing out those purposes include:

- Doing a psychosynthesis exercise in which the client becomes her fat (Ask her as the fat what she offers and what she wants.)
- Asking her to imagine herself thinner and co-exploring the feelings and turmoils that now arise
- Co-investigating differences in her life as they relate to different weights

One range of purposes that overweight often serves is "counting" to self and others. It is a way of having power, of assuring that one's opinions "carry weight." If to be "weightless" is to be/feel "worthless," having lots of weight can be a way of being/feeling substantial and full of worth.

There is considerable room for validation here, for the woman who uses weight for this purpose has a handle on something very real indeed. The slimness that is imposed on us is indeed part and parcel of our trivialization as women. And it indeed does diminish our standing and our strength. The client deserves appreciation for her perception, her resistance, her strength. At the same time, it is important to problematize the "overkill." As well, help her accept that the strength and worth are intrinsic to her and do not belong to the fat. And co-explore other ways of resisting.

For some women, excess weight is a way of avoiding unwanted sexual feelings or of warding off unwanted sexual advances. Again these purposes are important, and it is critical to validate them. Other work that might be called for include:

- Co-exploring the sexual fear and the experiences that may underlie them
- Addressing unresolved feelings of shame and guilt
- Helping the client explore other ways of dealing with fear
- Helping her explore and feel more comfortable with her body
- Helping her feel progressive ownership of and exclusive entitlement to her body
- Practicing other ways of saying no

Alternative or additional communicative purposes that the fat may serve are announcing:

1. "I am in trouble. I need help." (an appeal)
2. "Just look at what has been made of me." (a protest)

Again our job is to hear and respond to the neediness, to hear and affirm the protest, and to help the client find other ways of communicating.

A final "weight-distressed" group that it is critical to be cognizant of are women who weigh more than is healthy for them, who try unsuccessfully to do something about it, yet who honestly are eating very little. Although all women need and deserve to be believed, these women especially need credence and validation. Again and again they meet with incredulity when they speak of how little they eat. People suspect them of "indulgence," of sneaking extra food, of having "no willpower." In light of their deprivational socialization as women, the recrimination and suspicions sting. We help by clearly believing and empathizing with their plight. They need assurance that they are not crazy, that they really are not eating much. They need help loving their bodies as they are. It is important as well to co-investigate the role that fat oppression plays in their plight and to help them better resist. Most of all, however, they need resources.

Minimally in these instances it is important to be aware of and share names of doctors and nutritionists who will believe and respect them, who have expertise in the area, and who are not going to suggest anything dangerous. Additionally the feminist resources specified earlier in the chapter may be helpful.

SUGGESTED READINGS

Hutchinson, M. (1985). *Transforming the body image: Learning to love the body you have.* Freedom, CA: Crossing.

Lawrence, M. (Ed.). (1987). *Fed up and hungry: Women, oppression, and food.* London: Women's Press.

Lawrence, M. (1989). *The anorexic experience* (rev. ed.). London: Women's Press.

Orback, S. (1979). *Fat is a feminist issue.* New York: Berkeley.

Orback, S. (1988). *Hunger strike: The anorectic's struggle as a metaphor for our age.* New York: Avon.

Szekely, E. (1988). *Never too thin.* Toronto: Women's Press.

NOTES

1. For evidence and further discussion of these generalizations and shifts, see Szekely (1988), pp. 32-51, 187-201.

2. For elaborations on the relationship between childhood sexual abuse and eating problems, see Chapter 7.

3. By way of example, see Lawrence (1989).

4. For good arguments against such an emphasis, see Lawrence (1989) and Orback (1988).

5. As readers familiar with Wooley are aware, what I am suggesting is at odds with the position outlined by Wooley, who does believe in charts and weighing-in scales. For an elaboration on Wooley's position, see Wooley and Wooley (1980, 1986) and Wooley and Kearney-Cooke (no date).

6. For one example of the following, see Lawrence (1989).

7. This equation is particularly overt with Ellen West. Ellen West was an anorexic woman in Europe who committed suicide in the first half of this century. Her plight was tragically misunderstood by the male psychiatrists who "treated her" and by Binswanger—the male existential analyst who later interpreted her struggle as simple "greed." See, in this regard, Binswanger (1958) and Burstow (1981).

8. For one example and discussion of this division, see Cooper (1987), pp. 187-190.

9. For further discussion of these points, see Hutchinson (1985) and Lawrence (1989).

12

Drinking Problems

Although common enough, it is androcentric folly to address women's drinking problems like men's. Like bulimia and cutting, our overdrinking fundamentally relates to the patriarchy and our role in it.

According to Sandmaier (1981), the highest rate of overdrinking among women occurs in the category "married women with jobs." In terms of our analysis of woman as laboring body, this means women who are subject to double labor. High rates also exist for the unemployed, isolated "housewife" (hardly a surprise), the marginalized lesbian, the poor, and specific oppressed racial groups. (Be careful of racist assumptions here. Many oppressed races have significantly lower rates.) The lower rate for the housewife than for the superwoman, of course, probably stems from the housewife's use of and encouragement to use alternative numbing substances like Valium. And the comparatively lower rate recorded for the housewife, the middle-class woman, and women from elite racial groups may reflect little more than their increased ability to hide the drinking.

Women need help understanding the connection between the oppressive context and their drinking. And they need help dealing with the oppression, their internalization of the oppression, and their immediate situation.

As with troubled eating and cutting, where women engage in troubled drinking, it is critical to explore the purposes served, while both affirming and problematizing. Drinking, like cutting, is a solution just as much as it is a problem. Counselor and client alike need to see what type of solution it is. And we need to help the client deal with the unresolved issues that underlie it.

Many of the meanings explored in the bulimic section apply here. Like the eating binge, the drinking binge does the following:

- Helps women push, swallow down, distract themselves from or anesthetize themselves against unpleasant feelings, thoughts, or memories (the loneliness of being with a typically unexpressive male partner, the knowledge of being with a batterer, the pain of being sneered at as a lesbian or as a woman of color, and particularly commonly, feelings and memories associated with childhood sexual abuse)
- Helps women avoid difficult decisions that they are not ready to make (leaving the abusive man, assuming a despised sexual identity)
- Helps women at once prove that they are bad and punish themselves for the "badness," thereby exonerating others and safeguarding their world
- Helps women experience strength and daring
- Offers comfort
- Gives temporary pleasure
- Is a way of indirectly communicating "Fuck you," "I need help," and/or "Just look at what you have made of me."

Additionally, overdrinking can be a way of doing:

- Sharing and/or staying with a partner who drinks
- Overcoming self-restraint and so being able to do, feel, and express directly what we women are not allowed to do, feel, or express (acting "unladylike," expressing fury, proclaiming the injustice of our situation, feeling sexual, etc.)
- Overcoming self-restraint so that we can engage in other coping that involves self-harm (cutting, prostituting, "slutting")
- Opting out of an impossible situation, saying no to some of the demands, getting a rest, and/or "going on strike"
- Getting revenge

It is important to co-explore these and other meanings and to help women alter their situation. Women especially need help setting limits and saying no. In the absence of work such as this, at best we are helping clients exchange one mode of self-injurious coping for another. And we are involved in a cover-up. Correspondingly, insofar as deeper issues like childhood sexual abuse underlie the drinking, and they generally do, in the long run at least, these issues need to be the PRIMARY FOCUS OF THE COUNSELING. It is unacceptable nonetheless to insist that such problems be the sole concern of counseling and to force women to go elsewhere for help with their alcohol intake.

Women with drinking problems need to feel better about themselves if they are to get out of the drinking trap. Any progress that they make around drinking less helps and is critical, but they also need help accepting themselves as they are. Our respect and appreciation of them—whether they drink or not—go a long way. Our respect again helps them respect themselves. Such respect does not mean having sessions with them when they are drunk. Therapy with someone drunk is futile and gives the client the message that drunkenness is unproblematic and that we are not seriously inviting them to shift. It does, however, mean not insulting them, not acting as if they have "misbehaved," not thinking/suggesting that they have let us down. And it means recognizing and validating the very real strength that they have.

Feeling better is also contingent on seeing through and rejecting the multiple levels of shame imposed on them. These include:

- The shame that comes simply from being a woman in a misogynous society
- The shame attached to any other relevant oppression
- The shame of being an "alcoholic" in a society that equates drinking with irresponsibility, laziness, and self-indulgence and sees all of these as despicable
- The shame of being a "female alcoholic" in a society that demands and exacts overresponsibility and decorum from woman and so is far more intolerant of female than male "alcoholics"
- The shame of being a "female alcoholic" in a society that sees women overdrinkers as "sluts," "unwomanly," "selfish," "bad wives," and "bad mothers" and condemns them accordingly
- The specific shame arising from childhood sexual abuse, being battered, and so on

The women need to hear that their problem is not irresponsibility but the killing overresponsibility that is demanded of women. Oppressive concepts like "sluts," "unwomanly," "selfish," "bad wives," and "bad mothers" need to be problematized. Women who are mothers are likely to need particular help dealing with self-blame in these days of mother-blaming. With the popularization of such A.A. derivatives as "Adult Children of Alcoholics," they correspondingly need our reassurance that they have not ruined their children for life. Indeed a number probably have given their children far more love and appreciation than the average man gives anybody.

Either a one-step-at-a-time or a cold turkey approach to the drinking itself is possible. If the woman is interested in going cold turkey, it is important that she knows what she is getting into and that this is what she wants. Often women are pressured into a cold turkey solution with little understanding of what is involved and go along with it to please others.

If a woman goes cold turkey, it is critical that she be relieved of other responsibilities during the withdrawal period. Although there are exceptions certainly, in most cases she is better off out of her present situation, away from her home. (By "away from her home" I mean her lodgings, not necessarily the city. The increased use of out-of-town, out-of-country facilities speaks more to capitalist influences than needs.) Where children are involved, partners, friends, or others should be assuming temporary responsibility for them. She is going to need considerable support during this time. Medical attention is preferable, for many already have extensive medical problems caused by the drinking, and further problems may arise from the cold turkeying.

A "treatment center" with an in-house program is a common and indeed a viable solution. One with a feminist understanding and an understanding of different races, cultures, and sexual orientations is far preferable, although not always available. One that does not adhere to a 12-step model is also preferable, though rare. Be prepared to advocate with center staff where necessary. In the long run it is also important to help women gradually (a) soften some of the "absolutes" that the staff may have fed them and (b) problematize such "diagnoses" as "multiple personality disorders," which many staff currently "dispense."

Realistically it tends to be far harder for women to get such help. Men are more able to pick up and go. If they have children, either a female partner or some other woman is often willing to assume full responsibility for the children, while he "gets treatment." Male partners, however, frequently object to being "dumped with the kids" and often downright refuse. Partners, relatives, and friends who have been blaming her for years for being a "bad wife" or "bad mother" may see what she is doing as another form of self-indulgence and further proof of her "irresponsibility." They may expect her to simply "pull up her socks." Husbands who batter may see the request itself as justification for further battery.

Given these responses and her socialization generally, a woman in this situation is likely to need help just feeling entitled to focus on and take care of herself. Redefine what she is doing here as being responsible, not irresponsible. It may be beneficial to do role plays in which she asks for assistance with children and the other responsibilities with which she is saddled. Women who cannot get such help, women with limited financial resources—especially single mothers—may also need us to advocate for them to get the money needed for child care and so forth. Women with battering partners may not realistically be in a position to make any requests, and other avenues may need to be pursued.

Whether the approach be cold turkey or not, culture-specific resources have the potential of being far preferable than the mainstream. A Native woman, for example, may benefit far more from sweat lodge ceremonies and other Native-run programs than from anything that the white oppressor has to offer. Pursuing such a route may also be a way of returning to and taking pride in her heritage. As such it has the added advantage of addressing what may be an underlying issue.

Women who cannot get assistance and/or do not wish to cold turkey may opt for a one-small-step-at-a-time approach. They may choose to reduce the amount they drink a little this week, a little more next week. Our job here is to be constant and have faith in her, to help her increase her awareness so that she does not simply "find herself drinking," to co-explore reasons behind "slips."

Despite the pronouncements of A.A. and the medical establishment, gradual withdrawal is a perfectly good approach that we can wholeheartedly support. In some ways it is preferable to traditional cold turkeying, for it does not foster the absolutist thinking that is part and parcel of the medical model.

The A.A. and the medical establishment claim "one drink away from a drunk" essentially rules out gradual decrease in alcohol consumption. The position is that "alcoholism" is an incurable "illness" that can only be controlled by complete abstinence. "Once an alcoholic," the model says, "always an alcoholic." And once the "alcoholic" takes one drink, she or he is utterly unable to stop. The person cannot reduce intake. Once off alcohol, correspondingly, the person can never resume drinking without becoming hopelessly at the mercy of John Barleycorn (skid row name for booze).

Studies by Davies (1963), Cahalan, Cisin, and Crossley (1969), Clark and Cahalan (1976), and Pattison, Sobell, and Sobell (1977) conclusively disproved these claims. I have worked successfully with many people who slowly reduced their alcohol intake. And many of my clients who have been unproblematic light drinkers for years were once "alcoholics." Again the medical profession is inventing and addressing fictitious disease.

Just as it opens up the possibility of alternatives avenues for withdrawal, the defeat of the medical model means that, for some people anyway, goals besides complete abstinence can be reasonably entertained. Examples of other goals that clients have chosen and successfully reached include:

- Drinking only a few drinks a week, while using the same type of alcohol
- Medium-term goal—going off alcohol totally; long-term goal—becoming an occasional drinker
- Shifting from their alcoholic beverage of choice to one that they are not fond of and becoming a light drinker of it

A client of mine who was part of the lesbian bar scene and did not want to lose either her friends or the scene successfully chose this last route. She felt awkward always sipping Coke while they drank booze. She was a heavy beer drinker who did not like wine. Her solution was seeing her friends at women's bars and nursing a single glass of wine while they drank many beers. She never ended up exactly liking wine and did not want to drink more. Her solution worked for *her*. Years later she began feeling less comfortable with friends who were overdrinking and with the bar scene. She slowly drifted away and saw less of certain old friends and more of new friends.

It is important not to be rigid here. Goals can be changed if they do not work or are no longer working. A variety of goals and means can work temporarily or permanently, and it is up to the client to choose. Our job is to help the client clarify her needs, to offer feedback, to help her hone the goal and means, and where they both strike us as feasible and at least somewhat better for her than what she has been doing to date, to help her pursue them.

In suggesting openness, I am not suggesting that these are goals that we should suggest or that we should collude with minimization. Nor am I suggesting that all options are equally open to everyone. Some people have way more trouble (a) dealing with the pressure of friends who are drinkers, (b) drinking either lightly or not drinking when around these friends, and (c) drinking lightly at all. Wherever we think that a woman is fooling herself and/or that abstinence is preferable, we have an obligation to say so.

After a client has stopped drinking totally or has significantly reduced her alcohol intake, life is going to get considerably harder for her and is going to stay harder for a long time. It is important to warn her about this so that she is not caught by surprise. The thoughts and feelings that she has been numbing out, the problems that she has avoided are now going to be demonstrably present to her and larger than life. Although she knew how to get through the day with a glass in her hand, it may seem utterly impossible to get through the day without one. She may not know how to handle the conflict that is everywhere around her. She may not know how to handle pressures that she was able to resist before by drinking. She may not know how to handle new expectations that come on her or other new responses that her changes meet with.

One solution that is always there and that most of our clients fall back on a number of times is overdrinking itself. It is important to help allay the shame she feels over this. Let her know that you have faith in her, that the "slip" does not nullify the progress she has made, and that you do not regard this as an irreparable failure but as feedback that more help may be needed. By co-investigating the slips, counselor and client can ascertain danger points and what extra resources and skills are needed.

Although some of the people in her life may be of enormous help, the woman with a drinking problem is likely to have others who attempt to undermine her efforts at sobriety. "Drinking buddies" are a special problem. They can inadvertently undermine simply by being who they are (people who continue to drink plentifully in her presence, who crack the familiar drinker jokes, who use the same old "watering hole" as a meeting place). Friends, partner, or relatives may sabotage deliberately. They may, for example, keep offering her a drink, suggesting that "just one" is not going to hurt anyone. They may try to goad her into drinking by implying that she is being "gutless," is acting "just like a straight woman," has become "too good for her old friends," or is turning into "an apple." Where close friends or the partner are drinkers themselves, the likelihood of sabotage increases, for the woman's sobriety alters the relationship and tends to be experienced as a betrayal and a threat.

Although some women may need help understanding the difficulty of the friends' or partner's situation here, the average woman is only too sensitive to it. She needs help clarifying her needs, making requests, and confronting. She needs to be able to make changes in the relating, to establish bottom lines, to decide how often and under what circumstances she is prepared to see certain friends, and in some cases to actually give up friends and hangouts. Correspondingly she may be faced with the difficult task of leaving a sabotaging or otherwise abusive partner.

Where the woman is a mother, many additional problems present themselves. Although the blame heaped on the drinking mother is blatantly misogynous, there is no question but that children are often profoundly harmed by the drinking. Generally the children themselves need help. Groups for children or drinking parents can be beneficial and might be suggested. Check them out, though. Many such groups are decidedly mother-blaming. And some leave children with the impression that they are "spoiled merchandise."

Mother and children, or mother, children, and partner may want family counseling. Where the partner is male, the danger is real that father will be idealized and mother blamed, and it is critical to guard against this.

Facilitating communication between the children and the mother is particularly important, although attending to other lines of communication is also critical. The bottom line is that the children need to tell their mother how the drinking has affected them, and they need mom to hear, take in, and own her part. The children may be haunted by all sorts of traumatizing events and may have borne all sorts of burdens that the mother is partially or totally unaware of. They may have come home on numerous occasions only to find her flaked out on the floor. They may have been heartbroken by an endless stream of broken promises, by finding bottles hidden away when she had assured them that she had gotten rid of all the booze. They may have been humiliated in front of friends. They may have been railed at, insulted. They may have had to deal with social workers intent on removing them from the home. They may have felt responsible for her welfare and spent the better part of their childhood helping her back to bed, removing bottles, worried what was going to happen next. They need to talk about all this, and the mother needs to really hear them.

Communication such as this may also be needed between partners, although it should be nowhere near so one-sided. Both are adults. And where the partner is a male, more often than not his sexism has played a formidable role.

Sometimes, moreover, not helping the woman communicate with her partner but helping her leave her partner is a more obvious direction.

In some cases one or more children—often the eldest child—actively sabotage the mother's attempt to stop drinking and to resume her role as parent. This is particularly likely to occur in single-parent families. We need to be on the lookout for it.

One example of such a dynamic occurred with my client Dora. Dora is a single mother who was a serious alcoholic for about 7 years. She had six children. During her binges her eldest child, Janet, assumed the role of parent. Janet fed the other children and made decisions for the family. When Janet was 14, Dora went to a treatment center and returned sober. Dora's expectation was that everyone would be happy that she was now sober and that she could comfortably resume her role as mother. She was in for a shock.

Janet resented Dora's attempt to resume the mother role. She saw Dora as interfering. Arguments ensued. Dora ended up yelling and issuing commands. Janet resented the commands and objected to being "bossed around." Janet repeatedly told Dora, "I can't stand you. Things were a whole lot better when you were a drunk." And Dora kept vacillating between being overly controlling and feeling guilt and so "letting everyone get away with murder."

As we were doing individual, not family, counseling, I was able to approach these issues only via Dora. What became clear was that Dora needed to learn how to keep her cool and not be "triggered." She needed to resume parenting more slowly, without jarring everyone. She needed to distinguish between what she could and could not reasonably expect, what she should and should not insist on. And she needed to learn how to share power and decision making, where appropriate.

Situations differ, of course, and different issues will occur with different families. When confronting situations like this, it is nonetheless helpful to remember the following:

- The children have been hurt and need to talk of their experiences and be heard.
- Mom needs to know what the children have experienced and to understand their plight.
- It is never possible for the family to simply return to where it was before the drinking.
- The extra pressure now coming from the family is very hard on this woman, and without considerable support, she is likely to return to drinking.
- Usually this woman needs to resume the mother role.
- Changes should be made slowly and gently, with everyone talking about the problems.
- Children who have assumed the parental role cannot be expected simply to be children again.

- Neither being an authoritarian nor being a laissez-faire parent is a viable solution.
- Mom needs to learn how to negotiate and to share power and responsibility.
- She needs to be able to say no, to establish consequences, and to carry through with those consequences.
- She needs help freeing herself from the guilt and making decisions from a guilt-free place.
- Consistency is vital.

Where the mother is still drinking, an added problem that the family may face is social workers threatening to remove the children. Loss of custody to the father is also a possibility if the parents have split up or are about to. In light of the oppressive nature of society, the dangers increase if the mother is working class, is of color, and/or is lesbian. Once again, being prepared to advocate and knowing a good lawyer are critical. Where such a threat does exist, it is correspondingly a good idea to advise the client to make use of or at least "be seen as making use of" the traditional "alcohol treatment programs" that social workers and judges understand.

SELF-HELP—A.A. AND OTHERS

Self-help groups can be very valuable in this area indeed, and encouraging selective use of them makes sense. Unfortunately, although the ones currently in existence have been pioneers and have made important contributions, the problems that they pose are considerable.

A.A. is the granddaddy (male connotation fully intended), and it is far more widespread and accessible than the rest put together. A.A. has enormous drawbacks, as well as benefits. I have already alluded to the problem of the medical model that A.A. pushes. This model flies in the face of research. It gives people a "sick" identity. It unduly limits options. It individualizes problems that are not individual. And it covers up the political context(s) of women's problems. Other serious problems also exist.

An umbrella problem is that, although A.A. addresses the elite male's situation and needs, it is fundamentally an androcentric organization. In many very basic ways it seriously conflicts with women's reality and needs.

By way of example, A.A. stresses the importance of greater humility, of not seeing oneself as all-powerful, of "giving oneself over to a higher power."[1] This may be sound advice for the traditional white male who sees himself as the center of the universe and as self-sufficient and who is forever trying to control everything and everybody. It is, however, the last thing that women need to do.

The dominant culture has taught women to undervalue and underestimate themselves. And women from all cultures are forever being robbed of their power and pressured to hand it over to "higher powers" (men, whites, etc.). WE NEED PRIDE—NOT FURTHER HUMILITY. WE NEED EMPOWER-MENT—NOT A FURTHER RELINQUISHING OF OUR POWER.

A parallel problem is that even while describing "alcoholism" as a disease over which people are helpless and seemingly rejecting a moralistic stance, A.A. teaches drinkers that they are selfish and need to accept more responsibility. Members are encouraged to be more responsible and to go around apologizing to everyone whom they have "wronged." Unlike men's problem, however, women's problem is not irresponsibility but *overresponsibility.* WE NEED TO STOP APOLOGIZING AND BECOME MORE ENTITLED.

The disproportionate number of males is also a problem. As Sandmaier (1981) has observed, women who attend A.A. frequently feel like they are setting foot in an "old boy's club." It does not "feel right."

The gender mix itself is a problem despite the ratio. In mixed groups men "win" and women "lose out." Men talk about their problems; women empathize. Men lecture and define reality; women take in. This dynamic reinforces oppressive sex roles and constitutes further victimization.

A related problem is the lack of physical nurture—an important female value that should be a human value. In some ways going to an A.A. meeting is like going out for "poker with the guys." Everyone sits around puffing on cigarettes, swallowing gallons of coffee, and binging sugar donuts and other junk food.

An additional problem is the shallowness of the approach. It not only has no political analysis—and this is immensely serious in itself—but also has very little of any kind of context. For example, it has no understanding of and makes no attempt to explore such underlying issues as childhood sexual abuse.

A final problem is the life sentence and ongoing life-style that A.A. tends to impose. Given the A.A. belief "once an alcoholic, always an alcoholic," A.A. members are encouraged to keep identifying as "alcoholics" and to keep coming to meetings. Many are terrified of what might happen to them if they stopped coming and so continue rigorously following A.A. precepts. Their development as human beings is thereby thwarted.

On the positive side, A.A. provides structure and routine. It offers usable formulae. It provides ample opportunity for learning problem-solving skills. It gives people a place to go. It provides new friends who can be relied on not to sabotage. It fosters a sense of belonging. Most important of all, it provides strong ongoing peer support; that is, it facilitates support by others who have been there. In some cases it even provides the homogeneity that oppressed people need (gay A.A. and Native A.A.), although again not the political analysis. And the groups themselves are always there when you need them. In light of the proliferation of A.A. groups, generally some local chapter is having a meeting on any given night.

All things considered, I cannot see recommending A.A. to women without qualifying the recommendation. It is an option that should be discussed nonetheless. And where women are making use of it and it is helping them, it makes sense supporting that use.

Generally I support the use, while gently countering messages that are at odds with women's reality and needs. As clients become increasingly secure and progressively question A.A.'s tenets and rigidity, I support the questioning, while affirming the original use of A.A., and to varying degrees slowly help the women move on.

An option that can be more wholeheartedly recommended is Women for Sobriety. It is a network of self-help groups specifically for women with drinking problems. It offers some of the same types of support that A.A. does, while attempting to gear itself to women's reality and needs. Women are encouraged to think of themselves as competent and to give to themselves and their sisters. And emphasis is placed on good food and nurture. The shortcomings are (a) a strong feminist analysis is lacking, (b) the focus on underlying issues is not a strong one, and (c) few chapters exist.[2]

Feminist self-help and other feminist groups that are not drinking-specific but that operate both on a deeper and more political level might also be considered. Unfortunately a network of feminist groups that operates deeply and politically and that provides the 24-hour-a-day help needed does not exist. Once again, lobbying and other political action are called for.

SUGGESTED READINGS

Conrad, P., & Schneider, J. (1980). *Deviance and medicalization: From badness to sickness* (pp. 73-109). St. Louis: C. V. Mosby.
Johnson, S. (1989). *Wildfire: Igniting the she/volution* (pp.129-159). Albuquerque, NM: Wildfire.
Sandmaier, M. (1981). *The invisible alcoholics: Women and alcohol abuse in America.* New York: McGraw-Hill.

NOTES

1. For further explication of these and other A.A. concepts, see Alcoholics Anonymous (1939, 1957).
2. For details on Women for Sobriety, see Kirkpatrick (1978).

13

Working With Psychiatric Survivors

Many feminist therapists decline to work with anyone whom they think of as a "psychiatric patient." The reasons that workers give for limiting their practice in this way include:

- The women are strange and incomprehensible.
- The women are dangerous.
- The women need "expert psychiatric help."
- Psychiatrized women cannot afford the therapy fee.
- Psychiatrized women are "too much trouble" (are needy, often call after hours, miss appointments, shout at the worker, etc.).

As feminists it is critical that we problematize these reasons. We need to be more open to our psychiatrized sisters.

Some (not most) of the issues listed here are reality-based. The solutions, however, are inadequate. By way of example, the average fee that most feminist therapists need to charge is indeed way above what most psychiatric survivors can afford. Few private practitioners, however, could not take in one or two such women at greatly reduced fees. And we all can lobby for subsidized services.

By the same token, although they are not invariably so, psychiatrized women tend to be needy, and women who are more needy generally tax us more. It is important that we take care of ourselves as practitioners, and this is a reason for setting limits. Excluding all psychiatric survivors because psychiatric survivors tend to tax us more, however, is as incompatible with feminism as turning away all incest survivors because survivors are forever splitting, forgetting, or asking for extra hours.

Other rationales are based on lack of knowledge and misinformation. The myth of the "dangerous psychiatric patient" is just that—a myth. The average psychiatric survivor is *less* likely than the nonsurvivor to harm another. With women considerably less likely than men to harm others, the combination "woman plus psychiatric survivor" is about as safe as you get. The "unusual appearances" that bother some workers are often neglect coming from depression or alienation. It may directly or indirectly relate to poverty and homelessness. The appearances that frighten some are for the most part simply drug reactions. Psychiatric drugs disfigure and disable people, causing them to shake, tremble, twitch, drool, slur their words, become flat, go "dazed," grow stiff. This is reason to fear psychiatry, not its victims.

Talk that seems disoriented and claims that seem far-fetched correspondingly are not equivalent with gibberish. Like all women, psychiatrized women have some basis for what they say and can be understood. The idea that some of these women really have "mental illnesses" and "need psychiatrists" is a cop-out. It speaks to brainwashing, fear, and the failure to identify.

Most feminist therapists who do see psychiatrized women—even those who have a good theoretic stance—fall into errors of this sort periodically, generally without recognizing that they do. Serving psychiatrized women better means becoming increasingly aware of these slips and addressing them on an ongoing basis. It means (a) rigorously dealing with our own fear(s), (b) identifying, (c) accepting difference, and (d) recognizing cop-out concepts when we or others fall into them and correcting ourselves or them. Examples of cop-out concepts are *speaking gibberish, needs drugs, mentally ill, needs institutionalization, paranoid,* and *dangerous.* What is especially important is that it means understanding how very little we know about a woman by virtue of her being a "psychiatric survivor."

Indeed I can think of few clients that we group together who are less homogeneous. Some have extreme problems in living that are independent of psychiatrists. Others do not. Some are horrified by the psychiatric intervention. Others regard it as life-saving and intend to continue on drugs for the rest of their lives. A woman's being a psychiatric survivor moreover does not tell us whether she is "out of touch" or "in touch," "coping well" or "just making it." And the woman may be absolutely anywhere on the violence, the eating problems, and the self-violation continuums. The different diagnoses themselves do not narrow down the field appreciably—at least not in the way supposed. The label simply tells us what two or three specific men called "psychiatrists" have thought about a certain woman and how they are likely to have treated her. Besides the diagnoses not being based on medical fact, as studies like Rosenhan's (1973) demonstrated, the diagnosing itself lacks consistency.

I am not suggesting that we refrain from generalizations. This is an area, though, where caution is particularly critical. This highly diverse group of women have had hordes of generalizations imposed on them. The generalizations are then reified. They are treated as facts, as symptoms, as diseases, as products of "diseases." If we are to empower and not add to the overdetermination and injury, we need to start with what we know and proceed with care.

A working definition that we can reasonably begin with is, a *psychiatric survivor* is

> anyone who has been in the position of "patient" in a psychiatric facility for more than 24 consecutive hours

AND/OR

> anyone who frequently goes or has gone to such facilities

AND/OR

> anyone "taken" to such a facility

AND/OR

> anyone who has been subjected to any part of the psychiatric system *and sees herself or is seen by others as a "psychiatric patient," "psychiatric inmate," or "psychiatric survivor"*

AND/OR

> anyone who has been subjected to any of the following: neuroleptics, antidepressants, ongoing use of minor tranquilizers, electroshock, psychosurgery, insulin shock

Despite psychiatric propaganda to the contrary, and despite popular misconceptions, THERE ARE TWO AND ONLY TWO COMMONALITIES THAT WOMEN PSYCHIATRIC SURVIVORS SO DEFINED NECESSARILY HAVE.

1. They are women in a patriarchal society.
2. Whether technically "voluntarily" or not, they have fallen into the clutches of the psychiatric system.

Of course the majority of psychiatric survivors, at least in the period leading up to their entry into the system, have or have had extreme problems in living. In working with psychiatric survivors, we need to keep this in mind. "Having or having had extreme problems in living," however, is not only *not* a defining characteristic but also is not even a universal accompanying characteristic. I have known a few psychiatric survivors whose problems are not and have never been extreme. I have known more whose only extreme problems were caused by psychiatry intervention. Such characteristics as these that are frequent but far from universal need to enter into our understanding and our work with our psychiatrized sisters as appropriate. Only these two characteristics, though, can reasonably form the basis of our understanding.

The first—being a woman in a patriarchal society—allows us to make sense of what might otherwise appear as inexplicable or a "symptom." It allows us to understand, appreciate, and validate modes of coping that might otherwise appear totally negative. And it suggests types of internalized oppression to be on the lookout for.

As women, psychiatrized women encounter the difficulties and cope in the ways described in Chapters 1 through 12 and 14. Insofar as we are operating well and not pathologizing these clients, this is the primary work that needs to be done. The point is that PSYCHIATRIZED WOMEN ARE WOMEN FIRST AND FOREMOST.

The second commonality—being subjected to the psychiatric system—constitutes what is in some ways an extension of that first oppression and in other ways a new oppression. Our job is to help the client (a) co-investigate this oppression, (b) redefine her situation, (c) reclaim her physical and emotional being, (d) recover/reclaim her identity, (e) discover her own strength, and (f) protect herself from further psychiatrization.

To do this properly, it is necessary to be aware of the ways in which psychiatry oppresses women and how that oppression is internalized. We need to be aware more explicitly (a) of what behavior is pathologized and why, (b) of the patriarchal vision, purpose, and means, (c) of how institutions work, (d) of what the drugs and other "treatments" actually do, (e) of the collusion of friends, family, and "mental health professionals," (f) of what pressures are put on women, (g) of the ways in which these women are encouraged to think about themselves, and (h) of the misinformation that the women are fed. Chapter 2 is a good introduction to some of this. Throughout this chapter I will be providing more. Counselors with little experience in this area might also read first-person accounts.

A good place to begin in building a radical feminist approach is to commit ourselves to going beyond mere liberal or libertarian understanding. Feminist therapists who theoretically see through medicalization and see psychiatry as patriarchal coercion still tend to be strangely liberal when it comes to the individual client. Except in extreme cases, that is, they see psychiatry as a problem only if the woman herself considers it a problem. If the woman is happy with past or current "psychiatric interventions" and is not so drugged that she cannot put two thoughts together, the therapist dutifully stays away from the whole area. Her reasons for doing so include:

- If Mabel is okay with it, who am I to decide that it harmed her?
- It's her choice, after all.
- She likes it and there is no point in my alienating her.

These reasons miss the point. Of course we do not want to alienate clients who love their psychiatrists. Of course we need to approach the subject slowly and carefully when women are happy with their psychiatrization. With many, we will never end up saying half of what we think. And of course we should not take choice away from the woman.

Consciousness-raising, however, is not "taking choice away." It is what makes authentic choice possible. Correspondingly the worry of alienating our client should no more keep us from ever touching on the issue than the worry of alienating an incest survivor who loves her father should stop us from ever beginning to problematize what her father did. To assume that the client's liking psychiatry means that she is not being hurt by it moreover is to lose sight of what we know about this institution and about internalized oppression generally.

The situation is akin to the situation of the battered woman who has internalized her oppression. Her spouse may often act very caringly toward her. She may see him as treating her reasonably well. She may even think that she *needs* the occasional beating. As counselors, though, we would in no way feel obliged to reach the same conclusions. Of course it would be unwise to say simply, "The guy's abusing you and you should ditch him." In the privacy of our own minds, we would nonetheless conclude that what was happening was oppressive, and we would want to help the woman slowly overcome the internalized oppression. We need to give ourselves the same permission with the woman who thinks well of her psychiatrist or the psychiatric drugs that she is on. As with the battered woman, we correspondingly need to keep in mind that the satisfied psychiatrized woman is not "less oppressed" than the unsatisfied. She has simply internalized the oppression more.

Concepts like *voluntary* further trip us up, and it is critical that we keep our balance. This language of choice covers up violence and deception. A woman who "voluntarily" admits herself to a psychiatric facility is generally freaking out and looking for a safe place. Alternatively she is attempting to pacify relatives or to prevent herself from being institutionalized involuntarily. She is not choosing to be systematically humiliated and stripped of her identity.

By the same token, a woman who "chooses" to take drugs because she is directly or indirectly threatened with incarceration if she does not is not exactly *choosing* the drugs. Under duress she is choosing to avoid a greater violation. A woman who takes drugs because she has been told that she will never be well enough to get out of the hospital if she does not is not "choosing" drugs. She is taking the threat seriously and/or is believing the "prognosis" and choosing to get out. A woman whose husband threatens to desert her if she does not take her lithium is not "choosing" the lithium. She is choosing to avoid a desertion that she has been trained to be terrified of.

Women who take drugs, moreover, almost never "choose" to be gradually poisoned, to incur neurological damage, to be "cured" of the ability to think, perceive, or feel. They do not "choose" to twitch and spasm involuntary. They do not "choose" to look like a "psychiatric patient" and so be invalidated by everyone. They do not "choose" to become addicted. At best they choose temporary relief with little idea of the costs. They are choosing to avoid madness under the psychiatrically reinforced misapprehension that this is their inevitable fate. They are choosing a low level functioning, having been told that this is the best that they can expect. Generally they are also choosing to treat an illness without knowing that they have no illness other than what the drugs themselves induce.

It is important that we not let this bogus language of choice or the bogus language of medicine blind us to the bullying, the lies, and the violence that the language covers up. Such language as this mystifies, disempowers, and co-opts the victims of psychiatric assault and their allies. A feminist approach is predicated on rejecting and demystifying.

A feminist approach is similarly predicated on:

1. A detailed understanding of the "spoiled identity" that many of these women have ended up with
2. A profound commitment to help them free themselves of this identity and what goes with it—the drugs, the helplessness, the way of life that is euphemistically known as "their career as mental patients"[1]

To varying degrees psychiatrized women have been fundamentally and systematically humiliated and invalidated. Life in mental institutions is routinized humiliation. Inmates are forced to wear pajamas. They are treated like infants. If they cross staff, they loose "privileges" (freedoms that are normally everyone's right by virtue of being adult human beings). Loss of privileges may mean a return to pajamas—an event that announces to everyone, "This woman is in disgrace. She has messed up again." Every oddity that they fall into is duly recorded, read, discussed ad infinitum by staff, and then thrown back in their faces as proof of their unreliability. They are forever told that they are "in the wrong." Those on the outside are spoken about in their presence by mental health officials and concerned family as if they are not there. Families and friends correspondingly use patronizing terms, talk down, let privileged others know that Sally is "not quite right."

More direct assaults on selfhood also occur. The psychiatric institution creates a visible break in a woman's life. It forces her to leave her identity behind. She no longer is in her familiar home. Often she is stripped of her clothes—that powerful outward sign of who she is. She no longer does the things that are routine for her—those daily habits by which we create and recognize who we are. More decisively, "treatments" such as drugs and shock rob her of what is most personal of all—her thoughts, her feelings, and indeed often the very memory or continuity that we all need to maintain a sense of self.

Systematic invalidation further robs her of her sense of having a capable self, of making sense, of having meaning. The words *mentally ill* give her a new self without selfhood, a new identity without validity. It serves as an explanation that forever robs her. If she is unhappy with her situation, it is because she is mentally ill; she is depressive. If she thinks that others are treating her badly, it is because she is mentally ill; she is paranoid schizophrenic. She is trained to believe that she is defective, that her judgments are worthless and indeed simply the product of an illness. Thoroughly "feminized," she is trained to place other people's judgments above her own. She is taught to accept herself as sick, to stay on her "meds," and to continually seek help from patriarchal psychiatry.

Psychiatrized women both accept and rebel against this new identity to varying degrees. Empowering work means helping them further this rebellion and make it work for them. This means, of course, helping them get off the drugs and away from the psychiatrists. It means, more fundamentally, helping them see through and cast off the sick identity, reject the "invalid status," and assume authorship (authority) over their words and their lives.

DETAILS OF THE COUNSELING

Most psychiatric survivors let counselors know right away that they have been psychiatrized, though they may be uncertain what drug dosage they have been on. Some avoid all mention of it. As our awareness of the psychiatrization generally and damaging treatments in particular can help us serve clients better, we need to be able to pick up on what signs are evident. My proviso is that the awareness not be used for stereotyping or pathologizing purposes.

There is no easy way to recognize a woman on a small drug dosage, for psychiatric drugging is recognizable primarily through the impairment. Where a number of the following occur, we may reasonably conclude that the woman is on a sizable dosage of psychiatric drugs, has been on them awhile, and *is being significantly disabled by them:* slurred speech, frequent lip-smacking, glazed-over eyes, drooling, frequent loss of thought in midsentence or other difficulty thinking, always feeling tired, perceptual problems, low affect, a shuffle-type walk, extreme rigidity, tremors/shaking, involuntary twitching or tics in the limbs or face. Another possibility is that she was once on heavy psychiatric drugs even though she is not now and that she has incurred long-term or permanent damage.

Possible indicators that she has been subjected to ECT include large gaps in her memory, reference to not recognizing old friends or family members, losing thoughts in midsentence or other difficulty thinking, weakening on one side of her body (this can occur with unilateral shock—shock in which both electrodes are placed on the nondominant hemisphere).

More generally, possible albeit far from conclusive indicators of psychiatrization include:

- Vagueness around or a reluctance to talk about a specific period in her life
- Asking for some assurance, as well she might, that we will not institutionalize her under any circumstances

Additional behaviors/backgrounds that increase the risk of psychiatrization, as well as the odds that a woman has been psychiatrized, include the following:

- A background of overt childhood sexual abuse
- Suicidal background
- Overt self-abuse that is not socially approved of (cutting, burning, etc.)
- Extreme problems with eating
- Other commonly pathologized modes of coping, such as splitting and fragmenting
- Seeing what others do not see or hearing what others do not hear
- Frequent reference to individual persecution
- Strong expressions of anger
- Clear sex role rejection
- Seeming fusion/confusion of the literal and the metaphoric
- Manifestly holding beliefs that "appear" illogical where those beliefs have not been socially sanctioned

Counselors sometimes attempt to maximize early information about psychiatrization by including a category like "Institutionalization" on the forms that they ask clients to fill out. I have a problem with this. It puts clients on the spot. They feel pressured to give the type of information that most professionals use against them. And it makes our forms frighteningly reminiscent of the forms imposed on them by institutional psychiatry.

Where forms are used, categories like "Previous Therapy Experience" and "Drugs You Are On" are far preferable. Psychiatrized women do not feel singled out. They may or may not see these categories as including their experiences with psychiatry. Where they do, they will generally feel less intimidated and more entitled to provide or not provide that information as they see fit.

Also helpful are handouts on approach that include an antipsychiatry statement and/or a promise not to cooperate with psychiatric interference. Without putting her on the spot, such statements introduce the topic and give the psychiatrized woman critical information about what she can expect. Generally I also say something directly about my positions. If I pick up on signs that the woman is a psychiatric survivor, I am especially likely to refer, however briefly, to my antipsychiatry position. Where the client is a survivor and reacts with alarm, I reassure her that I understand her alarm and that although I will introduce different ideas from time to time, I will not pressure her.

Where we have a strong reason to suspect psychiatrization and the client herself does not raise the issue, raising it ourselves makes sense as long as we are prepared to back off. Similarly, where the client appears to be dropping hints, we can pick up on those hints and ask the question directly.

Generally it is wise to proceed slowly and gently when problematizing the psychiatrization. We need to know where the client is at and what she is ready to hear at any given time, and to pace ourselves accordingly. I am not suggesting that we should ever simply restrict ourselves to the client's position. We need to operate sensitively, though, to understand how threatening it may be to entertain what we are saying and to respect the client's timing.

The extreme situation—and one that unfortunately is very common—is that the survivor sees herself as "mentally ill," has been on heavy-duty drugs for years, and thinks that her well-being depends on taking her "meds" religiously. These women are terrified of themselves and of what might happen to them. They may be frightened of the voices that they heard prior to psychiatrization. They may be freaked out by vague memories of incest and other abuse that strike them and others as hallucinations. They are scared of "losing control" and "going mad again." They may have been supported by friends and family ever since "accepting their disease" and may be afraid of losing that support. Generally and understandably, they are afraid of giving up a rationale that helps them make sense of their experience and absolves them of guilt.

Women in this situation need to know that we are not going to rob them of their psychiatric solution. It is critical to spend time clearly taking in and empathizing. Let them know that we recognize their terror and are not going to pressure them into anything. And affirm that they are not guilty. Slowly we should nonetheless take what "in's" we have to begin problematizing the psychiatrization.

Even in extreme situations, we always have "in's," for no survivor is ever 100% sold on the psychiatric understanding of "treatment." Some are concerned about the "side effects" of the drugs. On some level most are irritated by how easy it is for others to dismiss their opinions. Although they may be afraid to think it for long, at some point an overwhelming majority have entertained thoughts like, "These people are supposed to be 'treating' us, but they're even crazier than we are." We help by empathizing with and affirming the protest and the discomfort on whatever level it occurs, while delicately extending the critique.

The following are examples of interactions in which this occurs:

Barbara	It's terrible. I know I'm schizophrenic and all that, but I don't like how people use it against me. Like, no one takes me seriously. When I disagree with Doug over anything, he tells me that I only think that way because of the paranoia and maybe I should ask the doctor about "upping my meds."
Therapist	That sounds awful. It's like you have no voice at all.
Barbara	I feel like I have to watch everything I say because Doug or Joanne can always come back with . . .
Therapist	You're just schizophrenic?
Barbara	Well, yes.
Therapist	You know, you and I disagree on schizophrenia; and that's okay. One thing though is clear. Whatever else it is or isn't, schizophrenia's a powerful label that is being used to discount you and keep you in line.

Lynne	I've had trouble concentrating ever since I was put on Librium. The doctor says it's just a minor side effect. Do you think I'm making too much of it?
Counselor	When you ask an antipsychiatry person a question like that, I assume it's because you want the answer that I am going to give. So let me give it. Of course you're upset. It's hard to do anything when you can't concentrate. And no, I don't think you are making a fuss about nothing. I can't imagine anything more central than being able to think and feel.
Lynne	Dr. Adams says it's just a minor side effect.
Counselor	How do you feel when he says that?
Lynne	I'm not sure. Like he's the expert and he knows; but he's saying it's minor and it doesn't seem, well . . .
Counselor	What doesn't it seem?
Lynne	It doesn't seem minor to me.
Counselor	Me either. And you know, there's a whole lot of people out there who would agree with you.

This pace may be accelerated as women question more. In the long run the messages that we want to impart include:

1. Psychiatric theory and treatment are without basis.
2. Drugs and shock do enormous damage. Damage increases in proportion to dosage, frequency, and duration.
3. Their compromised status as "mental patients" is an extension of their compromised status as women.
4. We want something better for them.
5. We know that they can lead a fuller, more independent life.
6. Alternative explanations make sense of their experience and leave them blameless without pathologizing them.
7. The terrifying experiences that they call "going mad" were their way of getting in touch with feelings and realities that they suppressed. If they understand what is going on and have support, they can work out what needs to be worked out without freaking out or landing "back in the system."
8. Drugs and shock prevent them from "working through."

Another common situation is that clients are critical but have significant doubt. One the one hand, say, they resent having spent the last few years in a hopeless stupor. They may see psychiatry as an attempt to control them. On the other hand, they are terrified that they may be wrong, that they may actually have a "mental illness."

In such instances we can move considerably more quickly. The client has a meaningful even if shaky critique. Generally a good part of why she is shaky is that significant others demonstrably disagree with her. They tell her she really is sick. They tell her that this is for "her own good." They remind her how she messed up in the past when she took things into her own hands. She desperately needs an ally to affirm her critique and to support her attempt to extricate herself. She needs us to say, "You are not imagining it. These drugs really are poisoning you." Other affirmations or clarifications that might be offered early or later on include:

- No, you are not "mentally ill."
- Not only do you not need these intrusive procedures now, but you also never needed them. What you probably needed and still need is help making sense of your situation and coping/resisting more effectively.
- There are ways of protecting yourself from the system, that is, . . .
- You are an adult human being with your own inner wisdom. No one has the right to invalidate or infantilize you.
- Experts—especially male experts—are far more a problem than a solution.
- Your body is your own. Only you should be determining what goes into your mouth.

- Like millions of others, you have been fed misinformation that is not in your interest.
- What happened to you constitutes unethical assault.
- You have a legitimate grievance against everyone who played an active role in or cooperated with this oppression.

Co-exploration of the formation of the sick identity and of the parts played by everyone is also helpful. Correspondingly she may end up needing concrete help withdrawing safely from drugs, casting off the sick role, and protecting herself from further intrusion.

Another common situation is that the client has been psychiatrized in the past, is appalled at what happened, and wants to forget the experience entirely. Generally she is telling herself something like: "What happened is dreadful, but it's over. I'm not like those others, who really are nuts. It's never going to happen again. So the best thing I can do is push it aside and get on with my life." This woman comes in with a specific agenda that does not include the psychiatrization. It may be getting ahead in her job. It may be "improving her self-esteem." Insofar as feasible, it is important to accept her agenda and help her address it. Sooner or later, however, in addressing the agenda properly, we are likely to come face to face with what she wishes to forget.

At this juncture, decent work entails inviting her to look at what she is avoiding. A disentitlement, a trauma, perhaps also other problems are going to sabotage her if she does not work them through. Minimally, moreover, at some point it is important to be up front and state:

1. Neither trauma nor embarrassment will disappear by forgetting about it.
2. Although very significant differences may exist, she does share some things with other survivors.
3. No one is completely invulnerable to psychiatric intrusion—women least of all.
4. Unjust though it is, the psychiatric intervention makes her more vulnerable to psychiatry than women spared these experiences.
5. Safety lies in remembering, identifying, and taking measures to protect oneself, not in forgetting and disidentifying.

A critical part of helping clients extricate themselves from psychiatry is helping them see through and dispense with psychiatric vocabulary. Throughout it is important to avoid psychiatric terms even if the client herself uses them. I am not suggesting that we always correct the client when she uses psychiatric jargon. Sometimes we may simply not follow suit. By way of example, if the client says, "I have an eating disorder," we can respond with, "You have a problem around food?"

Our rigor in avoiding psychiatric jargon (a) tempers our tendency to pathologize, (b) announces gently that there are other ways of thinking about her experiences, (c) is a sign that we genuinely dislike psychiatry and are less likely to pathologize her, and (d) helps both client and counselor unhouse the psychiatrist within.

To do the job properly, we need to listen to ourselves vigilantly and to systematically exchange demythologizing language for hegemonic language.

The information in Table 13.1 may be used as a beginning or temporary guideline. Where the replacement suggestions are too lengthy to be part of speech, they might nonetheless be used as an aide to demystification.

Where feasible, survivors should be invited to create their own replacement terms. Renaming is a critical part of resistance. It is a reclaiming of vision and the power to name.

Although validation is critical to empowerment with all women, it is especially so for psychiatric survivors because their views and stories have been subject to extra invalidation. It is important to affirm repeatedly whatever we can affirm. It is particularly important to affirm those beliefs that others have invalidated (they really never did recover full memory after shock; they really were punished and manipulated in the institution; it really was not safe to "share"; overwhelming and mindless work really was imposed on them at home; etc.). Hearing from someone whom they find credible that they are not crazy and that their story makes sense to us helps survivors believe themselves and believe *in* themselves.

Most feminist counselors have little trouble validating a woman who says that the staff were patriarchal or that the drug hurt her. We are far more reluctant, however, to validate a woman who says that

the CIA is sending her messages via the television set

OR

voices outside her door every night criticize her

OR

her husband, father, grandfather, and great-grandfather (long deceased) are trying to murder her

OR

in a secret lab far out in the country, government officials manufacture viruses that give people cancer, Alzheimer's, and so on; they place these in test tubes and then infect the population with them

TABLE 13.1 Demystifying the Psychobabble

Psychiatric Jargon	Possible Replacement Terms/Demystification
psychiatric patient	psychiatric inmate; psychiatric survivor
psychiatric hospital	psychiatric prison or institution
psychiatrist	medical agent of the state licensed to declare someone of danger to self or others and imprison her under the name of help; M.D. who pathologizes nonconformity and problems in living; professional with a license to hunt
mental illness, mental disability, mental disorder	deep emotional problems or problems in living; alternatively, behavior or thoughts that psychiatrists and others with power dislike and see you as not responsible for
mental health	emotional or psychological well-being; alternatively, thoughts or behavior that psychiatrists like
normal	being seen by psychiatrists and others as having no "mental disorder"; alternatively, conforming and/or being seen as responsible for one's behavior
grandiosity or delusion of grandeur	thinking we have more power(s) than others with more credibility think we have
hallucination	seeing or hearing what others do not see or hear
psychiatric treatment	psychiatric violation; psychiatric assault
psychosurgery	lobotomy; severing parts of the brain
chemotherapy, psychiatric medication	psychiatric drugging
electroconvulsive therapy	electroshock; shock; electrocution
side effects	primary effects; the effects that are actually being sought
remission/recovery	recently acting or thinking in ways that psychiatrist in charge is more comfortable with
prognosis	wild psychiatric guess what you will be like in the future; alternatively, psychiatric decision on how to treat you in the future
diagnosis	specific pathologizing label
multiple diagnosis	multiple pathologizing labels (Subtext: The psychiatrist is showing off; or the psychiatrist cannot make up his mind.)
informed consent	consent on the basis of inaccurate information; consent within the context of violence
voluntary admission	caving in to the pressure to enter a "psychiatric facility"; admitting oneself without proper information
suicidal ideation	considering ending one's life
threatening suicide	talking about considering suicide

Psychiatric Jargon	*Possible Replacement Terms/Demystification*
acting out	resisting in ways that upset psychiatric staff
uncooperative	challenging the psychiatric staff; disagreeing with the psychiatric staff
cooperative	internalizing the oppression; looking as if you are going along
rationalizing	having a different explanation
obsessive/compulsive /obsessive compulsive	repeatedly thinking or doing what you do not want to be thinking or doing
depressed	sad; low energy
manic	extremely happy; extremely "high"
manic-depressive	common patterns of extreme high followed by extreme low and vice versa
gender identity disorder	wrestling with one's sexual identity; wanting the power and/or the sexual access to women which men have; acting or dressing in ways that do not fit the roles imposed by patriarchy
histrionic personality disorder (hysterical)	being more emotional or spontaneous than androcentric males are comfortable with
multiple personality disorder	coping with childhood sexual abuse by splitting, dissociating, disidentifying
conduct disorder, oppositional defiant disorder, borderline personality disorder	rebelling, resisting; rejection of female gender role in particular
paranoid, paranoid schizophrenic	terrified that others are out to harm you (The psychiatrist either disagrees that they are or finds it irrelevant that they are.)
eating disorders	problems with eating

OR

she is a dead person pretending to be alive

OR

she needs to kill herself so that she can reach planet Zob and become a "fibro-burescalatogical" engineer

These women too need to be listened to and validated. In fact they need it more, for they are subject to greater invalidation. With these women too validation is correspondingly absolutely in order.

What I am saying here has two levels. On one level, I am suggesting that a few seemingly or blatantly irrational beliefs do not invalidate everything a person is saying. A woman who makes such statements as these is still right, say, when she says that the drugs are poisoning her or that her family colludes against her. In fact, 98% of what she says may literally be true, albeit disbelieved by all and sundry.

On the second level, far-fetched and seemingly nonsensical statements are not simply falsehood or gibberish. We can be mistaken about reality, and it is important to remember this. More significantly, though, truth is often spoken through fiction.

The point is that human beings distort and get confused where (a) they have been violated and invalidated fundamentally, and (b) for safety reasons they have had to hide from self or others what was going on.[2] Where they have been punished in the past for speaking truth, they may, for example, retreat to a figurative level. In time this may lead to a general fusion/confusion of the figurative and the literal. Where they desperately need to say something that they have been forbidden to say, they may correspondingly introduce nonsensical or seemingly nonsensical words and then later forget the origin, nature, and purpose of these terms. Or they may shift where and when the unspeakable happened and who did it. Or they may have hidden what happened from themselves successfully, only to be experiencing it in the present. On some level, nonetheless, what they are saying is meaningful and true. Our job is to seek out and affirm that truth on whatever level it occurs and in whatever way possible. This search and affirmation should be coupled with a detailed co-exploration of the various oppressive situations that these seemingly bizarre beliefs are at once pointing to and covering up.

By way of example, the woman who says that the government is poisoning its citizens with vials of diseases that it creates is speaking a figurative truth. The government indeed invents and disseminates propaganda that poisons our minds. The government also supports businesses that pollute the atmosphere and that manufacture junk food—all of which make us susceptible to disease. Telling the woman that she is mistaken is accordingly inaccurate. Ignoring it is just another way of invalidating. A more reasonable response is, "Yes, of course, the government harms us. I know myself that it poisons us with misinformation and all sorts of things and that it hides what it is doing." We might then reach for the meanings that *poison, disease, hidden,* and *far out in the country* have had in her life. It would be important as well to co-explore who silenced her in the past, how she was silenced, what precisely she was silenced about, and how she coped with being silenced. As trust builds, the information so gleaned could be used to help her better understand herself, sort through confusions, and alter her coping.

By the same token, in all likelihood the woman who claims to be dead is perfectly correct on an affective level. She has numbed herself and feels dead.

She may have had to deaden herself to survive childhood sexual abuse, battery, double messages, or ongoing invalidation. Our job is to affirm the reality of that "deadness" and to co-explore what the deadness is about.

Similarly the woman who hears voices criticizing her is correct. Although in all likelihood voices are not shouting at her now, chances are that she has been bitterly criticized in the past. Like the incest survivor, she is reexperiencing what occurred. By the same token, the woman who thinks that three generations of males in her family are out to kill her is right on one level at the very least. Men do try to kill women's spirits. Moreover she may have been raped by all three generations.

In each case, we need to affirm and find out more. Even the woman who talks of killing herself to get to planet Zob can be affirmed. She is stating that there are major obstacles to her doing what she wants. We can agree that there are and that on some level we all want to escape from the limitations placed on us. This affirmation could lead to a further exploration of what her obstacles really are, what she wants to do, and alternative routes.

Affirming and co-exploring what the client is saying are the surest ways of helping her gain clarity. This approach contrasts with the biological approach of drugging women into forgetting or wiping away certain beliefs with electroshock. It contrasts as well with the more traditional approach of attempting to demonstrate that certain of her beliefs are illogical. This too I recommend against.

Such arguments miss the point and close the door to co-investigation. The client knows that a reality she vitally needs to hold on to is being denied. She may say nothing because she is being double-binded again and there really is nothing to say. She may go along on the outside, while doing whatever she can to hold on to her truth on the inside. In either case, we have succeeded only in furthering the oppression and the splitting and in silencing her. Alternatively she may decide to argue with us. An endless and futile battle of wits thereby ensues. Or she may logically draw the opposite conclusion from each piece of evidence that we muster.

The folly of such an approach is amply demonstrated in an ableist joke that was popular in the 1970s:

Schizophrenic   I am dead.

Shrink   Let me prove to you that you can't be dead.

Schizophrenic   Anything you say.

Shrink   Dead people don't bleed. See this pin here. I'm going to prick you with it. And just see what happens. Just see if you don't bleed.

(Shrink pricks client with pin and client bleeds)

Schizophrenic   Oh, so dead people *do* bleed!

If we affirm and invite co-exploration instead, clients generally co-explore with us, move away from the figurative, and over time make whatever other alterations they need. Once co-exploration is well under way and sufficient trust has been built, sometimes we can additionally (a) discuss how and why reexperiencing and fusion/confusion happens, and (b) co-identify clues that the client can use in determining when she is reexperiencing and when fusion/confusion of the literal and figurative is occurring.

If a seemingly "irrational idea" persists regardless, I would not worry about it unless it is causing the client a real problem. The idea is serving a purpose. If it presents a major problem, co-explore how to deal with it or sidestep the problem.

Freak-Outs and Safe Places

A survivor who is freaking needs the same sort of help that anyone else who is freaking needs. She needs greater contact and reassurance. She needs ways of dealing with triggers and grounding herself. She needs help making sense of and normalizing what is happening to her. And she needs a support network to draw on.

A shelter where she can go, be fed, and looked after for a few days to a few weeks may also be helpful from time to time. If she is considering "hospitalizing herself," it is important to be clear about the problems that hospitals pose and to suggest shelters and other safer resources.

Whether they are freaking out or not, familiarize survivors with safe places. Optimally they should be ones that will not call in psychiatrists if the going gets tough and that are feminist. Practically, we often have to settle for ones that are simply unlikely to call in psychiatrists and are not blatantly sexist.

Protecting Self
From Future Psychiatric Intrusion

Because labels and past institutionalizations make psychiatric survivors particularly vulnerable to psychiatric intrusion, helping them become better able to protect themselves is an essential part of our job. They need to be so clear about their rights and how to access them that they can protect themselves even when terrified or in a drug stupor. Providing survivors with a copy of the new revised mental health act in their area or telling them where to get one can be helpful. Where the client dislikes or has trouble understanding legalese, copies of more accessible statements on rights are preferable. Copies with extra-large print are a good idea, for people on psychiatric drugs may have blurred vision. Combining written information with verbal clarification is optimal. Referrals to workshops on rights and legal avenues may also be helpful.

Rights vary from jurisdiction to jurisdiction. Rights that pertain in most states and provinces and that it is important to be aware of and to clarify include:

1. The right to appear at a designated body (review board) to contest involuntary committal
2. The right to appear at the designated body (review board) to contest a certificate of renewal (Commitment is authorized for a set period only. When that period is up, the psychiatrist must submit a certificate of renewal form if he or she wishes to extend the commitment.)
3. The right to refuse any "treatment" so long as the survivor is deemed "competent" to decide on treatments and/or "treatment" is not being used as a temporary means of restraint (Even where the survivor is considered "competent," the psychiatrist may appeal to a designated body [review board] for permission to treat against the survivor's will. Theoretically this permission is only given if the client's life is in jeopardy or, in some jurisdictions, if the board is convinced that the client's condition will seriously deteriorate if she does not receive "treatment." Where the psychiatrist appeals for permission to treat without consent, again the client has the right to appear at the hearing and contest.)
4. The right to appear at the designated hearing and contest the psychiatrist's application to have her declared incompetent to make decisions about treatment questions or incompetent to manage her estate
5. Where deemed incompetent to manage one's own estate, the right to apply to be in charge of one's estate again on release (Where this right has been lost, it is important to at least consider applying for it on release. Women without this right are powerless to make financial decisions and may be critically impeded in decisions that are not obviously financial.)
6. The right to be given adequate information on which to base informed consent (Unfortunately, what constitutes adequate or even accurate information is dictated by psychiatric hegemony.)
7. The right not to be held in restraints longer than a set period
8. The right to see and be represented by a lawyer

In some jurisdictions the following additional rights also apply:

• When "competent to choose on treatment matters," the right to authorize another to be his or her substitute consent giver (The substitute consent giver is authorized to consent or refuse treatment on behalf of the person should that person ever be judged incompetent to decide on treatment.)
• The right not to be subject to psychosurgery or shock without consent, whether deemed competent to make choices about treatment or not
• The right to appeal the decision of the board to a district court
• The right to see a psychiatric patient advocate if in a provincial or state "mental health center"

These are spelled out in local mental health acts. Other possible legal avenues for self-protection that are not embedded in mental health legislation but that may be worth exploring are (a) constitutional challenges to involuntary committal or specific "treatments," and (b) use of a living will (a signed, dated, and duly witnessed document that states that the person is competent (physician's signature needed here) and that it is her living will that _____ never occur to her should she ever be deemed incompetent to decide on treatment matters).

Survivors who get terrified or have trouble standing up for themselves can greatly benefit from role plays in which they get in touch with their own strength and gently but persistently refuse the drugs being pushed on them. Also helpful are role plays in which they ignore dire warnings of what is likely to happen if they do not "cooperate." For every, "But you really must take this if you are going to get well, dear," the survivor needs to be able to respond, "Thank you for your advice. And I am declining according to my rights under section _____, subsection _____ of the Mental Health Act."

Should the survivor be interested in having a substitute consent giver, looking into this while on the outside makes sense. She should use someone who is easily located. Family members are not necessarily the best choice. Although some certainly may be, family members are often in conflictual relationships with the survivor. The survivor may be the family scapegoat. Having her psychiatrized may be welcome proof that the family is "all right." Even where this is not the case, family may be beside themselves because of the current turmoil and easily duped into signing anything by a reassuring psychiatrist who is ready to shoulder the responsibility.

Husbands in particular frequently sign for "treatment" that wives would never want. The men are upset by what is going on. They desperately want everything "back to normal," with "normal," as we know, not being in the women's interest. And for obvious reasons they tend to trust patriarchal institutions.

Some very imperfect guidelines here are:

- Friends tend be more reliable than family.
- Friends who are not also friends of the family are better than friends of the family.
- Friends whom the survivor does not live with are more reliable than friends they live with, as built-up frustrations will not as likely figure into their judgment.
- People who are propsychiatry are an immense mistake.
- People who are slightly critical of psychiatry are better than people who are not critical.
- People who have a history of being antipsychiatry and of fighting for rights are optimal, whether they are friends or not.

A woman who is considering checking herself in voluntarily should be clearly apprised that "voluntary" does not mean "she can always check herself out if she does not like what is happening to her." Make sure she is aware that psychiatric facilities have the legal right to and often do change women's status from "voluntary" to "involuntary." In fact, deciding to leave when the hospital does not want her to leave is one of the surest ways of having her status switched to "involuntary."

If a client is institutionalized, whether "voluntarily" or "involuntarily," recommend that she encourage visits. We should also check in on her ourselves. Women who have others looking out for them are treated more carefully. Inmates who additionally challenge psychiatric decisions with the help of a lawyer tend to get out quicker regardless of what decisions the review board makes. So it is important to encourage challenges.

An updated list of lawyers that we can recommend is an invaluable asset. Common failings that lawyers have and that it is important to advise clients about include:

1. Not being knowledgeable in mental health legislation
2. A belief in "mental illness" (They think that the psychiatrist really knows best. Accordingly they try to talk the inmate into going along with what the psychiatrist wants or with some unacceptable compromise.)

Where such problems arise, encourage the client to find another lawyer and offer help finding one.

Survivors "on the outside" who are trying to get out of the system may find themselves intruded on by a system that does not like people to break loose. If so, they will need to know how to deal with the attempts to rein them in.

A typical scenario: A woman goes off the lithium. The "doctor" discovers that "something is amiss" when (a) she persistently breaks the standard appointments to have her lithium level checked, or (b) she attends the appointments and the psychiatrist discovers that her lithium level is zooming downward, or (c) someone blows the whistle on her, or (d) she tells him that she has gone off. At this point he is likely to try to coax her back on. When coaxing fails, the survivor, her family, or those around her may begin getting calls from "community mental health workers" or "psychiatric social workers." A standard line that they give is, "We'd just like to come down for a visit to see whether everything is all right."

Where a situation such as this materializes, it is important to let her know loudly and clearly that greatest safety lies in refusing this visit. If she, her family, or those around her swallow the bait and the worker comes, the chances of her being reinstitutionalized rise dramatically. The best line for everyone to take is some version of, "Thank you, but everything is just fine. We do not want a visit." If family or those around her look as if they might waver, we might offer to talk with them ourselves. If family or others are actively colluding with the system and/or the calls persist, a lawyer should be contacted forthwith. If family, friends, or people cohabiting with her are already part or likely to become part of the problem, a possible long-term change of residence and at the very least a temporary stay at a shelter should be considered.

Problems may similarly arise where others are uncomfortable with how the survivor is acting. In these cases as well, direct advocacy, change of residence, and legal assistance may be needed.

Some additional rough guidelines that we can offer survivors are:

- No one can be trusted who is trying to thwart her attempts to break free and/or is patronizing her.
- Wherever possible, it is best that she not let people whom she is not certain of know that she has gone off psychiatric drugs—at least not until she has been off them for a long time.
- If people are trying to interfere with her freedom, this is not a time to be polite or to "just sit down and talk things over."
- At such times, statements like, "We just want to take you somewhere you can rest" or, "Let's just go for a quiet drive" are a smoke screen. The real destination is a "mental health" official or a psychiatric institution.
- If an ambulance is on the way or turns up, look for a police officer.
- If any serious intrusion is under way, she should calmly state her rights and contact her lawyer as quickly as possible.[3]

Bona fide medical problems also place survivors in jeopardy, and it is critical that therapist and client be aware of this and know how to deal with the problem. If the survivor self-mutilates deeply, infects herself, and needs medical attention, such attention can easily turn into a one-way trip to the "psych ward." She is safer if she does not go to the emergency room but to a clinic that has a reputation for not pathologizing or overreacting. Having someone accompany her who is clear and is prepared to stand up for her is advisable.

Having been stigmatized, she is also in special jeopardy when she has "real" diseases. Doctors who are aware of her history are more likely to interpret what is going on as psychosomatic, to pathologize her distress, and to trivialize her complaints. Where viable, not letting them know her psychiatric record makes sense. And she should feel free to confront and change doctors.

If she is hospitalized for an illness, the sight of the hospital itself may traumatize her. Staff may respond to the trauma by calling in a psychiatrist. Whether she is traumatized or not, complaints may be interpreted as an indication of a "return of the psychosis," and again a psychiatrist is called in. Knowing and insisting on her rights here are critical. Again it is important that we keep close contact with her, help her stay calm, and be prepared to advocate for her.

An important proactive safety measure is becoming better able to size up "whom to trust with what, and when." The survivor who wants to go to the planet Zob may or may not shift her understanding. But she needs to know that, unfair though it is, most people would find these beliefs bizarre. Speaking out of them outside a trusted circle accordingly risks stigmatization and institutionalization. She needs to be able to identify which other beliefs people react to similarly. She needs to be able to assess how specific people are reacting to specific thoughts that she shares and to gear herself accordingly. Helping clients become more adept at making these judgment calls is time well spent.

Life Changes

Many survivors are in a rut and need help changing their lives. Often the early pressure, invalidation, or interference that predated the psychiatrization was never dealt with. After psychiatrization the situation grew worse. Dealing with it means confronting people. It may mean insisting on a more equitable chore division. It generally means stopping others from interfering and from making decisions for her. For many it means leaving home, putting some distance between themselves and the people who pathologize them, and making their own way.

We help by wanting more for our clients, by advocating for them where necessary, and by helping them plan and evaluate. Express confidence in their ability to form new liaisons, to cope, to learn whatever they have to learn. They need to know that they can take risks, that they can afford to rock the boat, that they really are not at everyone else's mercy, despite how vulnerable they feel and despite the oppressive reality. Small steps once again are critical, for these women need successes if they are to have the courage to go on.

It is generally worthwhile spending time sharpening communication skills. Many survivors are passive or passive-aggressive. They need to be more assertive, to ask for what they want, to give feedback, to clarify what they will and will not do. Some survivors also need help lowering their demands on others and respecting boundaries. It is not uncommon for survivors to use others as dumping grounds for their problems and as 24-hour rescue units. They may talk about their problems nonstop. They may keep turning up at all hours, stating that they cannot go on. They do so because they genuinely are needy, vulnerable, and subject to ongoing crises. And indeed they do get temporary relief this way. The long-term results nonetheless are catastrophic. Friends and family feel used, become overburdened, and progressively pathologize the survivor. Some look to psychiatry to relieve them of the burden. Some get into the practice of avoiding the survivor whenever possible. Some retreat altogether. Others end up responding only if the emergency is particularly dire, with the definition of what is "dire" getting progressively tougher.

A critical problem here is the client's very real neediness and her limited ways of addressing it. By listening and continuing to be patient and supportive ourselves, we at once take some of the burden off these relationships and give the survivor some of the consistency and concentration that she so desperately needs. It is equally critical to help her explore different ways of coping and to familiarize her with a variety of resources. Otherwise she may remain dependent on a few and vulnerable.

It is a mistake to raise her friends' dilemma early in the counseling relationship. She needs to know that we are concerned with her and her only. Our job, and let's be clear about this, is taking her side against the world. Once our relationship is solid, nonetheless, to the extent that she is open to it, it makes sense offering suggestions on these relationships and how to stop relationships from turning sour.

A change in financial situation and accommodations is a particularly important goal for many survivors. Despite our tendency to focus on the internal, in many cases poverty and poor accommodations are the most pressing problem that these women face. All too many survivors just make it from month to month, making do on the bare minimum. Some live on the street. Many live in crowded, dirty, rat-infested boarding houses. These houses are often within four blocks of the "mental hospital," and staff are highly intrusive, force women to "take their meds," and facilitate quick returns to "the hospital." Many survivors have rotting teeth that have not been attended to and ailments that they have not addressed. Few are living this way out of choice. They are in the situation because they have been dumped by male partners and others. They are here because psychiatric social workers have placed them here. They are here because they do not have the financial and other assistance that they need. It is hard for women to deal with anything else while faced with practical problems that are this dire. While they are living "like ex-patients," they are hardly likely to get free of the "patient identity."

Affirming their right to a more comfortable and freer life is important, for many women have so internalized the oppression that they are convinced that this is all they "deserve." More concrete ways that we can help include (a) directly intervening to get them the finances they need, (b) helping them challenge certificates of incompetence to manage their own estates, (c) arranging for free medical and dental services, (d) helping them secure emergency shelter, (e) helping them get into group homes (Homes run by survivors are a real plus.), (f) helping them secure other inexpensive but reasonable accommodations that are not near "THE HOSPITAL," and (g) lobbying for better financing and programs generally.

Alienation and loneliness as well are problems for many survivors. We help by encouraging them to reach out to others, by facilitating the brainstorming and planning necessary, and by assisting with any problems that arise. It is important additionally to familiarize women with local drop-in centers, recreation centers, survivor groups, women's groups, self-help groups, and so on.

A number of these programs can double as resources for clients seeking a place to discuss their experiences and to hear from others. Co-exploration with others who have been similarly injured can be enormously empowering. Some factors to keep in mind are:

- Survivor-led resources are often preferable to their professionally run counterparts.
- Groups that are critical of psychiatry are definitely preferable. Groups that are propsychiatry encourage an ongoing patient identity and may sabotage much of the good work that the woman is doing.
- Psychiatric ghettoization is a problem in its own right.
- Women in mixed groups face the same problem that women always face. Men talk and get support; women listen and empathize.
- For the most part, psychiatric survivors who have been subject to extreme sexual abuse or battery, who have severe eating problems, or who cut get more from women's groups that build on their identity as women and specifically address these issues.

Enhancement of educational and employment opportunities is also important for many. Once again encourage women to believe in themselves and help them reach for more.

"Offing the Meds"

Because psychiatric drugs materially impede feeling, perception, thought, and action, going off these drugs is one of the most liberatory acts that survivors can perform. If they are to effect this change successfully, they need to go about it carefully. As counselors it is critical that we understand what is involved and advise clients accordingly.

If the women are in a shelter or between housing, this is not a good time to go off. Where at all possible, they should have some permanence. They need a safe place. Ideally they should also have friends assisting who understand what they are up against and who are determined to see them through. Where feasible, friends who are lukewarm should not be told about what is going on, let alone used as support. They are too likely to blow the whistle.

Going off cold turkey is a common error. It is potentially lethal if the drug in question is a minor tranquilizer, for it can result in cardiac arrest. Although not a lethal hazard if it is an antidepressant or neuroleptic (major tranquilizer), it is nonetheless enormously inadvisable for a woman who has been on these drugs for a couple of months or longer.[4] When someone cold turkeys, her body goes into shock. A rebound reaction occurs. Her body now dramatically overproduces the amines whose production or transmission was being inhibited by the drugs. The longer she has been on the drugs and the greater the dosage, the greater the rebound reaction. Some combination of the following generally occurs: (a) night after night of sleeplessness, (b) enormous anxiety, (c) feeling "high as a kite," (d) feeling "as if one is going crazy," and (e) utter terror. The woman freaks out. She ends up reinstitutionalized. And she is put on an even higher dosage than she was on initially.

This is a major setback physically and psychologically. And it is avoidable. As workers we have a responsibility to warn women about it. Indeed some people do cold turkey successfully; that is, they do not completely freak out, they do not end up hospitalized, and they do not break down and "go back on their meds." These, however, are THE EXCEPTION—NOT THE RULE. Placing oneself in such jeopardy and making the experience harder than it has to be are not ways of taking care of oneself.

Women who want medical assistance in coming off are in some luck when it comes to the minor tranquilizers. "Addiction" centers regard such drugs as Valium as highly "addictive" and include them in in-house and other programs. The down side is that these centers are not feminist and may be quite intrusive, and women frequently emerge with a number of new "diagnoses" added to their list.

The situation is bleaker when it comes to the heavy-duty psychiatric drugs. The prevailing medical position is, "There is no difficulty with withdrawal per se. The symptoms of the mental illness simply return once the medication is no longer doing its job." Some liberal medical practitioners who buy into the medical model are nonetheless concerned with what is euphemistically called "overmedicating." They know that lowering the dosage appreciably is difficult, and they will help women with it. A smaller number who are critical and more responsible agree to help the women come off slowly. It is good to have a list of these doctors, but do not be overly optimistic. For a number of years, I tried every doctor anyone recommended to me in the Toronto area. In each case, when the client began having any real difficulty, the doctor got scared, became uncooperative, and in many cases pushed a higher dose on her or him. I have stopped using doctors accordingly.

If the client is on more than one psychiatric drug, she should be withdrawn from only one drug at a time. If one of the drugs is an antiparkinsonian (a drug used with the neuroleptics to stop involuntary twitching and spasming), the neuroleptic should be withdrawn from first. Where any drug was introduced to counteract the effects of another, the primary drug should be withdrawn from first.

With extremely long-acting injections like Prolixin (6 weeks), not taking the next injection will result in a reasonably slow withdrawal. Where feasible, it is preferable nonetheless to get a final injection at a reduced dose or switch to pills and then use the standard formula. With the rest (the majority), the standard inmate wisdom is Richmond's (1984) $\frac{1}{10}$ guideline: The client reduces the original dosage by $\frac{1}{10}$, stabilizes at that amount, then reduces by $\frac{1}{10}$ again. One eighth is also viable. I recommend holding the new dosage for at least 5 days before lowering it again.

If the client experiences considerable trouble at some new dosage, one option is returning to the previous dosage for at least a week. Where she is feeling reasonably safe, I suggest trying to weather the new dosage for a while, as I find that many people end up having to "go through the wet blanket" sooner or later in their attempts to get off. In such instances, 24-hour support is highly advisable. Where real problems such as this occur, it is wise to wait for 2 weeks after the difficulty subsides before decreasing again.

Before clients embark on the withdrawal process itself, it is important to explain the withdrawal symptoms (rebound reactions, etc.) that may occur. Provide them with written handouts. Besides needing to know what they may be getting themselves into before finalizing a choice like this, having something to refer to makes the process a lot easier. Problems that are expectable and that it is especially important to alert them to include:

- Nausea, vomiting, sweating, diarrhea, restlessness, headaches, general aches and pains
- In the case of neuroleptics, parkinsonian reactions such as muscle rigidity, tremors, involuntary twitching around the mouth and in the limbs
- The feeling of going crazy (known as "withdrawal psychosis")
- Sleepiness
- Anxiety
- The "wet blanket feeling"[5]

Women may experience only a few or many of these difficulties. And the degree of difficulty experienced ranges widely from very minor to reasonably severe. I recommend the slow withdrawal that I do, precisely because people tend to have a much easier time of it if they come down more slowly. Again my overwhelming preference is that women not experience a nightmare when they do not have to and that withdrawal be as gentle as possible.

Further ways of easing withdrawal that are easy enough to follow and that we can safely recommend include (a) increasing protein intake (fish, fowl, grains, legumes), (b) cutting back stringently on fatty foods (red meat, dairy products, etc.), (c) avoiding caffeine, sugar, and junk food generally, (d) taking mineral and vitamin supplements, (e) drinking herbal teas, and (f) taking other natural relaxants like valerian. Consulting "alternative medicine" practitioners is also a good idea.

Women who attempt to go off drugs altogether but stop short are sometimes ashamed. They think that they are cowards, that they have copped out, that they have let people down. It is critical to reframe what has happened. No one has been let down. What the women were doing, they were doing for themselves. And it is their own wisdom and readiness that they need to consult. Far from being cowards, moreover, they have had the courage to defy medical advice and do some heavy-duty reclaiming. And they have successfully lowered their drug intake.

Women who return to the original dosage similarly have had the courage to explore in defiance of androcentric medical advice, and that is no small feat. They are not ready to carry through with something like this, and that is fine. Many take a number of stabs at quitting before they get off. Some do the same with "hospitals." This is a reasonable process, and it should be respected.

Communal Protest

Becoming part of a movement and protest, whether peripherally or centrally, is another life change open to survivors. It is of enormous benefit to many. Simply from reading the literature, they recognize stories and feelings. They feel less alone. They become far more secure in their conviction that they are not now or never were "ill." They uncover new information about so-called "treatments." They learn new ways of defending themselves. At antipsychiatry events, even while just observing, they receive the comfort of being with others who share common experiences.

As survivors participate more actively, empowerment grows. Writing, speaking, and testifying with other survivors allow them to cut through the psychiatric mumbo jumbo to a degree that "therapy" never can. In public hearings, they directly contradict psychiatric testimony and make statements like:

> Dr.'s X and Y are not telling you the truth when they claim that modified shock does not cause long-term memory loss. I had modified shock 6 years ago. To this date, I get confused in midsentence and have gaps in my memory. What has happened to me should never happen to anyone, and it has to be stopped.

They hear others making similar claims and similar demands. In conferences and in their writing they extend the analysis further. Progressively they come to have faith in their own personal truth—their own collective truth. They also come to see that they have always been part of a collective resistance. When they laughed with other inmates at some staff member, this was collective resistance. When they "covered" for another inmate, this was collective resistance. They become aware of their early history of resistance and are able to build on it.

Turning up at demonstrations—protesting in front of the places of torture—adds to the empowerment. They grow less frightened. The system's power to intimidate them wanes.

Additionally, as part of a network, they are better protected from psychiatric invasion and they know it. They begin to effect real changes in law and belief. Any shift, however small, further protects them. It protects all survivors and indeed society as a whole. As such it adds to their sense of self. And it allows them to wrest dignity, purpose, and meaning out of what was originally a meaningless nightmare.

Most psychiatric survivors whom we work with are unlikely to become strongly involved in the liberation movement during the time they are seeing us, if they get involved at all. And as always, pushing makes no sense. In light of the enormous benefits that can accrue, nonetheless, it is important to plant seeds. Concrete ways we can help include:

- Giving individual women specific copies of survivors' writings that have special relevance for them
- Talking from time to time about what survivors have achieved
- Letting women know about local antipsychiatry demonstrations, survivor workshops and conferences, public hearings, evenings of testimony and speeches, and so on
- Mentioning specific activist groups or organizations and, where women seem interested, encouraging them to make contact
- Celebrating any efforts that they make
- Understanding the terror that they may have and providing extra support as needed

Of course, women—especially women who are triply and quadruply oppressed—can be oppressed in their own right in a movement that has few immigrants or people of color in it and that is so mainstream male in orientation. (Note in this regard such prevalent movement beliefs and stances as: Our only problem is the shrinks; just back off and leave us alone and everything will be fine.) It is important to support clients in challenging these beliefs and stances and to encourage efforts to link up with or create events that address their specific oppressions.

Laying Charges

Laying charges, as always, can be very empowering, and it is important for us to encourage it where appropriate. It can also be enormously humiliating, terrifying, and disappointing. Psychiatrists' authority as experts is enshrined in the law. And the "patient status" gives the psychiatric survivor even less credibility than the average survivor of childhood sexual abuse. The defense may try to play on this bias by making her look like a "babbling crazy woman." She is likely to hear demeaning half-truths taken as fact. Logical arguments that the client is pinning her hopes on may have only a slim chance of winning. It is our responsibility as counselors to do what we can to ensure that a client considering charging has realistic expectations and is prepared to deal with the indignities and disappointments that may occur.

Realistically, on the one hand, as abusive as shock and other so-called treatments are, no one is going to be convicted of anything for performing what is seen as "standard psychiatric practice." Charges involving clear-cut violations of the mental health act of the time, on the other hand, will "fly." Charges under the mental health act have the best chance of winning. Other legislation that is sometimes successfully used includes mental hospitals acts, health disciplines acts, libel legislation, court challenges, the criminal code (criminal assault, etc.), and injury under civil law.

Charges under mental health acts and health disciplines acts have severe time limits on them. By the time most people feel strong enough to sue, that limit is up. We need to be aware of those limits and alert clients to them.

When documenting, special note should be taken of the date that the client became aware that her rights were violated. (Awareness figures in some of the time limits.) Of relevance also is evidence of intellectual impairment and emotional suffering—especially impairment and suffering that interfere with the client's ability to pursue interesting, well-paid work.

THE LARGER COMMITMENT

We have an obligation to do what we can to oppose psychiatry and to sever our connection with it. Individual feminist counselors will have to make their own choices how best to go about this. I would not, however, use comfort as a guide. It is always more comfortable to go only slightly beyond conventional wisdom. We thereby alienate almost no one, but we achieve almost nothing.

My own recommendations/invitations are:

1. Publicly declare yourself antipsychiatry.
2. Do not identify as a "mental health professional." Our heritage is the witches and the midwives, not the doctors who usurped their power and declared them "mad." It is a wonderful heritage. Let's reclaim it.
3. Do not work in a psychiatric facility or with psychiatrists.
4. Do not refer people to psychiatrists or to any people or agency that places them in danger of psychiatrization.

5. Do not serve on the board of any human service agency that is not prepared to begin actively questioning psychiatry.

6. Place antipsychiatry squarely on the agenda of any new agency that you are helping to plan and any agency that you are currently part of; challenge people whenever they try to water down the concept; and keep raising the question of psychiatry despite the efforts of others to avoid it.

7. Encourage agencies you are involved with to replace psychiatrists who consult for them with other consultants.

8. Challenge both propsychiatry and liberal positions.

9. Point out and challenge "mental health" language and concepts, especially when used by colleagues.

10. Offer or arrange antipsychiatry presentations and workshops.

11. Publicly advocate for the end to forced institutionalization.

12. Oppose the use of neuroleptics, antidepressants, and shock.

13. Participate in antipsychiatry demonstrations and protests.

14. Present antipsychiatry testimony at public hearings, and write critiques of proposed "mental health legislation."

SUGGESTED READINGS

Becker, H. (1973). *Outsiders: Studies in the sociology of deviance.* London: Free Press.

Burstow, B., & Weitz, D. (1988). *Shrink-resistant: The struggle against psychiatry in Canada.* Vancouver: New Star.

Chesler, P. (1972). *Women and madness.* New York: Avon.

Goffman, E. (1961). *Asylums: Essays on the social situation of mental patients and other inmates.* New York: Anchor.

Laing, R. D. (1965). *The divided self: An existential study in sanity and madness.* New York: Penguin.

Millett, K. (1990). *The loony bin trip.* New York: Touchstone.

Richmond, D. (1984). *Dr. Caligari's psychiatric drugs.* Berkeley, CA: Network Against Psychiatric Assault.

NOTES

1. Concepts like *spoiled identity* and *career of a mental patient* come from labeling theory. Labeling theorists have argued, and I would suggest correctly, that it is the "mental health system" that creates "mental patients." And they have outlined the process by which this designation and this transformation occur. For informative analyses in this regard, see Goffman (1961) and Becker (1973).

2. For further discussions of these situations and their aftermath, see Bateson, Jackson, Haley, et al. (1956) and Laing (1965).

3. For a valuable first-person account that sheds light on a number of these, see Millett (1990).

4. Richmond (1984) suggests that lithium is an exception and can be cold turkeyed. I know some people who got really high when they did so, then became terrified, and ended up institutionalized. I have worked with others who had no problem at all. I do not recommend treating it as an exception.

5. These specific problems may persist for several months. In extreme cases, where the drugs have produced tardive dyskinesia, they may not disappear. Going back on drugs will continue to mask the reactions for a while but at the expense of worsening and accelerating the TD. See Chapter 2 for more information on TD.

14

Clients Who Are Considering
Ending Their Lives

Sadly, feminist counselors act much like other counselors when working with clients seen as "suicidal." Although they may modify or soften it, counselors essentially follow a "safe," recognizable "party line." The line is: Empathize strongly with the client. If the contact is by phone, try very hard to find out her number and location. Say whatever you can to "talk her out of it." Assess the "degree of danger" (translation, the likelihood that she will follow through and end her life in the foreseeable future) by asking questions like, "Have you ever tried to end your life before?" and, "Do you have a concrete plan for how to go about it?" If you think she is in any immediate danger, call the police or ambulance. Use whatever trickery you can to get her to divulge the necessary information. Use trickery and/or force to keep her in your office or on the phone long enough for an ambulance to reach her. Alternatively drive her to a "psych" ward.

I have no problem with empathizing, attempting to size up the situation, or introducing other options. THERE IS SOMETHING ENORMOUSLY AMISS, HOWEVER, WITH WHAT IS HAPPENING HERE. On the one hand, as feminists we are saying that we respect women's right to choose, that we are not going to impose in the way male "professionals" do, and that we believe in openness and sharing. On the other hand, we are buying into a process that imposes life on women whether they want it or not; we are complicit with having them dragged into a misogynous and violent psychiatric ward where they are likely to be drugged and shocked in an effort to sustain their lives against their will. And we are willing to lie, evade, and trick them in the process. There is a contradiction here. We need to bring our work more in line with our principles.

A number of relatively unexamined beliefs, among other things, underlie the contradiction. Moving in a more feminist direction means problematizing these beliefs.

One key set of beliefs from which counselors act out when they take this line is some combination of 1 through 4 as below, followed by 5.

1. Taking one's own life is morally wrong.
2. People do not have the right to take their own lives.
3. "Suicide" is "poor thinking." (Better options are always available.)
4. If a woman is seriously entertaining killing herself, at least at this point she is not of sound mind and not responsible.
5. Given 1 through 4, and given both the finality and the enormity of the act, we are right to stop her and to use any means necessary.

The first two beliefs are patriarchal moralism. We are saying that however dreadful someone's life is, she is morally bound to stick it out. Such beliefs have their origins in a tyrannical male god who has sole authority over life and death and who forbids "suicide." It is also part and parcel of patriarchal capitalism. The patriarchal and capitalist state purports to own the bodies in its jurisdiction. Patriarchal capitalism values quantity and devalues quality. These beliefs and values are incompatible with feminism.

As feminists we are committed to "not owning" people. There is no "higher authority" that people are obligated to obey. And *quality of life* is the overriding value. It follows that it can be moral and that we do have a right to take our own lives.

The right to kill ourselves is in fact integral to freedom. It is part and parcel of owning our own bodies, of making choices about our bodies and our selves. Insofar as we and we alone have the right to make choices about own living or dying, it follows that no one else has the right to deprive us of this choice whether through force or trickery, whether called "therapist" or "jailer."

The finality of the decision, while it understandably strikes us with dread, is in no way relevant to the ethical issue. Part of our awe stems in fact from a common sense misunderstanding about acts. "To act" is always "to do something that is final." Although we can act again and modify consequences, we can never go back and "not have done" what we have done. Real freedom, as opposed to empty or imaginary freedom, is precisely about finality. It is about being able to make choices in a real world where our actions are of consequence and where nothing is ultimately "erasable."[1] It is partially because suicide is so definitive and the results unmodifiable that existentialists and other philosophers have taken the choice to kill ourselves as paradigmal of human freedom.

The enormity of the decision similarly, while it terrifies us, is irrelevant to the rights issue. If we are the proper authority when it comes to ourselves, we are the proper authority whether the decision is minimal or monumental, of limited consequence or of such overriding consequence that it wipes out our very being.

Counselors who base their action on the third or fourth belief (followed by the fifth) avoid extreme moralism but also fundamentally err. The extreme psychiatric version of this error is that people who seriously entertain ending their lives are "mentally ill." This version is upheld by mental health law, which treats suicide as a subset of "danger to self" and makes "danger to self" sufficient criterion for institutionalization. Such a belief "justifies" the psychiatric violation that follows. What is happening here is that incarceration and an injurious bogus medical procedure are being inflicted on someone on the basis of a bogus illness. It is a sham. It is evasion. And it is opportunism.

The nonmedical version that many feminist therapists take is not opportunistic, but it is still mistaken. While not necessarily approving of very much that psychiatry does, many feminist therapists "accept" that "highly suicidal" women are "not in their right mind" and should be stopped. And they reluctantly use the "imperfect means" available. Significantly, many women who are not suicidal and who are clearly "rational" state uncategorically that they would rather die than ever be institutionalized again. Even if therapists were right that the decision is irrational, in other words, the solution is unacceptable. If you will excuse a problematic metaphor, regardless of the truth of the original premise, it cannot conceivably justify imposing a "cure" that is worse than the "disease."

What is more fundamental is that *the underlying premise is incorrect*. At some point in her life, almost every woman I have ever known has seriously entertained killing herself. Philosophers throughout the ages have regarded suicide as a fundamental human choice. These people cannot all be dismissed as temporarily "unsound."

The truth is that people do not consider suicide because they are deranged. People consider suicide because they are miserable (and who better to determine this than they?) and because they deem their lives not worth living (and as feminists, how can we conceivably substitute our assessments for theirs? external assessments for assessments based on lived experience?). This is the case whether people blatantly have a strong grasp on reality or present confused.

It is even the case with extreme confusion—something that is atypical but presented as paradigmal to justify intrusive policies. Consider in this regard the woman referred to in the last chapter who wanted to kill herself to get to the planet Zob. She fused the literal and the metaphoric. And she was extremely and blatantly confused. She was a deeply unhappy woman nonetheless—indeed an unhappy woman whom a series of well-intended helpers had not succeeded in making an iota happier. Without a doubt her thoughts about the planet Zob were wishful thinking. This notwithstanding, the choice that she was contemplating had a basis in reality. A still more obvious basis exists with the vast majority of humankind who approach suicide with no such fantasies and no wishful thinking.

The same kinds of flaws exist with the moderate position that does not posit "unsound mind" but nonetheless holds that we should stop women from killing themselves because suicide is irrational or poor thinking. An assumption being made here is that preferable options are always available. Acting rationally, according to this position, means realizing this and not killing oneself. The woman, it is assumed, is not in a position to realize this because she is upset or depressed.

This belief trivializes women's agony and misdescribes reality. In many cases options that are obviously better are not available. The woman who is racked with pain from a degenerative condition does not "obviously" have a better option. Even where the situation is less blatantly dismal, moreover, the client's decision to kill herself may be perfectly reasonable.

A common situation familiar to us all is: A woman who has been unhappy all her life considers killing herself. She may be a survivor of childhood sexual abuse who has spent most of her time terrified. She may have been invalidated since day one. She is considering killing herself because she believes that life is not going to get much better. Although it is perfectly understandable that we would prefer she not kill herself, and, say, let us try to help her first, her belief *is not irrational.* Whether right or wrong, her prediction has a basis in fact. Indeed the sad truth is that the prediction may be correct. Our certainty that it is not is naïveté, arrogance, or both.

What happened to Bruno Bettelheim is instructive. Bettelheim was a clinician who spent a good part of World War II in a concentration camp. After the Holocaust, he continued to be plagued by the experience. He kept finding himself in a sweat—reliving the nightmare. According to the standards by which we normally judge success, he became a dazzling success. He continued working on "his problem." He made use of "the problem," comparing his own experiences in the camp to the experiences of troubled children. And he developed new important clinical approaches on the basis of it. This notwithstanding, the terror did not greatly subside. After about 35 years of struggling with it, Bettelheim killed himself. Although it is impossible to know what Bettelheim was thinking, my guess is that he predicted that the agony would continue and decided that it was too awful to bear. If so, he surely had ample reason to believe what he believed. The decision was totally rational.

What if he had come to this same decision 4 months after his release from the camps? If a clinician had been around, that clinician would almost certainly have put such thinking down to "trauma" and stopped Bettelheim, claiming that the trauma had resulted in an irrational decision and that it his Sacred Duty to "save" Bettelheim. Bettelheim's decision would nonetheless have been rational at that time as well. And indeed his prediction would have been right.

Without even attempting to predict the future, moreover, a person can reasonably decide, "What I am going through now is just too awful. Even if I knew with certitude that I was going to be fine in a year, going through this is not worth it." Such decisions break our hearts. We encourage people to hold on, and understandably so. Nonetheless we are not inside their experiences and cannot definitively say that they are wrong. I am not even sure what "wrong" means in this instance.

Moreover, *even if we could know with certitude that better options existed and that if we stopped a woman from killing herself now she would agree with us a year down the road, that would not change the ethical issue.* Freedom means the right to make incorrect decisions—even lethally incorrect decisions. The right to make only "correct" decisions is no freedom at all. Whether the woman would agree with us later is not the point, although it is an important issue for the woman herself to consider. The person who is faced with a choice and is authorized to choose is not some person who does not yet exist. It is the person we are encountering now.[2]

Alongside and interweaved with these beliefs are a number of very difficult feelings and concerns that feminist therapists necessarily struggle with but are currently dealing with poorly. None of us want to see someone else die when we think that she has better options. And as caring women and helpers, we thankfully do not have the aloofness to simply walk away and say that it is "her choice." (How masculine and alienated the civil rights position by itself can be!) We want to help our sister who is in desperate straits and legitimately so.

Feelings of helplessness, correspondingly, are understandably common. I have seen sensitive counselors feel enormously helpless when a woman says to them, "Thank you for your help, but I don't need it now. I've made my decision, and I'm going to kill myself." We find ourselves wanting to do something to get rid of this powerlessness, to save her, to alter a situation that we do not want to exist.

We suspect—I think sometimes correctly, sometimes not—that something better is possible for these women and that if we could help them through the next few weeks or months, we could discover or create it together. We suspect— and I think correctly—that the majority of "suicidal women" who contact us are not fully intent on killing themselves. Generally most are ambivalent. Even when they present otherwise, generally at least part of them is hoping that we can relieve some of the burden, can help them find another way. That is why they are talking to us in the first place. We believe that, minimally, a lower suicide rate would be preferable.

When a woman whom we have been working with introduces the possibility of killing herself, we tend to doubt ourselves. We ask ourselves questions like: "How have I failed her? Would she have been better off with someone more skillful? Is she about to pay with her life for going to someone who is inadequate? Is there something—ANYTHING—I can do now?" This is often about the time that counselors blow the whistle.

Similarly, counselors who have had clients kill themselves are often plagued with guilt. They feel that they should have done something more. They do not want to "repeat the same mistake." Better bring in the boys in white, they argue, than face this tragedy again.

Additionally therapists are understandably afraid of what is going to happen to them if a "suicide occurs" and it becomes known that they have not followed "the party line." The first time I presented a feminist position on suicide at a women and psychiatry conference, the pervasiveness and impact of that fear was obvious. Counselor after counselor said, "Yes, Bonnie, I see what you are saying. And I agree with you. But I'm afraid of being charged." Additionally some who worked in agencies expressed a worry of being fired, a fear of what would happen to the agency, and so on.

All of these concerns are perfectly understandable and enormously empathiz-able. We have no reason to be ashamed of them. So many are based in our caring as women that we would be greatly diminished and indeed less human if we were not troubled. Some of the concerns are realistic, some unrealistic. Many call for "something" from us. The "something" that they call for, however, is quite different from intrusion. None warrant intrusion.

Although we can absolutely never know for certain, indeed with many women, we have at least some reason to think that something better is possible, whether in the short or long run. Wherever this is the case, something large indeed is required of us. We are called on to try as hard as we can to help the woman hold on, to take in support, to co-explore and build other ways. That is what suicidal counseling is about. But we still have to respect choice. And we are not justified in intruding.

We are right when we similarly see "contacting us" as a call for help. Women who are clear that they are going to kill themselves, who have closure, and who know how they are going to "tie up loose ends" have little reason to call counselors. A call for help, however, does not always mean that the client is ambivalent. Moreover it should not be interpreted as a call for interference. This is true even in the extreme case in which the woman is virtually handing herself over to us and saying, "Do something." Women who appeal desperately for help, who ask us to save them and to relieve them of responsibility want a great deal more responsibility from us, but they do not exactly want rights overridden. And they are often enormously shocked when this is what transpires.

Our sadness, our worry that someone who could have a better life is really "going to end it" is inevitable. And it is unproblematic. It is only problematic when we try to ease our fears and sadness at the expense of our client's freedom. We need to learn to live and deal with our own sadness and apprehension.

The sense of powerlessness per se has two dimensions. Both have something to do with blurring the distinction between the client and ourselves. And we can do something about them.

The first dimension involves "taking on" the client's feelings of powerlessness. I do not mean simply getting a feel for what the client is going through. I mean actually internalizing and getting stuck in her panic—her sense of being "out of control." Again it is important that the client not pay for our panic—our fusion. Calling emergency is a way of defusing our panic—feeling in control again. Getting back control by wresting control from our client will not do. We begin helping ourselves directly and our client indirectly by understanding what is happening to us. That understanding helps us clarify our boundaries—something we can do without being uncaring. Stronger boundaries in turn give us some relief and make it easier not to intrude. Significantly it also makes us much better able to function as skillful counselors. The bottom line is that no client can get clean and reliable help from a therapist "in crisis."

The second dimension that adds to our overwhelming sense of our powerlessness comes from exaggerating our own power and then discovering the real limits of that power when we most desperately want to have an impact. With clients all too often "going along" with us, we can forget that clients are their own people. They are not "our creatures" or even fundamentally "our clients." We cannot "get them" to agree to anything. It is partially frustration in bumping into these limits in a life-and-death situation that predisposes otherwise respectful therapists to intrude. We need to accept and value the limits even when they most dumbfound us. If we accept and work in terms of them instead of expecting them to disappear, we stop feeling as powerless and do better work.

This acceptance similarly defuses the issue of competence. We stop kicking ourselves for not finding that "magical word" that will "save them." And we are less likely to blame ourselves for choices that sadden us.

We can legitimately hold on to our conviction that a lower suicide rate is preferable and that fewer women would kill themselves if they got the help needed. What we need to take in, however, is that besides interference being unethical, IT DOES NOT EVEN ACHIEVE THE ENDS INTENDED. There is simply no reason to believe that interference lowers the suicide rate. The history of ECT is instructive in this regard. Throughout the history of this "treatment," its use has been justified on the basis that it "prevents suicide." As psychiatric researchers have demonstrated, however, after years of attempting to prove that it does, there is no indication whatever that ECT prevents suicide.[3] So with other interference.

We may forcibly prevent a woman from killing herself now, only for her to kill herself later. In that case our interference has only added to her agony. A woman who is institutionalized today to prevent "suicide" may in fact not have killed herself if we had not intervened. And she may be more likely to kill herself later because the brain damage inflicted on her has made her life substantially more difficult. (Women who are institutionalized for "suicidal ideation" are prime candidates for the most damaging of psychiatric treatments.) The fact that no one subsequently charges the psychiatrist and that the psychiatric intervention is still viewed as lifesaving is a testimony to psychiatric hegemony, not a vindication of the practice.

Ironically, moreover, rather than ensuring that women will get the help they need, *our interference prevents women from getting decent help.* Many women who are thinking of killing themselves want help but do not reach out precisely because they are worried that we will interfere.

Two fundamental rights are being violated here: (a) their right to kill themselves, and (b) their right to decent help, whether they are thinking of killing themselves or not. By violating the first, whether in the name of help or not, we are also fundamentally violating the second. Additionally, I suspect, by honoring both, we lower the risk of suicide. Significantly I have alsways used a nonintrusion policy while working clients who are suicidal. Although I suspect that sooner or later someone will kill herself, to date no one has.

The issue of our own protection is real enough. Let us approach it though with an unequivocal feminist commitment. Let us agree not to sacrifice our clients' freedom to protect ourselves or our agencies. Once we make that commitment, we can find other ways.

Not exaggerating the risk is helpful, for it reduces the possibility of imposing out of fear. Despite fears, the likelihood of any individual counselor being charged for not reporting a "potential suicide" is negligible. I have never known a single counselor who was charged. Even if someone were charged, it would be very difficult to prove that the counselor had sufficient reason to believe that a "suicide" was about to occur. The more strongly and publicly we advocate noninterference, of course, the greater the likelihood that the old boys' network will eventually become alarmed and that some charges will ensue. Even should this happen, however, it is still difficult to prove much. The chances of any given therapist being charged are minimal. And if someone does get charged, it is likely to be someone like me who is publicly promoting this policy—not someone who is following it and advocating it quietly within the feminist community.

A protective measure that we might offer each other is the agreement to stick together. Counselors who adopt a nonintrusion policy need to know that the feminist counseling community will back her if "the shit hits the fan." Correspondingly, if we are to beat patriarchal intrusion and to ensure that women workers are not punished for their refusal to be co-opted, we need solidarity.

Agencies do well to spell out their suicidal policy so that individual counselors cannot be sued. Both the individual and the agency can gain further protection by articulating a "feminist obligation of care" that explicitly prohibits interference. This is a task to address collectively with other feminist agencies. Insofar as a number of agencies together define *feminist obligation of care* in a way that prohibits interference, they all thereby gain protection. One possible suit against an agency that does not report a potential suicide is that the agency or the professionals therein did not live up to their obligation of care. A commonly held articulation of a feminist obligation of care that rules out interference significantly weakens the chance of such a suit winning.

DIRECT PRACTICE

Sometimes clients directly tell us that they have decided to kill themselves or are thinking about killing themselves. When clients directly speak of "suicide," we have an immediate "in." More commonly, clients "hint." They are indirect because they are ambivalent. On the one hand, they desperately want us to know because they are frightened, are terribly alone, and do not know where else to turn. On the other hand, they want to hide the truth because they are unsure how we will react. We can help by picking up on the hints, by asking the client openly and caringly whether she is thinking about killing herself, and by assuring her that we are okay with what she is saying and want to hear more. It is a relief to have the secret out and to be able to talk about it. It is a relief to know that the counselor whom she is turning to is not afraid to face the situation at hand and is at least going to try to understand.

The essence of good crisis work (and generally it is crisis work we are about here) is the bond—the dialogue. We need to truly care. We need to take in the enormity of the pain. We need to listen to our sister's story with the whole of our being. Our caring—our being there for her—helps her hang in. Remembering some time when we ourselves were in similar straits can help us connect. Counselors who ask the traditional questions to assess the likelihood of someone killing him- or herself need to make sure that these questions proceed out of, not disrupt, the dialogue.

It is important to take the client's thoughts, plans, and semiplans seriously and to let her know that we take them seriously. Be clear that you appreciate her situation and can understand why she is considering ending her life. Whether she asks about it or not, I always make a point as well of assuring the client that I respect her right to kill herself and that however much I may want something different for her, I will honor that right.

The validation and affirmation let clients know that we are safe to talk to and have some sense of what they are going through. Generally, though not invariably, it also deescalates the situation. The knowledge that we respect and accept is freeing. It makes it less threatening to consider other options. Not having to defend her direction gives the client the liberty to reconsider. If it is "okay to kill oneself," "not killing oneself" is conceivable.

The exceptional situation is where the client has made or is making a carefully reasoned choice and is not in crisis. In such an instance the client may want help clarifying, problem solving, achieving closure, saying "good-bye." It is our job to provide that help. If she seems unaware of how to protect herself from interference, advising her about this is critical.

More commonly the client is in crisis. She is despairing and/or panicking. And we ourselves suspect that if she held on longer, in the long run she could make the necessary changes for life to feel worthwhile. It is important to share such thoughts with the client, while being clear that we are not inside her pain or her life and cannot ultimately know. Correspondingly, while empathizing with the woman who wants to die and trying to provide relief, it is critical to reach for and attempt to ally with whoever within wants to go on. Significantly, as noted earlier, on some level most clients are ambivalent. That ambivalence is a resource.

Where I am at a loss, I sometimes solicit the client's help with requests like:

> I really need your help here. I've been talking to the Glenda who is sure that there is no other way. And I feel for her. Right now, though, I need to talk to the Glenda who is less sure—who thinks that there just may be a way.

Sometimes a less despairing person responds and we can begin teasing out other options. Sometimes the client does not think that such a part exists but is able to reach it with help. (Guided fantasy can be a real asset here.) Sometimes the client states definitively that no such part exists; I take this as an indication to back off.

Such approaches as these are most reliable with women who are currently but not habitually in crisis. It is harder with deeply injured women whose lives vary between very extreme crisis and extreme crisis. You may be "doing everything right" yet only occasionally hear a hopeful response. She may get only limited relief, and that relief may fade into thin air by the next conversation. You may be frustrated by someone who shrugs her shoulders, "yes buts" you, will not try anything, and keeps breaking appointments, saying, "I had best just kill myself and get it over with."

When we start feeling frustrated with women in this position, it helps to remember how much more frustrated they themselves must be. Anticipating the likelihood of such responses and understanding why it happens also helps. *Of course* the client does not want to try anything. All her life she has been trying what other people have suggested, and just look at where she is! The things that we suggest can moreover sound so very naive. *Of course* she "yes buts" us. Besides that "yes butting" giving women with limited power an experience of power, it conveys the hopelessness that she desperately needs us to take in. Moreover, in a very real way, "yes but" is her experience. Her life experience is that anything we can suggest REALLY WILL NOT WORK BECAUSE . . . *Of course* she shrugs her shoulders. It seems pointless to her. She is sick to death of hearing helpers prattle on about "better options." Even when we are extremely sensitive, what we say may remind her of what insensitive others have said before. And *of course* advances appear to vanish. When she leaves us, she returns to an unhappy life.

It is important that we not take the shrugs and the "yes butting" personally. If we are to help in the long run—and sometimes we cannot—this is the thorny route that we are forced to go through. For some time, we are not likely to see quick changes or changes that appear to last. Not seeing them, however, does not mean nothing is happening. Advances may be followed by setback after setback, with meaningful shifts nonetheless occurring in the background.

With a client whose life has been one endless crisis, the relationship is especially critical. Although our suggestions may seem irrelevant for a long time, little by little our caring is "warming" her. We need to keep in touch with that caring and keep expressing it.

Disempowering messages that some of the women considering "suicide" have been given and are giving themselves include:

1. I am not important. And what happens to me is not important.
2. I am so awful that I deserve to die.
3. Everyone else is better off without me.
4. I cannot do anything. I am helpless/hopeless.

Both external and internalized sexism are evident. In the short run, we need to counter these messages in whatever ways we can. In the long run, more stringent co-investigation and action are called for.

A common problem to be alert for—especially with women whose lives have not been endless crises—is: The suicidal language itself is trapping the client and half-creating its own reality. Many times people initially adopt suicidal language at least partially as a way of expressing their distress and the enormity of their plight. Little by little the language propels them farther down a path that they never fully chose. And it intensifies the terror, the loneliness, the despair. Gradually shifting the language helps. Without questioning the seriousness or the intention, we can gently alert clients to the problem and encourage more direct expressions and descriptions. A cautionary note: The client still needs to be able to talk about killing herself. And it is critical that this not be a ploy to avoid facing the situation ourselves.

It is important to let the "suicidal" client in crisis know repeatedly that we want her to live. Frequently the client is thinking, "No one gives a damn whether I live or die." In an alienating world in which human beings are trivialized and ravished, this belief makes perfect sense. It can make a difference having someone around who clearly wants her to go on, even if it is only a counselor. Our expression of our wish additionally serves as an invitation to life.

Clients in extreme crisis often need considerable help just getting through the next few days or the next few weeks. A key part of our job is helping her create as strong a support network as possible. The ideal is a few trustworthy friends who can take turns sleeping over and/or staying up with her at night, people who will call in, and one or more persons who will take over some of the practical tasks currently burdening her. It is important that the people be chosen carefully and that no one be overburdened. Otherwise people will withdraw and/or blow the whistle.

The minimum needed is someone who will phone in regularly and spend time listening. Sadly, for some it is hard to secure even the minimum. And for some the minimum is woefully inadequate.

Sometimes women have friends who really could help and are unlikely to freak, but the women are reluctant to call them because they do not wish to burden them. Again the traditional "female" belief "I am not important" is playing a part. So too is womanly caring. It is now working against her, but it may be able to be turned around.

One way of helping with this is facilitating an imaginary reversal. Although counselors need to go with their own style, I can recommend some version of the following:

1. Imagine that your friend ____ were experiencing a similar aloneness and desperation.
2. Imagine that she decided not to call you and risked killing herself instead because she could not bring herself to burden you.
3. How do you feel? What would you like to tell her?
4. Now give that same caring and that same message to yourself.

Besides helping them gain access to help, such exercises as these reduce alienation and help them get in touch with their own significance. Where clients still cannot reach out and cannot turn it around—and this is fairly common—they generally benefit from such exercises nonetheless. The overt messages that they are giving themselves and us may be, "It doesn't work. I'm not worth it. I can't do it." Very often, though, the covert is, "It is sad that I cannot feel at all the same about myself. And it would be nice to get to a point where I could."

Where no such friends can be found, where she will not ask, or where additional help is needed, outside resources should at least be considered, though again we need to accept the client's "no". Feminist hostels, which are caring and where she can stay a few days, can be a real plus. Where the client is thinking of using "mental health facilities," recommend other services and make sure that she knows what she is getting into and how to safeguard her rights.

Whatever the other resources, it is important that we ourselves keep in close contact. The fewer the resources that women have (and some have next to none), the more critical this contact is. Doubling up on sessions for the time being and providing daily (or biweekly) phone contact can help, though counselors will have to check in with themselves to see what works for them. We need to be sensitive to our own needs here. In crisis situations, we are sometimes pulled to offer more than we can reasonably give. It is critical that we not deplete ourselves or offer what we cannot follow through on. A fine line exists between supporting and rescuing anyway. We can help people stay alive and can even "fight for their lives." But ultimately we cannot "save" anyone.

Where the client declines further contact with everyone—counselor included—I would make it clear that she can always change her mind. Something more might be offered here as well, though again counselors will have to work out how far they are comfortable going.

I state and offer some version of the following:

> I respect your right not to have contact. At the same time, I am worried about you, don't want you to kill yourself, and don't want you to be any more alone than you have to be. So what I'm going to do is make contact easily available. Every evening (or second evening) around 8:30 this week, I'm going to call. You don't have to pick up the phone if you don't want to. You can even unplug it if it's bugging you. It is important to me, though, that you know that I am there and that you have the option of talking. Does that feel okay?

Clients get some reassurance. And it serves as a lifeline.

Throughout the process our calm and our ability to see other possibilities are critical, for it is out of these that we help clients gain steadiness and explore further. If you find yourself taking on the client's panic or despair, take a step back and disidentify. If you are working in an agency where staff escalate each other's panic, for the time being get some distance from them. In the long run, alert co-workers to the dynamic and begin addressing it together.

Clients who have been in crisis may emerge from the crisis and nonetheless decide to kill themselves. We need to accept this and support them. A client may kill herself in the midst of the crisis. Although we will inevitably go through our own grieving and soul searching, and I in no way wish to trivialize the process, this too we need to accept. Table 14.1 lists my recommendations for handling some crisis situations.

TABLE 14.1 Difficult Situations

The Situations	My Recommendations
The client asks for the name and number of an organization that will provide her with information on painless, effective ways to kill oneself.	I would begin by exploring the situation, and I would roughly follow the process outlined in this chapter. If the client remains clear that she wants this number, I would provide it. Besides having a right to kill themselves, clients have a right to information to safeguard themselves against pain, failure, interference, and unintentional disabling. Screening out unethical and otherwise poor services is essential. I would refer only to those organizations whose ethicality you feel okay with, that automatically include help sorting through and examining other options, and that offer reliable information.
A client who has said that she is going to kill herself turns up for her appointment. She has overdosed and begins losing consciousness.	It is our responsibility to respect the choices that clients make as long as there is someone there choosing. If the client is unconscious, losing consciousness, or too drugged to function, she is not present as a chooser. We have no right whatever to make a point of turning up at such times and using this state as a justification for intervening. That is not what is happening here, however. The client herself has turned up and for all intents and purposes has placed herself in our hands. No one else is present who can function as chooser. We are responsible. I would choose life and call an ambulance. Needless to say, this decision entails being prepared to advocate for her and to safeguard her rights.
The client appears to be deluded about what is going to happen to her after she kills herself.	I would try particularly hard to help her gain clarity. This is one of those times when I sometimes dispute specific aspects of reality, if I sense that this direction will help. In one case I said to a client, "You say that your previous therapist really hurt you. There is no question she did. And it was wrong. Your plan to slit your throat on her veranda, however, is just not going to give you what you think. It is not going to plague her day in and day out for decades. I know we all imagine things like this, but reality tends to be far different. You will become someone she occasionally thinks about, no doubt with certain regrets, and that will be about it. As far as I'm concerned, your life is worth a whole lot more than that."

Whether I dispute reality or not, and whether the "illusion" is common or unusual, I make a point of holding on to the knowledge that we are all deluded and all make our way, using what awareness we have. |
| The client had a suicide pact with her partner. The partner kept his or her part of the bargain and is now dead. She is upset and confused. And she thinks that she is obliged to kill herself. | The client needs help with grieving and with guilt. It is important to assure her that she is not responsible for her partner's death and that she is not obliged to kill herself. The bottom line is: Despite any agreement, each is responsible for her own life. At any point each had the right to change her mind, even at the last minute, when it is too late to tell the other.

The client is clearly ambivalent about killing herself, and I would reach for and work with that ambivalence. If she calls |

TABLE 14.1   Continued

The Situations	My Recommendations
	what happened "cowardice," work at renaming/reframing. Also find out more about the relationship itself and how her ambivalence was dealt with earlier. Sometimes the person who does not kill herself was "talked into going along." Unearthing what happened and the power dynamic in the relationship generally can help her regain her entitlement.
The client is badly fragmented. One part is threatening to kill the whole and has the power to do it.	Like many women who are thinking of killing themselves, this client is ambivalent. She needs help exploring that ambivalence. She needs help accessing any parts that object to "suicide" and making sure that their voices are heard. If one part announces that she is afraid that another part is going to kill her, <ol><li>Facilitate a dialogue between everyone within that you can locate.</li><li>Make a special effort to locate someone within who can explain what is going on and mediate.</li><li>Be prepared to champion the fearful part and speak on her behalf.</li><li>Keep an open mind about what is happening here. Although there is talk of "killing," and this certainly is how it is being experienced, what is scaring the client might be neither "suicide" nor "murder" *as we know it*. It might be the extinction of a subpersonality, whether by engulfment or fusion. And the change may be a good thing.</li></ol>
The client keeps ending conversations by stating, "Well, I had better go now. It's time for me to slit my throat. So, good-bye."	The client is undoubtedly getting some delight out of rattling the counselor. What is more significant is that she is in enormous pain. And one of these times she really may kill herself. In the long run, in fact, she is far more likely to do so than the average "suicidal client." It is important not to say anything provocative here, for the result can be lethal. Calmly empathize with her pain. Reestablish contact in a few days or at a previously agreed-on time. Our steadiness here is something that the client can hold on to, and it sets the groundwork for shifts in the future.

ATTENDING TO OURSELVES

In light of the uncertainty, grief, frustration, and fear that so often accompanies work of this sort, it is absolutely critical that those doing it take care of themselves. Throughout I have been offering suggestions on how to go about it. Some additional thoughts follow.

If in private practice, where possible do not overload the practice with a large number of women who are contemplating killing themselves or are otherwise in crisis. We are isolated and can easily become exhausted and overwhelmed. It is a good idea to reduce the isolation regardless, whether by networking with other therapists who do this type of work or by seeking supervision. It is just too hard without people around who can support us and offer suggestions.

Although social service workers do not suffer from similar isolation, their plight is every bit as severe and indeed, arguably worse. A very high percentage of the clientele are women in crisis. As a social service worker you moreover are not only carrying your own very difficult load. To a significant degree, you are also affected by every woman who comes into the agency and by every woman whom your co-workers talk about and actively worry over. Agency problems that can result include (a) the staff are forever in crisis, (b) staff burn out quickly, (c) staff get triggered by clients and trigger each other, and (d) staff end up desensitizing themselves to the women in crisis.

It helps to set aside time at staff meetings to surface such problems, to co-explore ways of dealing with them, and to support one another. Be prepared to make structural and other proposals to the board. Where agencies cater to clients who are likely to be in crisis, additionally taking on an external consultant is wise.

SUGGESTED READINGS

Camus, A. (1955). *The myth of Sisyphus and other essays* (J. O'Brien, Trans.). New York: Vintage.
Sartre, J. (1961). *The age of reason.* New York: Penguin.

NOTES

1. For an important existential novel that explores the relationship between freedom and finality, see Sartre (1961).

2. What I am saying here constitutes a refutation of the "Thank you, doctor" position. According to this popular and self-serving position, any "involuntary" treatment is justified if the psychiatrist has reason to suspect that down the road the "patient" may come to agree with it and say, "Thank you, doctor." Indeed women who are badly damaged by drugs and shock often do just that!

3. See Eastwood and Peacock (1976) and Avery and Winokur (1976).

APPENDIX

Example of a Client Handout

WORKING TOGETHER

This sheet is intended to give you some general information about my background, what I believe, and how I work. My hope is that it will be of some help to you in deciding whether to work with me and in clarifying what you might expect of me and what I expect of you and that it will generally assist us in creating a good working alliance. If you disagree with any of the views, ideas, or ways of operating, and/or you are not sure what I mean, let's discuss it and see what we can work out together.

EDUCATION

I have a Ph.D. and an M.Ed. in Adult Education and Counseling from Ontario Institute for Studies in Education (OISE), as well as a second master's degree. I have also taken training from Toronto Psychosynthesis Institute, The Bioenergetics Institute, and Toronto Institute for Human Relations and have done an internship at the Counselling and Development Centre at York University.

EXPERIENCE

I have been in private practice since 1979. I have done considerable agency work, supervising and training counselors. I have taught social work as a full-time faculty member both at the BSW program at the University of Manitoba and the MSW program at Carleton University. I supervise many therapists in private practice. And I have published extensively in the areas of counseling and psychotherapy.

OVERALL PERSPECTIVE

I am a structuralist/feminist. What this means is that although I will not necessarily stress the political,

1. I see external systemic oppression (sexism, racism, classism, ageism, ableism, and heterosexism) as fundamental to the problems that we find by living in the world.
2. I see the internalizations of oppression as fundamental to our problems in living.
3. I do not regard myself as The Expert, nor you as the Passive Recipient of My Expertise. I regard us both as adults, each with our own knowledge and skill, who are working together on issues that are meaningful to you.

APPROACHES

1. The counseling modalities that I draw on tend to be from the political and the humanistic streams. I draw primarily on radical therapy and secondarily on transactional analysis, gestalt, Rogerian, bioenergetics, dialogical, psychosynthesis, and existential analysis. I do not adhere to a single modality but rather go between modalities, trying to use whatever seems helpful to a client at any particular time.

2. I believe that genuine dialogue is the hallmark of good counseling, and I try to ground myself in dialogue. In other words, I share what I am thinking and feeling.

GUIDELINES, GENERAL EXPECTATIONS, INVITATIONS, AND REQUESTS

1. Deciding to work together is dependent on our both sensing that a fit exists between what I can offer and what you need and/or want. I will ask the questions that I need to ask in order to arrive at my decision. Please feel free to ask any questions that you may need to ask to arrive at yours.

2. Deciding not to have counseling and/or therapy is a perfectly respectable decision. It is an option, accordingly, that I often explore with clients.

3. These sessions are *for you*. Make sure that you get what you want out of them. It is your goals, not mine, that are ultimately the most meaningful. Please come in with your own agenda and feel free to change the agenda. If you disagree with something that I have said or have suggested, don't just go along with it. If you feel uneasy about how I have responded to something, please give me feedback. "Disagreement" is not a "sign of resistance." It is the reality of being separate human beings.

4. If I say or do anything that is oppressive, whether it be ethnocentric or ableist, please let me know about it so that I can shift. Nothing of this nature is insignificant or "too small to mention."

5. Except when conferring with a colleague (and here I try to be careful that you not be identifiable), and/or except when someone else's life is in danger, these sessions are

absolutely confidential. That is, I will not divulge to anyone that you are seeing me. I will not discuss you with your family or friends unless you explicitly ask me to do so. I will not testify against you at a court of law even if required by law to do so.

6. Because I view psychiatry as fundamentally oppressive, I do
   A. not consult with a psychiatrist.
   B. not assist anyone wanting to institutionalize anybody.
   C. not use medical backup, because that could leave a client vulnerable to unwanted psychiatric intervention.

7. I have a sliding scale to be as sensitive as possible to people's different financial situations. Insofar as possible, I try to let people place themselves within the range. I can take only a certain number of people within each of the lower fee categories, so it may sometimes happen that no vacancies are available for a certain fee category. When this occurs, and when a low fee is in order, I will go to the next available fee.

8. It is important that we be able to rely on each other. Except in the event of a genuine emergency, I give and expect at least 24 hours' notice of a cancellation or change of appointment.

9. If you are having trouble and wish to talk with me between sessions, feel free to call. A good time to call would be after 10:00 a.m. and before 9:00 p.m.

10. Please do not feel restricted to the once-a-week formula that has tended to typify counseling. Although this is most people's preference, I have had clients who have chosen to come as seldom as every 4 months and others who have come as often as twice a week. It is all a question of your specific needs or wants.

11. People often remain in therapy that is not helpful to them, or long after it has ceased to be helpful, or after the returns have greatly diminished. I do not think that this is in the client's best interests. Accordingly I build in periodic evaluations.

12. I see termination as an important part of the counseling process. When the time comes for our sessions to end, let's give this part of the process its due. As with any kind of important relationship, we will not be able to get closure with each other unless we take the time to say "good-bye."

References

Agel, J. (Ed.). (1973). *Rough times.* New York: Ballantine.

Alcoholics Anonymous. (1939). *Alcoholics Anonymous.* New York: A. A. World Services.

Alcoholics Anonymous. (1957). *Alcoholics Anonymous comes of age.* New York: Harper & Row.

Allen, P. G. (1986). *The sacred hoop: Recovering the feminine in American Indian traditions.* Boston: Beacon.

American Psychiatric Association. (1987). *Diagnostic and statistical manual of mental disorders* (3rd ed. rev.). (*DSM III R*). Washington, DC: Author.

Avery, D., & Winoker, G. (1976). Mortality in depressed patients treated with electroconvulsive therapy and antidepressants. *Archives of General Psychiatry, 33*(9), 1029-1037.

Baldessarini, R. S. (1978). Chemotherapy. In A. Nicholi (Ed.), *Harvard guide to modern psychiatry* (pp. 387-432). Cambridge: Harvard University Press.

Bandler, J., & Grinder, R. (1976). *The structure of magic* (Vol. II). Palo Alto, CA: Science Books.

Bargmann, E., Wolfe, S., Levin, J., et al. (1982). *Stopping Valium.* New York: Warner.

Barry, K. (1979). *Female sexual slavery.* New York: Avon.

Bateson, G., Jackson, D., Haley, D., & Weakland, J. (1956). Toward a theory of schizophrenia. *Behavioral Science, 1,* 251-264.

Beck, E. (1991). Therapy's double dilemma: Anti-Semitism and misogyny. In R. Siegel & E. Cole (Eds.), *Jewish women in therapy: Seen but not heard* (pp. 19-30). New York: Harrington Park.

Becker, H. (1973). *Outsiders: Studies in the sociology of deviance.* New York: Free Press.

Bell, L. (Ed.). (1987). *Good girls/bad girls: Sex trade workers and feminists face to face.* Toronto: Women's Press.

Bemis, K. (1978). Current approaches to the etiology and treatment of anorexia nervosa. *Psychological Bulletin, 85*(3), 595-617.

Bercuson, D. (1985). *A trust betrayed: The Keegstra affair.* Garden City, NY: Doubleday.

Berne, E. (1973). *Games people play.* New York: Ballantine.

Binswanger, L. (1958). The case of Ellen West: An anthropological-clinical study. In R. May, E. Angel, & H. Ellenberger (Eds.), *Existence: A new dimension in psychiatry and psychology* (pp. 237-364). New York: Basic Books.

Blackbridge, P., & Gilhooly, S. (1988). Still sane. In B. Burstow & D. Weitz (Eds.), *Shrink-resistant: The struggle against psychiatry in Canada* (pp. 44-51). Vancouver: New Star.

Boston Lesbian Psychologies Collective (Ed.). (1987). *Lesbian psychologies: Explorations and challenges.* Chicago: University of Illinois Press.

Bouhoutsos, J. (1989, February 15). *Sexual involvement with clients*. Workshop presentation, Toronto.

Breggin, P. (1979). *Electroshock: Its brain-disabling effects*. New York: Springer.

Breggin, P. (1983). *Psychiatric drugs: Hazards to the brain*. New York: Springer.

Brill, H. E., Crumpton, S., Eiduson, H. M. (1959). Relative effectiveness of various components of electroconvulsive therapy. *Archives of Neurological Psychiatry, 81*, 627-635.

Broverman, I. K., Broverman, D. M., Clarkson, F. E., et al. (1970). Sex role stereotypes and clinical judgments of mental health. *Journal of Counselling and Clinical Psychology, 34*(1), 1-7.

Brown, L., & Root, M. (Eds.). (1990). *Diversity and complexity in feminist therapy*. New York: Hawthorne.

Browne, A. (1987). *When battered women kill*. New York: Free Press.

Burch, B. (1982). Psychological merger in lesbian couples: A joint ego psychological and systems approach. *Family Therapy, 9*, 201-207.

Burch, B. (1985). Another perspective on merger in lesbian relationships. In L. Rosewater & L. Walker (Eds.), *Handbook of feminist therapy: Women's issues in psychotherapy* (pp. 100-109). New York: Springer.

Burstow, B. (1981). A critique of Binswanger's existential analysis. *Review of Existential Psychology and Psychiatry, 17*, 245-291.

Burstow, B. (1982). Psychiatry's assumptions are biased and unscientific. *Phoenix Rising, 3*(1), 35-38.

Burstow, B., & Weitz, D. (1984). Electroshock: A cruel and unusual punishment. *Phoenix Rising, 4* (3 and 4), 10A-12A.

Burstow, B., & Weitz, D. (Eds.). (1988). *Shrink-resistant: The struggle against psychiatry in Canada*. Vancouver: New Star.

Cahalan, D., Cisin, I. H., & Crossley, H. M. (1969). *American drinking practices*. New Brunswick, NJ: Rutgers Center of Alcohol Studies.

Caplan, P. (1987). *The myth of women's masochism*. New York: Signet.

Caplan, P. (1989). *Don't blame mother: Mending the mother-daughter relationship*. New York: Harper & Row.

Chesler, P. (1972). *Women and madness*. New York: Doubleday.

Chorodow, N. (1978). *The reproduction of mothering: Psychoanalysis and the sociology of gender*. Berkeley: University of California Press.

Clark, W. B., & Cahalan, D. (1976). Changes in problem drinking over a four-year span. *Addictive Behavior, 1*, 251-259.

Conrad, P., & Schneider, J. (1980). *Deviance and medicalization: From badness to sickness*. St. Louis: C. V. Mosby.

Cooper, T. (1987). Anorexia and bulimia: The political and the personal. In M. Lawrence (Ed.), *Fed up and hungry: Women, oppression, and food* (pp. 175-192). London: Women's Press.

Cooperstock, R. (1980). Special problems of psychotropic drug use among women. *Canada's Mental Health, 28*(2), 3-5.

Daly, M. (1978). *Gyn/ecology: The metaethics of radical feminism*. Boston: Beacon.

Davies, D. L. (1963). Normal drinking in recovered alcoholic addicts. *Quarterly Journal of Studies of Alcohol, 24*, 109-121, 331-332.

Davies, E. K., Tucker, G. J., & Harrow, M. (1971). Electroconvulsive therapy instruments: Should they be reevaluated? *Archives of General Psychiatry, 25*, 97-99.

De Beauvoir, S. (1964). *The second sex*. New York: Knopf.

Disabled Women's Network. (1990). *DAWN Toronto brochure*. Toronto: Author.

Dollars and Sense Editorial Board. (1983). Single parent families. *Dollars and Sense, 2*, pp. 12-15.

Doucette, J. (1990). Redefining difference: Disabled lesbians resist. In S. Stone (Ed.). *Lesbians in Canada* (pp. 61-72). Toronto: Between the Lines.

Dworkin, A. (1974). *Woman hating.* New York: E. P. Dutton.

Eastwood, M. R., & Peacock, J. (1976). Seasonal patterns of suicide, depression, and electroconvulsive therapy. *British Journal of Psychiatry, 129,* 472-475.

Foucault, M. (1988). *Madness and civilization: A history of insanity in the age of reason.* New York: Vintage.

Freire, P. (1970). *Pedagogy of the oppressed.* New York: Seabury.

Freud, S. (1973a). *Introductory lectures on psychoanalysis* (J. Strachey, Trans. and Ed.). The Pelican Freud Library, Volume I. New York: Penguin.

Freud, S. (1973b). *New introductory lectures on psychoanalysis* (J. Strachey, Trans and Ed.). The Pelican Freud Library, Volume II. New York: Penguin.

Fulani, L. (1988). *The psychopathology of everyday racism.* New York: Harrington.

Goffman, E. (1961). *Asylums: Essays on the social situation of mental patients and other inmates.* New York: Anchor.

Goldner, V. (1985). Feminism and family therapy. *Family Process, 24,* 31-46.

Goodrich, T., Rampage, C., Ellman, B., & Halstead, K. (1988). *Feminist family therapy: A casebook.* New York: Norton.

Goodwin, F. K., & Ebert, M. H. (1977). Specific antimanic-antidepressant drugs. In M. Jarvis (Ed.), *Psychopharmacology in the practice of medicine* (pp. 257-273). New York: Appleton-Century-Crofts.

Green, J. (1982). *Cultural awareness in the human services.* Englewood Cliffs, NJ: Prentice-Hall.

Greenspan, M. (1983). *A new approach to women and therapy.* New York: McGraw-Hill.

Halmi, K., Falk, J., & Schwartz, E. (1981). Binge-eating and vomiting: A survey of a college population. *Psychological Medicine, 11,* 697-706.

Holyroyd, J., & Brodsky, A. (1977). Psychologists' attitudes and practices regarding erotic and nonerotic physical contact with patients. *American Psychologist, 32,* 843-849.

Hooks, B. (1984). *Feminist theory: From margin to center.* Boston: South End.

Hucker, S. (1985). *Oak Ridge: A review and an alternative.* Report to the Ontario Ministry of Health.

Hutchinson, G. (1985). *Transforming the body image: Learning to love the body you have.* New York: Crossing.

Johnson, S. (1984). Testimony on electroshock. *Phoenix Rising, 4* (3 and 4), 21A-22A.

Johnstone, E. C., Deakin, J. F. W., Lawler, P., et al. (1980, December 20-27). The Northwick Park ECT trial. *Lancet, 9,* 1317-1320.

Kardener, S., Fuller, M., & Mensh, I. (1973). A survey of physicians' attitudes and practices regarding erotic and nonerotic contact with patients. *American Journal of Psychiatry, 130*(10), 1077-1081.

Kelly, L. (1988). *Surviving sexual violence.* Minneapolis: University of Minnesota Press.

Kirkpatrick, J. (1978). *Turnabout: Help for a new life.* New York: Doubleday.

Koedt, A., Levine, E., & Rapone, A. (Eds.). (1973). *Radical feminism.* New York: Quadrangle.

Laing, R. D. (1965). *The divided self: An existential study in sanity and madness.* New York: Penguin.

Lambourne, J., & Gill, D. (1978). A controlled comparison of simulated and real ECT. *British Journal of Psychiatry, 113,* 514- 519.

Lawrence, M. (1989). *The anorexic experience* (rev. ed.). London: Women's Press.

Lobel, K. (Ed.). (1986). *Naming the violence: Speaking out about lesbian battery.* Seattle: Seal Press.

Lorde, A. (1982). *Zami: A new spelling of my name.* Freedom, CA: Crossing.

Lorde, A. (1984). *Sister outsider.* Freedom, CA: Crossing.

Lowen, A. (1976). *Bioenergetics.* New York: Penguin.

Lowen, A. (1977). *The way to vibrant health: A manual of bioenergetics exercises*. New York: Harper & Row.

MacKinnon, C. (1982). Feminism, Marxism, method, and the state: An agenda for theory. In N. Keohane, M. Rosaldo, & B. Gelpi (Eds.), *Feminist theory: A critique of ideology* (pp. 1-30). Chicago: University of Chicago Press.

Masson, J. (1984). *The assault on truth*. Toronto: Collier.

Masson, J. (1988). *Against therapy: Emotional tyranny and the myth of psychological healing*. New York: Atheneum.

Meyerson, A. (1942). In F. Ebauch, H. Clarke, & K. Neubuerger. Fatalities following electric convulsive therapy. *Transactions of the American Neurological Association, 68*, 36-41.

Millett, K. (1990). *The loony bin trip*. New York: Touchstone.

Minuchin, S. (1974). *Families and family therapy*. Cambridge, MA: Harvard University Press.

Nicarthy, G., & Davidson, S. (1989). *You can be free: An easy-to-read handbook for abused women*. Seattle: Seal Press.

Ontario Coalition to Stop Electroshock. (1984). *The case against electroshock*. Submission to the Ontario government's Electroconvulsive Therapy Review Committee.

Orback, S. (1979). *Fat is a feminist issue*. New York: Berkeley.

Orback, S. (1988). *Hunger strike: The anorectic's struggle as a metaphor for our age*. New York: Avon.

Pattison, E. M., Sobell, M. B., & Sobell, L. D. (1977). *Emerging concepts of alcohol dependence*. New York: Springer.

Pope, K., & Bouhoutses, J. (1986). *Sexual intimacy between therapists and patients*. New York: Praeger.

Pope, K., Levenson, H., & Schover, L. (1979). Sexual intimacy in psychology training: Results and implications of a national survey. *American Psychologist, 34*, 682-689.

Pope, K., Keith-Spiegel, P., & Tabachnick, B. (1986). Sexual attraction to clients: The human therapist and the (sometimes) inhuman training system. *American Psychologist, 41*(2), 147-158.

Ramsey, S. (1984). Double vision: Nonverbal behavior east and west. In A. Wolfgang (Ed.), *Nonverbal behavior: Perspectives, applications, intercultural insights* (pp. 139-167). New York: Hogrefe.

Redstockings Collective. (1978). *Redstockings: Feminist revolution*. New York: Random House.

Rhodes, D., & McNeill, S. (1985). *Women against violence against women*. London: Onlywomen Press.

Rich, A. (1986). *Blood, bread, and poetry: Selected prose 1979-1985*. New York: W. W. Norton.

Richmond, D. (1984). *Dr. Caligari's psychiatric drugs*. Berkeley, CA: Network Against Psychiatric Assault.

Rivera, M. (1988). Am I a boy or a girl?: Multiple personality and gender differences. *Resources for Feminist Research, 17*(2), 41-46.

Rosenhan, D. (1973). On being sane in insane places. *Science, 179*, 250-258.

Rosewater, L., & Walker, L. (Eds.). (1985). *Handbook of feminist therapy: Women's issues in psychotherapy*. New York: Springer.

Samunda, R., & Wolfgang, A. (Eds.). (1985). *Intercultural counselling and assessment: Global perspectives*. New York: Hogrefe.

Sandmaier, M. (1981). *The invisible alcoholics: Women and alcohol abuse*. New York: McGraw-Hill.

Sartre, J. (1956). *Being and nothingness: A phenomenological essay on ontology*. New York: Pocket Books.

Sartre, J. (1961). *The age of reason*. New York: Penguin.

Savage, H., & McKague, C. (1988). *Mental health law in Canada.* Toronto: Butterworths.

Schoener, G., & Gonsiorek, J. (1989). *Sexual involvement with clients: Intervention and prevention.* Minneapolis: Walk-In Counselling Centre.

Scull, A. (1977). *Decarceration: Community treatment and the deviant: A radical view.* Englewood Cliffs, NJ: Prentice-Hall.

Showalter, E. (1987). *The female malady: Women, madness, and English culture, 1830-1980.* New York: Penguin.

Sinclair, D. (1985). *Understanding wife assault: A training manual for counsellors and advocates.* Toronto: Publications Ontario.

Small, E. F., Sharpley, P., & Small, J. G. (1968). Influences of Cyclert upon memory changes with ECT. *American Journal of Psychiatry, 125,* 837-840.

Smith, D. (1975). Women and psychiatry. In D. Smith & S. David (Eds.), *Women look at psychiatry* (pp. 1-17). Vancouver: Press Gang.

Smith, D., & David, S. (1975). *Women look at psychiatry.* Vancouver: Press Gang.

Sprenger, J., & Kramer, H. (1948). *Malleus maleficarum* (M. Summers, Trans.). London: Pushkin. (Original work published 1496)

Statistics Canada. (1988). *Canada yearbook 1988.* Ottawa: Author.

Steiner, C. (1975). *Scripts people live: Transactional analysis of life scripts.* New York: Grove.

Sterling, P. (1979, December 8). Psychiatry's drug addiction. *New Republic,* pp. 14-18.

Sternhell, C. (1985, May). We'll always be fat but fat will be fit. *Ms,* pp. 66, 68, 142-144, 146, 154.

Striegel-Morre, R., Siberstein, L., & Rodin, J. (1986). Toward an understanding of risk factors for bulimia. *American Psychologist, 41*(3), 246-263.

Sturdivant, S. (1980). *Therapy with women: A feminist philosophy of treatment.* New York: Springer.

Szasz, T. (1974). *The myth of mental illness: Foundations of a theory of personality conduct.* New York: Harper & Row.

Szasz, T. (1977). *The manufacture of madness: A comparative study of the Inquisition and the mental health movement.* New York: Harper & Row.

Szasz, T. (1987). *Insanity: The idea and its consequences.* New York: John Wiley.

Szekeley, E. (1988). *Never too thin.* Toronto: Women's Press.

Templer, D. I., Ruff, C. E., & Armstrong, G. (1973). Cognitive functioning and degree of psychosis in schizophrenics given many electroconvulsive treatments. *British Journal of Psychiatry, 123,* 441-443.

Walker, L. (1979). *The battered woman.* New York: Harper & Row.

Wine, J. (1989). Sexual abuse in therapy: A call for participants. *WCREC Newsletter, 1*(1), 1.

Wolfgang, A. (Ed.). (1984). *Nonverbal behavior: Perspectives, applications, intercultural insights.* New York: Hogrefe.

Wooley, S., & Kearney-Cooke, A. (no date). *Intensive treatment of bulimia and body image disturbance.* Cincinnati, OH: University of Cincinnati, Psychiatry Department, Eating Disorders Clinic.

Wooley, S., & Wooley, O. (1980). Eating disorders: Obesity and anorexia. In A. Brodsky & R. Hare-Mustin (Eds.), *Women and psychotherapy: An assessment of research and practice* (pp. 134-158). New York: Guilford.

Wooley, S., & Wooley, O. (1986). The Beverly Hills disorder: the mass marketing of anorexia nervosa. *International Journal of Eating Disorders, 1*(3), 57-69.

Wyckoff, H. (1975). Banal scripts of women. In C. Steiner (Ed.), *Scripts people live: Transactional analysis of life scripts* (pp. 210-234). New York: Bantam.

Wyckoff, H. (1980). *Solving problems together.* New York: Grove.

Index

About the Author

Bonnie Burstow was born in 1945. She is a third-generation Ashkenazi Jewish woman of lower-class origins. She grew up largely in the exciting, poor, multicultural north end of Winnipeg of the 1940s and 1950s. Like most north end Winnipeg Jews, she is a political activist. She has been active for decades in the women's movement, the antipsychiatry movement, and the prison abolition movement. She is also an academic, psychotherapist, consultant, and supervisor. She has been a full-time member of the social work faculty at Carleton University, where she taught in the MSW program, and at the University of Manitoba, where she taught in the BSW program. Her areas of specialization as a therapist and supervisor include working with survivors of childhood sexual abuse, psychiatric survivors, and women who self-mutilate. She currently supervises a number of therapists in Toronto, where she now lives, does intermittent faculty liaison work for Carleton University, and is a consultant for a number of feminist organizations. She is a contributing editor of *Issues on the Left* and has written and published extensively in the areas of psychotherapy, social work, education, antipsychiatry, and philosophy. Recent publications include *Shrink-Resistant: The Struggle Against Psychiatry in Canada*, co-edited with Don Weitz; "How Sexist Is Sartre?" in *Philosophy and Literature*; "Freirian Codifications and Social Work Education," in *Journal of Social Work Education*; "Toward a Freirian Approach to Counselling," in *Canadian Journal for the Study of Adult Education*; and "Humanistic Psychotherapy and the Issue of Equality," in *Journal of Humanistic Psychology*.